The Book of MACROBIOTICS

The Book of MACRO-BIOTICS

The Universal Way of Health, Happiness, and Peace

MICHIO KUSHI

with Alex Jack *· Completely Revised and Enlarged Edition*

Japan Publications, Inc.

Note to the reader: Those with health problems are advised to seek the guidance of a qualified medical or psychological professional in addition to qualified macrobiotic teacher before implementing any of the dietary or other approaches presented in this book. It is essential that any reader who has any reason to suspect serious illness seek appropriate medical, nutritional or psychological advice promptly. Neither this nor any other related book should be used as a substitute for qualified care or treatment.

Published by JAPAN PUBLICATIONS, INC., Tokyo and New York

Distributors:
UNITED STATES: *Kodansha International/USA, Ltd., through Harper & Row, Publishers, Inc., 10 East 53rd Street, New York, New York 10022.* SOUTH AMERICA: *Harper & Row, Publishers, Inc., International Department.* CANADA: *Fitzhenry & Whiteside Ltd., 195 Allstate Parkway, Markham, Ontario, L3R 4T8.* MEXICO AND CENTRAL AMERICA: *HARLA S. A de C. V., Apartado 30–546, Mexico 4, D.F.* BRITISH ISLES: *International Book Distributors Ltd., 66 Wood Lane End, Hemel Hempstead, Herts HP2 4RG.* EUROPEAN CONTINENT: *Fleetbooks—Feffer and Simons, 61 Strijkviertel, 3454 PK de Meern, The Netherlands.* AUSTRALIA AND NEW ZEALAND: *Bookwise International, 1 Jeanes Street, Beverley, South Australia 5007.* THE FAR EAST AND JAPAN: *Japan Publications Trading Co., Ltd., 1–2–1, Sarugaku-cho, Chiyoda-ku, Tokyo 101.*

First edition: January 1987
Second printing: April 1989

LCCC No. 85–081363
ISBN 0–87040–667–1

Printed in U.S.A.

Dedication

This book is dedicated to humanity's everlasting dream—past, present, and future—of realizing health, happiness, and peace.

This book is also dedicated to those known and unknown who have devoted their lives to inspiring the human family, ancient and modern, Eastern and Western, Northern and Southern.

This book is further dedicated to all our ancestors and to all unborn generations, as well as to all living children and parents.

This book is offered in a spirit of love and gratitude to George and Lima Ohsawa; my parents Keizo and Teru Kushi; my wife Aveline; my children Lillian, Norio, Haruo, Yoshio, and Hisao, and their families; to Alex's parents Esther and Homer; his friend Gale and her son Jon; to his sister Lucy and her family; and to all of our friends and associates around the world who share our common dream of building One Peaceful World.

Daily Dedication for One Peaceful World

When we eat, let us reflect that we have come from food which has come from nature by the Order of the Infinite Universe, and let us be grateful for all that we have been given.

When we meet people, let us see them as brothers and sisters and remember that we have all come from the infinite universe through our parents and ancestors, and let us pray as one with all of humanity for universal love and peace on earth.

When we see the sun and moon, the sky and stars, mountains and rivers, seas and forests, fields and valleys, birds and animals, and all the wonders of nature, let us remember that we have come with them all from the infinite universe. Let us be thankful for our environment on earth and live in harmony with all that surrounds us.

When we see farms and villages, towns and cities, arts and cultures, societies and civilizations, and all the works of humanity, let us recall that our creativity has come from the infinite universe and has passed from generation to generation and spread over the entire earth. Let us be grateful for our birth on this planet with intelligence and wisdom, and let us vow with all to realize endlessly our eternal dream of One Peaceful World through health, freedom, love and justice.

Prayers by Michio Kushi

We all have come from infinity.
We all live within infinity,
We all shall return to infinity,
We are all manifestations of one infinity,
We are all sisters and brothers of one infinite universe,
Let us love each other,
Let us help each other,
Let us encourage each other,
And let us all together continue to realize
The endless dream of one peaceful world.

—*May 1976*

Having come from, begin within, and going towards infinity,
May our endless dream be eternally realized upon this earth.
May our unconditional dedication perpetually serve for the creation of love and peace.
May our heartfelt thankfulness and devotion be universally shared with everyone, everything, and every being.

—*June 1977*

From this infinite, this food has come to us.
By this food, we realize ourselves on this planet.
To this food we are grateful.
For nature and people who have brought this food, we are thankful.
This food becomes us.
By eating together we become one family on this planet.
Through this food, we all are one.
Let us love each other in this life.
Let us realize our endless dream.

—*August 1984*

I AM GRATEFUL

I am grateful to my parents and ancestors,
I am grateful to my spouse and partner,
I am grateful to my children and offspring,
I am grateful to all people and all beings.

I am grateful to the foods I am given,
I am grateful to the nature that I am within,
I am grateful to the universe in which I am manifested,
I am grateful to all phenomena and all beings.

I am grateful to my sickness,
I am grateful to my ignorance,
I am grateful to my enemy,
I am grateful to my difficulties,
I am grateful to my suffering.

I am nothing, yet I have been given all,
Therefore, I am rich, equal to the whole universe.
I am endlessly grateful to my being here and now.

—*December 1984*

Preface

In August, 1945, World War II ended following the destruction of large parts of Europe and Asia. Hundreds of millions of people suffered and died during the long years and miseries of this war. Soon after the war ended, other wars began to break out in various areas of the world. Concurrently, with the increasing technological prosperity of modern civilization, the degeneration of humanity began to accelerate.

During my late teenage years, I often visited shrines, praying for the spirits of dying soldiers, many of whom were my friends, wondering why we had to fight on this beautiful earth. Later I was drafted into the army, and passed through Hiroshima just before and after the atomic bombing, as well as helped survivors from Nagasaki. These experiences made a deep impression on me. In my early twenties, my questioning was extended to various other undesirable human affairs, including sicknesses, disagreements, selfishness, and egocentricity, searching for the universal way of health, happiness, and peace.

I am grateful that I could meet George Ohsawa, the modern founder of macrobiotics, while I was a World Federalist studying in the graduate school of Tokyo University and later at Columbia University; Rev. Toyohiko Kagawa, a Christian leader; Professor Shigeru Nanbara, Chancellor of Tokyo University; Toyohiko Hori, Professor of Tokyo University; many other seniors in Japan; and Albert Einstein, Thomas Mann, Upton Sinclair, Norman Cousins, Robert M. Hutchins, and other seniors in the United States. I am also grateful that after coming to America in 1949 I could have various work experiences—as dishwasher, bellboy, night watchman, interpreter, retailer, trader, restaurant operator, and correspondent. Throughout this period, I continued to study various sciences to be utilized for the development of human biological and spiritual evolution. Oriental philosophy, medicine, and culture needed to be synthesized with modern Western sciences for a comprehensive understanding of human destiny and its reorientation in a peaceful direction.

In order to bring about a unified world, it is necessary to establish a unifying principle that covers all domains of religion, philosophy, science, and culture, as well as all physical, mental, spiritual, and social phenomena. The universal principle of change, yin and yang, which forms the background of all Oriental societies and ways of thought and has counterparts in traditional Western philosophy, should be verified and confirmed by modern research and experimentation.

I began to lecture in New York in 1955. With many friends, I continued to talk about the way of life according to the Order of the Universe. I have been living day and night with the unchanging dream of achieving One Peaceful World. Especially since 1963, many of my student friends have started to spread the way of life for health, happiness, and peace throughout America, Europe, and other parts of the world. For the same dream, we have promoted the natural foods movement along with macrobiotic principles, and we have tried to cultivate the social, cultural, and philosophical ground for enduring world peace through the harmonious meeting of East and West, North and South.

Since the mid-1960s, nearly ten thousand stores in North America have started to carry natural foods, as well as several hundred restaurants, and many organic farms have begun. Our dietary and environmental approach has begun to be recognized by modern medicine, and traditional practices such as shiatsu massage, acupuncture, palm healing, meditation, and visualization have been spreading in modern society. Peaceful biological revolution has begun to help humanity recover from degeneration toward the reconstruction of the world. Macrobiotics has spread to every continent and most major countries and regions.

This book is a simple introduction to the principles of health, happiness, and peace through an understanding of natural order and an application of the universal laws of change and harmony, especially as they relate to dietary practice, human relations, the prevention and relief of physical and mental disorders, the transformation of society, and spiritual development.

This book was originally compiled ten years ago as a distillation of about five thousand lectures and seminars given over the years in America and Europe. It has been translated into many languages including German, French, Italian, Spanish, Portuguese, Dutch, Danish, Norwegian, Japanese, and Hebrew. There is also a braille edition available from the Library of Congress in Washington, D.C. Over the last decade Aveline and I, along with our associates, have written many books devoted to various aspects of macrobiotics introduced in this volume, such as the dietary approach to cancer, visual diagnosis, pregnancy and child care, and world peace. However, *The Book of Macrobiotics* still remains the basic, most comprehensive introduction and overview of our teachings as a whole.

In the last ten years, we have given several thousand more lectures and seminars, and our own understanding and practice have continuously developed. Year by year, season by season, we have gradually changed our content and altered our presentation. Studying and understanding unfold endlessly, and no matter how long we have been practicing macrobiotics, we still feel we have so much to learn and that we will never reach the end.

This new edition of *The Book of Macrobiotics* retains the same general content and order of the original but has been completely revised in light of our current understanding. It has also been expanded to include new material on the history of macrobiotics, the structure of the universe and celestial cycles, yin and yang and the five transformations, the origin and destiny of humanity, the challenge of biotechnology, and relations between man and woman. Two new chapters have been added on medical and scientific studies (summarizing almost one hundred macrobiotic medical, nutritional, and other research experiments over the last decade) and on the spiritual world (introducing material presented in Spiritual Training Seminars at our new retreat center in the Berkshire Mountains).

Many new tables and illustrations have been furnished, and the food composition charts in the appendix have been expanded to include nutritional information on dozens of macrobiotic-quality foods such as tempeh, seitan, rice cakes, arrowroot, and amazake not previously available. The governments of the U.S., U.K., and Canada, as well as national and international medical bodies, have issued dietary guidelines in the last ten years moving in the direction of macrobiotic eating, and these are assembled in the appendix, along with an index of modern society's current biological, social, and environmental decline. For easy reference, a chronology of macrobiotic developments in North America and abroad has been compiled, and an annotated East West reading list has been provided for further study and enjoyment.

I am grateful to Alex Jack, who has co-authored *The Cancer-Prevention Diet*, *Diet for a Strong Heart*, *Macrobiotic Diet*, and *One Peaceful World*, for help in putting together this new edition as well as correcting my broken English which, alas, does not seem to improve with the years. Olivia Oredson and Janet Lacey assisted in the original edition, for which I am thankful. Christian Gautier has provided new diagrams and illustrations that gracefully complement Peter Harris's original artwork. The president and vice-president of Japan Publications, Inc., Mr. Iwao

Yoshizaki and Mr. Yoshiro Fujiwara, have faithfully overseen this book and many other macrobiotic publishing projects over the years, and I am grateful for their kindness, valuable suggestions, and hard work. Gale Beith, a wonderful macrobiotic counselor and cooking teacher from Dallas, Texas, inspired and assisted Alex during the preparation of the manuscript, for which I know he is most appreciative. To Donna Cowan, my personal secretary, Mary Brower, Marlene Sciascia, and other office staff I am indebted for their tireless devotion and assistance. Anna Ineson made valuable suggestions on revising the nutritional tables, and Edward Esko helped with the chronology.

To my teachers, family, associates, students, and friends all around the world, I wish to express my boundless joy and gratitude for being on this beautiful planet at this stage in our infinite journey together. I pray that we will continue to help and love one another in this life and the next and together realize our endless dream.

MICHIO KUSHI

Brookline, Massachusetts
St. Valentine's Day, 1986

Contents

List of Figures

List of Tables

Introduction: The Regeneration of Modern Humanity

Unknown time has elapsed since our galaxy was formed by whirlpool motion in the infinite ocean of space. As the earth developed to its present condition, more than four billion years have passed. Biological life has existed on this planet for more than three billion years, and human beings have developed physically and spiritually for probably over 20 million years. Although it is uncertain how the ancestors of our present human species lived and adapted to their environment, during our recent development as *homo sapiens*, especially within the span of recorded history, we have seen the rise and fall of more than twenty civilizations.

During these constant vicissitudes, humanity has experienced health and sickness, stability and chaos, peace and war, prosperity and poverty, happiness and unhappiness, as if we have been riding upon waves. Our present world civilization and this modern age are not exempt from these fluctuations.

Our modern civilization offers material wealth and technological conveniences to the majority of the world's population, together with rapid communication and the dissemination of knowledge. At present we are seeing the blossomings of such benefits: worldwide distribution of food for everyone's survival and enjoyment; transportation that enables us to be on the opposite sides of the globe within the same day; communications systems through which we can know instantaneously what has happened on other continents; well-organized religious and education programs; universal control of governmental administration; and an impressive degree of scientific and technological development. It is no longer only a daydream that we may colonize other planets. From the far depths of the ocean to the uncharted polar regions, from impenetrable equatorial rain forests to the frontiers of space, our explorations are advancing everywhere. From the microscopic world of atoms and subatomic particles to the macroscopic world of galaxies and constellations, our understanding is expanding. It appears that we are approaching the realization of the Golden Age envisioned by poets and artists, prophets and utopian thinkers, throughout history.

However, when we examine our surroundings more carefully, we find that increasingly there is sickness instead of health, chaos instead of stability, war instead of peace, poverty instead of prosperity, unhappiness instead of happiness. The huge expenditures of major governmental and public programs are not being applied for the creative development of human potential but rather are being used up simply in defensive measures against perceived threats to the modern way of life. The negative aspects of modern civilization include:

- *Constant Expansion of the Defense System:* While we are enjoying world trade and exchange as well as global travel, every nation is constantly manufacturing weapons and strengthening its military forces to prepare to destroy other nations. The potential power of destruction possessed by modern nations can destroy the entire earth within a few hours.
- *Constant Expansion of Medical Care:* At the same time that we are making great advances in medical research and emergency care and relief of pain, we see more people suffering from disease—physical, mental, and spiritual. Heart disease, cancer, diabetes, mental illness, sexual and reproductive disorders, and other degenerative conditions have reached epidemic levels in the industrialized countries and are on the rise in developing areas. AIDS and other immune-deficiency diseases are also on the increase, for which there is no medical relief. Many large hospitals are fully crowded with patients, and many drugstores are visited from morning to evening by a constant stream of people.
- *Constant Expansion of the Insurance and Welfare Systems:* While life expectancy has been prolonged due to the control of infant mortality and infectious diseases and while social security for the elderly has been almost assured, various insurance systems are expanding to offset rising losses from sickness, accident, injury, unemployment, fire, theft, property damage, and death. Nearly every modern person has two or three insurance policies on the average. Meanwhile, public welfare, pension, and support payments for the sick, the disabled, the retired, and others continue to increase, making it more difficult for ordinary families to maintain their households and pay their taxes.
- *Constant Expansion of the Legal, Judicial, and Police Systems:* Despite the spread of modern education, violence, greed, selfishness, and

crime prevail, requiring more and more powerful judicial and police control to regulate undesirable behavior and conduct. Violence and distrust are particularly widespread within the school system itself. Though most basic labor benefits have been secured, relations between employees and management are often disharmonious. Health conditions and medical benefits are a rising source of friction in the workplace. Personal injury lawsuits are soaring, especially those by patients against their doctors. Moreover, community and organizational loyalty has all but vanished, as business executives, authors, athletes, entertainers, and others commonly retain lawyers to negotiate new contracts on the basis of the highest financial gain.

• *Constant Increase of Family Decomposition:* While worldwide communication systems are developing in modern society, understanding among family members is becoming increasingly difficult. Only half a century ago, separation and divorce of married couples was uncommon. Today one out of every two marriages meets with divorce and separation. Relations between spouses, between parents and children, between grandparents and families, and other family relations are generally declining. With modern society's increased mobility and opportunities to relocate, family members typically live long distances from each other, further contributing to a loss of family tradition and rootlessness.

• *Constant Sexual and Reproductive Disorders:* Despite reduced societal restrictions on sexual orientation and behavior, harmonious sexual relations are declining, and men and women are losing basic connection with the natural order. Harmful birth control practices, including vasectomy and tubal ligation, as well as the artificial birth control pill, are on the rise, besides sexually transmitted diseases (STD), infertility, prostate and ovarian tumors, and other reproductive and sexual disorders. Male sperm counts have fallen dramatically over the last several decades, and as a result of cardiovascular disease or diabetes many men are impotent. By age sixty one half of American women have had their uteruses surgically removed. To offset this wave of voluntary and involuntary sterilization, artificial birth procedures such as test-tube babies, sperm bank fathers, and surrogate mothers have been introduced, contributing to the further decline of natural family relations.

• *Constant Decline of Traditional Values:* Religious traditions that have inspired people's consciences for many centuries have declined, and churches, synagogues, mosques, and temples have lost their attraction for many people. Schools, colleges, universities, and other educational institutions that have guided social awareness in the past have lost their influence, and their function has changed to one of primarily dispensing information and promoting competition among themselves. Family and community heritage—the traditional soil that has nourished the human spirit for endless generations—has all but disappeared.

Despite modern society's unparalleled material prosperity and advantages, most people today are full of fear and anxiety, seeking vainly for happiness and fulfillment, doubtful whether there will be a world for their children to inherit. What mistakes have we made in the process of building modern civilization that we should come to this sorrowful end? For what we are confronting is the biological, psychological, and spiritual degeneration of humanity. If present trends continue, modern civilization will be destroyed either by 1) gradual extinction as the result of heart disease, cancer, mental illness, AIDS, and other degenerative disorders or 2) rapid extinction through nuclear war.

Everyone in the modern world—and all future generations to come through us—face destruction through universal fire—global thermonuclear war—or through universal flood—the consumption of unnatural food, contaminated water, polluted air, and disharmonious electromagnetic vibrations and thoughts. In the ancient world, salvation during time of universal conflagration was achieved by building an Ark. Where can we find the Ark to save our lives and those of posterity? Today salvation lies within our own physical, mental, and spiritual constitutions. We need to self-reflect deeply to discover our mistakes, and we need a biological revolution so that we may change our own constitutions, reverse the trend toward degeneration of our species, prevent world war, and create a new planetary order based on love and trust. This peaceful revolution will not be accomplished by the work of the government; it is not the mission of the church or temple; and it is not the duty of the school. This revolution arises out of our own personal effort to change the quality of our blood and bodily fluids, improving every one of the billions of cells in our body and brain, and developing our physical health, mental clarity, and spiritual awareness.

The self-revolution to reestablish our biological, psychological, and spiritual health and well-being rests on two foundations: 1) an understanding of what humanity is, what life is—our origin and our destiny—and as a whole, the understanding of the Order of the Universe, and 2) the biological, psychological, spiritual, and social application of the Order of the Universe, commencing with proper dietary practices according to everchanging environmental and personal conditions.

This revolution is the most peaceful and effective way to restore the earth. Through it we are able to save ourselves and our families and friends from the vast current of degeneration sweeping the globe. We are even able to turn the general trend of modern civilization in a more healthy, constructive direction. And, ultimately, we are able to enter the gateway of the new world, the Era of Humanity, with health and peace, justice and freedom, leading toward the unlimited happiness of all humanity for endless generations to come.

1. The Order of the Universe

Though a river streams endlessly,
Yet the water of the stream is not the same.
Foam floating on the stream appears and disappears and does not last long.
People and their homes in this world are changing constantly.

—Chomei Kamo
Writings in a Small House
13th Century

The voice of the gong coming from Gionshoja [ancient temple of Buddha] echoes a sound of ephemerality.
The color of the flowers on the tree of Shara-Soju suggests that the destiny of the prosperous is inevitably to decline.
Those who are powerful do not last and disappear like a dream in the spring night.
Those who are violent perish like dust in the wind.

—*Tale of the Heike*
13th Century

Life Is Vanity

The Order of the Infinite Universe—the eternal principles of change—are nothing but the different names of the living God or the moving infinite creation. When the name of God is used, it is often misunderstood as a static personality, and when the term Infinity is used, it is difficult for many people to comprehend. The infinity of God is neither a person nor a phenomenon; it is a universal oneness, embracing everything—every being, every phenomenon—and it is the endless universe itself. Other names for this limitless source or process are Beauty, Truth, Love, Righteousness, and Peace. The universe does not remain in one state but is changing constantly—transforming continuously, transmuting eternally from the beginningless beginning to the endless end. The infinite universe is a process of absolute dynamic change within which countless relative changes are arising everywhere in every dimension and at all times.

Without knowing the Order of the Universe, it is fruitless to talk about life or truth, and it is senseless to speak of human existence and life. Without understanding the Order of the Universe, no one can achieve health, freedom, and happiness through his or her own initiative. No society can achieve order, progress, and harmony. No country can complete its security, prosperity, and development, and no world can establish peace and justice.

Where there is no understanding of the Order of the Universe, there is no true love, no real truth, and no true happiness. It may appear from time to time that there is love, peace, and happiness among people, but it shall pass away in vain as the poets tell us like morning dew or the foam on a stream. Needless to say, there were in the past, and there are at present, many teachings of a religious and spiritual nature, many discourses of a scientific and intellectual nature, and a cornucopia of knowledge of a social and cultural nature. Love is sought everywhere, health is discussed everywhere, peace is yearned for everywhere, and grace and salvation are spoken of endlessly. And yet, far and near around us, there are really very few seekers of the Order of the Universe and the principle of eternal change. As a result, all religious and spiritual teachings have decayed, all theoretical and aesthetic cultural movements have declined, and all human races and societies have been unable to escape the miseries of disease and poverty, selfishness and war.

Here and there throughout the world, we hear voices of consolation and whispers of encouragement. They are calling now as their ancestors called in the past, "Come to us. Your rest is here." But despite that there are few teachings that reveal the perpetual Order of the Infinite Universe, and even fewer teachings that demonstrate how to practice it. Unless we know ourselves as a manifestation of the Order of the Universe, we are unable to realize our endless dream.

We may see around us injustice practiced upon naive, innocent, and good people. We see sickness suffered by those who appear to be practicing the proper way of life. We see people suffering from daily hardships that appear unreasonable for them. We ourselves at any time may meet with an unexpected accident, unforseeable misery, or sudden death. We may consider all these things unfair and unreasonable, but actually there is nothing excepted from the Order of the Universe. As infinitesimally small inhabitants of an infinitely large cosmos, we are unable in our ignorance to see the larger currents of cause and effect, the movement of eternal life encompassing our own small existences. Everything and anything happens with a certain order by a definite cause and process. From the absolute perspective, there is nothing that is unjust, unrighteous, and improper because all things have arisen and shall vanish according to the endless Order of the Infinite Universe or what we might call the law of God. Therefore unless we know that order, or what has been called the justice of the Kingdom of Heaven, and how to practice it, all of what we are doing in this life, and on this planet, shall turn to ashes. This is the meaning of the famous passage in Ecclesiastes: "Vanity of vanities, saith the Preacher, vanity of vanities; all is vanity. What profit hath a man of all his labor which he taketh under the sun? One generation passeth away, and another generation cometh: but the earth abideth forever. The sun also ariseth, and the sun goeth down, and hasteneth to his place where he arose. The wind goeth toward the south, and turneth about unto the north; it whirleth about continually, and the wind returneth again according to his circuits. All the rivers run into the sea; yet the sea is not full; unto the place from whence the rivers come, thither they return again."

The Principles and Laws of the Universe

The universal principles and laws of change have been understood by traditional cultures since ancient times and have been enshrined in various ways in their scriptures, myths, systems of agriculture and food production, architecture, and folk arts. In the modern age, they have been rediscovered and expressed, usually in more fragmented form, by various philosophers, scientists, authors, and artists. In this century, they were comprehensively outlined by George Ohsawa and further simplified by the author and his associates through their experiences and observations of nature and society during the past thirty-five years.

The eternal Order of the Universe can be viewed and understood in two ways, according to seven universal principles and twelve laws of change. These two perspectives complement each other and are apprehended by our intuitive understanding or what we might call native common sense. We experience them daily wherever we are, at all times, and under all circumstances. Everything proceeds in accordance with this universal order, and all phenomena change according to these precepts.

- *The seven principles of the infinite universe are:*

1. Everything is a differentiation of one Infinity.
2. Everything changes.
3. All antagonisms are complementary.
4. There is nothing identical.
5. What has a front (i.e., a visible side) has a back (i.e., an invisible side).
6. The bigger the front, the bigger the back.
7. What has a beginning has an end.

- *The twelve laws of change of the infinite universe are:*

1. One Infinity manifests itself into complementary and antagonistic tendencies, yin and yang, in its endless change.
2. Yin and yang are manifested continuously from the eternal movement of one infinite universe.
3. Yin represents centrifugality. Yang represents centripetality. Yin and yang together produce energy and all phenomena.
4. Yin attracts yang. Yang attracts yin.
5. Yin repels yin. Yang repels yang.
6. Yin and yang combined in varying proportions produce different phenomena. The attraction and repulsion among phenomena is proportional to the difference of the yin and yang forces.
7. All phenomena are ephemeral, constantly changing their constitution of yin and yang forces; yin changes into yang, yang changes into yin.
8. Nothing is solely yin or solely yang. Everything is composed of both tendencies in varying degrees.
9. There is nothing neutral. Either yin or yang is in excess in every occurrence.
10. Large yin attracts small yin. Large yang attracts small yang.
11. Extreme yin produces yang, and extreme yang produces yin.
12. All physical manifestations are yang at the center, and yin at the surface.

The terms *yin* and *yang* do not represent certain phenomena, nor are they pronouns of certain things. They are showing relative tendencies compared dynamically and therefore are to be understood comprehensively. In daily life on this planet, for example, we experience them in the following ways: in tendency yin is more expansive, while yang is more contractive. In dimension, yin is more spatial, while yang is more temporal. In position, yin is more outward, while yang is more inward. In direction, yin is more ascending, while yang is more descending. In color, yin is more purple, blue, and green, while yang is more yellow, brown, orange, and red. In temperature, yin is colder, while yang is hotter. In weight, yin is lighter, while yang is heavier. In natural influence, water results in yin, while fire results in yang.

In atomic structure, electrons and other peripheral particles are more yin, while protons and central particles are more yang. In the world of elements, oxygen, nitrogen, potassium, phosphorous, and others are more yin, while hydrogen, carbon, sodium, arsenic, and others are more yang. In the realm of light, yin is darker, while yang is brighter. In physical construction, yin is more surface and peripheral, while yang is more interior and central. In vibration, shorter waves and higher frequency waves are more yin, while longer waves and lower frequency waves are more yang.

In work, yin is more psychological, mental, and spiritual in orientation, while yang is more physical, material and social. In attitude yin is more gentle, passive, and receptive, while yang is more aggressive, active, and outgoing. In the biological world, the vegetable kingdom is more yin, while the animal kingdom is more yang. In the botanical world, yin manifests as branches, leaves, and flowers and plants that are taller, juicier, and more tropical in origin, while yang manifests as roots and stems and plants that are shorter, drier, and more northern or colder in origin. In sex, yin is more manifested in female, while yang is more in male. In body structures, softer and more expanded organs such as the stomach, intestines, and bladder are more yin, while harder and more compacted organs such as the liver, spleen, and kidneys are more yang. In the nervous system, peripheral nerves and the orthosympathetic system are more yin, while central nerves and the parasympathetic system are more yang. In taste, spicy, sour, and strongly sweet are more yin, while salty, bitter, and mildly sweet are more yang. In seasonal influence, hot summer creates a yin expanding influence, while cold winter creates a yang contracting influence.

As we can see, everywhere and in everything, in whole or in part, every manifestation in nature can be observed and experienced, compared and understood, as relatively more yin or more yang, the two antagonistic and complementary forces and tendencies that are constantly harmonizing with each other. The proportion of yin and yang is continually in flux, and yin and yang change constantly into one another. As energy contracts, becomes smaller, and hardens, the pressure of yang increases. Inside motion speeds up, generating heat. When heat is generated, expansion arises. This energy becomes larger, bigger, softer, and slower—more yin. Then as coldness arises, contraction develops and the cycle begins anew. Thus everything eventually turns into its opposite. Hot summer changes into cold winter; youth changes into old age; action changes into rest; the mountain changes into the valley; land changes into ocean; day changes into night; hate changes to love; the rich and powerful decline while the poor and meek prosper; civilizations rise and fall; species come and go; life changes into death and new life is reborn; matter changes into energy; space changes into time; galaxies appear and disappear.

Arising out of Infinity or God, yin and yang are the eternal forces and tendencies governing all phenomena, visible and invisible, individual and group, part and whole, past and future. To know the principles and laws of change is to reach the Tree of Life, to drink the water from the River of Life, and to live with the justice of the Kingdom of Heaven. When we know these principles and laws, all spiritual and religious concepts, all scientific and philosophical ideas, and all individual and social efforts are unified and understood to be complementary aspects of a larger whole. Across the ages, these principles and laws have been described in various ways and have been known under different names and forms. Understanding them is humanity's greatest achievement. The laws of change and harmony are the natural birthright of us all. Healthy human beings intuitively think and act in terms of yin and yang. These forces and tendencies are a compass enabling us to realize all possible dreams. By knowing them, we can turn sickness into health, war into peace, conflicts into harmony, misery into happiness, chaos into order. They are the invincible, eternal constitution of the infinite universe, as well as of all phenomena within it, including our life and destiny, and all worlds—past, present, and future (see Table 1).

Table 1. Examples of Yin and Yang

	Yin ▽*	Yang △*
Attribute	Centrifugal force	Centripetal force
Tendency	Expansion	Contraction
Function	Diffusion	Fusion
	Dispersion	Assimilation
	Separation	Gathering
	Decomposition	Organization
Movement	More inactive, slower	More active, faster
Vibration	Shorter wave and higher frequency	Longer wave and lower frequency
Direction	Ascent and vertical	Descent and horizontal
Position	More outward and peripheral	More inward and central
Weight	Lighter	Heavier
Temperature	Colder	Hotter
Light	Darker	Brighter
Humidity	Wetter	Drier
Density	Thinner	Thicker
Size	Larger	Smaller
Shape	More expansive and fragile	More contractive and harder
Form	Longer	Shorter
Texture	Softer	Harder
Atomic particle	Electron	Proton
Elements	N, O, P, Ca, etc.	H, C, Na, As, Mg, etc.
Environment	Vibration . . . Air . . . Water . . .	Earth
Climatic effects	Tropical climate	Colder climate
Biological	More vegetable quality	More animal quality
Sex	Female	Male
Organ structure	More hollow and expansive	More compacted and condensed
Nerves	More peripheral, orthosympathetic	More central, parasympathetic
Attitude, emotion	More gentle, negative, defensive	More active, positive, aggressive
Work	More psychological and mental	More physical and social
Consciousness	More universal	More specific
Mental function	Dealing more with the future	Dealing more with the past
Culture	More spiritually oriented	More materially oriented
Dimension	Space	Time

* For convenience, the symbols ▽ for Yin, and △ for Yang are used.

Macrobiotics in Eastern Thought

Everything in the universe is eternally changing, and this change proceeds according to the infinite Order of the Universe. This Order of the Universe was discovered, understood, and expressed at different times and at varying places throughout human history, forming the universal and common basis for all great religious, spiritual, philosophical, scientific, medical, and social traditions. The way to practice this universal and eternal order in daily life was taught by Fu-Hi, the Yellow Emperor, Lao Tzu, Confucius, Buddha, Nagarjuna, Moses, Jesus, Muhammad, and other great Far Eastern and Near Eastern teachers in ancient times and has been rediscovered, reapplied, and taught repeatedly here and there over the past twenty centuries. In his multi-volume *Science and Civilization of China*, historian Joseph Needham describes the ancient art of health and longevity—in both East and West—as *macrobiotics.*

From observation of our day-to-day thought and activity, we can see that everything is in motion or, in other words, everything changes: electrons spin around a central nucleus in the atom; the earth rotates on its axis while orbiting the sun; the solar system is revolving around the center of the galaxy; and galaxies are moving away from each other with enormous velocity, as the universe continues to expand. Within this unceasing movement, however, an order or pattern is discernible. Opposites attract each other to achieve harmony, and the similar repel each other to avoid disharmony. One tendency changes into its opposite, which shall return to the previous state. During the day we stand up and are active, while at night we lie down and rest. We repeat this pattern. From a single fertilized cell we grow into an embryo, then follow the processes of birth, growth, maturity, and death; then new life repeats the same pattern. These cycles occur everywhere throughout nature.

In the Book of Genesis, we read, "In the beginning, God created the heaven and the earth." This reveals that One Infinity polarized itself into two complementary and antagonistic forces of yang and yin. Genesis then proceeds to describe the subsequent manifestations or transformations of energy resulting from this polarization, through the stages of vibration (light and darkness), subatomic particles (the firmament or ionosphere above the earth), the world of elements (dry land and water), the vegetable kingdom (grass and herb-bearing seeds), and the animal kingdom (creatures in the water, on the earth, and in the air), reaching finally humanity, as represented by Adam and Eve, the first man and woman. This entire process of creation encompasses seven days, or stages, of development.

Observing the genesis of the universe and reflecting on our origins, we see that our humanity is the terminus of a huge spiral of life arising in the ocean of One Infinity or God. The animal kingdom, at whose apex humanity stands, exists within the vegetable kingdom, on which it depends directly or indirectly for its life and sustenance. There is no clear borderline between these two realms, since the vegetable kingdom is continuously transforming itself or changing into the animal kingdom. Thus one continuing orbit of the spiral leads to the next orbit within it. Further, the world of plants appears originally from the world of elements: soil, water, and air, which are continuously transforming themselves into vegetative life. The movement of atoms in the world of elements arises from the manifold spiral motion of electrons, protons, and other subatomic particles which further originates from waves of vibrational energy. The movement of energy or vibration ultimately appears from two polar tendencies, yin and yang, which are antagonistic and complementary to each other. In turn, as we have seen, yin and yang are the primary manifestations of One Infinity, or the ultimate origin of all phenomena.

Simply speaking, One Infinity differentiates into yin and yang, which begin an inward-moving spiral process of physical and material manifestion through six further continuously transforming worlds of energy or vibration, subatomic particles, elements, plant life, and animal life, of which human beings are the last result. Upon becoming human, we then start to return to Infinity through an outward-moving spiral of decomposition and spiritualization, melting personal and individual identities and ultimately achieving union with the Eternal One (see Figure 1).

In ancient China, this same understanding was taught by Fu-Hi (approximately 2500 B.C.), the legendary sage whose understanding of the Order of the Universe forms the foundation for the *I Ching* or *The Book of Changes.* According to legend, the Eight Trigrams symbolizing the endless cycle of change were revealed to him in the markings on the back of a great tortoise in the Yellow River. Fu-Hi and his successors used the terms *Tai-Kyoku,* which means "ultimate extremity," and *Mu-Kyoku,* which means "non-polarization" or "non-extremity," to express One Infinity. Ultimate reality, in turn, polarizes into *Tai-In,* or Great Yin, and *Tai-Yō,* or Great Yang. These forces or tendencies were symbolized, respectively, by a divided line (— —) and an undivided line (——). From this initial polarization, it was observed that yin and yang again divided into two, resulting in four; and further, these four again divided, resulting in eight possible combinations or stages of change. This pattern was symoblized as eight sets of three divided and undivided, or yin and yang

Figure 1. The Spiral of Creation

Spatial Representation: From the view of infinity, an expanding yin force creates the universe. This is represented by a centrifugal spiral (back view▽). However, from our view the universe is created by a contracting yang force or centripetal spiral (front view△).

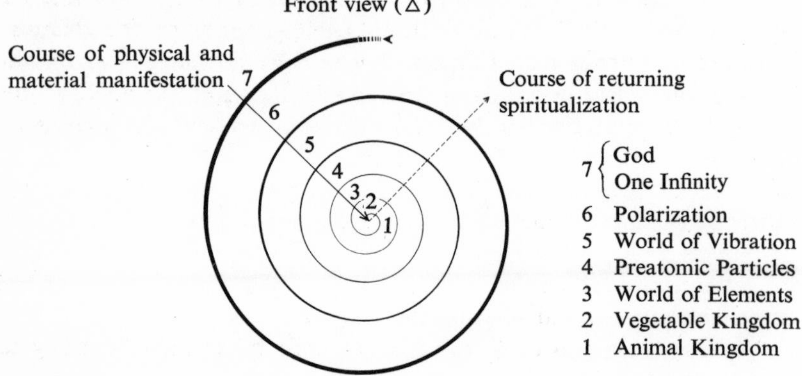

The space outside of the spiral is the unmanifested, undifferentiated ocean of Infinity, and the worlds within the spiral are the relative and ephemeral worlds.

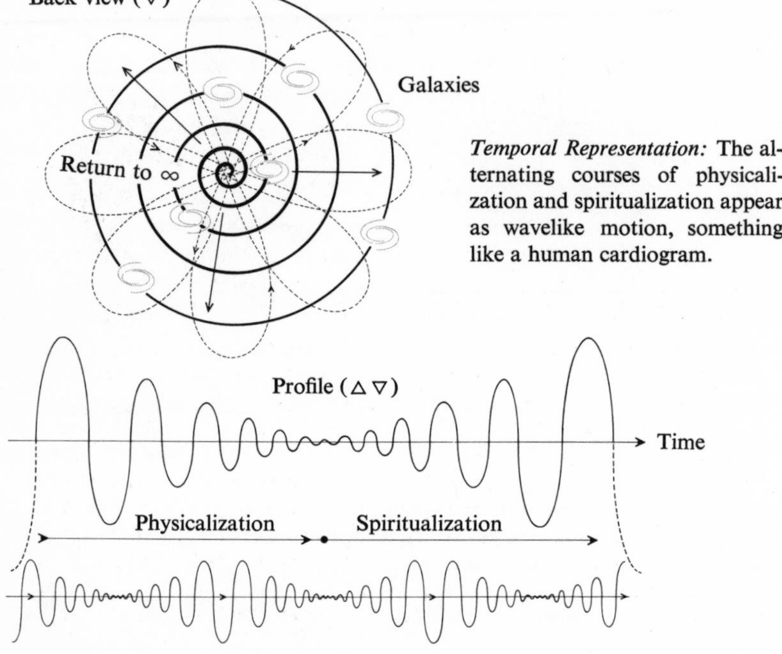

Temporal Representation: The alternating courses of physicalization and spiritualization appear as wavelike motion, something like a human cardiogram.

lines, which form the trigrams (see Figure 2).

The teaching of Fu-Hi was further developed by many philosophers and statesmen in ancient China and later became the basis for the sixty-four hexagrams of the *I Ching* or *The Book of Changes*. Both Confucius (551–479 B.C.) and Lao Tzu (*c.* 604–531 B.C.) studied these laws of change and based their teachings on the underlying principle of yin and yang. The work of Confucius includes Commentaries on the *I Ching*, which are traditionally published with *The Book of Changes*, and Confucianism calls the Order of the Universe by the term *Ten-Mei*, or the Heavenly Order. In the *Tao Te Ching*, Lao Tzu wrote of the process of eternal creation:

> Tao produces One,
> One produces Two,
> Two produce Three,
> Three produce all phenomena.
> All phenomena carry the Yin on their backs and the Yang in their embrace,
> Deriving their vital harmony from the dynamic balance of the two vital forces.

Figure 2. The Eight Trigrams

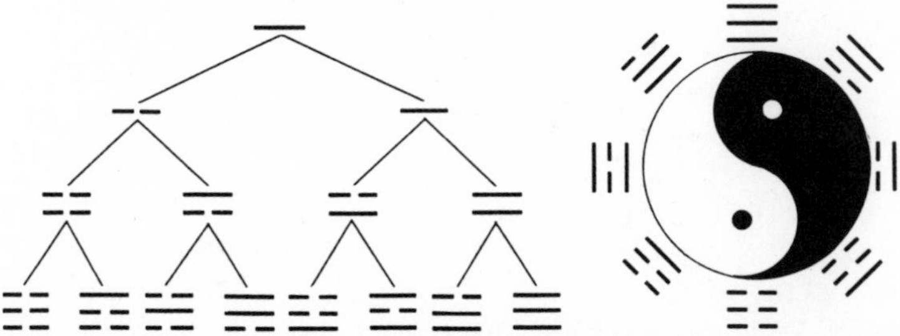

Chart at left shows *Tai-Kyoku* or *Mu-kyoku* differentiating into Great Yin and Great Yang. Great Yin further differentiates into Greater Yin and Lesser Yin, while Great Yang further differentiates into Greater Yang and Lesser Yang. Each of them further differentiates into two, forming altogether eight categories of phenomena. From left to right, each trigram or symbol represents: Earth, Mountain, Water, Wind, Thunder, Fire, Lake, Heaven. They also represent different directions, character traits, human relations, and various other natural and social, physical, and psychological manifestations. The drawing at right shows the eternal cycle of yin and yang, manifesting into these eight stages. On a universal scale, this chart has been traditionally used to describe and interpret compass directions, seasons, calendars, and other natural and social cycles.

From their understanding of the Order of the Universe—yin and yang—there developed Confucianism and Taoism, which have profoundly influenced life in Far Eastern countries for more than twenty-five centuries. The universal principles of change and harmony are also expressed in Japanese Shintō (or Shin-Do), the way of God and the ancestors. The *Kojiki*, or *Book of Ancient Events*, and the *Nihon-Shoki*, the *Book of Japanese History*, dating to the early eighth century, were composed from ancient records, legends, and mythologies. These books tell the story of the universe's creation from Ame-No-Minakanushi-No-Kami, or the Heavenly Central God. From this supreme being, who represents One Infinity, two divinities were manifested: Takami-Musubi, the God of Centrifugality, and Kami-Musubi, the God of Centripetality. From these two deities, all lesser gods and spirits, matter and energy, and other phenomena appeared. In Oriental countries there have been many outstanding individual thinkers who advocated the spirit and practice of the macrobiotic way of life. Among them in Japan were Ekiken Kaibara in the 17th Century, Shyoeki Ando in the 18th Century, and Sontoku Ninomiya and Kenzo Futaki in the 19th Century.

In Japan the word for Tao—the way of unifying oneself with the infinite Order of the Universe—is *Do*. The way to harmonize yin and yang by serving tea is called *Sa-Do*, or the Tea Ceremony. The application of yin and yang to brush writing, or calligraphy, is called *Sho-Do*. Together the martial arts are known as *Bu-Do*; while the art of swordsmanship is *Ken-Do*; the art of physical adaptation to the opponent, *Ju-Do*; the art of harmonizing *ki*, *Aiki-Do*; and the art of archery, *Kyu-Do*. Far Eastern medicine is known as *I-Do*, the art of harmonizing one's life with the environment.

For thousands of years, Oriental people have also used yin (or *in* in Japanese) and yang (or *yō* in Japanese) to describe nature and to express their thoughts and ideas in words and in daily conversation. The sun is called (*Tai-Yō*), the Great Yang, and the moon is called *Tai-In* (Tai-Yin), the Great Yin. The solar calendar is called *Tai-Yō-Reki* and the lunar calendar is called *Tai-Yin-Reki*. In Japanese, *Yin-Sei* and *Yō-Sei* refer to the nature of people, things, and the atmosphere. *Yin-Sei* means yin nature—gentle, slow, dark and humid, and sometimes depressive. *Yō-Sei*, or the nature of yang, represents the active, positive, bright and gay, and sometimes aggressive. The yin nature of vibration, energy, and atmospheric influences is called *Yin-Ki*, while the yang influences are called *Yō-Ki*. In daily conversation, many common expressions are used in this way such as *Yin-U*, meaning damp, humid rain, and *Yō-Kō*, or bright happy sunshine. Similar expressions are used very widely even in modern sciences such as the study of electricity and magnetism. *Yin-Kyoku* represents the minus pole and *Yō-Kyoku* the plus pole. In Japan the electron is called *Yin-Denshi*—yin electric particle—and the proton *Yō-Denshi*—or yang particle.

In the ancient Indian philosophy of Vedanta, which underlies Hinduism and Buddhism, we find the principle of dualistic monism expressed in the image of Brahman, or the Absolute, differentiating into Shiva and Parvati, Krishna and Radha, and other pairs of primordial male and female divinities. We see the same understanding of the universal principle further in the mythology of the ancient Sumerians and Egyptians in the Middle East—as in the stories of Astarte and Tammuz and of Isis and Osiris—as well as among the Zoroastrians.

In the Middle East, the teaching of Jesus was based on the same underlying principle known as yin and yang in the Orient. The New Testament relates many examples of this teaching, as when Jesus fed the multitude with two small fish and five loaves of barley bread. The two fish represent yin and yang and the five loaves of bread symbolize the doctrine of the five transformations (a further refinement of yin and yang and the universal cycle of change). Jesus is not just feeding people physically. He is also teaching them the Order of the Infinite Universe, or what he referred to as the justice of the Kingdom of Heaven.

The Gospel According to Thomas, *The Gospel According to Philip*, and other early Christian texts discovered in Egypt in the 20th Century contain many further accounts of Jesus's nondualistic teachings. In Thomas's account, for example, when he is asked to explain his teaching, Jesus replies, "If they ask you 'what is the sign of your Father in you?', say to them: 'It is a movement and a rest.'" Movement and rest are traditional qualities of yang and yin. In another passage, he tells his disciples how to live within the infinite universe:

> When you make the two one, and when you make the inner as the outer and the outer as the inner and the above as the below, and when you make the male and female into a single one, so that the male will not be male and the female not be female, when you make an eye in the place of an eye, and a hand in the place of a hand, and a foot in the place of a foot, and an image in the place of an image, then shall you enter the Kingdom.

By this, in our terminology, Jesus meant that when his disciples could change yin into yang and yang into yin, and achieve harmony through the unification of both, then they could become one with the Order of the Universe and live in health, freedom, and happiness.

The universal principle of yang and yin, movement and rest, or other complementary opposites is the intuitive common understanding of all the world's great religions, including Confucianism, Taoism, Shintoism, Buddhism, Zoroastrianism, Judaism, Christianity, and Islam (see Figures 3 and 4). Together with these religious adaptations, we are able to see the same understanding embodied in traditional astronomical and calendrical observations, in architecture and public construction, and in many arts and crafts. From megalithic times through the farming revolution, from the rise of civilization until the eve of modern times in about the 16th Century, the Order of the Universe was intuitively known and expressed, guiding the day to day lives of countless families and individuals, tribes and cultures, societies and civilizations, around the world.

Figure 3. Traditional Ways of Life

All of the ancient and traditional cultures, religions, mythologies, and cosmologies listed above shared a comprehensive, dynamic understanding of reality as the interplay of two opposite, yet complementary forces originating from One Infinity or God.

Figure 4. Religious Symbols

Symbol of Judaism: The Star of David, a symbol of God, shows the harmony between complementary opposites.

Symbol of Taoism: Yin and yang rotate and alternate. The center of the yin half has a yang nucleus, while the center of the yang half has a yin nucleus.

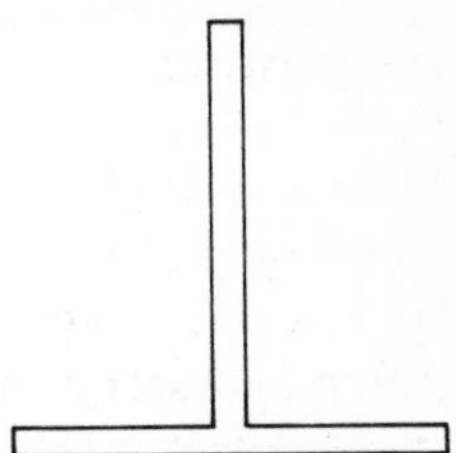

Symbol of Shintoism: The Divine Tree, Himo-Rogi, or the vertical line, makes harmony with the Earth, Iwa-saka, or the horizontal line.

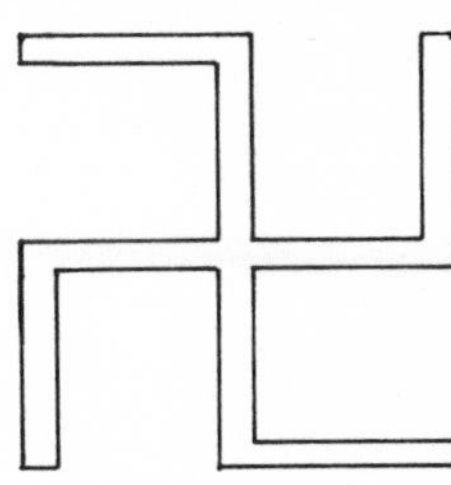

Symbol of Buddhism: Yin vertical energy and yang horizontal energy combine together and rotate, representing universal reincarnation.

Symbol of Christianity: The yin vertical arm of the cross and the yang horizonal arm harmonize, showing the unity of all phenomena.

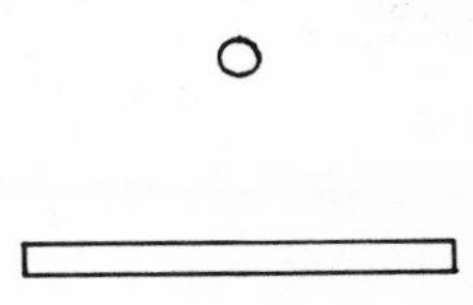

Symbol of Zoroastrianism: The yang condensed dot and the yin extended line, always together, show universal antagonism and complementarity.

Chart of the Universe of Zoroastrianism: The alternating 32 yin white squares and 32 yang black squares signify the 64 stages of transformation, corresponding to the 64 hexagrams of ancient China.

Macrobiotics in Western Thought

In the West the universal principle of change and harmony has also been observed and applied, directly or indirectly, by all previous civilizations and cultures. These include ancient Greece and Rome, the Celts of northern Europe, and the Scandinavians. In the Western Hemisphere, native peoples from the Arctic to the Yucatan peninsula, as well as in the Andes and Amazonian regions of South America, embodied views essentially similar to yin and yang in their legends of universal creation and the origin of human life. As in the Far East, the common vocabulary included many words, expressions, and concepts reflecting the harmony of opposites and the nondual nature of reality.

Many individual Western philosophers and thinkers have also developed insight into the Order of the Universe. In ancient Greece, Empedocles held that the universe is the eternal field of play for two forces, which he called Love and Strife. Although only fragments of his work survive, we find passages that remind us very much of the *Tao Te Ching*, which was composed about the same era:

> I shall speak a double truth; at times
> one alone comes into being;
> at other times, out of one several things grow.
> Double is the birth of mortal things and double demise . . . .
> They [Love and Strife] are for ever themselves, but running through each other they become at times different, yet are for ever and ever the same.

In the ancient Hellenistic world, teachings based on a deep understanding of the Order of the Universe came to be known as *macrobiotics*, after the common Greek words for "Long Life" or "Great Life." The term *makrobios* was first used by Hippocrates in the 5th Century B.C. The Father of Western medicine introduced the word in his essay *Airs, Waters, and Places* to describe a group of young men who were healthy and relatively long-lived. Hippocrates, who himself lived to over age one hundred, taught a natural way of life emphasizing harmony with the environment, especially the selection and preparation of daily food. His philosophy was summed up in the aphorism, "Let food be thy medicine and medicine thy food." The Hippocratic Oath, still taken by modern doctors, states in part: "I will apply dietetic measures for the benefit of the sick according to my ability and judgment; I will keep them from harm and injustice. I will neither give a deadly drug to anybody if asked for it, nor will I make a suggestion to this effect. . . . I will not use the knife [surgery]. . . ."

Other classical authors, including Herodotus, Aristotle, Galen, and Lucian, also used the word *macrobiotics* in discussing health and longevity. In early Western literature the term became synonymous with a simple, natural way of life, including a diet largely centered around whole grains and vegetables. The ancient Ethiopians, the Thessalians, Biblical patriarchs such as Abraham, and other long-lived people were described respectfully as macrobiotic, and the term entered the common vocabulary. During the Renaissance, for example, Rabelais, the French humanist, has a chapter on macrobiotics in *Gargantua and Pantagruel*, his satire on the foibles and follies of approaching modern civilization.

In more recent times, macrobiotics found a spokesman in Christolph W. Hufeland, M.D., an 18th Century German philosopher, professor of medicine, and physician to the poet Goethe. At a time when the leaders of the age were fighting to establish republics and nation-states, Hufeland proclaimed himself "a citizen of the world." Going against the scientific tide, he devoted his life to promoting a simple grain and vegetable diet, warned of the health hazards of meat and sugar, and promoted breast-feeding, running and other exercise, and self-healing. *Macrobiotics or the Art of Prolonging Life*, Hufeland's most famous book, was published in 1797 and was translated into many foreign languages. In this book, Hufeland pays tribute to Hippocrates and other early proponents of a simple grain-based diet such as Luigi Coronaro, the 15th Century Venetian architect and author of *The Art of Living Long* who also lived to be over one hundred.

Meanwhile, in England, at the end of the 18th Century, the essayist Walking John Stuart wrote up his walking tours across Europe, the Near East, and Tibet. "Discover that moral and physical motion have the same double force, centripetal and centrifugal, and that, as the celestial bodies are detained in tranquil orbits . . . so moral bodies . . . move . . . in the orbit of society."

In Europe, a number of creative thinkers contributed to a more integrated Western understanding of the Order of the Universe. In Germany, the philosopher Georg Wilhelm Friedrich Hegel, in his interpretation of dialectical development, postulated that human affairs develop in a spirallic form from a phase of unity, which he termed *thesis*, through a period of disunity, or *antithesis*, and on to a higher plane of reintegration, or *synthesis*, Hegel's principle of dialectics was later studied by Karl Marx, Friedrich Engels, and their associates, and formed the basis of their philosophical speculations in the area of politics, economics, and science. Marx's theory of social change, with its emphasis on *praxis* or practical activity, was very comprehensive and dynamic, but his understanding of universal order emphasized the principle of disharmony rather than harmony and neglected nonmaterial reality. Nor was he able to apply dialectics to practical aspects of daily life, such as personal health and happiness. As a result of chronic degenerative illness that ultimately took his life, Marx was unable to complete *Das Kapital*, and most of his family and Engels died of cancer.

In the 20th Century, Sigmund Freud also helped reintroduce a dynamic understanding of change. The founder of psychoanalysis identified two basic energies which he named *libido* and *thanatos*, or the life instinct and the death instinct. In the well-adjusted individual, these two basic drives balance each other, while if these energies are blocked neurosis results. Freud further divided the human personality into three parts: the *id* or unconscious instinctual drives, the *superego* or inner censor or conscience, and the *ego* or mediator between the id and superego and between the individual and society. In some ways, thanatos and id correspond to yin, libido and superego correspond to yang, and the ego represents a harmonious balance of both. Freud and his successors began to rediscover the connection between mind and body that had been severed with the rise of modern science and the mechanistic theories of Hobbes, Newton, Descartes, and Darwin. However, psychoanalysis failed to incorporate dietary, environmental, and various vibrational factors into its approach so that its therapy remains very limited. As a result of imbalance in his personal life, Freud was plagued by illness and ultimately died of cancer.

In the physical sciences, Albert Einstein, among many other scientific thinkers, sensed the complementary antagonism between the visible world of matter and the invisible world of vibration, or energy, and based on this insight formulated his universal law of relativity, in which he stated that energy is constantly changing into matter and matter is continuously transforming into energy. Thanks to Einstein's theories, the modern scientific view of reality is changing further in a more holistic direction. However, Einstein died without fully discovering the laws of spirallic development and the principles of yin and yang that would have explained the unified field theory that he devoted the last half of his life to developing. Also instead of devising practical applications of his theories to harnessing natural electromagnetic energy for peaceful purposes, to his lasting regret Einstein allowed his name and formulations to be used to split the atom and develop highly destructive artificial energy sources.

In the social sciences, Arnold Toynbee based his study of history on the alternating movement of complementary opposites which he expressed as *challenge* and *response*. In the opening of his multi-volume *Study of History*, he explains that his understanding originated from a study of yin and yang:

> Of the various symbols in which different observers in different societies have expressed the activity in the rhythm of the Universe, Yin and Yang are the most apt, because they convey the measure of the rhythm directly and not through some metaphor derived from psychology or mechanics of mathematics. We will therefore use these Sinic symbols in this study henceforward.

Other social commentators with insight into the process of historical and social change include Pitirim Sorokin, the sociologist and author of *Social and Cultural Dynamics*; Alexis Carrel, the biologist and author of *Man's Destiny*; and F. S. C. Northrop, the philosopher and author of *The Meeting of East and West*.

In Western art, music, and literature, there are many great men and women who have demonstrated a deep understanding of the Order of the Universe. These include Homer, Dante, Shakespeare, Leonardo da Vinci, Bach, Beethoven, Sir Walter Scott, Tolstoy, George Eliot, Lewis Carroll, Samuel Butler, Edward Carpenter, Cézanne, Monet, and Georgia O'Keeffe.

Modern Macrobiotics

In a second-hand bookstore in Kyoto, Japan in 1913, a young man of eighteen named Yukikazu Sakurazawa suffering from terminal tuberculosis came upon a small book entitled *The Curative Method by Diet*. The author, Sagen Ishizuka, M.D., claimed that nearly all infectious and degenerative illnesses could be relieved by discontinuing the consumption of meat, sugar, white rice, white flour, and other refined foods of modern civilization and eating instead a traditional diet of brown rice and other whole cereal grains, miso soup, cooked vegetables, sea vegetables, and other customary foods. To young Sakurazawa's surprise the diet worked, and after curing himself of tuberculosis he went on to devote his life to understanding the relation between food, environment, and human health. Under the pen name George Ohsawa, he wrote many books and gave many lectures on the Order of the Universe, especially the application of dietary and environmental principles to achieving individual and family health and realizing world peace.

In the late 1950s and early 1960s, during travels to Europe and the United States, Ohsawa introduced the term "Zen Macrobiotics" to refer to his teachings. Balanced dietary practices were traditionally kept by Zen practitioners. Since Zen was then popular in the West, Ohsawa hoped to bring this aspect of Zen practice to public attention, though his own teachings were not limited to Buddhist practices. Also, about this time, in his comparative history of science and civilization in East and West, Professor Needham compared the traditional Far Eastern approach to health and longevity, based on the principles of yin and yang and emphasizing dietary factors, with the Western tradition that came down through Hippocrates, Hufeland, and others. Needham referred to these twin historical streams as *macrobiotics*. As a result of these influences, the traditional term *macrobiotics* again began to take root in modern society.

After studying with George Ohsawa in Japan following the Second World War and after beginning to teach the philosophy of yin and yang in the United States, I adopted "macrobiotics" in its original meaning, as the universal way of health and longevity which encompasses the largest possible view of not only diet but also all dimensions of human life, natural order, and cosmic evolution. Macrobiotics embraces behavior, thought, breathing, exercise, relationships, customs, cultures, ideas, and consciousness, as well as individual and collective ways of life found throughout the world. In this sense, macrobiotics is not simply or mainly a diet, though that is the first step and usual introduction to this way of life for many people. Macrobiotics means the universal way of life with which humanity has developed biologically, psychologically, and spiritually and with which we will maintain our health, happiness, and peace. Macrobiotics includes a dietary approach but its purpose is to ensure the survival of the human race and its further evolution on this planet.

As this brief historical review shows, macrobiotics is not an abstract concept but a living reality. It has evolved from generation to generation from the time of the earliest human cultures and civilizations on this planet. It encompasses eating and sleeping, acting and resting, thinking and feeling. Macrobiotics involves respect for parents and ancestors, love and nurturing of children and offspring, caring and helping of brothers and sisters, admiring the beauty and miracle of flowers, trees, mountains, rivers, and stars, and marveling at the infinite Order of the Universe. The macrobiotic spirit is inseparable from serving other people and community, working for family and society, and devotion to build-

Figure 5. Macrobiotic Forebears

Following the expanding spiral (spiritualization): Hippocrates, Hufeland, Sagen Ishizuka and George Ohsawa.

ing a healthy, peaceful world.

Macrobiotics is not the limited philosophy of one time or place, one country or people, one teacher or organization. It is universal in its scope and eternal in its duration. It encourages the East to learn from the West, and the West to learn from the East. It recognizes that both the North and the South have much to teach each another. All antagonisms are seen as complementary: analysis and synthesis, reason and intuition, traditional and modern, spiritual and material, male and female. Macrobiotics recognizes that our understanding and practice are not fixed but constantly growing and developing. Following a general separation from the natural world and a pattern of general dietary decline over many centuries, it may take humanity possibly several hundred years to fully recover its health and develop the theoretical side of modern macrobiotics relating to technology, communications, new energy sources, and space travel, as well as to reorient society in a more healthy and peaceful direction.

Under many names and forms, macrobiotics will continue as long as human life continues to exist, as its most fundamental and intuitive wisdom. It offers a key to restoring our health, a vision for regenerating the world, and a compass for charting our endless voyage toward freedom and enduring peace.

2. Spirals of Everlasting Change

"The substance of the Great Life completely follows Tao."
—Lao Tzu

The Spiral: The Universal Pattern

Our study of humanity's origin and destiny is based on a view of life that encompasses the entire universe while revealing the order which operates at every level within it. At the foundation of this understanding is the logarithmic spiral of the universe. This basic form, which appears throughout nature, reveals the mechanism of creation and the fundamental unity and interconnectedness of life. This simple but comprehensive form enables us to unify all of the seeming contradictions in our modern science and in all other domains of modern thought, including the origin of the universe and biological life, the course of human history, and the development of consciousness.

Observing the movement of yin and yang—the antagonistic and complementary forces that make up all phenomena—through time and space, we discover that their motion appears in the pattern of a spiral when viewed from the front, while their motion is helical when viewed from the side. About eighty percent of the galaxies, including our Milky Way, are spiral in form, and this universal pattern is also observed in the currents of wind and ocean upon the earth, the growth and development of plants, the construction of shells found on the beach, the flow of water in rivers and kitchen sinks, in the whorls of our fingertips, the helical structure of DNA, the construction of our ears, and the spiral pattern of hair growing on our heads (see Figure 6).

Spirals are initially created by a yang centripetal force from the periphery to the center, moving towards physicalization and materialization. Upon reaching its most contracted state, this centripetal force turns

Figure 6. Examples of Natural Spirals

Nature forms many beautiful logarithmic spirals.

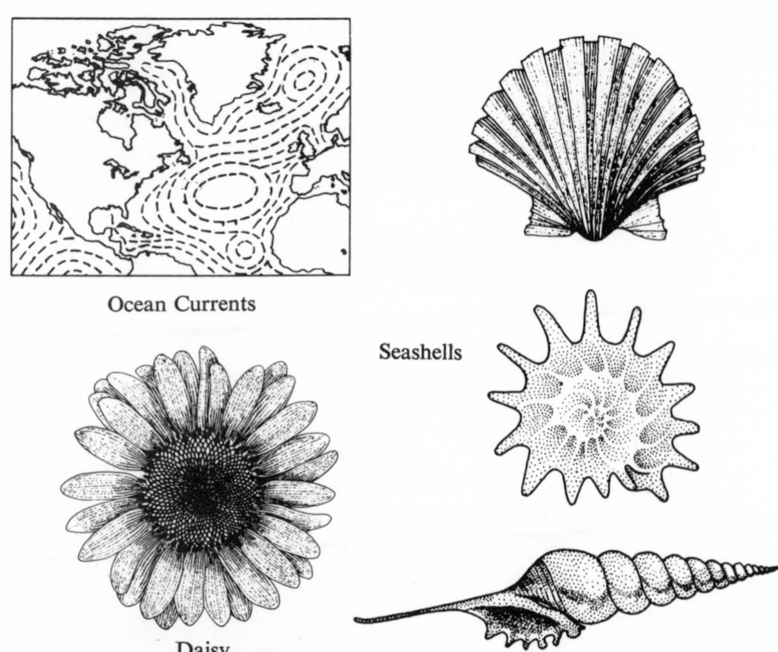

Ocean Currents

Seashells

Daisy

Figure 7. The Expanding Universe

Milky Way Galaxy

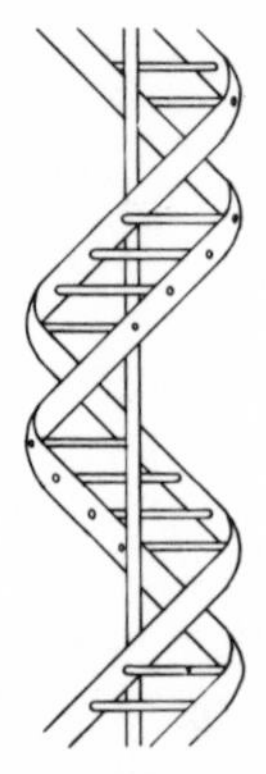

DNA Molecule

The universe is expanding not by a big bang but by a logarithmic spiral. As a result, galaxies here and there appear to be flying away from each other.

to its opposite, and a yin centrifugal force, expanding from the center back to the periphery, develops moving toward decomposition and dematerialization. The periphery, being more expanded, is the more yin region of the spiral, while the center, being more condensed, is the more yang region. The ultimate periphery is the infinite space of the universe itself—the greatest yin. The ultimate state of condensation is infinitesimal matter—the greatest yang.

The modern theory of creation is a misinterpretation of the logarithmic spiral. Because galaxies appear to be moving away from each other at high speed, scientists have postulated a primordial Big Bang (see Figure 7). In actuality, the universe is expanding spirallically and did not begin with a violent explosion. Nor will it end with one. Eventually everything dies out peacefully and vibrations cease, but then a new universe will appear again. Einstein's theory that space is curved and light bends comes close to discovering the logarithmic nature of the universe. However, his assumption that the speed of light is constant violates the basic principle that everything changes. Light also moves in a spiral, and its speed changes inversely with the distance from its source, approaching infinite velocity. In coming years, as science develops and rediscovers the unifying principle of yin and yang, the structure of the universe will become better understood.

Meanwhile, the relative movement between yin and yang has been partially noticed by science and medicine and applied in limited form to other domains. The world of electricity and magnetism, for example, is commonly understood to involve a flow of current and charge between plus (+) and minus (−) poles. The balance of blood is maintained between alkalinity and acidity as well as between a ratio of red-blood cells to white-blood cells. Autonomic nerve reactions covering the extensive area of automatic motion throughout the human body are subdivided into orthosympathetic and parasympathetic functions. Chemical structures, including the composition of DNA, are known to contain alternating groups of elements and compounds. All physical phenomena are conditioned by the relations between time and space, mass and energy, and many other relative factors.

In some cases, the spiral pattern governing these phenomena has been discovered by modern science. For example, when electrons and protons are examined in detail, it is clear that they are not discrete particles but are regions within the spiral field of moving energy known as the atom where the condensation of energy is particularly dense or highly charged. In the case of the proton, this condensed energy is positively charged and centrally located, and therefore we may classify it as yang. In the case of the electron, this spiral cloud of condensed energy is negatively charged and located at the periphery, and therefore yin. However, electrons are moving at a much greater speed than protons. From this perspective, their activities are more yang in comparison with the slower-moving protons. Thus, the proton's greater size is compensated for by the electron's more rapid motion, thereby achieving a dynamic balance between their yin and yang qualities (see Figure 8).

Figure 8. Formation of Subatomic Particles

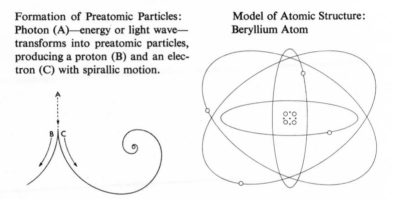

Formation of Preatomic Particles: Photon (A)—energy or light wave—transforms into preatomic particles, producing a proton (B) and an electron (C) with spirallic motion.

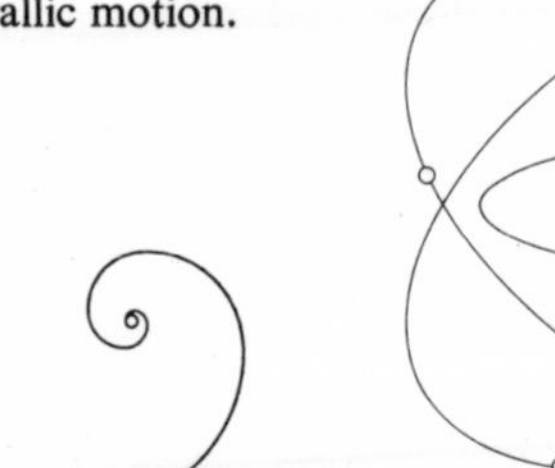

Model of Atomic Structure: Beryllium Atom

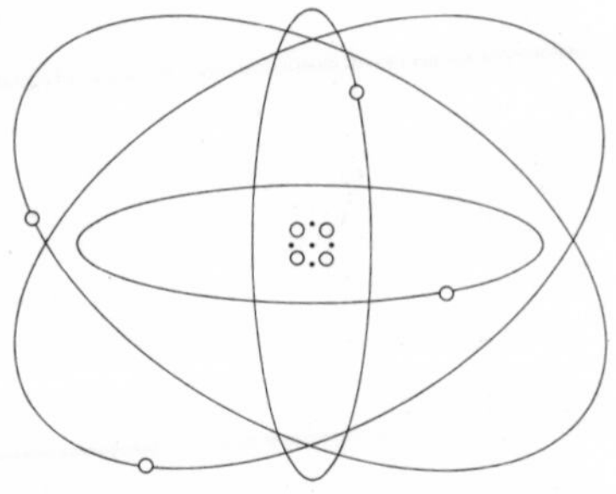

The spiral construction of the universe has left many traces within the human form, though this basic pattern is not fully appreciated by modern science and medicine (see Figure 9). The basic form of human life is spirallic, though this form can be most clearly seen in embryo. The two main complementary-antagonistic spirals in our bodies function through the nervous and digestive systems. While developing in the womb, the digestive system is originally more yang, being in a central or inward position, while the nervous system, being at the periphery, is more yin. Among the nutrients that nourish the fetus through the blood in the mother's placenta, protein and other more yin factors are attracted primarily to the yang digestive system. As a result, this system eventually becomes more yin (i.e., soft and expanded). In a similar manner, calcium and other minerals which are more condensed or yang in structure are attracted more to the peripheral yin nervous system. Eventually the nervous system becomes more yang (i.e., hard and compacted), forming the spine.

The formation of the arms and legs is also spirallic (see Figure 10). Consider their curled position during the period of embryonic development as well as in a newborn baby. The arms and legs are each composed

Figure 9. Spirallic Human Development: Embryo to Adult

In each of the three diagrams, A (the inner system) represents the digestive and respiratory systems. B (the peripheral system) represents the nervous system. C (the middle system) represents the circulatory and excretory systems, which result from the interaction of systems A and B.

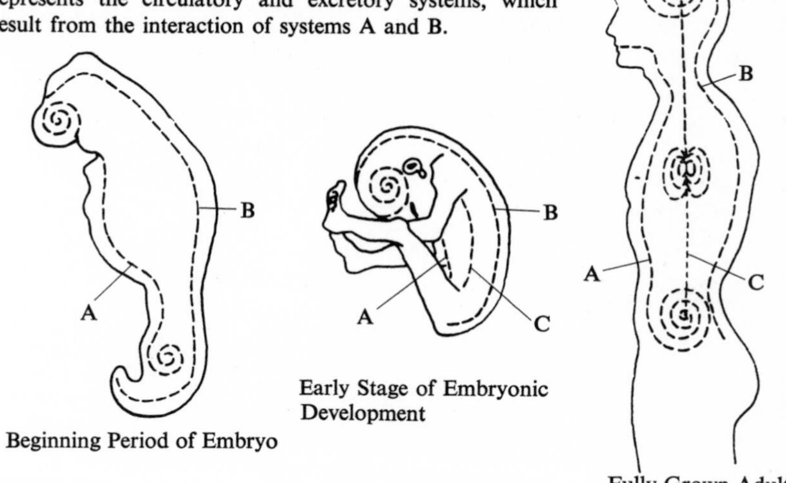

Beginning Period of Embryo

Early Stage of Embryonic Development

Fully-Grown Adult

Figure 10. Spirals in the Arm

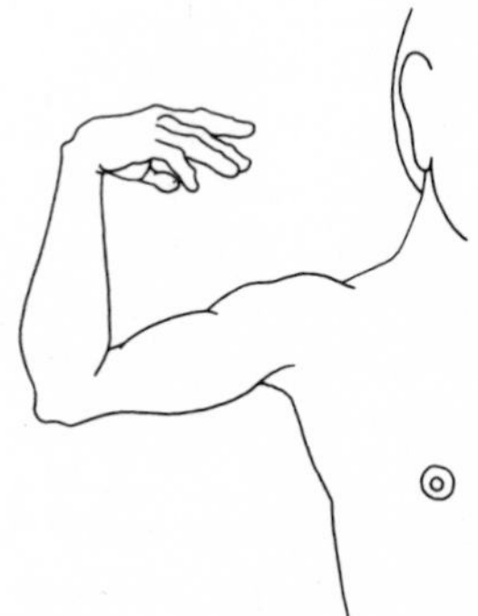

Each arm is composed of seven-orbital logarithmic spirals. Each orbit later develops as a section of the arm. The tip of the fingers are the innermost part of the spiral.

of seven concentric logarithmic spirals. The logarithmic spiral with seven orbits is the universal shape of all fully developed forms in the universe. In the arm, the first orbit extends from the region of the collarbone to the shoulder-blade. The second orbit extends from the shoulder to the elbow. The third goes from the elbow to the wrist; the fourth from the wrist to the knuckles; the fifth, sixth, and seventh from the three joints of the fingers. The distance from the shoulder to the elbow is about one half the distance from the shoulder to the tips of the fingers. The distance from the elbow to the wrist is about one-half to two-thirds the distance from the elbow to the tips of the fingers. The distance between the wrist and knuckles is about one-half to two-thirds that of the wrist to the tips of the fingers. The distance between the knuckles to the first joint of the fingers is about one-half to two-thirds that between the knuckles and the tips of the fingers. The distance between the first and second joints of the fingers is about one-half to two-thirds that between the first joint and the fingertips. In a logarithmic spiral, the ratio between successive orbits remains constant; each orbit is about two to three times larger than the previous turn.

From the surface of the earth to the reaches of endless space, from here to eternity, everywhere at any time, logarithmic spirals appear and disappear in all dimensions of the boundless ocean of universal energy. Our world of vicissitude governed by two antagonistic and complementary forces, yin and yang, is the relative world sensed, perceived, and experienced by everyone in everyday life. From a tiny flower in the field to large movements of the entire universe, from a shadow of a smile on our face to the huge scale of natural catastrophe, every being and every phenomenon is spirally governed between expansion and contraction, in the relation of front and back, of inner and outer, and in the balance between the beginning and the end.

The Spiral of Life

Within the infinite ocean of the universe, a spiral of life has arisen moving inwardly through seven orbital stages (see Figure 11). Infinity, the first stage, is the primary source and origin of all phenomena. It is known variously as God, Brahman, *Tai-Kyoku*, or Oneness. Polarization, the appearance of yin and yang, is the second stage. These forces and tendencies manifest as centrifugality and centripetality, space and time, and are the origin of all relative worlds. Movement or motion begins between these two poles, and energy and vibration, the third stage, manifests in the relative world as the primary field or state before and after the appearance of physical and material forms. Preatomic or subatomic particles, the fourth stage, appear next in the form of numerous particles of spirally moving energy. The world of elements or atoms, the fifth stage, is formed by the orderly manifestation of subatomic particles into spirallic atomic structures. Elements also appear in molecular state in solids, liquids, gases, and plasmas, which in turn manifest

Figure 11. The Spiral of Life

1st Stage: Seventh Heaven, One Infinity, God, Brahman, *Tai-Kyoku*, Oneness.
2nd Stage: Polarization, Yin and Yang, beginning of the Relative World.
3rd Stage: Energy and Vibration, beginning of the Phenomenal World.
4th Stage: Preatomic Particles, beginning of the Material World.
5th Stage: World of Elements and Physical Nature.
6th Stage: The Vegetable Kingdom, beginning of the Organic World.
7th Stage: The Animal Kingdom, culminating in Human Beings.

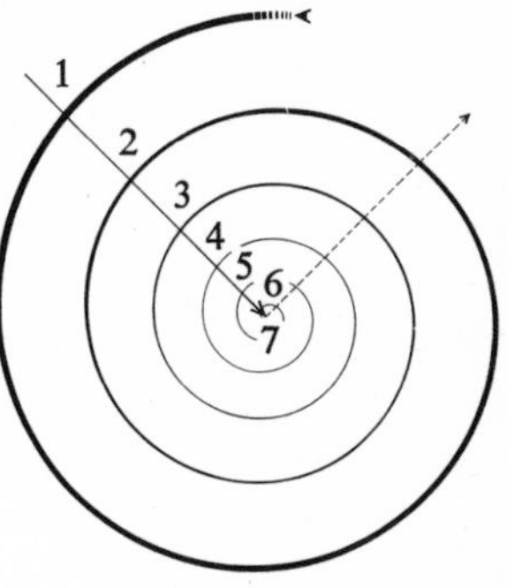

as soil, water, air, and fire. The world of plants is the sixth stage. From the world of elements, organic life arises upon the surface of the earth. Charged electromagnetically by heaven's and earth's forces, the vegetable kingdom grows and decays according to laws of spirallic expansive and contractive motion. The animal kingdom, the seventh stage, develops out of the vegetable world as a more highly charged and activated order of life. At its apex, human beings have evolved as the most conscious and physically active species.

The inward-moving centripetal spiral of life reached the center of the spiral with the creation of *homo sapiens* and other highly evolved animal species. At the center, however, the spiral starts to reverse its course, returning again towards One Infinity with which it ultimately merges. By rotation, yang heaven's force changes into yin earth's force. Thus the universal process of physicalization changes into its opposite, dematerialization or spiritualization, giving rise to an outward-moving spiral leading to union with God.

During the last phase of physicalization upon the earth, after millions of billions of years of transmutation, human life emerges and takes in various energies, particles and elements, and organic chemical compounds absorbed and arranged in the form of vegetables—the preceding stage in the spiral of life. We call this process eating, and it includes the digestion and absorption of food and liquid through our digestive vessels. The nutrients we ingest are absorbed into the blood and other bodily fluids, which in turn form body cells, including the reproductive cells. The formation of the ovum, or egg in a woman, is a result of inward spirallic motion of follicles in the ovaries, while the formation of sperm in a man is the result of the outward differentiation of reproductive cells. These processes are, respectively, yang and yin, and therefore in accordance with the law of harmony attract and fuse with each other to create the beginning of new life. During the embryonic period of approximately 280 days, four major stages take place in the mother's uterus. The first process is fertilization and implantation, which occurs over a period of about seven days. Second, the formation of the major systems takes place, over a period of about 21 days. Third, the major organs and glands become formed along the systems, taking about 63 days. The fourth period of approximately 189 days sees the formation of appendages and continuous development, up to the time of birth. These stages unfold logarithmically, with each stage taking about three times longer than the previous stage.

The Spiral of Consciousness

During the embryonic period, our growth and development proceed through autonomic, mechanical functions that we may call the primary and basic judgment of our life. Upon birth and for the duration of our life, this primary judgment continues to function through all parts of our body such as unconscious nerve reactions, digestive and respiratory functions, circulatory and excretory activities, and in various other ways. However, soon after our birth, we begin to develop sensory consciousness or judgment to deal with various kinds of stimuli from the other stages of spirallic life: a sense of touch for the solid environment, a sense of taste for the liquid environment, a sense of smell for the gaseous environment, a sense of hearing for the vibrational environment, and a sense of sight for the world of light. The sensory experience further involves discriminating various physical states such as hunger and thirst, pain and comfort, and heat and cold.

In the third stage, we continue to develop our sensory to emotional judgment, which deals with the feeling and distinction of beauty and ugliness, love and hate, joy and sadness, like and dislike, emotional attachment and detachment, sentimental agreement and disagreement. This is the world of most literature and film, popular music and romantic feeling. We may call this stage of development in the more refined apprehension, aesthetic consciousness.

Through the repeated experience of sensory and aesthetic rise and fall, we grow and develop our judgment and consciousness to the fourth level: assumption and speculation, conceptualization and organization, analysis and synthesis, evaluation and definition, and other more objective mental activities. In this level, which we may term the intellectual, logical concepts are formed, reasoning images are structured, organized systems are conceived, and comparative values are defined. This is the world of modern science and technology as well as social administration.

Our consciousness further expands toward understanding the relations among people and among groups of people, including societies and the world as a whole. From individual human relations we further develop to understand and balance family relations; from family relations to community relations; from community relations to relations among humanity and other species. This level of consciousness may be called social judgment. The problems of ethics and morals, harmony and peace, world law and world order are among many other concerns at this level. From this stage we view personal life from the perspective of society and national life from the perspective of benefiting the world as a whole.

From many experiences and challenges, successes and failures in the first five levels, our consciousness further develops to the level of philosophical thought. We think deeply about such basic questions as: What is life? Where have we come from? Where are we going? What is the purpose of life? Who am I? We start to reflect upon the meaning of our own life, search for the secret of the universe, and strive to become one with the eternal truth. The sixth level of consciousness is a door to the last level of consciousness. All traditional religions, spiritual doctrines, and teachings of the way of life begin at this level.

Through the constant search for universal truth, the meaning of life, and the origin and destiny of creation, we finally reach universal consciousness, which may be called Supreme Judgment. At this level we understand the Order of the Universe and the achievement of universal love and absolute freedom. Living at the universal level has been described by different traditions as attaining *Satori*, reaching Nirvana, or entering into the Kingdom of Heaven. This consciousness does not conflict with any circumstances or point of view, embracing all contradictions in the relative world as complementary, understanding the paradoxical constitution of the entire universe, and beginning to exercise our real freedom. At that time, our consciousness starts to merge with One Infinity. We move or play freely among the previous six levels of judgment. We live with the spirit of endless gratitude and love and pray for all beings to realize eternally their endless dream.

These, in brief, are the seven levels of consciousness through which a natural human being passes while living upon this earth (see Table 2).

Table 2. Levels of Judgment and Consciousness

Levels of Judgment		Name of Infinity in Each Level	Products in Each Level
7th Supreme	Universal and eternal consciousness; all-embracing, unconditional love and acceptance; endless gratitude, complete freedom.	Freedom	Eternal happiness with the spirit of "One Grain, Ten Thousand Grains." Living in *satori*, nirvana, or grace.
6th Philosophical	Awareness of justice and injustice, righteousness and unrighteousness, spiritual and material, invisible and visible.	Justice	Religions, philosophical doctrines, spiritual disciplines.
5th Social	Awareness of right and wrong, suitable and unsuitable, proper and improper, flexible and rigid.	Peace	Ethics, moral codes, family, culture, civilization, politics, economics.
4th Intellectual	Awareness of reason and unreason, proved and unproved, general and specific, causes and effects.	Truth	Theories, concepts, organizations, systems, sciences.
3rd Emotional	Awareness of love and hate, joy and sadness, likes and dislikes, harmony and disharmony.	Love	Poetry, novels, music, art, theater, dance.
2nd Sensory	Awareness of pleasure and pain, beauty and ugliness, comfort and discomfort.	Desire	Tools, crafts, machines.
1st Mechanical	Spontaneous, automatic response.	Adaptability	Instincts, drives, habits, impulses, and other responses to environmental stimuli.

There is a spirallic relationship among the different levels of judgment and consciousness. In terms of time, mechanical responses change instantaneously, usually in a matter of seconds. Sensory changes take longer, usually a matter of minutes. Emotional feelings persist over a period of days, while intellectual theories can keep their influence for years. Social ideas can last over a century, while philosophical products such as religions and doctrines can last a millennium. In terms of space, the lower types of judgment influence a fewer number of people over a narrower space, while the higher judgments influence a larger number of people over a wider space. Yet all results and influences produced by the first six levels of consciousness are relative, ephemeral, and all eventually disappear, producing the opposite effects. Supreme judgment or consciousness alone acts beyond the limits of time and space, and its influence is universal and everlasting.

However, the majority of modern people limit themselves only to developing sensory or aesthetic consciousness, seeking emotional gratification or ephemeral love and beauty in the changing world. Few among us enter into the fourth level of intellectual judgment and fewer still grow to the fifth and six levels of social and philosophical consciousness, concerning ourselves with problems of world peace and spiritual growth. From time to time, every several hundred years in the modern era, there appears someone who is able to attain universal consciousness. However, Supreme Judgment is in reach of all who know the Order of the Universe and its endless mechanism of change, yin and yang. Together with this understanding, of course, we must know how to apply yin and yang, physically, mentally, socially, and philosophically, anywhere, at any time, and for this we must develop qualities of infinite patience and life-long perseverance to realize our dream.

Macrobiotics—the way of health, happiness, and peace through biological and spiritual evolution—is the universal means to practicing and harmonizing with the Order of the Universe in daily life. Macrobiotics does not deny any traditional way of life, expression, or view but encompasses all human thought and behavior in an orderly whole. Macrobiotics recognizes that human life on this planet is one manifestation of the eternal Spiral of Life unfolding from infinity to the infinitesimal world, from the infinitesimal to infinity. Yin and yang are a compass to guide us all toward health and happiness, freedom and justice, during our life on this wonderful planet and in the course of our endless journey through the stars.

The Spiral of Evolution

It is impossible to record and document the actual changes that stars go through in the course of their lives, since stars may exist for hundreds of billions of years. Present assumptions about the evolution of galaxies, stars, and planets are speculative, based largely on fragments of observed data and on mathematical possibilities. However, from our understanding of the Spiral of Life, we discover that galaxies are created and subsequently held in balance by two huge forces: a more yang, centripetal force generated by the periphery of space inward toward the galactic center, and a yin, centrifugal or expanding force generated outward from the center of the galaxy toward the periphery.

Stars are born and live within these galactic environments, and their development also occurs in the form of a spiral that is governed by the interplay of yin and yang (see Figure 12). The development of a star generally takes place in three phases which correlate with the spiral: 1) a phase of condensation or materialization in which the star coalesces out of a diffused cloud of interstellar gas; 2) a phase of stability, during which the star maintains a degree of equilibrium within the main sequence; and 3) a phase of decomposition or dematerialization, in which the star becomes increasingly unstable and experiences alternating phases of expansion and contraction, discharging most of its material substance off into space.

Figure 12. The Origin and Development of Stars

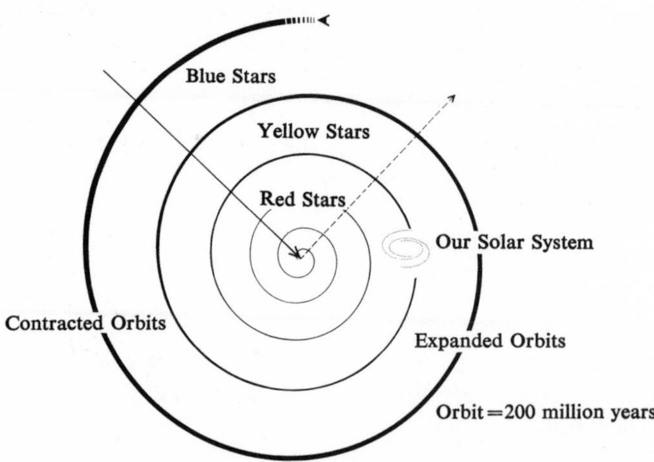

As stars spiral in toward the center of the galaxy, they change from blue to yellow to red classifications. One orbit of our solar system takes about 200 million years.

Our sun, for example, was created when the centripetal force coming in from the periphery of the galaxy and the centrifugal force coming out from the center of the galaxy intersected within a cloud of intersteller gas and dust, creating a huge inward, centripetal spiral. The gaseous cloud then began to condense, guided by the energy lines that are formed within this huge spirallic motion. With continuing contraction, the pressure inside the proto-star began to rise, along with its temperature. Eventually, the contracting process stopped as centrifugal outward energy generated in the internal regions of the star counterbalanced the inward centripetal energy. The sun may actually be more like a terminus of centripetality and the beginning of centrifugality rather than a shining body that is independent from the planets and comets. As the center of the solar system, the sun was born as a center of energy change, where the direction turns from incoming energy generated by combustion into outgoing heat, light, and pressure generated by solar wind and radiation.

Our solar system, one of hundreds of millions of similar systems in the Milky Way galaxy, also forms a spiral when viewed as a whole. The field of planets, including the orbits of Mercury, Venus, Earth, Mars, Jupiter, Saturn, Neptune, Uranus, and Pluto, falls within the nucleus of the spiral. Beyond the planetary region, more than one hundred million comets are constantly streaming in toward the sun in an extended field about four thousand times larger than the field of planets—a dimension of about four light years. The peripheral field of comets may gradually be increasing in density in the center of the system, where eventually comets may enter into the planetary field and change into planets (see Figure 13).

Figure 13. The Cometary and Planetary Field

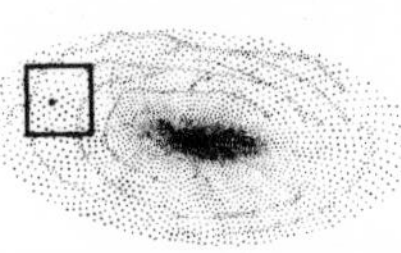

Oblique view of the Milky Way galaxy. Dot shows approximate position of the solar system.

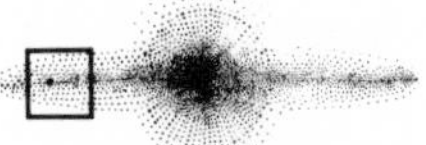

Side view of the Milky Way galaxy. Dot shows approximate position of the solar system.

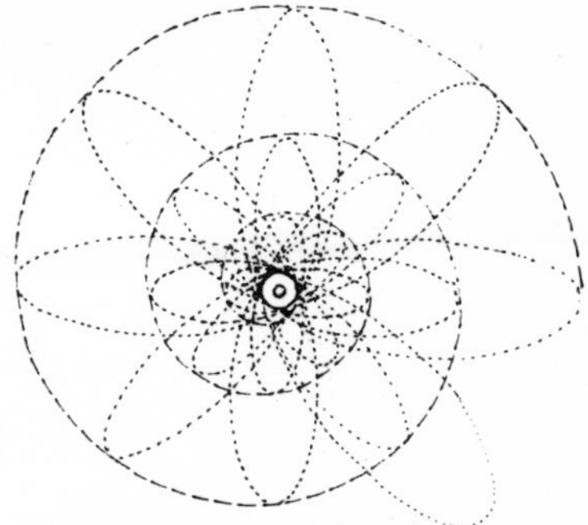

Schematic structure of the solar system. Central circle shows the position of the sun; next circle shows the planetary field; spirallic petal design indicates orbits of various comets. All the planets are slowly spiralling in toward the sun.

Within the solar system, nearly 4 billion years ago, our earth was a gaseous spiral. Within the cloud, which was highly charged with intensive thunderstorms of electromagnetic activity, various light elements were produced: hydrogen, helium, lithium, beryllium, boron, carbon, nitrogen, and oxygen. Fusions among them created further, heavier elements, and their combinations made molecules and chemical compounds.

Relatively heavier elements, molecules, and compounds gradually gravitated toward the center, eventually forming the solid core of the earth, while others of lighter weight gradually formed the periphery of the earth, eventually becoming the atmosphere (see Figure 14). In between that solidifying matter and the expanding atmosphere, water (a compound of more yin oxygen and more yang hydrogen) started to appear, and it covered the entire surface of the solid earth.

Figure 14. The Spiral of the Elements

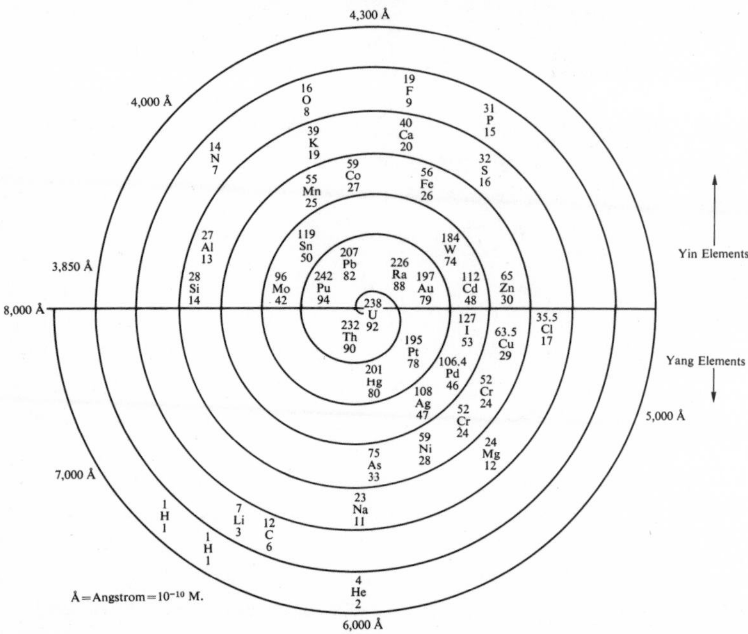

• This spirallic arrangement of major elements is made according to the spectroscopic examination of color waves. Approximately 8,000 Å to 5,000 Å is the area of yang elements, and approximately, 5,000 Å to 3,500 Å of yin elements. According to this chart, elements occupying the positions in opposite orbits—e.g., hydrogen (H) and oxygen (O)—can combine easily due to the principle of attraction between yin and yang; and elements occupying a similar position—e.g., hydrogen (H) and helium (He)—have difficulty combining with each other unless technical changes of temperature, pressure, or nature are applied.

• Elements occupying peripheral areas are more yin and lighter—e.g., hydrogen (H) and helium (He)—while elements located at more central areas are more yang and heavier—e.g., zinc (Zn) and iron (Fe). Elements belonging in the most centeral orbits—e.g., uranium (U)—are radioactive, tending to return to the outer orbits in the same way the sun is radiating its energy outwards in the solar system. Most balanced elements are found in the fourth orbit, and some of them are magnetic, such as iron (Fe), cobalt (Co), and nickel (Ni).

• The chart reveals that lighter elements are gradually transmuting toward heavier elements and heavier elements are in turn transmuting back into lighter elements, though it may take some thousands to millions of years to do so naturally. The transmuting speed of peripheral elements is much slower than that of central elements.

• The precise chart of classification of the elements by yin and yang should be considered together with this spectroscopic examination, including other factors such as the nature of chemical reactions and freezing, melting, and boiling temperatures. Knowing the yin and yang natures of elements, we are able to discover all laws and phenomena—chemical and biochemical, geological and biological—as well as the order of change.

Within the gaseous cloud activated by electromagnetic storms, primitive organic molecules—carbohydrates, proteins, viruses, and bacteria—began to appear and continued to evolve mainly in the gradually forming water toward more highly evolved organisms. In general, out of the primary common molecule, two streams of life began to evolve: 1) the vegetable kingdom accelerated more by the centrifugal expanding force (yin) and 2) the animal kingdom, stimulated more by the centripetal contracting force (yang) (see Figure 15). They continued to change, transform, and differentiate into various species of life, mainly in water and later on land, over a period of more than 3.2 billion years of organic life.

In the water, during the Precambrian era, various water mosses and invertebrates started to appear. Both primitive vegetables and animals depended upon each other: the former as the food of the latter, the latter as nourishment to the former. This period may have continued nearly 2 billion years with gradual transformation of the organisms and their environment toward the next stage of development.

During this long period, the surrounding water gradually accumulated minerals that condensed and crystallized, creating salt water. Along with this yang process of transformation, the water plants changed toward mineral-rich seaweeds and the invertebrates, taking in minerals within their bodies, developed toward vertebrates, which are the ancestors of most of our present marine animals. In this biological stage, evolution continued for approximately 0.8 billion years.

As the next great change, the land arose above the water, following repeated shattering of the earth. Over the course of millions of years as land was created, water plants and water animals were transported to the land and exposed to the air. Some sea plants adapted to the land atmosphere becoming land moss and primitive grasses. Some sea ani-

Figure 15. The Spiral of Evolution

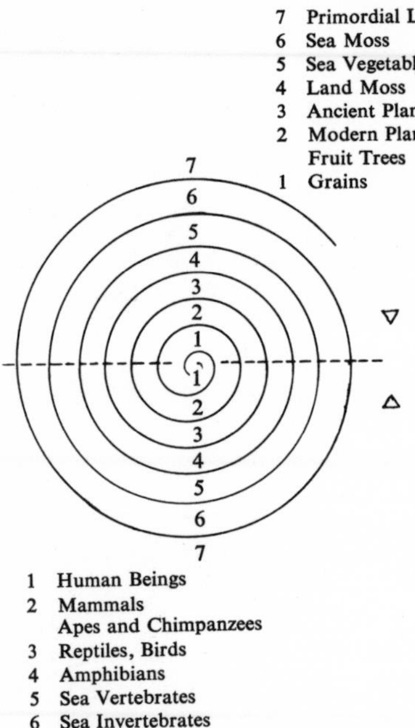

This chart illustrates another approach to understanding the development of life on earth. Overall, the entire period of biological development has taken over 3 billion years in accordance with geological and celestial change. The entire process unfolds spirallically in seven stages or orbits. The upper half of the drawing shows botanical development (more yin), and the bottom half shows zoological development (more yang). Plants tend to come out during warmer climatic periods in the earth's history, while animals develop more during cooler climatic periods. Human beings, in the center of the spiral, the most yang, contracted form of life. Our species is the turning point between the long inward course of physicalization and the return outward course of spiritualization. We can take all domains of biological life as food; in the right proportion, this secures our health and consciousness for further stages in our evolutionary journey.

mals evolved toward amphibians which are able to live in both water and air. Since then, evolution has proceeded on the land, beginning approximately 400 million years ago (see Figure 16).

As the next development in the progressive evolution of land species, a variety of ancient plants and a variety of primitive reptiles and birds began to appear about 200 million years ago. With the increasing temperature and humidity on the surface of the earth following that period and with the more intensified solar radiation, these species grew eventually into the ancient giants—fern trees, horsetails, conifers, dinosaurs, flying reptiles, and others. The dominion of ancient plants as well as ancient birds and reptiles reached its zenith about 100 million years ago.

From that time, the atmospheric temperature of the earth turned gradually colder. The age of modern plants—the ancestors of most present vegetables—and the age of mammals, depending upon these plants directly or indirectly for food, began about 64 million years ago

Figure 16. Evolutionary Development

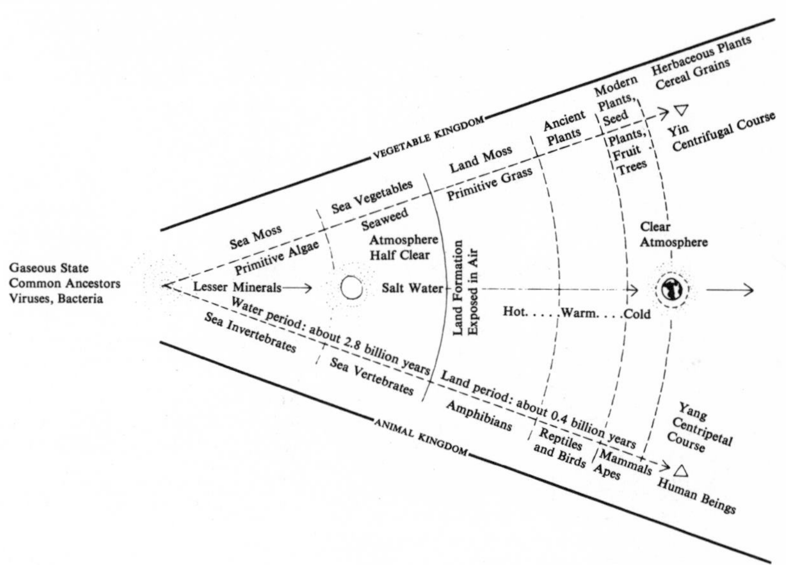

with the rapid extinction of the preceding giant forms of life. The biological modern age continued about 50 million years, during which most of the present species of plants and animals appeared.

As the earth continuously became colder, seed-bearing plants started to appear. The fruits and leaves that were once huge and juicy in the era of ancient plants contracted in the colder climate, becoming smaller, harder, and drier. In the forests, the species eating these fruits, playing from tree to tree, evolved into apes. In the fields, various herbaceous plants continuously produced smaller grains with harder shells as the climate became successively colder. The species eating cereal grains—the most biologically developed plants, combining the fruit and seed together—gradually evolved into human beings. The ancestors of *homo sapiens,* standing upright like the wild grains they consumed, may well have emerged about 20 million years ago.

Since then, the atmosphere of the earth has tended as a whole to become colder, with minor fluctuations alternating between warmer and cooler eras. In the most recent period of geological change, during a period of about 1 million years, the cycle of ice ages began, with four great glacial and interglacial periods up to the present time (see Figure 17). With these repeated periods of coldness, together with the eating of herbacious grains and other plants, *homo sapiens* developed an intelligence superior to any preceding species upon the earth.

As the cold climate covered a larger territory of the earth during the ice age, human beings began to adapt to their environment through the use of fire and salt. First, fire and salt were applied to food to improve digestion, provide strength and vitality, and contribute to clear, focused thinking. Secondly, fire was applied to the production of tools and dwellings, including weapons used to hunt animals as a supplementary source of food during times of hardship and occasionally against other human beings. The use of fire produced the birth of human culture and now today, less than a million years later, its misuse threatens to end it.

Figure 17. The Ice Ages

▽ Colder Glacial Period

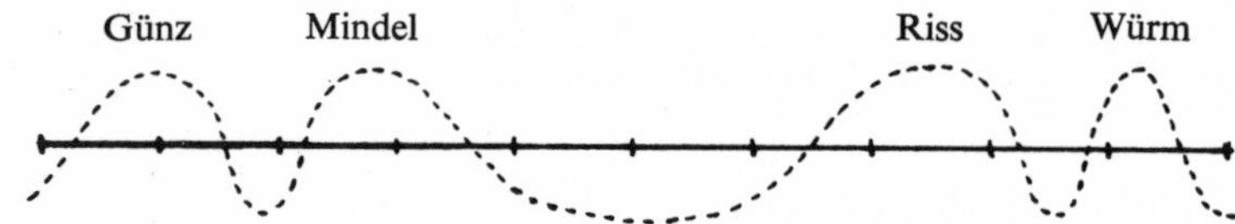

△ Warmer Interglacial Period

Dotted line shows the approximate alternation of glacial and interglacial periods during the past million years. About 12,000 to 20,000 years ago, the fourth glacial period, the Würm, ended. We are now in a warmer, interglacial period.

The Galactic Spiral

While biological life has progressed in its evolution for a period of more than 3.2 billion years, our solar system has been constantly revolving, with neighboring groups of similar systems, in orbit around the center of our galaxy. Our solar system is moving at present with the speed of about 186 miles (300 kilometers) per second, making an entire orbit in about 200 million years. Though the duration of the orbit may gradually change, we may assume that biological life on earth has experienced sixteen orbits or more in the course of organic evolution.

During each 200-million-year orbit, the distance from the center of our galaxy to our solar system changes just as the distance of the earth from the sun changes in its yearly cycle. When the distance shortens, the dimension of our solar system tends to contract slightly, resulting in a slight shortening of the distance between the sun and the earth. When it lengthens, the solar system tends to expand slightly, resulting in the lengthening of the distance between the sun and the earth. During the shorter period, the earth receives more intensified solar radiation, becoming hotter and more humid, while during the longer period it becomes colder and drier. The warmer and hotter periods may be referred to as Galactic Spring and Summer, while the cooler and colder periods correspond with Galactic Autumn and Winter (see Figure 18). Each season lasts approximately 50 million years. The change in the earth's climate during this time appears to be the major influence in the change of atmosphere that resulted in the gradual change of biological species.

Figure 18. Galactic Seasons

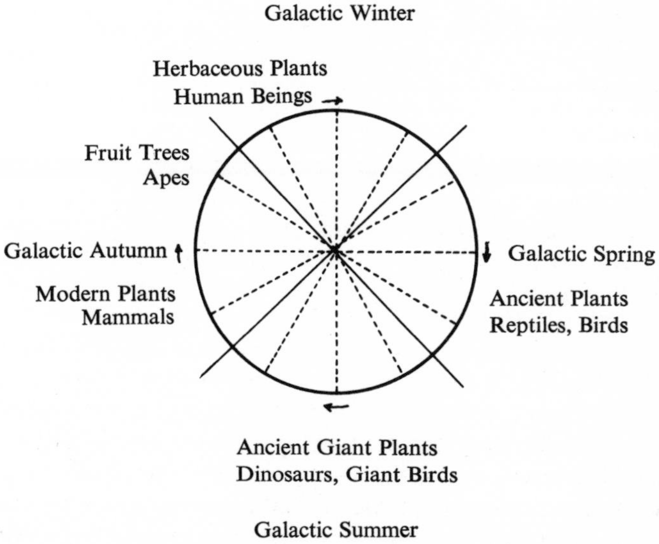

The arrows show the direction of the solar system orbiting around the center of the Milky Way galaxy, taking approximately 200 million years—one Galactic Year—for one orbit. Each season lasts about 50 million years. Each dotted section, representing galactic months, is approximately 16.6 million years. During Galactic Summer, biological life became more expanded and cooler (cold-blooded), while during Galactic Winter, it became more contracted and warmer (warm-blooded). Humanity is a product of Galactic Winter.

About 150 million years ago, during Galactic Spring, when the earth's surface was mild and moist, ancient plants and animals, including reptiles and birds, appeared. As the planet continued to warm up, plants and animal species grew larger in size, culminating in the dinosaurs and giant ferns during Galactic Summer. Since that time, plants and animals have continuously become smaller and harder as the earth cooled down and grew drier. Modern plants and mammals began to appear about 50 million years ago in Galactic Autumn, and herbaceous plants, especially whole cereal grains, and the human species appeared at the beginning of Galactic Winter. Our species will continue to experience increasing coldness for many millions of years, with shorter cycles alternating between cold and warm climates. To sum up: in Galactic Spring and Summer, biological life became more expanded and cooler (cold-blooded), while in Galactic Autumn and Winter, it became contracted and warmer (warm-blooded). How to adapt to our changing evolutionary environment, especially in respect to eating and the use of fire in the preparation of food, are matters of essence and survival for the continued survival and development of *homo sapiens* for millions of years to come.

The Spiral of the Northern Sky

Vibration coming from the periphery of the solar system, or during nighttime, is stronger than energy coming from the sun, or during daytime, because this more powerful influence is coming from the centripetal force that created the solar system, of which the radiation of the sun is only a result.

The same is true in the case of the northern and southern skies. Our solar system is inclined at approximately a 90-degree angle within the Milky Way and is about two-thirds out from the center of the galaxy. The earth's south pole is thus facing the center of the galaxy and is receiving the more localized influence of that area, while the north pole faces the outer rim of the galaxy and beyond, directly receiving vibration from the infinite universe itself. This is why the cycles of the northern skies have such a profound influence on human civilization.

As a result, the intensity of electromagnetic charge in the northern and southern hemispheres is somewhat different, with a greater intensity of charge existing in the north. It is for this reason that practices such as palm healing developed more in the northern hemisphere, particularly on mountainous islands like England and Japan, which are at the edge of a big continent and where the charge of natural electromagnetic energy is more active.

As the earth spins on its axis and revolves about the sun it also moves in an important cycle called the Precession of the Equinoxes. Gyrating like a spinning top, the earth's polar axis constantly changes position in relation to the plane of the galaxy (see Figure 19). Extending from the North Pole in a line out to the stars, we can see that this motion traces a great circle in the northern sky called the path of the Northern Ecliptic. This cycle takes about 25,800 years to complete, during which time the Pole Star slowly changes (see Figure 20).

Figure 19. Precession of the Equinoxes

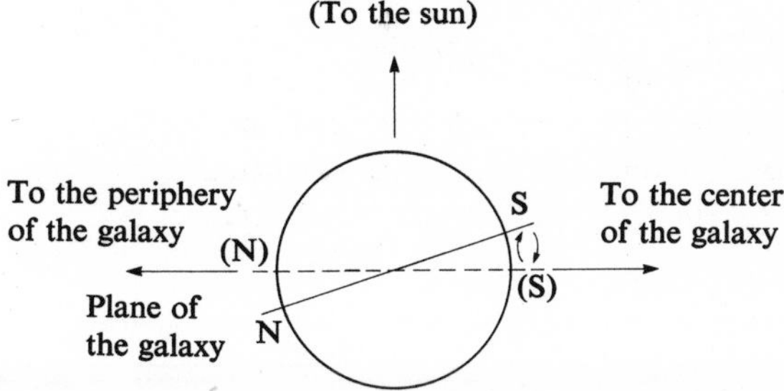

The turning of the earth's axis traces a great circle of major celestial influences in the Northern Sky.

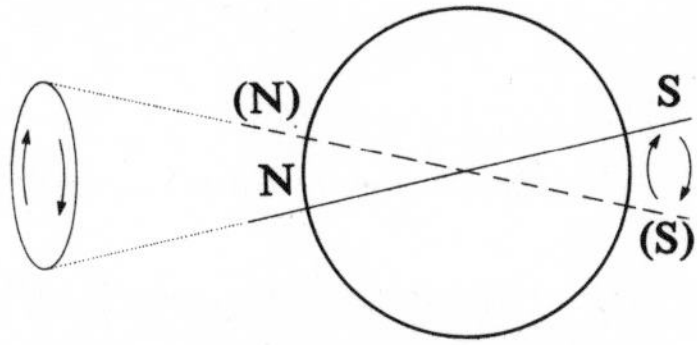

The earth's axis rotates, moving in and out of the plane of the Milky Way galaxy in a cycle of 25,800 years.

During this cycle the earth passes through different stages with various stars and constellations shifting directly overhead. As a whole, the earth is surrounded by a vast protective belt of electromagnetic fields, but the area over the North Pole is relatively open. The shower of energy from these particular stars therefore exerts a strong influence on the earth; as they slowly shift position (see Figure 21), the stars or constellations in this region produce a regular change of electromagnetic charge on the earth.

Figure 20. Constellations of the Northern Sky

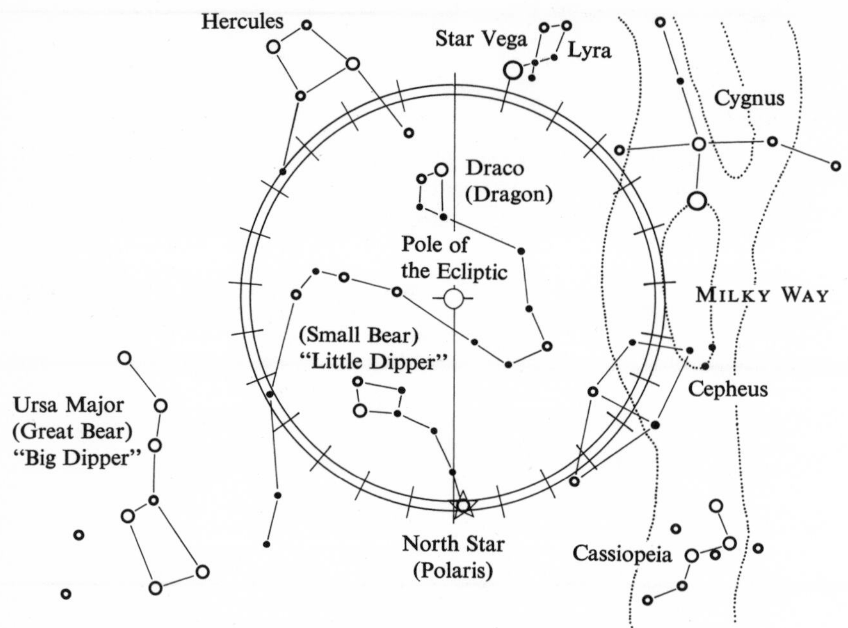

Stars in different constellations serve as the Pole Star on account of the Precession of the Equinoxes. Six thousand years ago, the Pole Star, Thuban, was located in the tail of Draco. Some 13,000 years ago, it was located in the constellation Vega. Today it is located near the Little Bear.

At present, the star Polaris is almost directly overhead; in about the year 2100 it will arrive at a position exactly over the north pole. This will signal the end of the preceding 12,900-year cycle and the beginning of a new half-cycle (see Figure 22). During the new 12,900-year cycle, the heavenly river of stars we call the Milky Way will dominate the northern sky.

Humanity last experienced this half-cycle from about 23,000 to 13,000 years ago. During that time, the earth's axis moved more into line with the plane of the galaxy, and the northern sky was covered with thousands of stars. We were constantly bathed in a shower of light and radiation, pouring in through our spines, energy centers, meridians, organs, tissues, and trillions of cells. We became very highly energized, and our consciousness developed heightened awareness and capacities.

Figure 21. Northern Electromagnetic Influence

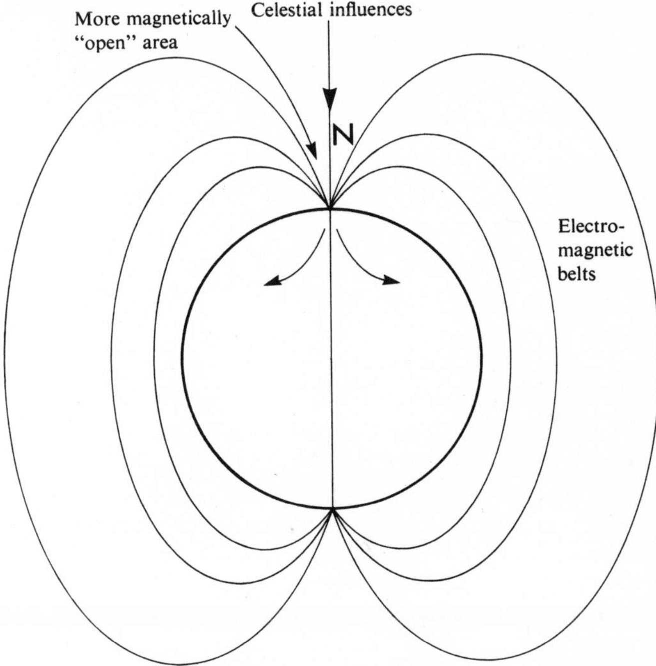

The northern polar stars and constellations exert a particularly stronger influence on the earth.

This era is remembered in myths and scriptures as the Age of Light or the Golden Age and was generally peaceful and prosperous, healthy and wise.

Then about 13,000 years ago, we moved out of the galactic plane as the star Vega of the constellation Lyra came overhead. Our consciousness gradually diminished, together with a decrease of the earth's electromagnetic charge. This was later chronicled as the age of Paradise Lost. While we cannot be sure of how life was organized in the previous Age of Light, the world's myths and scriptures almost universally record that humanity reached advanced cultural, spiritual, and scientific levels and maintained a worldwide peaceful, unified civilization. This ancient spiritual and scientific world community then collapsed through a series of natural catastrophes that ushered in the next 12,900-year half-cycle, the Age of Darkness.

Figure 22. The Vega/Polaris Cycle

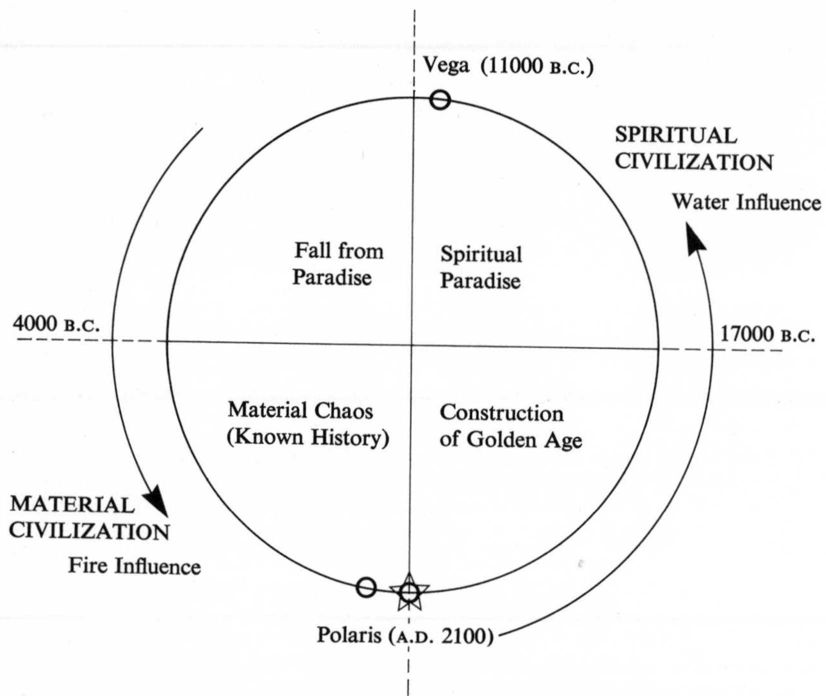

In approximately A.D. 2100, Polaris, the current North Star, will be directly overhead, marking the beginning of a new Era of Humanity.

The Spiral of History

World history moves in a spiral. There is as marvelous an order and unity to human affairs, including the rise and fall of civilizations, as there is to the helical development of galaxies, solar systems, plants and animals, DNA, and subatomic particles.

The Spiral of History can be divided into twelve sections (see Figure 23). They are not actually equal but because the spiral is logarithmic become increasingly smaller in size and shorter in time. The first sections span over a thousand years in length, while the last section lasts less than fifty years. Because of the spirallic nature of historical development, history actually does repeat itself to an extent. For example, the Crusades and the Mongol invasions of the Middle Ages fall in the same

Figure 23. The Spiral of History

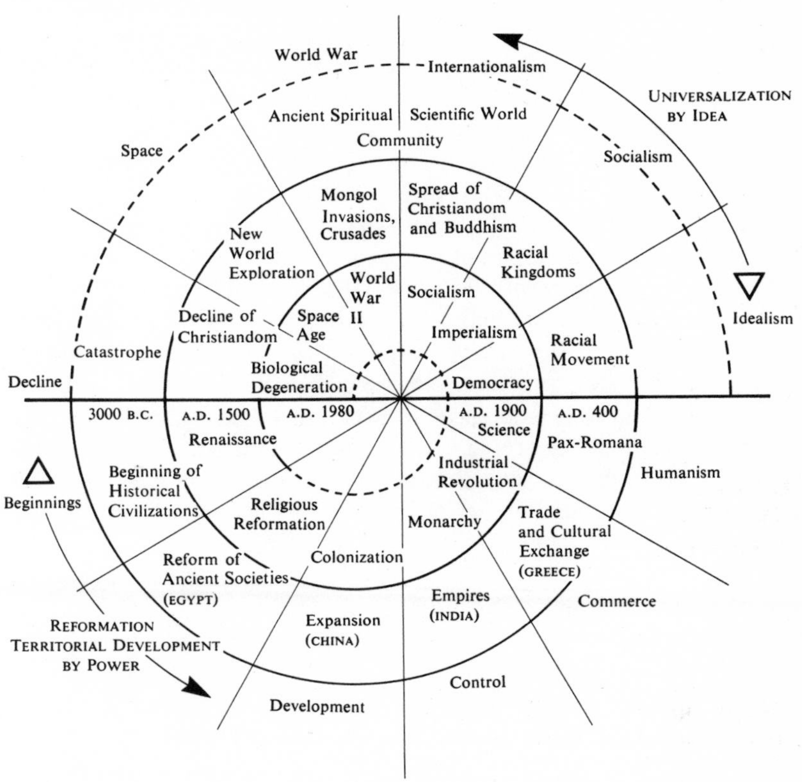

section as the World Wars in our era. The quality of each section is the same; the main difference is that previous ages spanned a longer period of time.

The Spiral of History alternates between periods of territorial expansion and conquest and periods of universalization by idea. Each half-orbit of the spiral encompasses a half dozen sections and corresponds with one of our historical ages. Each successive orbit of the spiral is approximately one third as long as the previous orbit. In other words, each period changes with three times the speed of the previous age. Life today is three times as fast-paced as it was a generation ago. It is nine times as rapid as a hundred years ago, and twenty-seven times more accelerated than during the Middle Ages. The seven ages include:

1. *The Age of the Ancient Spiritual and Scientific World Community*, about 23000 B.C.–3000 B.C.

Ancient civilization appears to have reached a peak about fifteen to twenty thousand years ago in an era when the earth was milder, vegetation was more fertile, and human consciousness received the full electromagnetic force of the Milky Way overhead. According to worldwide myths and legends this age declined when the celestial energy of the northern sky diminished and catastrophic changes ensued. The first of these great natural disasters probably took place twelve or thirteen thousand years ago during the era when Vega became the Pole Star. Over the next several thousand years almost all traces of this ancient civilization disappeared with flooding, volcanic eruptions, earthquakes, a possible partial axis shift, and other natural calamities, including melting of the glacial ice sheets across most of the northern half of the world.

Prehistoric standing stones, pyramids, ziggurats, and other megalithic structures have long been associated with funeral and burial practices. A new view is now emerging that these monuments embody a high degree of mathematical precision in their construction and advanced astronomical knowledge in their alignment to solstices, equinoxes, and other celestial events. It is also now increasingly recognized that some of these structures were laid out in patterns along lines of relatively intense electromagnetic energy in the earth or atmosphere. It is believed that standing stones can transmit electromagnetic impulses and waves across fields and forests like acupuncture needles placed along meridians of energy in the body to stimulate various internal organs. In some cases, the stones and monuments appear to have been used to collect, generate, and transmit natural energy and radiation from the sky and earth for use in farming, energy production, and healing (see Figure 24). A common theme in ancient myths and legends is the misuse of technology, triggering natural catastrophes and an end of the ancient world community.

New methods of calculating tree ring growth, as well as revisions in radiocarbon dating, have pushed the chronologies of early cultures and civilizations thousands of years further back. The discoveries of archeologists, anthropologists, astronomers, linguists, mythologists, and other researchers are beginning to reveal the existence of an ancient worldwide civilization that was much more developed and peaceful than previously imagined. However, since we cannot be certain about life in the ancient world, this era is outlined with a broken line in the diagram.

2. *The Ancient Age*, 3000 B.C.–A.D. 400

Recorded history began about five thousand years ago. A period of

Figure 24. Ancient Technology

Standing stones, pyramids, ziggurats, and other ancient structures appear to have been used to collect and generate natural electromagnetic energy.

milder climate stimulated new territorial developments in northern China, northwest India, Mesopotamia, the upper Nile and Mediterranean regions, as well as in Mesoamerica and the northwestern part of South America. This age was characterized by the rise of agriculture, the domestication of livestock, and the spread of bronze and some iron technology, as well as the formation of empires. The Ancient Age ended about A.D. 400, around the time of the fall of Rome.

3. *The Medieval Age*, A.D. 400–A.D. 1500

The age was characterized more by religious and ideological control than by political, social, or economic power and expansion. In Europe, Christianity inherited the mantle of authority following the collapse of Rome. Racial kingdoms formed including those of the Angles, Saxons, and Normans. Two global wars, the Mongol invasions from east to west and the Crusades from west to east, occurred during this time. This era ended with the exploration and discovery of new territories in Africa, Asia, and the Americas, followed by the decline of Christiandom in Europe and the rise of modern science.

4. *The Modern Age*, 1500–1900

This era began with the Renaissance at the end of the 15th Century and the birth of modern science. In Europe, religious reformation led to the split between Protestants and Catholics. In Asia, Buddhism and Confucianism also split into different sects over religious doctrines and practices at this period. Western powers colonized various areas of the world. The Hapsburgs, Bourbons, Romanovs, and other monarchies prospered. However, monarchism declined following the rise of the bourgeoisie, and democracy developed out of the political and industrial revolution and the humanist movement. This era ended in the early 1900s on the eve of the First World War and the Russian Revolution.

5. *The Recent Age*, 1900–1980

The 20th Century began with the spread of democratic principles and the formation of modern nations. Communist, socialist, and imperialist movements also developed on an international scale. Industrial technology spread around the globe, and advances in transportation and communication contributed to a more unified world. Space exploration began during this period, and with the establishment of the League of Nations and United Nations humanity's consciousness of being citizens of one planet started to evolve. However, during this age, social, political, economic, and ideological conflicts intensified, leading to two world wars, recurrent racial and religious struggles, and the nuclear arms race. Pollution increased, contributing to the destruction of cropland, oceans and rivers, and the atomosphere. The Recent Age drew to a close with the spread of cancer, heart disease, and other degenerative illnesses, the widespread decomposition of families, the decline of religious and spiritual values, and the failure of educational systems, as well as the decline of human physical, mental, and spiritual health and vitality.

6. *The Biotechnological Age*, 1980–2030?

About 1980 we entered a new era, the last fifty years before the Spiral of History reaches its center. During this period, the threats to human survival will reach their climax. The proliferation of nuclear technology and weapons, the threat of nuclear terrorism and blackmail, the accumulation of nuclear waste, escalation of the nuclear arms race into space, and other related aspects of the atomic dilemma are already of widespread concern. Parallel to this external threat to human survival is an internal one. Every year it is more apparent that the human race faces an unparalleled crisis of biological degeneration resulting from increased consumption of artificial foods and beverages, environmental pollution, and an unnatural way of life.

To slow the present epidemic spread of cancer, heart disease, diabetes, mental illness, AIDS and other immune-deficiency diseases, infertility, herpes and other sexually transmitted diseases, and other degenerative disorders, modern civilization is turning increasingly to genetic engineering and other artificial methods that could result ultimately in the loss of our basic human quality and spirit and creation of an artificial species.

At a recent conference, a group of futurists described this coming period as the Age of Bionization and foresaw that it would begin in 1980 and last into the next century. Organ and gland transplants, as well as artificial body parts, will become commonly available. Silicon chips have been fused with the human nervous system for the first time in order to control certain nervous disorders. With the development of test tube pregnancies, artificial insemination, surrogate mothers, sperm bank fathers, and other forms of genetic manipulation, birth will increasingly be removed from the hands of parents, and the traditional family unit will further decline. Computers and robots will rapidly replace the industrial work force, making humanity even more dependent on automation and artificial technology.

Along with the increased mechanization of the body, the last turn of the spiral will witness more widespread control of the mind. This process has already been initiated in schools, hospitals, and prisons with the use of tranquilizers, sedatives, and other drugs to modify behavior. In the future, drugs and chemicals may be introduced to control common moods, feelings, perceptions, and possibly even program beliefs, opinions, and basic human values such as love, truth, and spirit. The latter part of this period, the Age of Psychonization and Ultrapsychonization, will probably reach a peak about 2030 or 2040. About this time, according to present trends, the natural human species as we know it will collapse and be succeeded by an artificial species that may bear some external resemblance to *homo sapiens* but have no natural link with millions of years of past human evolution.

7. *The Dawn of the Era of Humanity*, about 2030–2100

Though modern civilization will rapidly decline in the next half century, natural human beings need not die out. At the same time that bionization and psychonization are proceeding, a new orientation of civilization will arise among those people who have individually reoriented their way of life according to the laws of nature and the Order of the Universe. Through their understanding and efforts, the construction of a new world of health and peace will begin, unifying all antagonistic factors in human affairs. This trend, of course, has already begun and will intensify between now and about A.D. 2100, when the Pole Star moves directly overhead, coinciding with the start of the bright half of the 25,800-year cycle.

During the last several thousand years, prophets and visionaries, such as Buddha, Confucius, Lao Tzu, Abraham, Jesus, Muhammad, Nostradamus, and Swedenborg have prepared humanity for the coming age of light. The start of the Era of Humanity will probably be signalled by the establishment of a world federal government or planetary commonwealth to oversee the elimination of nuclear and conventional weapons, to preserve the earth's natural environment, and to promote the biological, psychological, and spiritual health and happiness of humanity. Existing political, economic, ideological, and cultural systems will be seen as complementary to one another and will be allowed to develop naturally as civilization as a whole develops in a more peaceful direction. We may anticipate that this era of peace and harmony will last for about ten thousand years as the celestial influence of the Milky Way increases. However, whether we pass through the center of the Spiral of History safely and build this glorious new era depends entirely upon each one of us. As with the ancient scientific and spiritual world community, this part of the spiral remains speculative, as indicated by the dotted line in the diagram.

In summary, universal will or, we may say, the consciousness of God travels with infinite speed, differentiating into yin and yang, time and space, life and breath. As this movement begins, a curving vibration is produced, and the relative world, including the worlds of stars and planets, elements and compounds, plants and animals, and human beings appears. Infinite consciousness manifests as wavelike motion, creating first simple spirals, then more complex spirals, and finally spirals within spirals, creating what is called atoms and particles, galaxies and clusters of galaxies, body and mind, male and female, nature and history. The universe is nothing but a beautiful flower with trillions of spiral petals, all unfolding in perfect harmony. By understanding the various spirals of creation, we come to know our eternal origin and destiny and become one with life as a whole.

3. Food and the Human Constitution

"All beings are evolved from food."
—Bhagavad Gita

"As the air I breathe is drawn from the great repositories of nature, as the light on my book is yielded by a star a hundred millions of miles distant, as the poise of my body depends on the equilibrium of centrifugal and centripetal forces, so the hours should be instructed by the ages and the ages explained by the hours. Of the universal mind, each individual man and woman is one more incarnation."
—Emerson

Centripetal and Centrifugal Force

During more than 3.2 billion years of biological development, the atmosphere surrounding the earth has gradually changed from a heavy, dense gaseous state toward a light, clear state as it progressed. Celestial radiation from the sun, the moon, the planets, and stars and galaxies has showered upon the earth with more intensified and varied radiation passing through the clearer atmosphere.

When the sun was the only shining celestial body sending its dim influence into the very ancient gaseous cloud of the earth, biological life consisted only of single-celled organisms. As the radiation from the moon and planets started to penetrate through the atmosphere, biological life began to differentiate and divide. As the natural electromagnetic radiation from hundreds of thousands of stars began to be felt, more complex multicellular organisms began to evolve. As the millions of celestial bodies in the heavens began to exert an influence from the depths of the darkness of space, highly evolved plants and animals began to appear.

The human constitution is a product and reflection of this celestial and terrestrial environment (see Figure 25). Our systems, organs, and functions reflect and correspond to the movement of groups of constellations and galaxies, as well as the influence of planetary motions. The whole body is a replica of the universe. Mountains, waterfalls, forests, and fields all have their counterparts in our physical makeup. The celestial galaxies, for example, are reflected in the human brain, each condensed cell representing a galaxy. In turn, each cell or organ represents the whole body. Each infinitesimal part reveals the whole. Without the influence of heavenly forces, human life would not exist, and without their influence the human body would not have its present form.

Figure 25. Solar Wind and Human Structure

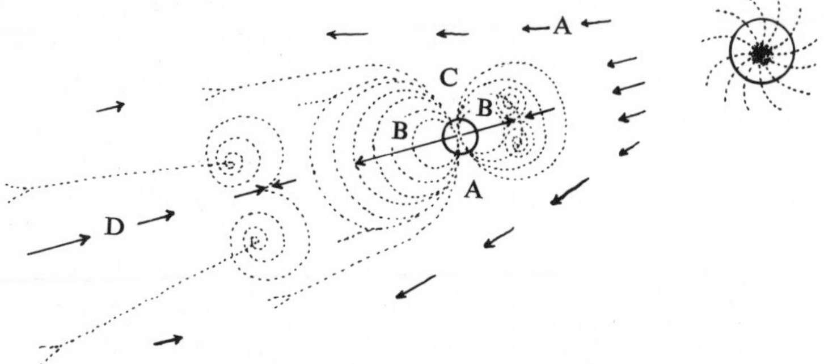

As the earth (C) rotates, electromagnetic orbits are generated and formed around the earth. Incoming solar wind (A) from the sun and the centripetal force from peripheral space (D) collide with the centrifugal force generated by the earth's rotation (B), and form an a humanlike aura of electromagnetic or plasmic energy around the earth.

The force of celestial influence showering upon the earth day and night is at present seven times stronger than the expanding force generated by the rotation of the earth. Escaping velocity from other planets, depending upon their distance from the sun, size, and rotation, varies from that of the earth. The 7: 1 ratio shows up in numerous natural phenomena. The formation of waves in the ocean, for example, reflects this proportion (see Figure 26). Recently developed biological species, especially human beings, have a relation of head to body of 1: 7. This ratio appears in the human structure in many aspects, as the average ideal proportion (see Figure 27).

Figure 26. Spirallic Ratios in Nature

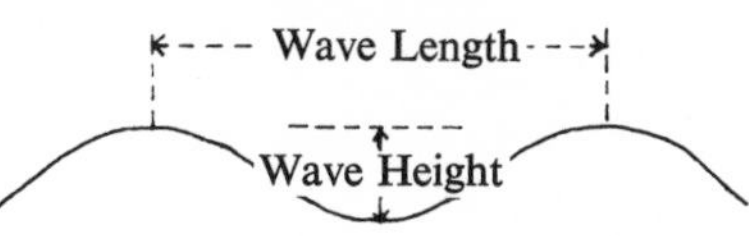

Natural wave height and wave length maintain an orderly 1: 7 ratio. Many other natural phenomena also show the 1: 7 balance in the forces of Heaven and Earth.

Figure 27. Spirallic Ratios in the Human Body

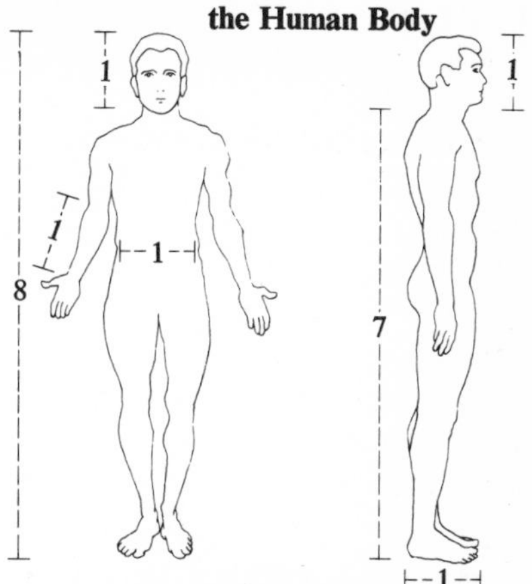

The 7: 1 proportion occurs in the relation of head to body and other ratios of the human body.

The 1: 7 ratio between centripetal and centrifugal forces found in nature suggests that our intake of the physical environment in the form of food, drink, and air should also follow this general proportion. Ideally, by comparative weight or volume, the ratio of minerals to protein in the diet is 1: 7; protein to carbohydrate, 1: 7; carbohydrate to water 1: 7; and water to air 1: 7. However, practically, this varies, of course, according to the environment and individual conditions, between 1: 5 in the colder, more northerly regions and 1: 10 in the warmer, more southerly climes.

By harmonizing with the environment in this way, human beings are able to maintain maximum balance and enjoy maximum flexibility in thinking and behavior. Observing logarithmic proportions in our way of life—such as the traditional golden mean—is the key to achieving health and longevity. Among the many kinds of food available for humanity, unrefined whole cereal grains generally contain the ideal 1: 7 ratio of minerals to protein and protein to carbohydrates. In combination with whole grains, soups, cooked vegetables, beans and sea vegetables, and occasional fruits, along with good quality spring water or well water for tea or other traditional beverages, provide the ideal proportion of liquid. Proper breathing exercises, meditation, prayer, and other forms of self-reflection, as well as physical activity and physical exercise, supply sufficient air to the organs and tissues, as well as electromagnetic energy, completing the spiral.

Ki, the Energy Centers, and Meridians

In ancient times, people referred to the centripetal force coming in from above as the force of heaven and the centrifugal force generated from below as the force of earth. Physically speaking, heaven is yin or expanded, but the force or energy which it generates is yang, centripetal, or coming in toward the core of the earth. On the other hand, physically the earth is yang, compacted and hard, but the energy generated by its rotation is yin, upward and expanding. Because some of the ancient texts on yin and yang took this paradoxical relationship for granted, it is easy to confuse yin and yang and the five stages of transformation originating from them (see Chapter 7).

Everything and every phenomenon upon the surface of our planet are composed of these two energies, though some manifest proportionately more heaven's force, appearing more contracted in shape, and others manifest proportionately more earth's force, appearing more expanded in size. Because of atmospheric conditions, heaven's centripetal force comes in strongest at the poles in a counterclockwise direction, while earth's centrifugal force is at its peak in a clockwise direction at the equator. Together the two forces were traditionally known in the East as *ki*, *chi*, or *prana*. We may call them by these terms or simply refer to them as natural electromagnetic energy and vibration.

In human beings, heaven's force enters primarily from above, especially at the center of the hair spiral on the top back of the head, moving downwards in the usual standing position. The force of earth enters the human body from below through the genital region and moves upward. Both forces pass through the innermost depths of the body, creating a channel of electromagnetic energy that we may call the Energy Channel or the Spiritual Channel. In addition to the two entrance points, the forces collide and charge five major areas in the Energy Channel, producing altogether seven major places of activated natural electromagnetic energy in the body (see Figure 28). In ancient India, these energy centers were called *chakras*. The seven energy centers include:

1. The region at the top of the head where heaven's force enters through the hair spiral. This energy center governs higher consciousness.
2. The innermost region of the brain, the area of the midbrain, from where the electromagnetic charge is distributed to millions of brain cells. When the brain is charged, the brain cells are capable of receiving natural electromagnetic waves, interpreting them into images and transmitting them. This process is similar to the radio, television, computer,

Figure 28. The Seven Chakras

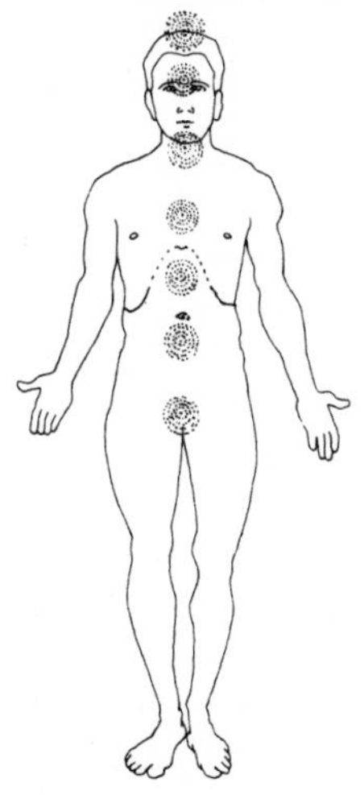

The seven energy centers, or chakras, form a vertical channel for the flow of electromagnetic energy between heaven and earth.

and other modern electronic devices that pick up and give out artificial electromagnetic waves and images. This energy center governs intuition and reason.

3. The region of the throat, charging and activating the secretion of saliva, the vibration of the uvula at the back of the throat, and the root of the tongue, as well as the operation of the thyroid and parathyroid glands, together with the rhythmical wave between inhaling and exhaling. This energy center governs speech and breathing.

4. The area of the heart, causing the formation of cardiac muscles, the rhythmical motion of the heart, and the smooth functioning of the entire circulatory system. In this region, heaven's and earth's force are most evenly balanced. This energy center governs the individual's overall destiny and especially love and emotional development.

5. The stomach area from where charges are distributed to such central organs as the liver, spleen, pancreas and kidneys, controlling and directing the operation of their rhythmical functions. This energy center governs courage, sympathy, patience, and other qualities of will and perseverance.

6. The center of the intestinal area below the navel. Known traditionally in the Far East as the *tanden* or *hara*, electromagnetic charges from this area are distributed to all parts of the small and large intestines as well as the bladder and genital areas, governing the smooth and

rhythmical processes of digestion, decomposition, and the absorption of food, water, and energy. This energy center maintains body equilibrium and overall vitality.

7. The genital region, charging the testicles in men or ovaries in women, as well as the other reproductive organs and the eliminatory system. This energy center governs reproduction and regeneration.

The seven energy centers maintain and coordinate various physiological and mental activities in each region. Incoming streams of yin and yang force branch out from the energy centers into fourteen channels of electromagnetic energy or meridians (see Figure 29). The meridians, which end in the arms and feet, have 361 major holes or points, traditionally called *tsubo*, connecting to the surface, outside, or physical functions. The meridians, in turn, subdivide, supplying energy to organs and functions, tissues and cells.

Figure 29. The Meridians

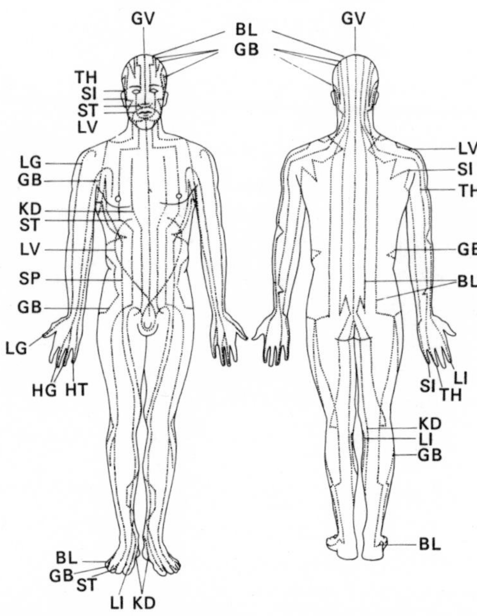

Circulation of ki or electromagnetic energy through the meridians. H=Heart, L=Lung, SP=Spleen, K=Kidney, GB=Gallbladder, B=Bladder, S=Stomach, HG=Heart Governor, SI=Small Intestine, LI=Large Intestine, GV=Governing vessel, TH=Triple Heater.

Thus our physical structure is nourished by an invisible nonphysical one. Energy comes from heaven and earth, and their charge gives life. In the chest cavity, the collision of these two forces causes our hearts to beat. Opposite hormones are secreted from glands along the Energy Channel, some more charged by heaven's force, others more charged by earth's force. The meeting of these two forces also makes for breathing. Breathing out is more contractive or yang, while breathing in is more expansive or yin. In reality our body is a spiritual entity. Cosmic or spiritual force is constantly nourishing our consciouness, as well as the organs, glands, functions, tissues, and trillions of cells that make up our physical constitution (see Figure 30).

Figure 30. The Triple Heater

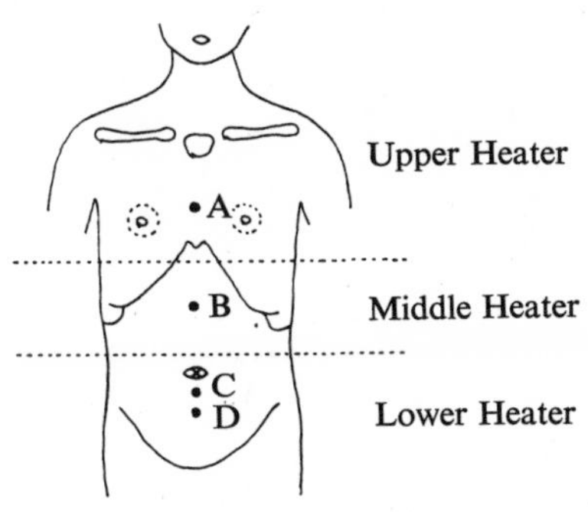

A. *Dan-Chu*—CV17
B. *Chu-Kang*—CV12
C. *In-Ko*—CV7
D. *Ki-Kai*—CV6

In Oriental medicine, three regions where heat is generated, represented by the heart, stomach, and intestine, are called *San-Sho* (三焦)—Triple Heater. Each of these regions has a central point as listed at the left; these points, situated in the center of the second, third, and fourth chakra, are used for diagnosis and treatment in acupuncture, moxibustion, shiatsu, massage, and palm healing.

The characteristics and functions of the human organism are exactly the opposite of plants. The leaves of a tree—more expanded or yin in structure—take in carbon dioxide and give out oxygen, while human lungs—more compacted or yang in structure—take in oxygen and give out carbon dioxide. In plants, the roots are located at the bottom and the fruit and flower are at the top because earth's force governs their formation and growth. In human beings, the roots and stem are situated in the head—the more yang, compacted brain cells and higher consciousness centers—while the flower and fruit—the reproductive sys-

Figure 31. Opposite Biological Structure

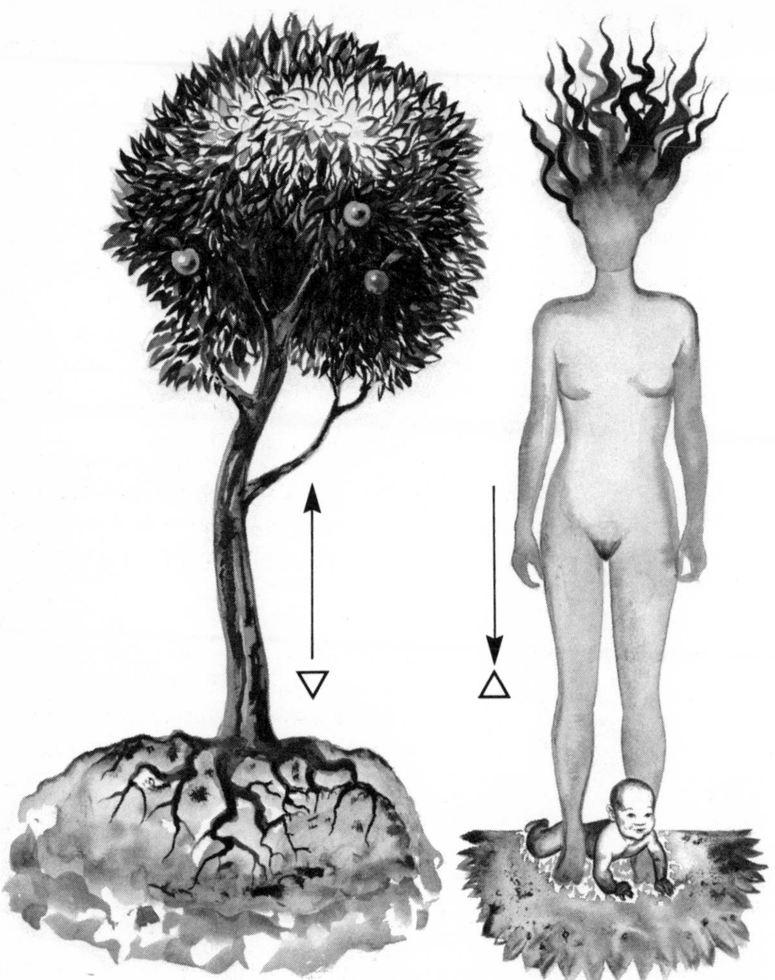

The roots of plants extend down to the earth and the fruits grow up toward heaven, while in human beings the roots, (brain cells) are above and the fruits (gonads) are below.

tem—are at the bottom (see Figure 31). Our cells are like leaves, though contracted rather than expanded. Each one is alive, energized and electromagnetized by the constant stream of *ki*. As human beings, the real source of our life is coming from the universe. It is more accurate to say that we hang down from heaven than stand up on earth. The head is our root, from which we develop our consciousness, realize our dream in life, and set out to return to the next world.

Materially, modern science has not yet detected the universe's spiritual structure or constitution. Because it is based on an extention of the physical senses, even the most advanced technology cannot measure the energy centers, meridians, and holes through which the *ki* or electromagnetic energy of the infinite universe flows. However, this energy can easily be perceived by the healthy and flexible mind. It is also readily measurable with the simplest of instruments. If we hold a small pendulum over the back of a man's head, the pendulum will start to rotate in a counterclockwise direction, showing the predominance of heaven's force. Over a woman it will start spiralling in a clockwise direction, showing the influence of earth's force. (In the Southern Hemisphere, these directions are reversed just as Australia enjoys spring and summer when we enjoy fall and winter.)

Internally the seven energy centers and meridians are vitalized by the stream of blood, which is also charged electromagnetically. Depending upon the volume and quality of the food and drink consumed, as well as the speed and frequency of breathing, the function of the energy centers changes. Hence to change consciousness or to develop physical coordination, it is important to maintain strong, healthy blood. Blood quality depends primarily on the day to day way of eating, though it is also influenced by breath and consciousness. The Energy Channel can become blocked by overeating, by taking food in improper proportions, or by taking poor quality food. Stagnation can also arise from unclean air, a disorderly or chaotic physical environment, mental or emotional disorders, or other forms of imbalance. Food serves to provide spiritual energy through the blood. The nourishment we receive from food depends primarily on its *ki*, or quality of natural electromagnetic vibration, not on its physical characteristics such as amount of calories, protein, vitamins, or other nutrients.

All traditional spiritual, religious, and social disciplines, as well as physical exercises such as yoga and tai chi ch'uan, began from this understanding of the energetic nature of life. The aim of meditation, for example, is to harmonize heaven's and earth's forces passing through the Energy Channel, thereby unifying and contributing to the smooth functioning of the mind and body at all levels. In the practice of meditation, however, there are many techniques to emphasize and activate certain energy centers. Zen meditation mainly focuses on the *hara*, Vedanta and Raja Yoga on the midbrain, and Judeo-Christian and Islamic prayer on the heart.

Traditionally, meditation, chanting, and breathing exercises were considered supplemental to harmonizing the daily way of eating. Food was understood to be the foundation on which everything else depended. In the *Taittiriya Upanishad*, we read:

> "He who knows this, after dying to this world, attains the self which consists of food, attains the self which consists of the vital breath, attains the self which consists of the mind, attains the self which consists of the intellect, attains the self which consists of bliss. Then he goes up and down these worlds, eating the food he desires, assuming the forms he likes. He sits, singing the chant of the non-duality of Brahman: 'Ah! Ah! Ah!'
>
> "'I am food, I am food, I am food! I am the eater of food, I am the eater of food, I am the eater of food! I am the uniter, I am the uniter, I am the uniter!
>
> "'I am the first-born of the true, prior to the gods, and the navel of Immortality. He who gives me away, he alone preserves me. He who eats food—I, as food, eat him.
>
> "'I (as the Supreme Lord) overpower the whole world. I am radiant as the sun.'
>
> "Whosoever knows this (attains Liberation). Such, indeed, is the Upanishad."

In the Far East, Buddhist temples, monasteries, and shrines traditionally observed *Shojin Ryori*, "cuisine for spiritual advancement." In the Near East, a simple grain and vegetable diet was also originally observed by the Jewish sages and the earliest Christians. Kosher cooking and fasting during Lent and avoiding meat on Fridays were instituted after the original principles of diet started to decline. These dietary codes and practices, though partial, helped to ensure the survival of the great world religions for thousands of years. At the present time, even these relatively modest attempts to balance society's way of eating are rapidly declining.

Human Beings Can Eat Anything

As the last and most recent development of the animal kingdom, human beings have taken within themselves all preceding qualities and stages of evolution, including the various species of animals and plants. Accordingly, human beings are capable of eating and taking in within themselves all levels of the animal and plant kingdoms in the form of food.

Biologically, we recapitulate the evolutionary process in condensed form whenever we eat a preceding species. In this sense, when we eat animal food, the animal becomes a part of the human species. The relation between more developed and less developed biological species was understood intuitively in former times. In *The Gospel According to Thomas*, for example, Jesus refers to this process when he says: "Blessed is the lion which the man eats and the lion will become man; and cursed is the man whom the lion eats and the man will become lion." Eating more primitive lives and being eaten by more developed beings are natural biological processes. Every day, the entire scope of evolution dating back over 3 billion years is repeated in the daily lives of countless animal and plant species as they transform into each other at very rapid speed. From protozoa to highly developed forms, from single-celled organisms to human beings, life is constantly changing in complexity and consciousness.

Through this process, protozoa transmute into fish, fish transmute into seagulls, flying birds transmute into mammals, and mammals transmute into human beings. On the contrary, if the lower species devour more evolved species, a process of degeneration or de-evolution begins. When human beings are eaten by other mammals or by mosquitoes or by bacteria and viruses, the natural order is reversed and biological degeneration is the result.

Many modern people are consuming a variety of biologically recent mammal species: cows in the form of beef; pigs in the form of ham and bacon; goats in the form of lamb; and their products in the form of milk, cheese, and other dairy food. Humans also eat more ancient animal species: many birds such as chicken, turkey, duck, and pheasant, with their eggs. Among reptiles, snakes and lizards are consumed in some regions, while among amphibians, frogs, turtles, snails and others are widely eaten. Among fish, many thousands of freshwater and deep-ocean varieties are consumed, as well as shellfish, squid, octopus, and other invertebrate sea life. Finally, human beings eat the most primordial form of animal life—bacteria, enzymes, yeast, and other microorganisms—that are found in fermented and processed foods as well as in the water and in the air.

The fact that we are capable of eating and taking in almost all preceding animal species, either in whole or in part, also suggests that we can eat almost all vegetable species. Actually animals are nothing but transmuted plants. Even carnivorous animals who eat only other animals are ultimately eating reprocessed vegetable matter.

Universally, human beings have eaten all kinds of grains and grain products such as rice, wheat, millet, oats, barley, rye, corn, and buckwheat, as well as leguminous plants such as soybeans, lima beans, kidney beans, chickpeas, lentils, split peas, and many others. Among biologically recent plants, human beings eat various seeds, fruits, and nuts. Among modern vegetables, we consume watercress, kale, carrots, turnips, potato, squash, pumpkin, radish, cabbage, Chinese cabbage, onions, scallions, and many others. Among plants of more ancient origin, we eat ferns, asparagus, and many fungi such as mushrooms. Further we eat sea plants including kombu, wakame, hijiki, dulse, Irish moss, and nori. Finally, among the most primitive plant life we eat molds, yeast, and the like.

Homo sapiens is really a universal eater. Humankind is the most capable among all animal species of eating so many varieties of food. Modern people have added to their food artificially processed and refined food, as well as chemicalized, industrialized, and mass-produced food. Moreover, human beings, unlike other species, change the quality of their food by applying methods of growing, selection, processing, combining, preserving, and cooking, as well as drying and watering, pickling, pressuring, heating, and freezing, storing and fermenting.

If we eat more variety, our biological development is usually greater, while eating less variety creates less genetic diversity and social evolution. Also a society with more refined cooking methods develops more culturally, while a society with more primitive cooking methods remains less developed. Through the ages, as human beings have learned more well developed ways of choosing, preparing, and cooking foods, they have been able to create cultures and civilizations that are more advanced. When we see cooking methods in a household, we can know its family's state of mind. When we see the general way of cooking in a country or an ethnic group, we can know its mental and psychological orientation.

In addition to animal and plant species, we also eat and drink minerals and water. Almost all elements exist in different degrees within our bodies, and 80 percent of our organs and tissues consist of water. We take these substances in the form of vegetable and animal food as well as in the form of salts, refined and unrefined, and we take many varieties of liquid in the form of juice fruits, vegetables, cooked grains and flours, and in the form of soup and beverage. Every day we take in part of our natural environment, including part of the animal, vegetable, and mineral kingdoms.

We further take in air, especially oxygen, eliminating a part of the food we use in the form of carbon dioxide. The intake of air is proportional to the quality and volume of what we eat. The more we eat, the more we breathe; the less we eat, the less we breathe. The more animal food we eat, the more we inhale and our breathing becomes labored and disharmonious, while the more vegetable-quality food we eat, the more harmonious our breathing becomes.

When we eat a certain variety of food, a certain quality of blood is formed. When we eat certain other types of food, certain other qualities of blood arise. However small the difference may be, a pinch of salt, a few drops of soy sauce, a slice of cheese, a few sections of orange, a half teaspoon of sugar, a cup of tea, each mouthful delicately influences and changes the quality and volume of blood. When the blood changes, the quality of cells, organs, and tissues of the body as a whole change, including the brain and nervous system. These changes automatically transform physical and psychological functions, influencing all behavior, expressions, thoughts and feelings. Physical movement and habits, as well as sensory perceptions, emotional responses, intellectual conceptions, social consciousness, and philosophical view of life are changing day to day because of the change in what we consume.

Like a television with inferior parts that is unable to receive and transmit into images and sounds a series of vibrations coming from a distant station, if our blood quality is heavy and stagnated from our daily way of eating, we are unable to perceive and respond to waves and vibrations coming from short and long distances. If our consciousness is sometimes clouded, it may be due to the change of environmental vibrations, but it is more largely due to what we are taking into our body by ourselves. We understand this process when we see that some person may react nervously but another person maintains normal responses under the same circumstances. Our psychological responses and variations are largely the result of what we consume daily.

We are what we eat, and we are totally responsible for our physical and mental condition. Whether we are active, healthy, and happy or whether we are inactive, sick, and unhappy on this earth depends entirely upon ourselves and upon no one else. We are always our own masters, and no one else can really control our personal destiny. Sickness and unnatural death, frustration and suffering, severe accidents and failures, are all caused by ourselves, as a result of our day to day way of eating, thinking, and living, but especially our way of eating over which we have almost complete control. The secret for realizing health and wisdom, freedom and happiness—all physical, mental, and spiritual well being as well as social harmony and world peace—is in front of us, day to day, in every dish we consume. How to choose food, how to prepare meals, and how to absorb and harmonize with our natural environment through food are keys to humanity's personal and collective destiny. We can eat everything, and yet we must maintain a certain order and proportion to what we eat. Proper eating is the turning point for our evolutionary development or decline.

Food of Embryo and Infant

Both man and woman constantly receive heaven's force, which is moving downwards towards the earth, and earth's force, which is moving upwards as a result of the rotation of the earth. These forces naturally course through the bodies of both man and woman. However, at the time of sexual union, the magnetism between the two poles is strongest, and the flow of these forces becomes more intensified. At that time, the male reproductive cell, the sperm which is more yin in structure, fuses with the female reproductive cell, the ovum which is more yang in structure. Fertilization and implantation occurs in the inner depths of the uterus, in the *hara* or *tanden*, which as we have seen is one of the chakras or energy centers. This process repeats in microcosm the primordial creation of life about 3 billion years ago when the earth was in a gaseous state.

Following fertilization, the egg develops into an embryo in the amniotic fluid. The first three months of fetal life see the formation of the structural systems. These include the inner digestive and respiratory systems, the outer nervous systems, and the central circulatory and excretory system. Organs and glands are also developed along these systems during this period. During the remainder of pregnancy, the embryo continues to grow and develop auxiliary parts and functions.

Altogether the entire embryonic period lasts approximately 9 months or 280 days. This process repeats in microcosm the evolutionary development of biological life in the ocean until the formation of land upon the surface of the water. According to modern science, this took about 2.8 to 3 billion years. Thus each day spent in the womb recapitulates about 10 million years of biological evolution. A similar logarithmic development takes place in the accelerating increase of the baby's body weight. From a very minor weight at the beginning of pregnancy, it usually reaches 6 to 8 pounds at the time of delivery—an increase of almost 3 billion times. Because of these evolutionary correspondences, the quality of the mother's diet largely determines the physical, mental, and spiritual constitution of her child. The quality and volume of the food that she takes day to day is passed on to the embryo through the blood and placenta. Each meal she eats during pregnancy represents about 3 million years of evolutionary development. Even though the DNA in the chromosomes, together with RNA, carry numerous hereditary factors (representing the past way of eating of the ancestors), it is essential that the mother's diet be balanced to secure the baby's smooth development. The constitution developed during the embryonic period is the foundation for the entire human life, from birth until death.

During the period of conception and gestation, if the mother keeps a peaceful mind, leads a moderately active life, eats properly, and lives in harmony with her environment, the coming birth will be smooth and rapid, and she can usually enjoy a natural delivery without the need of any drugs, chemicals, or other artificial intervention. (However, in some instances, depending on her past way of eating and lifestyle, medical assistance may be required.) A baby who is born smoothly through natural birth has the native potentiality to grow healthy and active in his or her physical and mental life. However, if the mother nourishes the baby in her uterus with improper quality and volume of food, the newborn life will usually suffer. Structural deformation or mental retardation may also result. Even without noticeable differences in form and function, the baby's potential physical, mental, and social abilities may be weakened, not only at birth and in childhood but also for the continuation of life. Many diseases attributed to heredity or physical and mental disorders that the child may experience in the period prior to adulthood are caused by the mother's improper food consumption or thoughts, as well as by the unnatural style of living of both parents as a family unit.

From ancient times, traditional societies have recognized the importance of the pregnancy period as a foundation for the entire life. In the Far East, people practiced *Tai-Kyō*, embryonic education. The aim of *Tai-Kyō* was to produce a physically and mentally sound baby during the nine months prior to birth. The parents, and especially the mother, were advised to observe a simple, harmonious way of life at this time. Specific steps included:

- Avoiding quarrels and conflicts among themselves and other family members.
- Wearing simple, neat clothing, preferably of vegetable quality such as cotton, next to the skin and keeping the clothing clean and sanitary.
- Keeping the household in order and keeping every part of the

house, beginning with the kitchen, clean and orderly.

- Avoiding activities or experiences that may cause unnecessary excitement and stimulation. These include violent scenes and pictures and loud disturbing music and sounds.
- Keeping active in daily life, either through housework or working, right up to the time of delivery.

Both parents, and again especially the mother, should observe proper dietary practices. Whole cereal grains, beans, and land and sea vegetables are to be consumed daily, though the mother may need small supplemental amounts of fruit, seeds, nuts, and animal food from time to time. Such a diet will provide the day to day energy, as well as clear, focused mind, necessary to practice embryonic education.

Birth corresponds with the period of biological evolution about 400 million years ago when the land rose from the sea and life was transferred from the world of water to the world of air. This natural event in the earth's history witnessed vast floods and great earthquakes. Similarly, the time of delivery brings a baby from a liquid environment to the air environment accompanied by the flow of water. The baby rapidly adapts to the new environment, contracting its physical body by means of the contraction of the uterus as it passes through the narrow birth channel. Excessive gas is released with the baby's cries, and a few days of fasting after birth complete the process of contraction. The period after birth repeats the process of biological evolution on land. The baby passes through stages of motion, crawling, and half-standing, corresponding with development as an amphibian, a reptile, a mammal, and ape. Gradually from these curved postures, the baby assumes an erect position. When it is able to stand up and the infant teeth have come in, the baby has completed the entire process of biological evolution, covering water and land life over the last 3.2 billion years.

During pregnancy and after birth, up to the development of an erect posture as a human infant, the baby is continuously eating food of animal quality. Before delivery, the baby is nourished through the placenta and umbilical cord, which are permeated with the mother's blood. This food is the most condensed form of animal substance in order to accomplish the entire scope of biological evolution in the span of only nine months. After delivery, the food changes into a sweeter and more dilute animal liquid, mother's milk, in order to complete the evolutionary process of land development in about a one-year period.

The quality of food that the baby receives during these two periods largely determines its constitution and destiny for the rest of its life.

For example, in the event the mother takes a tranquilizer or unusual chemical during her pregnancy, it may well affect the quality of the amniotic fluid and the blood that the embryo absorbs for several days. Similarly, after birth, if the mother gives her baby cow's or goat's milk instead of breast milk, or if artificial and chemically produced food are given, the baby's development will be greatly impaired. Many cases of deformity, retardation, congenital defects, and weak constitutions result from such practices. Human life begins in the womb, and the food that the baby receives before and after birth shapes his or her future happiness.

Food for Human Beings

After completing the process of development from a single-celled fertilized egg to a multicelled evolved human infant, the need for eating food of animal quality has ended. Animal food—in the form of the mother's blood and breast milk—was necessary to shorten the process of development and recapitulate the entire course of biological evolution in the womb and during the first year of life in the air world. However, when we reach the stage of human beings, we should start to consume human food, which consists primarily of whole grains and vegetables.

Nature is continually transforming one species into another. A great food chain extends from bacteria and enzymes to sea invertebrates and vertebrates, amphibians, reptiles, birds, mammals, and human beings. Complementary to this line of animal evolution is a line of plant development ranging from bacteria and enzymes to sea moss and sea vegetables, primitive land vegetables, ancient vegetables, modern vegetables, fruits and nuts, and whole cereal grains. Whole grains evolved parallel with human beings and therefore should form the major portion of our diet, just as nuts and fruits developed with chimpanzees and apes and formed the staple of their diet and as giant ferns and other primitive plant life evolved in an earlier epoch in conjunction with the dinosaurs. The remainder of our food as human beings may be selected from earlier evolutionary varieties of plants and animals, including land and sea vegetables, fresh fruit, seeds and nuts, fish and seafood, and soup containing fermented enzymes and bacteria representing the most primordial form of life in the ancient sea.

In selecting supplemental food of animal quality, species that are more primordial are preferable to those that are more recent. Thus fish and seafood are preferable to chicken or turkey, and chicken and turkey are preferable to beef and pork. If animal food is eaten regularly, water animals are preferable to land animals, especially mammals, because they are the most further away from us in evolutionary development.

In the course of evolution, as we have seen, the period of water life, approximately 2.8 billion years compared with the period of land life, approximately 0.4 billion years, produces a spirallic ratio of 7: 1. Since human beings are the most recent species to develop upon the land, the composition of our food should be reversed—generally seven parts land quality and one part water quality. If we eat animal food, preferably fish and seafood, this suggests that the ratio of vegetable food to animal food also be in a ratio of 7: 1.

The structure of the human teeth (see Figure 32) offers another biological clue to humanity's natural way of eating. The thirty-two teeth include twenty molars and premolars for grinding grains, legumes, and seeds; eight incisors for cutting vegetables; and four canines for tearing animal and seafood. Expressed as a ratio of teeth designed for grain use, for vegetable use, and for animal use, the proportion comes to 5: 2: 1; and of all vegetable quality to animal quality, 7: 1. Other examples of comparative anatomy, such as the length of the intestines, show that the human constitution is suited primarily to the consumption of vegetable-quality food (see Table 3). Except in cold, northern climates where the growing season is less and a source of stronger energy is needed to balance the temperature, animal food is not essential to human development. It provides variety and enjoyment to those in usual good health and may be regarded as optional.

Figure 32. The Human Teeth

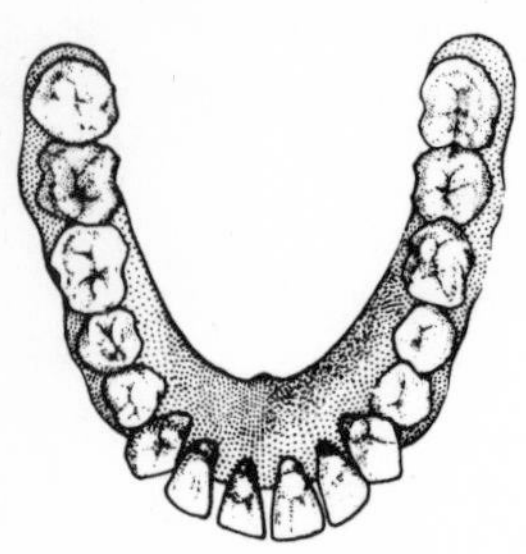

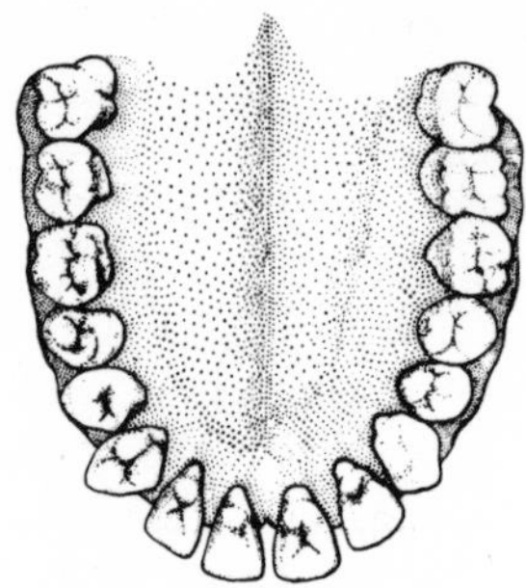

Canines (4 teeth)
Incisors (8 teeth)
Molars and Premolars (20 teeth)

Table 3. Comparative Anatomy of Herbivores and Carnivores

Trait	Herbivores	Carnivores
Vision:	Keenly developed (for spotting motionless food, i.e., vegetables)	Less developed
Smell:	Less developed	Highly developed (for tracking moving prey)
Taste:	Highly refined (because of varied diet)	Less refined
Hearing:	Less refined	Keen (for hearing game)
Movement:	Physique adapted for climbing, slower movement	Streamlined physique adapted for very high speed movement
Orientation:	Vertical	Horizontal
Limbs:	Hands equipped for grasping (e.g., primates, racoons)	Claws for tearing and striking
Teeth:	Flat for grinding	Sharp for tearing
Jaw:	Rotational for chewing plants	Only up and down for devouring mostly game
Digestive System:	Built for frequent, relatively small meals or constant eating; milder digestive juices and assimilation slower and more even; long colon	Adapted to huge feasts, followed by fasts of many days; stronger digestive juices and food rapidly assimilated; short colon
Saliva:	Contains ptyalin for predigestion of starches	Does not contain ptyalin and cannot predigest starches
Perspiration:	Sweat pores for heat control and elimination of wastes	Extruding the tongue and rapid breathing
Liquids:	Taken by suction through the teeth	Lapped up

From these observations and the actual experience of traditional cultures and civilizations for thousands and thousands of years, we may conclude that our daily meals in the temperate zones of the world ideally should be composed of the following categories and proportions of food:

- 50 to 60 percent or more of our daily food, by volume, should consist of whole cereal grains and their products, representing the most advanced species of vegetable life. These include brown rice, whole wheat, barley, oats, rye, millet, corn, buckwheat, sorghum, and other traditional consumed wild and domesticated grasses.
- 5 to 10 percent of our daily food may be taken in the form of soup (one to two bowls). The soup broth is made frequently with miso or tamari soy sauce, which are prepared from naturally fermented soybeans, sea salt, and grains, to which several varieties of land and sea

vegetables may be added during cooking. The enzymes in miso and tamari soy sauce represent the most primordial form of life.

- 25 to 30 percent vegetables prepared in various ways, representing modern, ancient, and primordial stages of vegetal life. These include daikon, carrots, cabbage, kale, watercress, squashes, onion, and many other modern varieties; lotus root and other ancient species; and mushrooms and other primitive species.
- 5 to 10 percent beans and bean products and sea vegetables representing more recent vegetable species from land and sea. These include azuki beans, chickpeas, lentils, pinto beans, soybeans and many others. Seaweeds and mosses include wakame, kombu, hijiki, nori, dulse, Irish moss, agar-agar, arame, and many others.
- Occasional use (15 percent or less) of animal food if desired, primarily fish and seafood, representing early animal life. These include cod, sole, trout, flounder, oyster, clam, shrimp, crab, and many others.
- Occasional use of fruit, nuts, and seeds in small volume, representing the most recent biological species prior to grains. These include apples, cherries, peaches, plums, apricots, berries, melons, almonds, walnuts, pecans, cashews, sesame seeds, sunflower seeds, and pumpkin seeds, and many others.
- Fermented food, especially that of vegetable quality, in small volume daily, representing the most primordial stage of biological life. Foods in this category containing beneficial enzymes and bacteria include miso, tamari soy sauce, koji (molded grain), natto, sauerkraut and other pickles, and many others.

The Natural Order of Eating

The way that food is prepared and the order in which it is eaten at the meal should also follow principles of biological evolution.

Principal food consisting of whole cereal grains and their products, including bread, noodles, and pasta, is traditionally eaten from the beginning to the end of the meal. Beans and seeds, since they are the most recent species next to cereals, may also be consumed at this time in small amounts or be included with principal food. For example, beans may be cooked as a small side dish or be served together with rice or other grains. Sesame seeds may be roasted and crushed, together with sea salt, to be used as a condiment to be served with the grain.

Soup, consisting of sea vegetables, sometimes land vegetables, beans, or grains, and occasionally fish or seafood, usually forms the first side dish of the meal. Such soup or broth, especially that containing sea vegetables and fermented enzymes with a slightly salty taste, is a condensed form of the ancient sea within which early life evolved.

Land vegetable dishes, containing root, ground, and leafy green vegetables, are generally served as the next side dish or dishes after soup. They may be prepared in a variety of forms, including boiling, steaming, sautéing, baking, and deep-frying and tempura. Vegetables of more ancient origin should be cooked longer, while those of more recent origin may be cooked less. Toward the end of the meal, a small volume of vegetables may be served in uncooked form such as salad or pickles.

Seaweeds and sea moss, cooked separately or together with some land vegetables or beans, may be served as a third side dish. They may also be served in soup.

Fish, seafood, and other animal food, if desired, can be prepared together with land and sea vegetables and be eaten as a second side dish during the meal. However, it is important that animal food be stopped part way through the meal, finishing with vegetable quality.

Fruits and nuts, locally grown and in season, may be served occasionally at the end of the meal, representing the food eaten by monkeys and small mammals just prior to the development of cereals and the invention of cooking by human beings. Fruits may be prepared fresh, cooked, or dried, while nuts are commonly roasted with sea salt to make them more digestible.

Finally, beverage, as the last part of the meal, may be taken alone or together with the dessert. The beverage is usually made by steeping a small amount of a modern herbaceous plant in hot water. However, it may occasionally be made with ancient plants or sea vegetables. To facilitate appetite and digestion, a fermented beverage, such as beer or other mild alcoholic drink, may be taken in small volume before the meal if soup containing fermented enzymes, such as miso soup, is not prepared.

4. Dietary Principles for Humanity

"Blessed art thou, O Lord, our God, Ruler of the Universe, who bringest forth bread from the earth."

—Jewish Prayer

"Give us this day our daily bread."

—Lord's Prayer

"Let humanity examine its food."

—Koran

Standard Macrobiotic Dietery Approach

As part of nature and the infinite universe, we are inseparable from our environment. Like other species on this planet, when our environment changes, we change. Eating is the most fundamental way we relate to our natural surroundings. By exercising consciousness over our selection and preparation of daily food we adapt to the changing environment. To choose and prepare food properly, we need to understand the laws of nature—the Order of the Universe. Through what we consume, we change the quality of our body, mind, and spirit. Each of us is responsible for his or her own life and destiny. We are our own masters, and no one else can chew for us.

Yet unless we know how to change and harmonize with fluctuating atmospheric, climatic, and weather conditions, we will soon die out and possibly be succeeded by some other species that is more adaptable. Throughout the centuries, there have been many philosophical, religious, and scientific suggestions to improve the quality of human life, and there have been many social and spiritual attempts to secure better living conditions through reform or revolution. However, unless such proposals change our way of thinking and behavior through simple. commonsense methods that everyone is able to practice, they are impractical. To change our way of thinking and behavior it is necessary to change the quality of our blood cells and our brain cells, as well as strengthen our Energy Channel, through the day to day foods we eat.

Without food, life would not exist. In all traditional societies and civilizations, extending back thousands and thousands of years, our ancestors left us teachings and sayings, customs and traditions, ceremonies and festivals revealing the fundamental importance of daily food. For example, the Grand Ise Shrine situated in Ise City, the most central shrine in Japan, contains a shrine dedicated to the Great Grain Spirit, *Toyo-Uke-No-Ookami*, symbolizing food and prosperity.

Standard Dietary Recommendations

Generally in the temperate climates of the world, where four seasons clearly alternate and where the vast majority of the world's population lives, the following way of eating, with necessary modifications and adjustments, is in harmony with the environment and traditional practice. They have been further modified with a view to enjoying, within moderation, the benefits and conveniences of modern civilization (see Figure 33).

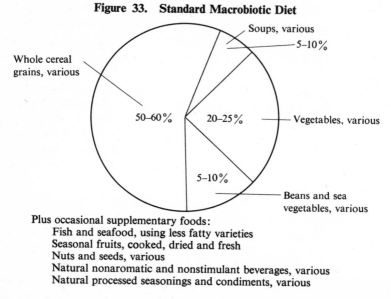

Figure 33. Standard Macrobiotic Diet

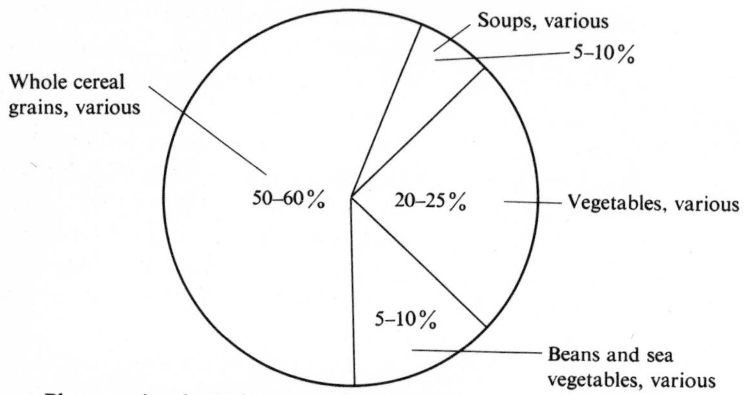

Plus occasional supplementary foods:
- Fish and seafood, using less fatty varieties
- Seasonal fruits, cooked, dried and fresh
- Nuts and seeds, various
- Natural nonaromatic and nonstimulant beverages, various
- Natural processed seasonings and condiments, various

1. Whole Cereal Grains: The principal food of each meal is whole cereal grain, comprising from 50 to 60 percent of the total volume of the meal. Whole grains include brown rice, whole wheat berries, barley, millet, oats, and rye, as well as corn, buckwheat, and other botanically similar plants. From time to time, whole grain products, such as cracked wheat, rolled oats, noodles, pasta, bread, baked goods, and other flour products, may be served as part of this volume of principal food. However, their energy and nutrients are substantially less than grain consumed in whole form, which ideally constitutes the center of each meal.

2. Soup: One to two small bowls of soup, making up about 5 to 10 percent of daily food intake, are consumed each day. The soup broth is made frequently with miso or tamari soy sauce, which are prepared from naturally fermented soybeans, sea salt, and usually grains, to which several varieties of land and sea vegetables, especially wakame or kombu, and other vegetables such as carrots, onions, cabbage, Chinese cabbage, daikon greens and roots, may be added during cooking. The taste of miso or tamari broth soup should be mild, not too salty nor too bland. Soups made with grains, beans, vegetables, and occasionally a little fish or seafood may also be prepared frequently as part of this category.

3. Vegetables: About 25 to 30 percent of daily food includes fresh vegetables prepared in a variety of ways, including steaming, various types of boiling, baking, sautéing, salads, marinades, and pickles. The vegetables include a variety of root vegetables (such as cabbage, carrots, burdock, and daikon radish), ground vegetables (such as onions, fall- and winter-season squashes, and cucumbers), and leafy green vegetables (such as kale, collard greens, broccoli, daikon greens, turnip greens, mustard greens, and watercress). The selection will vary with the region, season, availability, personal health, and other factors. More than two-thirds of the vegetables are served cooked and up to one-third may be prepared in the form of fresh salad or pickles. Vegetables that historically originated in the tropics, such as tomato and potato, are avoided.

4. Beans and Bean Products: A small portion, about 10 percent by volume, of daily food intake includes cooked beans or bean products such as tofu, tempeh, and natto. These foods may be prepared individually or be cooked together with grains, vegetables, or sea vegetables, as well as served in the form of soup. Though all dried and fresh beans are suitable for consumption, the smaller varieties such as azuki beans, lentils, and chickpeas contain less fat and oil and are preferred for regular use.

5. Sea Vegetables: Sea vegetables, rich in minerals and vitamins, are eaten daily in small volume, about 5 percent or less. Common varieties including kombu, wakame, nori, dulse, hijiki, arame, and others may be included in soups, cooked with vegetables or beans, or prepared as a side dish. They are usually seasoned with a moderate amount of tamari soy sauce, sea salt, or brown rice vinegar.

6. Animal Food: A small volume of fish or seafood may be eaten a few times per week by those in good health. White-meat fish generally contain less fat than red-meat or blue-skin varieties. Currently, saltwater fish also usually contain fewer pollutants than freshwater types. To help detoxify the body from the effects of fish and seafood, a small volume of grated daikon, horseradish, fresh ginger, or mustard is usually consumed at the meal as a condiment. Other animal-quality food, including meat, poultry, eggs, and dairy food, is usually avoided, with the exception of infrequent cases when it may be recommended temporarily for medicinal purposes.

7. Seeds and Nuts: Seeds and nuts, lightly roasted and salted with sea salt or seasoned with tamari soy sauce, may be enjoyed as occasional snacks. It is preferable not to overconsume nuts and nut butters as they are difficult to digest and high in fats.

8. Fruit: Fruit is eaten by those in usual health a few times a week, preferably cooked or naturally dried, as a snack or dessert, provided the fruit grows in the local climate zone. Raw fruit can also be consumed in moderate volume during its growing season. Fruit juice is generally too concentrated for regular use, although occasional consumption in very hot weather is allowable as is cider in the autumn. Most temperate-climate fruits are suitable for occasional use such as apples, pears, peaches, apricots, grapes, berries, melons, and others. Tropical fruits such as grapefruit, pineapple, mango, and others are avoided.

9. Desserts: Dessert is eaten in moderate volume two or three times a week by those in good health and may consist of cookies, pudding, cake, pie, and other sweet dishes. Naturally sweet foods such as apples, fall and winter squashes, azuki beans, or dried fruit can often be used in dessert recipes without additional sweetening. However, to provide a stronger sweet taste, a natural grain-based sweetener such as rice syrup, barley malt, or amazake may be used. Sugar, honey, molasses, chocolate, carob, and other sweeteners that are refined, extremely strong, or of tropical origin are avoided. A delicious seaweed gelatin called kanten made with agar-agar and various cut-up fruit, nuts, or beans is very popular and served often.

10. Seasoning, Thickeners, and Garnishes: Naturally processed, mineral-rich sea salt and traditional, nonchemicalized miso and tamari soy sauce are used in seasoning to give a salty taste. Food should not have an overly salty flavor, and seasonings should generally be added during cooking and not at the table, though occasionally personal adjustments may need to be made at the table in which case a moderate amount of seasoning may be added. Other commonly used seasonings include brown rice vinegar, sweet brown rice vinegar, umeboshi vingegar, umeboshi plums, and grated gingerroot. The frequent use of spices, herbs, and other stimulant or aromatic substances is generally avoided. For sauces, gravies, and thickening, kuzu root powder or arrowroot flour is preferred over other vegetable-quality starches. Sliced scallions, parsley sprigs, nori squares or strips, fresh grated gingerroot, and other ingredients are commonly used as garnishes to provide color, balance taste, stimulate the appetite, and facilitate digestion.

11. Cooking Oil: For daily cooking, naturally processed, unrefined vegetable-quality oil is recommended. Dark sesame oil is used most commonly, though light sesame oil, corn oil, and mustard seed oil are also suitable. Less occasionally or for special occasions, other unrefined vegetable-quality oils such as safflower oil, olive oil, and walnut oil may be used. Generally fried rice, fried noodles, or sautéed vegetables are prepared several times a week using a moderate amount of oil. Occasionally, oil may also be used for preparing tempura, deep-frying grains, vegetables, fish, and seafood, or for use in salad dressings and sauces.

12. Condiments: A small amount of condiments may be used on grains, beans, or vegetables at the table to provide variety, stimulate the appetite, and balance the various tastes of the meal. Regular condiments include gomashio (roasted sesame salt), roasted seaweed powders, umeboshi plums, tekka root vegetable condiment, and many others.

13. Pickles: A small volume of homemade pickles is eaten each day to aid in digestion of grains and vegetables. Traditionally fermented pickles are made with a variety of root and round vegetables such as daikon, turnips, cabbage, carrots, and cauliflower and are aged in sea salt, rice or wheat bran, tamari soy sauce, umeboshi plums or shiso leaves, or miso.

14. Beverages: Spring or well water is used for drinking, preparing tea and other beverages, and for general cooking. Bancha twig tea (also known as kukicha) is the most commonly served beverage, though roasted barley tea, roasted brown rice tea, and other grain-based teas or traditional, nonstimulant herbal teas are also used frequently. Grain coffee, umeboshi tea, mu tea, dandelion tea, and other nonaromatic root and herbal teas are prepared occasionally. Less frequently, green tea, fruit juice, vegetable juice, soymilk, beer, wine, sake, and other grain, bean, vegetable, and herbal beverages are served. The consumption of black tea, coffee, herb teas that have stimulant or aromatic effects, distilled water, soft drinks, milk and dairy beverages, and hard liquor is usually limited or avoided.

The Standard Macrobiotic Diet is not limited to the above examples. An almost infinite variety of meals can be created from the standard suggestions. The amount, volume, and proportion of food in each category may also be adjusted slightly for each person or family member depending upon changing environmental conditions such as climate and weather, as well as age, sex, ethnic background, constitution and condition of health, and social and personal need. The macrobiotic dietary approach is very flexible, always looking at the needs of the individual or family as a whole. The development of intuition is essential to balanced cooking and food preparation. Our health and happiness depend upon our practical understanding and application of yin and yang.

Yin an Yang in Daily Food

Food is the mode of evolution, the way one species transforms into another (see Tables 4 and 5). To eat is to take in the whole environment: sunlight, soil, water, and air. The classification of foods into categories of yin and yang is essential for the development of a balanced diet. Different factors in the growth and structure of foods indicate whether the food is predominantly yin or yang:

Table 4. Yin and Yang in the Vegetable Kingdom

	Yin (▽) Centrifugal	Yang (△) Centripetal
Environment:	Warmer, more tropical	Colder, more polar
Season:	Grows more in spring and summer	Grows more in autumn and winter
Soil:	More watery and sedimentary	More dry and volcanic
Growing direction:	Vertically growing upward; expanding horizontally underground	Vertically growing downward; expanding horizontally above the ground
Growing speed:	Growing faster	Growing slower
Size:	Larger, more expanded	Smaller, more compacted
Height:	Taller	Shorter
Texture:	Softer	Harder
Water content:	More juicy and watery	More dry
Color:	Purple—blue—green—yellow—brown—orange—red	
Odor:	Stronger smell	Less smell
Taste:	Spicy——sour——sweet——salty——bitter	
Chemical components:	More K and other yin elements Less Na and other yang elements	Less K and other yin elements More Na and other yang elements
Nutritional components:	Fat——protein——carbohydrate——mineral	
Cooking time:	Faster cooking	Slower cooking

Table 5. Yin and Yang in the Animal Kingdom

	Yin (▽) Centrifugal	Yang (△) Centripetal
Environment:	Warmer and more tropical; also in warm current	Colder and more polar; also in cold current
Air humidity:	More humid	More dry
Species:	Generally more ancient	Generally more modern
Size:	Larger, more expanded	Smaller, more compacted
Activity:	Slower moving and more inactive	Faster moving and more active
Body temperature:	Colder	Warmer
Texture:	Softer, more watery and oily	Harder and drier
Color of flesh:	Transparent——white——brown——pink——red——black	
Odor:	More odor	Less odor
Taste:	Putrid——sour——sweet——salty——bitter	
Chemical components:	Less sodium (Na) and other yang elements	More sodium (Na) and other yang elements
Nutritional components:	Fat...............Protein...............Minerals	
Cooking time:	Shorter	Longer

YIN Energy Creates:	*YANG Energy Creates:*
Growth in a hot climate	Growth in a cold climate
More rapid growth	Slower growth
Foods containing more water	Drier foods
Fruits and leaves, which are more nurtured by expanding energies	Stems, roots, and seeds, which are more nurtured by contracting energies
Growth upward high above the ground	Growth downward below ground
Sour, bitter, sharply sweet, hot, and aromatic foods	Salty, plainly sweet, and pungent foods

Figure 34. Plant Growth According to Yin and Yang

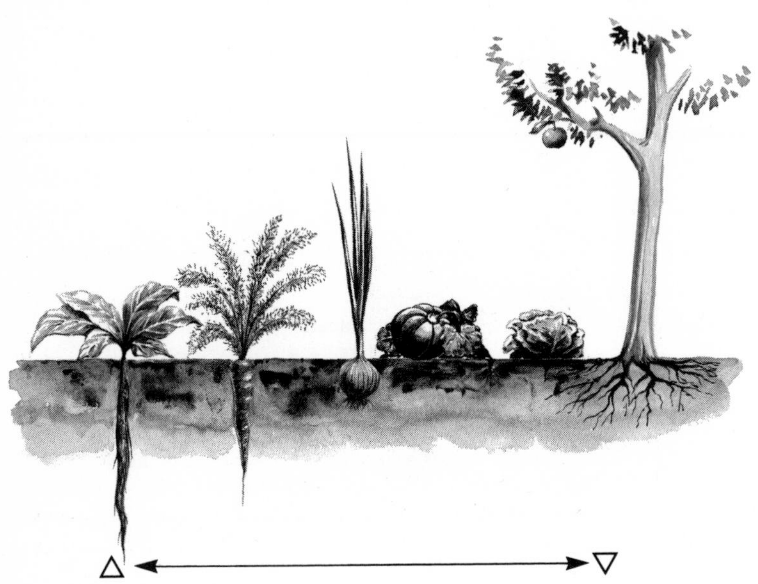

Natural order governs the plant kingdom. Foods that are condensed and grow below ground such as burdock, carrot, and other root vegetables are yang, those that are expanded and grow on the ground such as onion and squash are more balanced, and those that grow above ground such as kale are yin. Fruits that grow high above the ground are even more yin.

Figure 35. Seasonal Diet

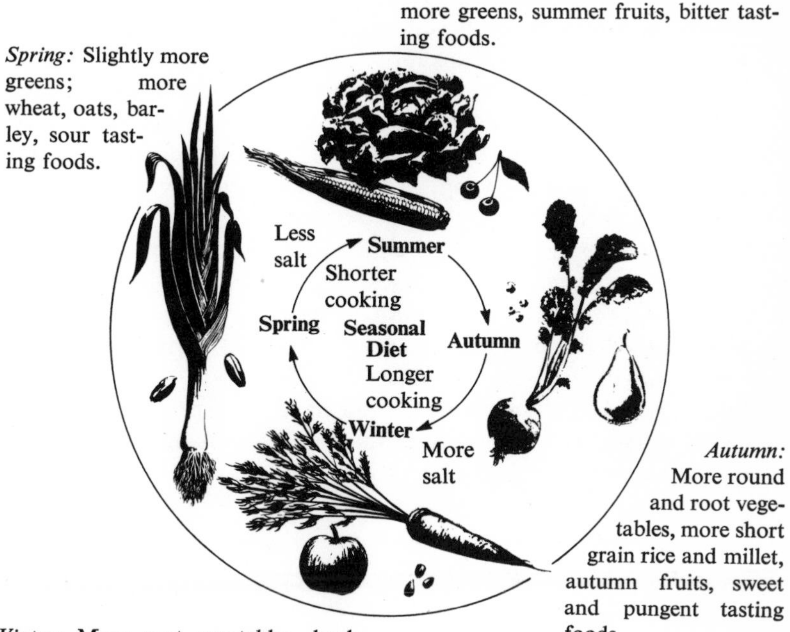
Summer: More corn, long-grain rice, more greens, summer fruits, bitter tasting foods.
Spring: Slightly more greens; more wheat, oats, barley, sour tasting foods.
Less salt
Summer
Shorter cooking
Spring
Seasonal Diet
Autumn
Longer cooking
Winter
More salt
Autumn: More round and root vegetables, more short grain rice and millet, autumn fruits, sweet and pungent tasting foods.
Winter: More root vegetables, buckwheat and rice more often, and easily stored and dried fruits.

To classify foods we must see the predominant factors, since all foods have both yin and yang qualities (see Figure 34). One of the most accurate methods of classification is to observe the seasonal cycle of growth in food plants (see Figure 35). During the winter, the climate is colder (more yin); at this time of year the vegetal energy together with the atmospheric energy descend into the root system. Leaves wither and die as the sap descends to the roots, and the vitality of the plant becomes more condensed. Plants used for food and grown in the late autumn and winter are drier and more concentrated. They can be kept for a longer time without spoiling. Examples of these plants are carrots, parsnips, turnips, and cabbages. During the spring and early summer, the vegetal energy together with the atmospheric energy ascend, and new greens appear as the weather becomes hotter (more yang). These plants are more yin in nature. Summer vegetables are more watery and perish more quickly. They provide a cooling effect, which is needed in warm months. In late summer, the vegetal energy has reached its zenith and many fruits become ripe. They are very watery and sweet and develop higher above the ground.

This yearly cycle shows the alternation between predominating yin and yang energies as the seasons turn. This same cycle can be applied to the part of the world in which a food originates (see Figure 36). Foods that find their origin in hot tropical climates where the vegetation is lush and abundant are more yin, while foods originating in northern or colder climates are more yang. We can also generally classify plants according to color, although there are often exceptions, from the more yin colors—violet, indigo, green, and white—through the more yang colors—yellow, brown, and red. In addition, we should also consider the ratio of various chemical components such as sodium, which is yang or contractive, to potassium, which is yin or expansive, in determining the yin/yang qualities of various foods.

In the practice of daily diet, we need to exercise proper selection of the kinds, quality, and volume of both vegetable and animal food. With some minor exceptions, most vegetable food is more yin than animal food because of the following factors (see Figure 37):

Figure 36. Diet and Climate

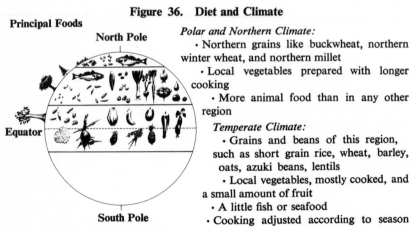

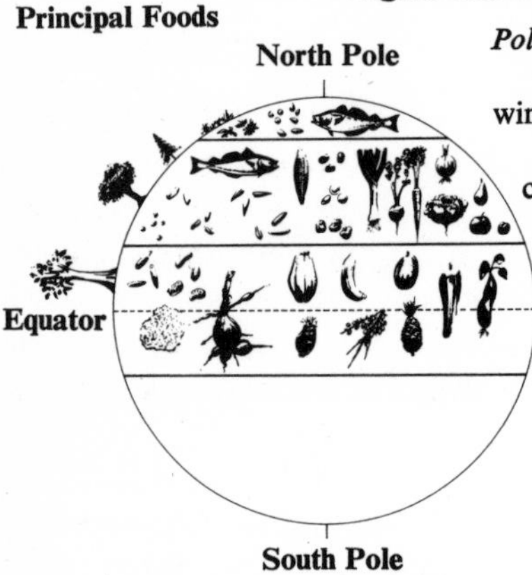

Principal Foods

North Pole

Equator

South Pole

Polar and Northern Climate:

- Northern grains like buckwheat, northern winter wheat, and northern millet
- Local vegetables prepared with longer cooking
- More animal food than in any other region

Temperate Climate:

- Grains and beans of this region, such as short grain rice, wheat, barley, oats, azuki beans, lentils
- Local vegetables, mostly cooked, and a small amount of fruit
- A little fish or seafood
- Cooking adjusted according to season

Southern and Tropical Climates:

- Southern grains such as medium and long grain rice; cassava, sago, and other roots and tubers.
- Larger beans, such as pinto, lima
- Local vegetables, with more salads, and more fruit than in any other region
- Little or no animal food
- Light cooking, with more oil and spices

Figure 37. Animal and Vegetable Cells

Green Plant Cell

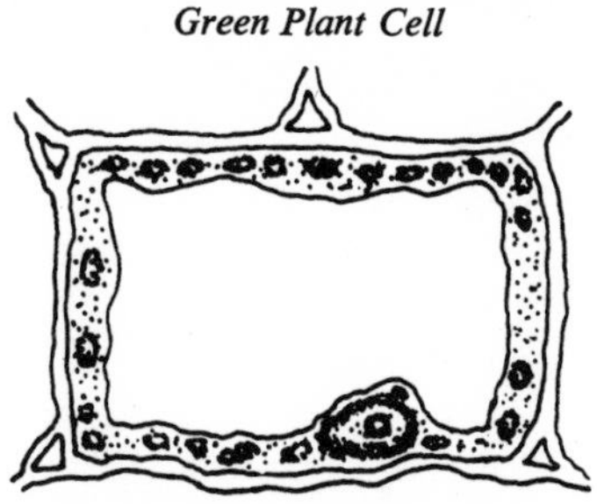

More expanded form—Yin

Typical Animal Cell

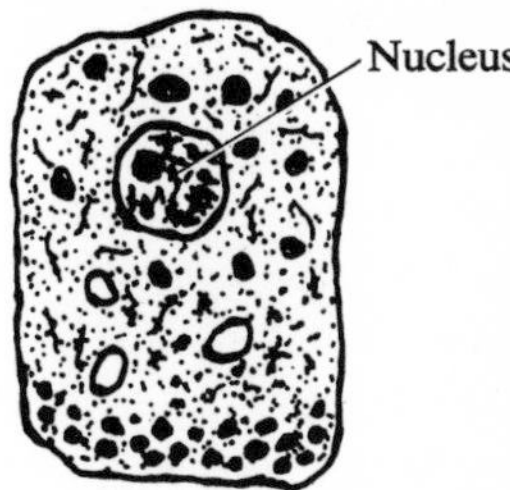

More contracted form—Yang

• Vegetable species are fixed or stationary, growing in one place, while animal species are independently mobile, able to cover a large space by their activity.

• Vegetable species universally manifest their structure in an expanding form, the major portion growing from the ground upward toward the sky or spreading over the ground laterally. On the other hand, animal species generally form compact and separate unities. Vegetables have more expanded forms, such as branches and leaves, growing outward while animal bodies are formed in a more inward direction with compact organs and cells.

• The body temperatures of plants are cooler than some species of animals and generally they inhale carbon dioxide and exhale oxygen (see Figure 38). Animal species generally inhale oxygen and exhale carbon dioxide. Plants are mainly represented by the color green, chlorophyll, while animals are manifested in the color red, hemoglobin. Their chemical structures resemble each other, yet their nuclei are, respectively, magnesium in the case of chlorophyll and iron in the case of hemoglobin.

Although vegetable species are more yin than animal species and animals are more yang than vegetables, there are different degrees even among the same species and within one body. We can distinguish these differences of quality in accordance with the following standard of judgment:

As a general principle, when we use plant foods in the warmer seasons of the year or in a warmer region, it is safer to choose those that are more yin in quality. Conversely, when we use them in the colder season or region, it is preferable to choose more yang quality. In temperate

Figure 38. The Opposite Characteristics of Plants and the Human Body

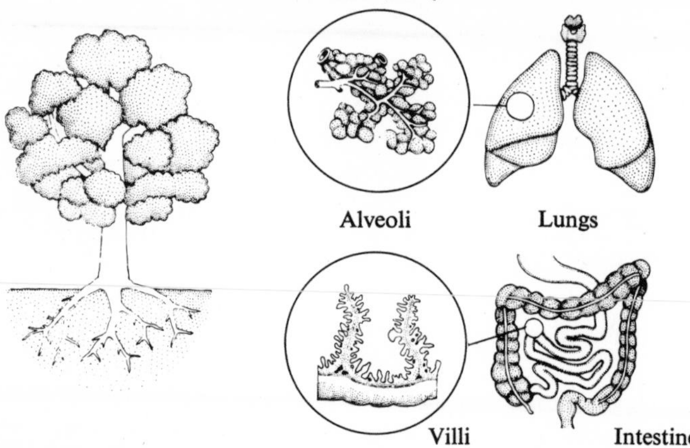

The leaves of the tree—expanded, yin structures—breathe in carbon dioxide (CO_2) and give out oxygen (O_2), while human lungs—compacted, yang structures—breathe in oxygen and give out carbon dioxide. Roots absorb liquid nourishment from the soil in the case of plants, while in the case of human beings, intestinal villi, which have an inverse structure, absorb the nourishment of food molecules. Many other opposite characteristics can be observed in the structures and functions of plants and the human body.

regions, vegetables whose quality is more yin as a rule should be cooked a slightly longer time than yang vegetables, with the possible addition of other yang factors including more heat, pressure, and salt. Similarly, vegetables whose quality is more yang can be slightly less cooked and more yin factors such as less heat, less pressure, and less seasoning can be applied. In general, when cooked, more yin plants expand the mind and body, slow down metabolism, and lower body temperature, while more yang plants contract the mind and body, activate metabolism, and increase body temperature. However, foods of extreme yin or extreme yang quality can produce opposite effects. For example, some very yin foods such as spices, stimulants, and aromatic plants and drinks can temporarily activate metabolism and raise body temperature, and some very yang root vegetables, especially those cooked with strong salt or other seasoning, can temporarily slow down the metabolism and lower body temperature.

In general practice, when we use animal quality food it is preferable to choose more yin quality animal foods, such as fish and seafood, and it is safer to use them together with vegetables to harmonize each other. Each plant and animal, moreover, has its own balance of nutrients:

carbohydrate, protein, fat, minerals, and vitamins in the case of vegetables and protein, fat, and minerals in the case of animals. It is therefore advisable to consume each type of food as a whole. For example, carrot roots with their green tops or dandelion roots and their leaves. In the case of animal food, smaller fish can be eaten whole, including head, bones, and tail. The exception to this principle is grains and fruits, because they have an independent unity separate from the other parts of the plant.

From our understanding of natural order, we are able to classify, from yin to yang or from yang to yin, the entire scope of food (see Table 6) as well as classify within each category of food. Celery, for example, grows in the warm season or climate; grows quickly; is long in shape; is fragile and watery; has a strong smell and taste; cooks quickly; and is pale green in color. We can easily see that celery has many yin characteristics. A carrot, meanwhile, is more hard and compact, takes a longer time to grow and continues growing in the cool season; is orange in color with a mild taste and odor; is a drier vegetable; takes a longer time to cook. Among vegetables, then, we may classify a carrot as more yang. As for a grain of wheat, it is very small and compact and may grow in cool climates and during a cool season; matures slowly; is more dry and hard; brown in color; with a very subtle odor and taste; a high carbohydrate content; and a need for longer cooking time. We see that wheat as well are other grains are relatively more yang in comparison with many other kinds of vegetable food. Among fish, the shrimp is small, red or pink, fast moving, and contains plenty of minerals and less fat. This places it on the more yang side of the seafood kingdom. On the other hand, a carp is large, soft, fat, slow moving, and lives in warm currents—all yin factors. Brook trout live in cold streams, move quickly, are hard and compact with less fat, so we may see that they are more yang than the carp. Using these criteria, we may develop the ability to judge the yin and yang qualities of all different kinds of food (see Table 7).

Environmental Modifications and Personal Adjustment

Although the standard dietary recommendations are universally applicable in the temperate regions of the world for people who are in general good health and leading a normal life, some modifications and adjustments may need to be made to take into account changing environmental conditions and personal requirements.

Table 6. Food Classification According to Yin and Yang

EXTREME YANG FOODS

SOME CHEMICALS, DRUGS, AND ROOTS

Refined Salt
Iodized Salt
Crude Gray Sea Salt
Ginseng
Insulin
Thyroxin
Various others

EGGS

Chicken Eggs
Duck Eggs
Caviar
Other Eggs from Poultry or Fish

MEAT

Beef
Lamb
Pork
Ham
Sausage
Bacon
Veal
Wild Game

POULTRY

Chicken
Duck
Goose
Pheasant
Turkey

FISH AND SEAFOOD

Bluefish
Salmon
Swordfish
Tuna
Other Red-Meat and Blue-Skinned Varieties

MODERATE

FISH AND SEAFOOD

Carp
Clams
Crab
Cod
Flounder
Haddock
Herring
Iriko
Lobster
Octopus
Oysters
Red Snapper
Scallops
Scrod
Shrimp
Smelt
Sole
Trout
Other White-Meat Fish and Seafood

CONDIMENTS

Gomashio
Sea Vegetable Powders
Tekka
Umeboshi Plum
Shio Kombu
Shiso Leaves
Green Nori
Yellow Mustard
Green Mustard
Cooked Nori
Roasted Sesame Seeds
Other Traditional Condiments

WHOLE GRAINS & GRAIN PRODUCTS

Brown Rice
Millet
Barley
Whole Wheat
Oats
Rye
Buckwheat
Corn
Sorghum
Wild Rice
Amaranth
Quinoa
Other Cereal Grains
Sweet Rice
Mochi
Bread
Chapatis
Tortillas
Soba
Udon
Somen
Noodles and Pasta
Couscous
Bulghur
Fu
Seitan
Oatmeal
Corn grits
Cornmeal
Arepas
Popcorn
Other Grain Products

SEEDS & NUTS

Almonds
Chestnuts
Filberts
Peanuts
Pecans
Pinenuts
Pistachios
Poppy Seeds
Pumpkin Seeds
Sesame Seeds
Squash Seeds
Sunflower Seeds
Walnuts
Other Temperate-Climate Varieties

BEANS & BEAN PRODUCTS

Azuki Beans
Black-Eyed Peas
Black Soybeans
Black Turtle Beans
Broad Beans
Chickpeas
Great Northern Beans
Kidney Beans
Lentils
Lima Beans
Mung Beans
Navy Beans
Pinto Beans
Soybeans
Split Peas
Whole Dried Peas
Other Beans
Miso
Natto
Okara
Tamari Soy Sauce
Tempeh
Tofu
Other Bean Products

PICKLES

Bran
Brine
Miso
Pressed
Rice Flour
Salt
Salt and Water
Sauerkraut
Takuan
Tamari Soy Sauce
Umeboshi
Other Traditional Types

SEA VEGETABLES

Agar-Agar
Alaria
Arame
Dulse
Hijiki
Irish Moss
Kelp
Kombu
Mekabu
Nekabu
Nori
Wakame
Others

SEASONINGS

Unrefined Sea Salt
Tamari Soy Sauce
Real Tamari
Miso
Rice Vinegar
Brown Rice Vinegar
Umeboshi Vinegar
Sauerkraut Brine
Mirin
Amazake
Barley Malt
Rice Malt
Grated Gingerroot
Grated Daikon
Grated Radish
Horseradish
Umeboshi Plum
Umeboshi Paste
Lemon Juice
Tangerine Juice
Orange Juice
Fresh Black Pepper
Red Pepper
Green Mustard
Yellow Mustard
Sesame Oil
Corn Oil
Safflower Oil
Mustard Seed Oil
Olive Oil
Sake
Sake Lees
Other Natural Seasonings

In a temperate climate, the Standard Macrobiotic Diet consists of a wide variety of foods and beverages from the moderate category, while those in the extreme yang and extreme yin groupings are limited or avoided. For further information on the origin, cultivation, preparation, use, and health benefits of these foods, please see *Macrobiotic Diet* by Michio and Aveline Kushi (Japan Publications, 1985).

FOODS

VEGETABLES

Root:
Beets
Burdock
Carrots
Daikon
Dandelion Roots
Jinenjo
Jerusalem Artichoke
Lotus Root
Parsnip
Radish
Rutabaga
Taro
Turnip
Others

Round/Ground:
Acorn Squash
Broccoli
Brussels Sprouts
Buttercup Squash
Butternut Squash
Cabbage
Cauliflower
Cucumber
Green Beans
Green Peas
Hubbard Squash
Hokkaido Pumpkin
Mushrooms
Onions
Patty Pan Squash
Pumpkin
Red Cabbage
Shiitake Mushrooms
Snap Beans
Summer Squash
Swiss Chard
Wax Beans
Zucchini
Others

White/Green Leafy:
Bok Choy
Carrot Tops
Celery
Chinese Cabbage
Chives
Daikon Greens
Dandelion Greens
Endive
Escarole
Kale
Leeks
Lettuce
Mustard Greens
Scallions
Sprouts
Turnip Greens
Watercress
Wild Grasses
Others

FRUITS

Fresh and Dried:
Apples
Apricots
Blackberries
Blueberries
Cantaloupe
Grapes
Honeydew Melon
Lemon
Mulberries
Nectarines
Olives
Oranges
Peaches
Pears
Plums
Raisins
Raspberries
Strawberries
Tangerines
Watermelon
Wild Berries
Other Temperate-Climate Varieties

GARNISHES

Grated Daikon
Grated Radish
Grated Horseradish
Chopped Scallions
Grated Ginger
Red Pepper
Other Traditional Garnishes

BEVERAGES

Regular Use:
Bancha Twig Tea
Bancha Stem Tea
Roasted Rice Tea
Roasted Barley Tea
Roasted Grain Tea
Kombu Tea
Spring Water
Well Water

Occasional Use:
100% Grain Coffee
Amazake
Dandelion Tea
Lotus Root Tea
Burdock Root Tea
Other Traditional, Nonstimulant, Nonaromatic Natural Herb Teas

Infrequent Use:
Fruit Juice
Cider
Soy Milk
Vegetable Juice
Barley Green Juice
Sake
Beer, Natural Fermented
Wine, Natural Fermented
Other Grain- and Fruit-based Mild Alcoholic Beverages of Natural Quality

SWEETENERS

Amazake
Barley Malt
Rice Syrup
Maple Syrup
Fruit Juice
Cooked Fruit
Dried Fruit

EXTREME YIN FOODS

TROPICAL FOODS

Asparagus
Avocado
Bananas
Brazil Nuts
Cashews
Coconut
Coconut Oil
Dates
Eggplant
Figs
Grapefruit
Green Peppers
Kiwi Fruit
Mango
Palm Oil
Papaya
Plantain
Potato
Red Peppers
Spinach
Sweet Potato
Tomato
Yams

DAIRY FOODS[1]

Butter
Cheese
Cream
Ice Cream
Kefir
Milk
Sour Cream
Whipped Cream
Yogurt

SWEETENERS[2]

Aspartame
Blond Sugar
Brown Sugar
Cane Sugar
Carob
Corn Syrup
Chocolate
Dextrose
Fructose
Glucose
Honey
Molasses
Nutra-Sweet
Raw Sugar
Saccharin
Sorbitol
Turbinado Sugar
White Sugar
Xylitol

STIMULANTS

Black Tea
Green Tea
Mint Tea
Other Stimulating, Aromatic Teas
Coffee
Decaffeinated Coffee
Cola
Soft Drinks
Chocolate
Cinnamon
Curry
Nutmeg
Other Spices

PROCESSED FOODS

White Rice
White Flour
Refined Grains
Instant Foods
Canned Foods
Frozen Foods
Sprayed Foods
Dyed Foods
Irradiated Foods
Foods Produced with Chemicals, Additives, Artificial Coloring, Flavoring, Emulsifiers, Preservatives, Stabilizers
Vitamin Pills
Mineral Supplements
Other Food Capsules, Tablets, and Similar Products

SOME CHEMICALS & DRUGS

Amphetamines
Antibiotics
Aspirin
Cortisone
Cocaine
LSD
Marijuana
Others

SEASONINGS

Margarine
Soy Margarine
Lard
Shortening
Animal Fats
Refined Vegetable Oils
Herbs
Spices
Wine Vinegar
Mayonnaise
Hot Pepper

[1] Brie, roquefort, and several other salted cheeses that have aged for a long time are classified as yang rather than yin.

[2] Soft drinks, candy, pastries, desserts, and other items containing these sweeteners should also be avoided.

Table 7. Yin and Yang Factors in Food Selection and Preparation

Foods in general may be categorized as strong yang, moderate, or strong yin as in Table 6. However, within each category, foods may be classified as relatively yin and yang depending upon their size, shape, growth, or other factors. Food selection as well as the application of different cooking methods, time, pressure, and seasonings can also change the quality of the meals we prepare.

	More Yang	More Yin
Beverages:	Warmer, nonaromatic, nonstimulating	Colder, aromatic or stimulating
Sugar:	Raw	Refined
Fruit:	Smaller, growing on the ground or in a colder climate	Larger, growing in trees or in a warmer climate
Nuts:	Less oily	More oily
Seeds:	Smaller	Larger
Vegetables:	Root and round	Leafy greens
Beans:	Smaller	Larger
Grains:	Smaller, rounder, and growing in a colder climate	Larger, more elongated, and growing in a warmer climate
Fish and Seafood:	Smaller and faster moving	Larger and slower moving
Poultry:	Smaller and higher flying	Larger and lower flying
Dairy:	Harder, saltier, less fatty	Softer, sweeter, more fatty
Red Meat:	Less fatty	More fatty
Eggs:	Smaller	Larger
Salt:	Refined	Unrefined
Cooking Methods:	Pressure-cooking, long time boiling, baking, pan-frying, tempura or deep-frying	Raw or uncooked, steaming, light or medium boiling, quick sautéing, broiling
Time:	Longer cooking	Shorter cooking
Seasoning:	More salt, miso, or tamari soy sauce; less oil, vinegar, herbs, or spices	Less salt, miso, or tamari soy sauce; more oil, vinegar, herbs, or spices
Volume:	Smaller serving	Larger serving

Modification According to Traditional Practice: Generally speaking, if we continue to live in a certain place throughout our lifetime or a large part of our life, we should follow the dietary practices that have been traditionally observed by the majority of people in that particular place. Like most traditional cultures throughout the world, the people of Hunza in Pakistan, the people of Vilcabamba in Ecuador, and the native Inuit people of the Arctic, have maintained certain patterns of eating that have enabled them to enjoy health and longevity down through the centuries.

However, if long-lived traditional societies begin to adopt foods from another climate zone or use manufactured food they inevitably lose their adaptability to their environment. This is happening in many cases today with the spread of sugar, white flour, soft drinks, hamburgers, and other highly processed foodstuffs.

The traditional way of eating has been developed through the centuries by the accumulated experience of many generations. In many parts of the world there developed religious and ceremonial customs dedicated to certain kinds of energy that food embodied, which their ancestors experienced through the long period of history as the foundation of their cultural and social life. Shintoism in Japan, for example, enshrined the spirit of rice and other grains. North and South American Indians developed an elaborate mythology relating to maize. The early Jewish and Christian people respected unleavened bread as a holy means to commune with God. The Greeks and Romans worshipped Ceres and Demeter, the goddesses of grains and the harvest. Through rituals and pageants such as these, ancient peoples handed down their understanding to offspring, teaching them about the way of eating in harmony with their environment and the unity of mind, body, and soul. In many cases, such traditions included special types of dishes and special types of cooking. Proverbs and parables were also left by early societies to tell future generations the importance of certain ways of eating in that environment.

Therefore, wherever we go and live we should respect and integrate into our own dietary practice the way of eating traditionally developed in that locality over many centuries. Of course, over the millennia, traditional cultures went through many cycles of growth and decay so that customs prevailing today are not necessarily those observed during more harmonious times. Moreover, today as modern world citizens, we are building a peaceful planetary society that is synthesizing various traditions and values from East and West, and North and South. As a result, our understanding and practice is broader and more universal than that of those who have come before, just as those who come after us will build and improve upon what they have inherited from our era.

Modification According to Climate: The world climate is generally divided into five climatic regions in respect to diet: polar, cool, temperate, semitropical, and tropical (see Figure 39). The polar climate generally has a colder atmosphere throughout the year. The cool climate has a long cold season and a short warm season. The temperate climate generally has four distinct seasons. The semitropical climate has a long

Figure 39. World Climate Zones

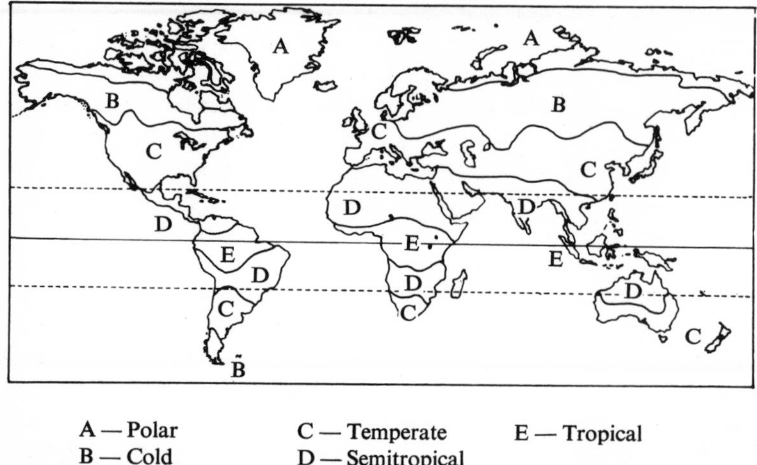

warm season and a short cool season, and the tropical climate has a hot atmosphere throughout the year.

When we live in different climates, our way of eating is naturally different. In a colder climate, we adapt ourselves to the more yin environment by making our food more yang. We select slightly stronger quality food, cook it longer, use more salt and other seasoning, and even use animal food to a larger degree. People who live in Mongolia and northern Manchuria, for example, have traditionally maintained their strength by eating heavily cooked food and by including animal food in their diet. Similarly, people in Scandinavia have used fish and seafood in their daily diet as well as a small volume of dairy food.

On the other hand, in a warmer climate we adapt ourselves to the more yang environment by making our food more yin. We select slightly more expansive food, use lighter cooking, use less salt and other seasoning, and use little or no animal food. In Africa, for example, people traditionally depended on sorghum, millet, tapioca, yams, and other indigenous grains and vegetables, using very little animal food. Similarly, in India, Southeast Asia, and southern China, people traditionally used lighter food, including more raw food and more spices, and generally avoided meat, dairy food, eggs, and other animal products.

People who live in the higher mountains have eaten differently from people who live in the lower plains. People who live in the interior of continents naturally differ in their way of eating from those who live on the seashore. Within food categories, the same principle applies. Though grain has been humanity's principal food for thousands of years, populations living in Russia, Eastern Europe, and other colder regions traditionally ate buckwheat, the most yang of the cereal plants. Those in southern Europe and other more temperate regions ate wheat and rice—more centrally balanced grains—and those in Central America, South America, and other warmer regions ate corn—the most yin grain. In North America, which includes several climate zones, people who live in California, Florida, and other southern areas cannot tolerate the dietary practices of New England for very long unless they modify their cooking methods, including lighter cooking and the more frequent use of some raw vegetables and fruits.

The following dietary guidelines are recommended for the varying climates of the world:

Polar Diet: In the colder regions of the world, the food should be primarily whole grains, land and sea vegetables, and a moderate proportion (up to about 30 percent) of fish, meat, and other animal products. Hardy grains for this climate include buckwheat, northern millet, and northern winter wheat. Vegetables are prepared with heavier cooking by using more fire, pressure, salt, and time. Fish and meat should be prepared traditionally and eaten in whole form as much as possible. In extremely cold weather, the larger portion of the meal may consist of animal food, though vegetable-quality food should normally be eaten whenever available.

Cool Region Diet: In cool climates, the food should be primarily whole grains, beans, land and sea vegetables, and a light to moderate proportion (up to about 20 percent) of fish, seafood, and other animal food, as well as small amounts of fruits native to this environment. Grains suitable for this climate include wheat, oats, barley, rye, millet, buckwheat, and a northern short-grain rice. Vegetables are to be native grown and generally well cooked, except during the warm summer season. Animal food is to be prepared according to traditional practices. The portion of animal food in the daily diet should be far less than vegetable-quality food, though it may be consumed frequently.

Temperate Diet: In temperate regions, the food should be whole grains, beans, land and sea vegetables, small supplementary amounts of animal food (up to 15 percent) two or three times a week if desired, and a small volume of fruits, seeds, and nuts. Grains and beans, as well as vegetables, can be chosen from among the many varieties growing in the same climate. Fruits should also originate in the same environment and be eaten in season. Cooking should be modified with the changing seasons, though generally fire, pressure, time, salt and oil should be moderate.

Semitropical Diet: In semitropical areas, the food should be whole grains, beans, land and sea vegetables, a small volume of fruits, and very infrequent use of animal food if desired. All foods should come from a similar climate, for example, medium- or long-grain rice, summer wheat, and middle sized beans. Cooking should be moderate to light, with a slightly higher portion of vegetables served raw in the form of salad or pickles.

Tropical Diet: In tropical regions, the food should be grains, beans, land and sea vegetables, and proportionately more fruits than in other regions. Almost no animal food is traditionally consumed in hot, humid areas. In general, cooking is much lighter, and oil and spices may be used in a larger volume than in any other region.

Modification According to Seasonal Change: In most parts of the world, we experience the change of seasons, from colder to warmer and from warmer to colder. In a temperate region, we experience this change more clearly in the alternation of the four seasons: spring, summer, autumn, and winter. The polar and tropical regions do not experience the clear change of seasons. In nature, various species of plants and animals change their qualities and numbers according to the change of season. Human beings, the vast majority of whom also live in areas where seasonal change is experienced, should also observe the order of the seasons. If we eat summer products such as melon and summer squash in the winter, we lose our adaptability to the immediate environment. Conversely, if we eat hearty stews and well cooked casseroles in summer, we soon become imbalanced in the other direction. Advances in transportation and food storage and preservation have made it possible today to import food from one climate to another. While this has provided variety and convenience, it has violated the natural order and is a major cause of loss of natural immunity to disease in the modern world.

Each season and each month, from spring to autumn, nature produces certain kinds of grains, beans, vegetables, and fruits. These products should be consumed in the season or month they are grown. During the winter season, when very little is naturally produced, we should consume foods that are stored by simple methods. Grains, beans, seeds, root vegetables, and many hard leafy green vegetables, as well as some autumn fruits, can be stored very easily for use throughout the winter. With the exception of food stored by traditional methods, including pickling, drying, and smoking, food preserved by canning, freezing, and other artificial and chemical methods should be avoided.

Modifications According to Geographical Conditions: Although the same pattern of food is generally applicable to people living in the same climatic region, people who live in a mountainous region should observe a diet that is particularly suitable to their locality. A mountain does not produce the varieties of plants usually found growing in the plain. For example, in the case of grains, mountainous regions in a temperate climate often produce buckwheat and millet and seldom wheat and rice. Those who live in a high habitat should generally eat those grains growing in their area and not trade with the villages on the plain for rice and wheat as their staple. Inhabitants of the mountainside should adjust their way of eating according to the altitude they are living in. For example, Mt. Kilimanjaro is located in a tropical region of Africa, but from the foot to the top, includes all climatic regions: tropical, semitropical, temperate, cool, and cold.

Similarly, people who live on the island or seashore near the ocean live in a salty environment and atmosphere. Vegetation in such areas is also more enriched with sodium and other minerals, and by eating locally grown plants they are better able to adapt to their environment. On the other hand, people living deep inland on large continents should consume primarily plants growing in their area.

In the same way, people who are living in drier air follow a way of eating different from those who live in areas of high humidity. In most of western Europe where it is less humid, people have traditionally used a smaller volume of salt than in the islands of the Far East, including Japan, Taiwan, and the Philippines, where it is more humid. In most of North America, more water and other beverages, as well as salad and fruits, are consumed than in western Europe where it is less dry.

The traditional observance of ecological eating has made people living on islands and the seashore smaller and more active (more yang) than those who are living in the inland areas of continents. Interestingly, stories of giants are almost always related to continents, while stories of dwarves come from islands, for example, the Leprechauns of Ireland; the Kappa of Japan; King Kong and Paul Bunyan from the American continent; and the Abominable Snowman from the Himalayas. Peninsular parts of continents have mixed stories, such as the Scandinavian fairy tales which include both giants and little people. People living in large continents tend to appreciate large structures, while people living on islands appreciate more refined arts and miniature objects. In terms of yin and yang, the continent covering a larger, more expanded space is yin, while the island enclosing a smaller, more contracted space is yang.

Modification According to Social Conditions: In comparison with modern societies, primitive societies maintain a much more traditional way of eating. Developing countries observe a more natural method of cultivation and way of preparing food, though this is rapidly changing in many areas of the world. In comparison with modern societies, inhabitants in these areas are consuming a quality of food similar to that which their ancestors ate for many centuries. Similarly, people living in the countryside are generally consuming a less artificial quality of food than people living in towns and cities. Meanwhile, in highly industrialized parts of the world, refined, highly processed, and artificial foods have almost completely taken over. Modern people no longer eat the same kind of foods their ancestors ate. As a result, their blood quality, way of thinking, way of acting, and understanding and life's dream are entirely different. In modern societies, we must be careful to select good natural quality food and to practice slightly lighter cooking than in developing areas. We must be especially cautious about eating unnatural, mass-produced commercialized food, including that available in schools, hospitals, the military, and business establishments.

Modification According to Personal Variation and Needs: Every person has a different constitution, level of activity, and occupation together with differences of sex and age. Those who are engaged in more mental activity such as teaching, writing, planning, accounting, designing, the arts, music, or religious activities should consume a slightly more yin quality of food, and those who are engaged in a more physical occupation such as farming, sales, speaking, politics, sports, labor, or driving should eat a slightly more yang quality of food. The former can take less quantity of food and liquid, while the latter may consume a larger volume of food and drink.

Man, according to his biological constitution and his comparatively wide social activities, may eat more variety of food than woman including a small volume of animal food (except in tropical regions). On the other hand, woman, according to her unique biological nature as the nurturer of life, may consume a smaller volume of food, which should consist almost exclusively of vegetable quality (except in cool or polar regions). Accordingly, man may take slightly more minerals and salt in his food, while woman may take slightly less.

During the early growing years, our food should be slightly more yin—more volume in proportion to the body size, especially in protein and carbohydrate, more volume of liquid, and more frequent use of natural sweets, as well as less use of salt. As we reach physical maturity, the volume of food we consume may become proportionately smaller, and as we reach old age, it should become smaller still. Animal food also generally becomes successively less in volume with aging. At about the early sixties in man and the middle fifties in woman, food should become almost exclusively vegetable quality in the temperate and warmer climate regions of the world. At the same time, the intake of salt and other seasoning, as well as fruits and sweets, gradually diminishes with age.

Knowing the Order of the Universe—yin and yang—allows us to change our way of eating and harmonize with our environment. At the same time, our understanding of natural order allows us to modify our physical and mental conditions at any time by adjusting our food. When we are able to change our thinking and behavior freely through applying yin and yang to our daily way of eating, we are exercising true freedom over our life and destiny. Health is the state of freely maintaining the balance between yin and yang. To sum up:

- In a more yin environment, we adapt by making ourselves more yang. In a more yang environment, we adapt by making ourselves more yin.
- To make ourselves more yang, we take more yang food or apply more yang cooking methods. To make ourselves more yin, we take more yin food or apply more yin cooking methods.

Principles of Cooking

For over three billion years, no other species on earth has developed the art of cooking. For millions of years, our ancestors ate wild cereal grains, which contributed to their advanced intellect, upright posture, and higher consciousness. During the ice ages, humanity started to use fire in order to adapt to the cooling environment. Fire gives energy, vitalizing physical, mental, and spiritual activities. Fire—for cooking and technology—created human culture and civilization.

In the beginning, fire was applied just to food. Then it was applied to produce clothing, to build dwellings, and to produce tools and equipment out of the natural surroundings. *Homo sapiens*' emotional, intellectual, social, and ideological consciousness developed rapidly from exposure to fire in the external environment (culture) and in the internal environment (cooked food) (see Figure 40). Humanity's unique use of fire has been the subject of many traditional myths and stories. The tale of Prometheus, for example, relates human destiny to the proper use of fire.

However, as the use of fire began to extend to other domains of life, a technological society arose and human beings started to lose their ability to manage fire flexibly and adapt to the natural environment through proper use of food, including proper cooking methods. Instead, human civilization has become increasingly enslaved by an artificial fire environment which has grown out of control.

Internally, modern populations are now suffering various physical and mental diseases caused primarily by long-time consumption of unnatural and artificial food and drink, as well as breathing polluted air and drinking contaminated water, which have all been produced by the use of fire. Externally, the world is beset with various social conflicts and struggles, wars and battles, which also have resulted from the misapplication of fire. Our species now faces possible extinction from this source.

To reverse this trend, it is essential that everyone understand the principles of cooking and apply them daily. Proper cooking will not only secure our continued survival on this planet. It will also contribute to the further development of our consciousness. Cooking is the highest art humanity has produced. There are many masterpieces, including the work of Leonardo da Vinci, Michelangelo, Mozart, and Beethoven. But only cooking is able to create and change daily life itself.

The purpose of cooking is to harmonize with the surrounding environment—minerals, water, biological life, atmosphere, pressure, and time. Preparing the simplest dishes in the most practical and delicately condensed form makes for our smoothest transformation into healthy, happy, free beings.

The principles of cooking may be summarized as follows:

1. All food materials should be chosen from natural or organic products growing in the same climatic region and in the same season.
2. Our daily meals should represent all the stages of biological

Figure 40. Fire and Civilization

The use of fire for cooking, fuel, and technology has governed the development of human culture and civilization.

development—mainly vegetable quality species in the case of normal adults not living in polar regions.

3. Food should be prepared as fresh as possible (not be picked or be kept alive until the beginning of cooking) and should be used in whole (e.g., leaves as well as roots in the case of vegetables and skin and bones as well as flesh in the case of fish).

4. The meal should center around whole grains and cooked vegetables. More ancient species should be cooked more; more recent species can be cooked less.

5. Before applying fire and water, chopped food materials should be kept separate—not mixed—to avoid premature interchange of quality.

6. When cutting food materials, it is preferable that each piece should represent both yin and yang qualities. (This art is taught in macrobiotic cooking classes.)

7. During the cooking process, we should refrain from frequent mixing and stirring and, as much as possible, simply allow foods to mix themselves during the natural process of cooking.

8. Excessive use of fire, water, pressure, and time, as well as the excessive use of salt, oil, and other seasoning, should be avoided.

9. Seasoning should be with natural quality products such as unrefined sea salt, unrefined vegetable oil, natural grain sweetener, and whole grain vinegar, and should be used moderately. The taste of the seasoning should not be evident but should only be used to bring out and enhance the natural taste of the food itself, which should be the predominant taste.

10. The same style of cooking and same type of dish should not be repeated too soon. It is preferable to change the style of cooking often, in order to adapt to the changing environment, as well as provide variety and enjoyment to the meal.

11. The best quality of fire to use for cooking is wood, though gas, charcoal, coal, or other natural fuel is also recommended and often more practical in a modern urban environment. Electric and microwave cooking that alter the natural structure of the foods and artificially step up the speed of cooking should be avoided.

12. The best quality of water is spring water, well water, or mountain stream water. Chemically treated municipal city water, as well as distilled water, are preferably avoided.

13. According to the climate, hot, fragrant spices should be avoided or minimized.

14. Dishes should be arranged beautifully at the meal. Serving dishes should complement the natural color of the foods and be placed con-

veniently according to the order of eating. Food should be served gracefully and consumed with appreciation.

15. The atmosphere of the kitchen and eating place should be kept clean and quiet. All those who cook, serve, and eat should maintain a peaceful mind.

Even though we use the same food, eat in the same place, and use the same utensils, each time we cook the food comes out differently. This depends largely upon our changing conditions, physical and mental. If our own condition is clean, calm, and orderly, the food we prepare contributes to the improved health and consciousness of all who eat it. On the other hand, if our condition is stagnant, disturbed, and disorderly, our meals will contribute to our family's deterioration. Those who cook, therefore, are required to have good health and a deep understanding of yin and yang, the order of nature and the universe, together with a practical knowledge of proper cooking techniques. Such a person is society's most valuable asset, and because of him or her, a household, a community, or a nation will become healthier and happier. Traditionally throughout history, both sexes, but especially women, have engaged in this most important role for human development. If we are to reverse the destructive march of modern civilization, it is essential that proper cooking be restored as soon as possible in every family, in every community, and in every country.

Modern Nutrition

The macrobiotic way of eating is based upon native common sense with an intuitive understanding of the relation between the environment and human life. It is also founded on a sense of balance and the dynamic harmony between antagonistic and complemental factors, yin and yang. The macrobiotic way of eating has been experienced and tested by billions of people over hundreds of generations in most parts of the world, whether under the name "macrobiotics" or some other traditional term.

Modern nutrition has made a valuable contribution to the symptomatic treatment of illnesses occasioned by the historic shift in our diet from whole foods and vegetables to refined and artificial foods. In traditional cultures, adoption of processed and chemicalized food has been accompanied by outbreaks of serious illness which modern nutritional science had helped stem. Deficiencies and imbalances in the standard modern diet are also corrected to a limited extent by following current guidelines in respect to calories, protein, vitamins, and other modern scientific categories of food composition.

However, as a whole, nutrition is a very young science, commencing only within the past two centuries. Modern scientific and nutritional studies are still immature and imperfect in many respects and will never reach a stage of perfection as long as they are based almost exclusively on analytical methods and overlook the dynamic relation of life and environment as an organic whole.

Modern nutritional science began in Germany in the 19th Century and developed around the dietary practices of Prussian men who were considered to be the physically strongest at that time. This way of eating, high in animal protein, saturated fat, and sugar, became the standard for nutritional guidelines in the United States, Europe, and Japan. However, history has shown that the modern diet, and the science of nutrition on which it is based, is dangerously imbalanced and has contributed to the current epidemic of heart disease, cancer, and other degenerative disorders, as well as the consciousness and thinking that led to two devastating world wars and the nuclear arms race.

Over the decades, recommended weight levels, caloric intake, and consumption of protein, fat, carbohydrate, vitamins, minerals, and other nutrients have been revised many times by dietitians and medical bodies, but the basic principles remain unchanged. Even today, many nutritionists still believe that animal-quality protein, sugar, enriched flour, polished rice, canned foods, foods containing chemical additives, and other highly processed substances are as healthy as, or even healthier than, whole natural foods.

In order to have a clear and practical understanding of this subject, we need to examine several issues raised by modern nutrition.

The Problem of Meat and Dairy Products: Meat, poultry, eggs, milk, cheese, and other dairy foods are the backbone of the modern diet. Physiologically, they give the human organism an immediate burst of energy and strength. It was this raw power that allowed nomadic tribes of Indo-Europeans to overrun traditional grain and vegetable-consuming cultures in ancient Greece, Italy, the Near East, and India. In the Americas, a heavy meat-centered diet enabled pioneers to level whole regions of the continent quickly and efficiently, though at high cost to native peoples and the environment.

While meat and other naturally processed animal quality foods are part of the traditional diet in colder and polar regions of the world, their regular consumption in temperate and tropical climates can have adverse effects on human health. Meat begins to decompose as soon as it is killed, even with traditional preservatives such as salt or with refrigeration to retard spoilage. Meat is harder to digest than plant foods and continues to putrefy in the digestive tract, taking about 4 to 4½ hours to be absorbed in the intestines versus 2 to 2½ for grains and vegetables. Putrefaction produces toxins and amines that accumulate in the liver, kidneys, and large intestine, destroys bacterial culture, especially those that synthesize the vitamin B complexes, and causes degeneration of the villi of the small intestine where metabolized foodstuffs are absorbed into the blood. Saturated fatty acids, from meat and other animal products, accumulate in and around vital organs and blood vessels, often leading to cysts, tumors, and hardening of the arteries. Saturated fat also raises the amount of cholesterol in the blood, further contributing to the buildup of atherosclerotic plaque.

To compensate for eating meat, poultry, eggs, and other animal foods, the body requires more oxygen in the bloodstream. The breathing rate rises after eating animal food, making it difficult to maintain a calm mind. Thinking in general becomes defensive, suspicious, rigid, and sometimes aggressive. A very narrow, analytical view is often the result.

Dairy food, which often accompanies meat consumption, contributes a soothing, stabilizing, and overall calming influence on a digestive and nervous system subjected to volatile red-meat elements. However, it can lead to illness in its own right or in combination with other factors.

Casein, the protein in cheese, milk, cream, butter, and other dairy foods cannot be assimilated easily and begins to accumulate in an undigested state in the upper intestine, putrefying, producing toxins, and leading to a weakening of the gastric, intestinal, pancreatic, and biliary systems, as well as mucous deposits. The inability to digest milk or other dairy products is known as *lactose intolerance* and is found in about 50 to 90 percent of the world's population groups with the exception of those of Scandinavian origin and of some other European ancestries.

Dairy food affects all organs and systems. However, because it is a product of the mammary gland, it primarily affects the human glands and related structures, especially the reproductive organs. The most commonly affected are the breast, uterus, ovaries, prostate, thyroid, nasal cavities, pituitary gland, the cochlea in the ear, and the cerebral area surrounding the midbrain. Its adverse effects first appear as the accumulation of mucus and fat and then the formation of cysts, tumors, and finally cancer. Many people who eat dairy food have mucous accumulations in the nasal cavities and inner ear, resulting in hay fever and hearing difficulty. Accumulation of fatty deposits from dairy food consumption in the kidneys and also gallbladder leads to stones. The development of breast cysts, breast tumors, and finally breast cancer follows a similar pattern. Common problems from dairy, in combination with other factors, also include vaginal discharges, ovarian cysts, fibrosis and uterine cancer, ovarian cancer, and prostate fat accumulation with cyst formation. Many diseases of the reproductive organs, including infertility, are associated with dairy consumption. In the case of the lungs, fat and mucous accumulation in the air sacs causes breathing difficulties. In combination with tobacco, dairy food can trap tars and other ingredients of tobacco smoke in the lungs, leading often to lung cancer.

Modern medical studies have begun to link milk and dairy food consumption with a wide variety of sicknesses including cramps and diarrhea, multiple forms of allergy, iron-deficiency anemia in infants and children, aggressive and anti-social behavior, atherosclerosis and heart attacks, arthritis, and several forms of cancer. Since more oxygen is needed to carry hemoglobin to cells enveloped with mucus, dairy food consumption contributes also to uneven thinking, dulled reactions, and emotional dependency.

Human milk is the ideal food for human infants. The chief nutrients for which cow's milk and dairy foods are often eaten, such as calcium and iron, are found in proportionately greater amounts in vegetable-quality foods as shown in the accompanying tables. If animal food is desired, fish and seafood may be taken occasionally. Marine products such as these contain unsaturated rather than saturated fat, and among them white-meat fish and slower-moving shellfish are less fatty than red-meat, blue-skin, or faster-moving varieties.

The Problem of Calories: Present recommendations of caloric intake made by scientific and medical institutions tend to overestimate the volume of calories required by the average person. The modern method of calculating the calories required for various activities is based upon expenditure of energy as measured by discharge following activities rather than the actual amount of calories really required to carry on those activities. Guidelines based on such analytical examinations result in progressively higher recommendations of caloric intake needed in prosperous countries, where people are eating more rich and refined food, and progressively lower recommendations in countries where the people are eating more simply.

According to the macrobiotic view, one's natural appetite for whole, natural, properly cooked foods and one's regular bowel movements are more practical barometers for determining the necessary volume of food as well as required calories. Caloric requirements vary generally between 1,400 and 1,800 daily depending upon age, sex, and personal condition and need, if the Standard Macrobiotic Diet is generally practiced in a temperate region, with two or three meals consumed per day. In contrast, the average American consumes about 2,400 to 3,300 calories daily.

Furthermore, it is necessary to consider that some foods convert into calories with higher speed than other foods. For example, sugar processed from sugarcane produces calories rapidly, but the caloric discharge soon ceases, while glucose metabolized from whole cereal grains burns slowly and produces caloric energy lasting longer. In this respect, a low-calorie diet centered around grains and vegetables is far superior to a high-calorie diet centered around meat and sugar.

The Problem of Carbohydrates: Carbohydrates are generally known as sugars, but in speaking of sugar we should specify the variety. Single sugars or *monosaccharides* are found in fruits and honey and include glucose and fructose. Double sugars or *disaccharides* are found in cane sugar and milk and include sucrose and lactose. Complex sugars or *polysaccharides* are found in grains, beans, and vegetables and include cellulose. In the normal digestive process, complex sugars are decomposed gradually and at a nearly even rate by various enzymes in the mouth, stomach, pancreas, and intestines. Complex sugars enter the bloodstream slowly after being broken down into smaller saccharide units. During the process, the pH of the blood remains slightly alkaline.

In contrast, single and double sugars (together known as simple sugars) are metabolized quickly, causing the blood to become overacidic. To compensate for this extreme yin condition, the pancreas secretes a yang hormone, insulin, which allows excess sugar in the blood to be removed and enter the cells of the body. This produces a burst of energy as the glucose (the end product of all sugar metabolism) is oxidized and carbon dioxide and water are given off as wastes. Diabetes, for example, is a disease charactered by the failure of the pancreas to produce enough insulin to neutralize excess blood sugar following years of extreme dietary consumption.

Much of the sugar that enters the bloodstream is originally stored in the liver in the form of glycogen until needed, when it is again changed into glucose. When the amount of glycogen exceeds the liver's storage capacity of about 50 grams, it is released into the bloodstream in the form of fatty acid. This fatty acid is stored first in the more inactive places of the body, such as the buttocks, thighs, and midsection. Then, if cane sugar, fruit sugar, dairy sugar, and other simple sugars continue to be eaten fatty acid becomes attracted to more yang organs such as the heart, liver, and kidneys, which gradually become encased in a layer of fat and mucus.

This accumulation can also penetrate the inner tissues, weakening the normal functioning of the organs and causing their eventual blockage as in the case of atherosclerosis. The buildup of fat can also lead to various forms of cancer, including tumors of the breast, colon, and reproductive organs. Still another form of degeneration may occur when the body's internal supply of minerals is mobilized to offset the debilitating effects of simple sugar consumption. For example, calcium from the teeth may be depleted to balance the excessive intake of candy, soft drinks, and sugary desserts.

In order to prevent these degenerative effects, it is important to avoid or minimize the consumption of refined carbohydrates, as well as naturally occurring lactose and fructose in dairy foods and fruits, and to eat carbohydrates primarily in the form of polysaccharides found in grains, beans and bean products, and vegetables from land and sea.

The Problem of Protein: Modern nutrition tends to greatly overemphasize the need for protein. While it is true that the human body consists in large part of protein—such as muscle, nails, and hair—the protein required by our body does not necessarily come from the protein we eat. Within the body, there is a constant interchange among protein, carbohydrate, and fat, so that reserves of carbohydrate and fat are often mobilized to supply the protein needed for body functions. Moreover, daily food is used primarily for energy in carrying on regular activities and only secondarily for the formation and maintenance of bodily functions. The ratio of food used for body construction to food used for daily activity is, on average, about 1: 7, which, of course, fluctuates according to our activities and climatic conditions from about 1: 5 to 1: 10. Generally, protein is used for body maintenance and carbohydrates for daily activity, though they are somewhat interchangeable. Therefore, under normal circumstances, carbohydrates are required in much greater volume in the diet than protein.

In the Standard Macrobiotic Diet, protein is supplied from whole cereal grains, various beans and bean products, sea vegetables, seeds and nuts, and the occasional use of fish and seafood. As part of a balanced diet, these foods supply all the essential amino acids needed by the body. Vegetable-quality protein, moreover, is more flexible than animal-quality protein in the ability to interchange between the needs of body construction and body energy for activity. Recently, medical researchers have begun to associate overconsumption of protein, as well as protein wastes from animal sources, with increased risk of cancer, heart disease, and other degenerative conditions. Excess animal protein consumption has also been associated with the current epidemic of osteoporosis (thinning of the bones) and fractures in later life. Medical studies have shown that too much protein intensifies the loss of calcium and possibly other minerals in the body.

The average American consumes about 100 grams of protein a day, primarily from animal sources. Macrobiotic persons consume about 40 to 60 grams a day, primarily from plant sources (see Table 8). Generally, beans and legumes have about the same amout of protein as a comparable volume of meat, poultry, and dairy food, while whole grains have about half the amount of animal foods. Soybeans and soybean products such as tofu, tempeh, and natto are particularly high in protein, containing about one and half times more protein than a similar volume of meat and three times as much as eggs. Seitan, made from wheat gluten, is also very high in protein and is enjoyed frequently in the macrobiotic diet.

The Problem of Fat: In modern societies, fat is consumed in much larger amounts than in countries where people are eating whole grains as their principal food. For example, in the United States, about 42 percent of the ordinary diet is composed of fat, while in rural Mexico among the Tarahumara, a native people renowned for their health and longevity, the amount is only 12 percent. About 15 percent of the Standard Macrobiotic Diet consists of fat.

Lipids are the family name for fats, oils, and fatlike substances including fatty acids, cholesterol, and lipoproteins (see Table 9). *Fats* are solid at room temperature, while *oils* are fluid. Solid lipids tend to contain more saturated fatty acids. Fatty acids are long chains of carbon and hydrogen atoms including an oxygen molecule at one end. *Saturated fatty acids* are bonded or saturated to hydrogen atoms. *Unsaturated fatty acids* lack at least one pair of hydrogen atoms. *Polyunsaturated fatty acids* are those in which more than one pair is missing.

Fatty acids are the building blocks of fats, just as simple sugars are the fundamental units of carbohydrates. In order to help digest fats, which are insoluble in water and form large globules, the liver secretes bile, a yellowish liquid stored in the gallbladder. In the intestine, bile serves to emulsify fats and enables them to be broken down into fatty

Table 8. Protein Content in Various Foods

Meat, poultry, dairy food, and seafood are noted for their protein content. Whole grains, beans, and bean products are also high in protein, and some plant foods such as soybeans contain almost 50 percent more protein than a comparable amount of animal food. Protein requirements vary. The U.S. RDA recommends 0.8 grams of protein per kilogram body weight per day, or about 52 grams for an average male and 44 grams for a female. The FAO/WHO international standards are lower, 37 and 29 grams respectively. (Figures per 100 grams, unit g. 100 g.=3.5 ounces, a typical serving.)

Whole Cereal Grains	Brown rice, various	7.4–7.5
	Wheat, various	9.4–14.0
	Oats	13.0
	Barley, various	8.2–8.9
	Rye, various	12.1–12.7
	Millet, various	9.9–12.7
	Buckwheat, various	11.0–14.5
	Corn, various	8.2–8.9
	Sorghum	11.0–12.7
Beans and Bean Products	Azuki beans	21.5
	Broad beans, various	25.1–26.0
	Kidney beans	20.2
	Lima beans	20.4
	Mung beans	23.0–24.2
	Peas, dried, various	21.7–24.1
	Soybeans, various	34.1–34.3
	Natto	16.9
	Tempeh, various	18.3–48.7
	Tofu	7.8
Seeds and Nuts	Various	11.0–29.7
Meat and Poultry	Beef, various	13.6–21.8
	Pork, various	9.1–21.5
	Chicken, various	14.5–23.4
	Other birds and poultry	18.5–25.3
	Eggs, various	12.9–13.9
Dairy Food	Cheese, various	13.6–27.5
Fish and Seafood	Fishes, various	16.4–25.4
	Shellfish, various	10.6–24.8
	Seafood, various	15.0–20.0

Sources: U.S. Department of Agriculture and Japan Nutritionist Association.

acids and glycerol by digestive enzymes.

Lipids are essential to digestion but can be harmful to the body, especially saturated acids like stearic acid, found in animal tissues, which coats the red-blood cells, blocks the capillaries, and deprives the heart of oxygen. One of the main constituents of lipids is *cholesterol,* a naturally occurring substance in the body which contributes to the maintenance of cell walls, serves as a precursor of bile acids and vitamin D and also a precursor of some hormones. Cholesterol is virtually not found in plants foods but is contained in all animal products, especially meat, egg yolks, and dairy products. Since cholesterol is insoluble in the blood, it attaches itself to a protein that is soluble in order to be transported through the body. This combination is called a *lipoprotein*. However, excess cholesterol in the bloodstream tends to be deposited in artery walls and as plaque eventually causes constriction of the arteries, reduces the flow of blood, and can lead to a heart attack, stroke, or peripheral artery disease. Normally, fat is absorbed by the lymph and enters the bloodstream near the heart. However, if excess lipids accumulate in the body, eventually some will become deposited in the liver. Such stored fat, primarily from meat, poultry, eggs, and dairy products, is usually the chief source of liver malfunctions. Excess fat, especially saturated fat, is also stored in and around vital organs, such as the kidneys, the spleen, the pancreas, and the reproductive organs and is a leading cause of cancer in these sites.

Because of the increased public awareness of the connection among cholesterol, saturated fat, and heart disease and cancer, many people have switched to unsaturated fats and oils, including vegetable cooking oils, mayonnaise, margarine, salad dressings, and artificial creamers and spreads. Today, these make up the largest single source of fat in the American diet. However, unsaturated fats, especially those of a refined quality, serve to redistribute cholesterol from the blood to the tissues and combine with oxygen to form *free radicals*. These are unstable and highly reactive substances that can interact with proteins and cause the loss of elasticity in tissue and general weakening of cells. *Hydrogenated* fats, moreover, such as dairy or soy margarine, are treated to remain

Table 9. Types of Oils and Fats

Saturated	*Monounsaturated*	*Polyunsaturated*
Beef	Olive oil	Whole grains
Pork	Peanut oil	Beans
Lamb		Corn oil
Chicken		Sesame oil
Lard		Soybean oil
Butter		Sunflower oil
Milk		Mustard seed oil
Dairy food		Safflower oil
Coconut oil		Many white-meat fish
Palm oil		and some seafood

solid at room temperature, a process that converts their unsaturated fatty acids into saturated fatty acids to a significant degree.

Whole grains, beans, seeds and nuts contain polyunsaturated fats and oils, but these are naturally balanced by the right proportion of vitamin E and selenium, which are usually lost in the refining process. Similarly, unrefined polyunsaturated cooking oils (in which the vitamin E remains) such as dark sesame oil are a balanced product and, if used moderately, will contribute to proper metabolism, including more flexible motion and thinking.

The Problem of Vitamins: Vitamins exist naturally in whole foods and should be consumed in whole form as a part of the food together with other nutrients. Vitamin pills and other nutritional supplements became popular in recent decades to offset the deficiencies, and in extreme cases deficiency diseases, caused by modern food processing. In essence, the vitamins and minerals that are taken out of whole wheat, brown rice, and other whole unrefined grains to make white flour, white rice, and other refined foods are sold back to the consumer in capsule form. When taken in this unnatural way as a supplement to our regular food, vitamin pills produce a chaotic effect on the body's metabolism.

For hundreds of thousands of years, humanity has taken vitamins in whole form. This practice is respected by the macrobiotic dietary approach and is beginning to find acceptance in some scientific quarters. Megadoses of niacin can cause a wide variety of symptoms including abnormal heart rhythms, headache, cramps, nausea and vomiting; excessive vitamin B_6 can cause severe nervous-system dysfunctions; too much vitamin C can cause mild diarrhea, abdominal cramps, and in some cases precipitate kidney stones; and large amounts of vitamin A or vitamin D can cause acute and chronic toxicity. In addition to the active ingredients, many vitamin and mineral pills, tablets, and capsules contain fillers, binders, disintegrating agents, lubricants, artificial colors and flavors, and synthetic coatings that may also cause harmful effects.

There are two general classes of vitamins: fat-soluble vitamins including A, D, E, and K, and water-soluble vitamins including thiamin (B_1), riboflavin (B_2), B_6, B_{12}, C, niacin, folic acid, biotin, and pantothenic acid. Fat-soluble vitamins are generally more yang, while water-soluble vitamins are generally more yin. (However, there are a few exceptions such as B_{12}, a water-soluble vitamin that is predominantly yang.) When our general food tends to become excessively yin in quality, with more salad, fruits, sugars, and beverages, more volume of yang vitamins with some yin vitamins such as thiamin and riboflavin are required. If our diet becomes excessively yang in quality, with the consumption of meat, eggs, more salted food, and more well-cooked food, more volume of yin vitamins is required. A theory is popular among some people eating a great deal of animal food—or vegetarians who previously ate a lot of meat—that the daily consumption of a large dose of vitamin C is healthful. For their overly yang condition, vitamin C (especially in whole foods rather than in vitamin capsules) may have a temporary beneficial effect. However, vitamin C doses are not suitable for people eating grains and vegetables, whose food is more balanced in quality, already rich in vitamin C. In capsule form, moreover, some vitamin C originates from potatoes, tomatoes, and other solanaceous (nightshade) plants high in this substance that are associated with arthritis and a wide variety of other diseases.

Table 10. Vitamin C Content in Various Foods

Citrus fruits are well known as a source of vitamin C (ascorbic acid). However, many green leafy vegetables are very rich in vitamin C, and some temperate-climate and sea vegetables contain modest amounts. The U.S. RDA is 60 mg./day and the FAO/WHO recommendation is 30 mg./day. (Figures per 100 grams, unit mg.)

Leafy Green Vegetables	Broccoli	113
	Brussels sprouts	102
	Cabbage leaves	47
	Cauliflower	78
	Chives	56
	Collard greens	152
	Daikon greens	90
	Kale	186
	Mustard greens	97
	Parsley	172
	Turnip greens	139
	Swiss chard	32
	Watercress	79
Citrus Fruits	Grapefruit	38
	Lemon	77
	Orange	50
	Orange juice	56
	Tangerine	31
Temperate-Climate Fruits	Apricot	10
	Nectarine	13
	Strawberries	59

Source: U.S. Department of Agriculture and Japan Nutritionist Association.

Vitamin C is readily available in a range of whole foods, though many people today believe that citrus fruits are the most efficient source of this nutrient (see Table 10). Such a belief depends largely upon commercial promotion and insufficient understanding of food composition. Many green leafy vegetables contain much more vitamin C than citrus fruits, which are largely tropical and subtropical in origin and can lead to loss of natural immunity if consumed regularly in temperate regions. Also, vitamin C is not destroyed as easily in cooking as generally believed. Large amounts of vitamin C are lost when cooking lasts longer than 8 minutes at 100 degrees C., the boiling temperature of water. In macrobiotic cooking, leafy green vegetables high in vitamin C are usually boiled or steamed from 30 seconds to 1 minute and in some cases 3 to 5 minutes, thereby retaining most of the vitamin C and other important nutrients.

There is also misunderstanding about vitamin B_{12}, which many people believe is found only in animal foods such as liver and eggs. Contrary to such belief, vitamin B_{12} is found in many fermented food products of vegetable origin such as miso, tamari soy sauce, tempeh, and natto, as well as in some sea vegetables (see Table 11). In modern society, B-complex vitamins are commonly recommended for various conditions of health, but this practice too has resulted from eating white bread, white flour products, and other refined grains as well as observing other imbalanced dietary habits that do not supply vitamins naturally within each food.

Table 11. Vitamin B_{12} Content in Various Foods

Until recently, scientists thought that Vitamin B_{12} was found only in foods of animal origin. However, for thousands of years, people in traditional societies have been eating vegetable-quality foods high in this nutrient. The U.S. RDA is 6 micrograms/day. (Figures per 100 grams, unit mcg. 100 g. = 3.5 ounces, an average serving unless otherwise noted.)

Tempeh	3.9
Natto	0.3
Miso (1 Tablespoon)	0.1
Spirulina (16 g.)	16.5
Kombu (15 g.)	4.1
Wakame (15 g.)	2.3
Swiss Cheese	1.8
Canned Tuna	2.2
Beef Liver	80.0
Eggs	2.0

Source: *East West Journal*, October, 1982

The accompanying charts list some common dietary sources of individual vitamins in the macrobiotic diet and show how they compare with foods in the usual modern diet. A balanced whole foods diet, containing various kinds of whole cereal grains, beans and bean products, vegetables, sea vegetables, fruits, seeds and nuts, and occasional animal food if desired, and using good quality unrefined sea salt and unrefined vegetable-quality cooking oil, supplies all essential nutrients in natural form.

The Problem of Minerals and Trace Elements: The human body contains various kinds of minerals such as calcium, phosphorous, potassium, sulphur, chlorine, sodium, magnesium, and iron as well as minute amounts of trace elements such as iodine, manganese, copper, nickel, arsenic, bromine, silicon, selenium, and others. Approximately 80 percent of the body consists of water, in which these minerals and trace elements are found, and our bloodstream and other bodily fluids are similar in composition to the primordial ocean in which life began.

Minerals and trace elements are essential to form bones, muscles, and other body structures. Like seawater that neutralizes various toxins streaming into the ocean from the land, the minerals in our circulatory system serve to maintain smooth metabolism by harmonizing the influx of excessive dietary factors. For example, excessive sugar intake results in the condition of acidosis in the blood, which is neutralized by using such minerals as calcium and is ultimately eliminated from the body in the form of carbon dioxide and water. Therefore, a constant supply of various minerals in the form of good quality unrefined sea salt, whole grains and vegetables, and especially mineral-rich seaweed is necessary and highly recommended for daily life.

Modern refined table salt is nearly pure sodium chloride, to which trace amounts of mineral compounds, dextrose (a form of refined sugar), and usually potassium iodide have been added. This product is unsuitable for meeting metabolic requirements, has been associated with high blood pressure, and is a primary reason why many modern people take mineral supplements. Another reason is to supplement minerals and vitamins lost from foods grown in mineral-poor soil that has been depleted by chemical fertilizers, pesticides, and other sprays. Scientific tests show that organic fruits and vegetables contain up to three times more minerals and trace elements than inorganic produce. Unrefined sea salt, the traditional type of salt used in macrobiotic cooking and food preparation, retains all the natural mineral compounds and trace elements (about sixty in number) found in the sea.

It is also commonly believed that milk and other dairy foods can supply more calcium than any other foods and that the best source of iron is liver or other animal-quality foods. The accompanying charts show that many other foods contain these nutrients and often in proportionately greater amounts than meat or dairy foods (see Tables 12 and 13).

Taken in supplemental form, megadoses of minerals—like vitamin pills—can sometimes block the absorption of other essential nutrients or at other times increase the body's normal requirements. Excessive amounts of zinc, for example, can cause anemia by inhibiting copper absorption and in some cases can interfere with proper calcium absorption. Similarly, too much iron or selenium can cause a zinc deficiency. As part of a balanced whole foods diet, these and other nutrients are naturally found in their proper proportion and measure.

The Problem of Acid and Alkaline: Our blood, under normal circumstances, is slightly alkaline, having a pH between 7.3 and 7.45. Acids are constantly produced in the body during metabolic processes, yet the blood remains relatively constant by the elimination of excessive acid conditions in the form of carbon dioxide through the lungs, the elimination of urine by the kidneys, and through the action of buffers in the blood that change strong acid into weak acid.

As a result of these reactions, some people today believe that food containing more acid (pH factor less than 7.3) should be avoided in daily eating. Sometimes this belief leads them to avoid consuming whole grains because they appear to be more acid than alkaline when reduced to ash in laboratory testing. In practice, however, living metabolism is different from laboratory experiments such as those measuring acid and alkaline content. Some alkaline foods such as sugar and fruits, for example, often produce excessive acid conditions, though acid foods such as meat and eggs also produce acid conditions. Whole cereal grains, though showing an acidic pH in the laboratory on account of their phosphorous content, produce an overall mild alkalizing condition in the blood, and the compound in whole grains containing phosphorous is used as a buffer to eliminate strong acids from the body.

In general cereal grains (acid in the laboratory) produce alkaline conditions in the body. Most vegetables (alkaline) produce alkaline conditions. Some vegetables, especially those of tropical origin (alkaline), produce acid conditions. Sugar (alkaline) produces acid conditions. Meat and other animal food (acid) produce acid conditions. Fat and oil (acid) produce acid conditions. Minerals (alkaline and acid) produce

Table 12. Iron Content of Various Foods

Foods noted for their iron content include liver and other organ meats, spinach, and molasses. However, whole grains, beans, green leafy vegetables, and seeds generally contain comparable amounts of iron, and sea vegetables are also a good source. The U.S. RDA varies from 10–18 mg/day. (Figures per 100 grams, unit mg. 100 g.=3.5 ounces, a typical serving unless otherwise noted.)

Whole Grains	Buckwheat	3.1
	Millet	6.8
	Oats	4.6
	Soba	5.0
	Whole Wheat, various	3.1–3.3
Beans	Azuki Beans	4.8
	Chickpeas	6.9
	Lentils	6.8
	Soybeans	7.0
	Tempeh	5.0
Green Leafy Vegetables	Beet Greens	3.3
	Dandelion Greens	3.1
	Mustard Greens	3.0
	Parsley	6.2
	Spinach	3.1
	Swiss Chard	3.2
Seeds (1 Tablespoon)	Pumpkin Seeds	3.2
	Sesame Seeds	3.0
	Sunflower Seeds	2.4
Sea Vegetables (1/4 cup, cooked)	Arame	1.5
	Dulse	1.6
	Hijiki	3.2
	Kombu	1.9
	Nori	5.6
	Wakame	1.3
Fish and Seafood	Herring	1.1
	Sardines	2.9
	Abalone	2.4
	Oyster	5.5
Meat, Dairy, and Poultry	Milk	0.1
	Beef	3.6
	Chicken	1.6
	Egg Yolk	6.3
	Beef Liver	6.5
	Calf Liver	8.7
	Chicken Liver, various	7.9
Refined Sugar (1 Tablespoon)	Molasses	1.7

Source: U.S. Department of Agriculture and Japan Nutritionist Association.

Table 13. Calcium Content in Various Foods

Dairy foods are known as a source of calcium, but many vegetable-quality foods are also rich in this element. Calcium needs vary with age and other factors. The U.S. RDA varies from 800–1,200 mg/day. Figures are for average servings.

Category	Food	Calcium
Leafy Green Vegetables (1/2 cup, cooked)	Beet Greens	72
	Broccoli (a large stalk)	246
	Collard Greens	177
	Daikon Greens	80
	Dandelion Greens	74
	Kale	103
	Mustard Greens	97
	Parsley	61
	Spinach	83
	Turnip Greens	126
	Watercress	90
Beans and Bean Products (1 cup, cooked)	Azuki Beans	37
	Chickpeas	75
	Kidney Beans	70
	Navy Beans	95
	Soybeans	131
	Miso (1 Tablespoon)	40
	Natto (3.5 oz.)	103
	Tempeh (3.5 oz.)	142
	Tofu (3.5 oz.)	128
Sea Vegetables (1/4 cup, cooked)	Agar-Agar	100
	Arame	146
	Dulse	137
	Hijiki	152
	Kombu	76
	Nori	100
	Wakame	130
Seeds and Nuts: (1 Tablespoon)	Sesame Seeds	331
	Sunflower Seeds	40
	Sweet Almonds	81
	Brazil Nuts	53
	Hazel Nuts	60
Grains	Buckwheat (1 cup, cooked)	57
Fish and Seafood (3.5 oz.)	Carp	50
	Haddock	23
	Salmon	79
	Sardines with Bones	372
	Shortneck Clams	80
	Oyster	94
Dairy Food	Cow's Milk (1 cup)	288
	Eggs (1 large)	27
	Goat's Milk (1 cup)	315
	Cheese, various (1 slice)	100–350
	Yogurt (1 cup)	272

Source: U.S. Department of Agriculture and Japan Nutritionist Association.

alkaline in some cases, acid in other cases, and buffer effects in still other cases.

In practice, yin and yang are much more useful concepts than acid and alkaline in evaluating the energy and nutrients of food, as well as their effect on living organisms. In general, we may say that excessively yin and excessively yang foods such as meat and sugar, dairy products and chemicalized foods, and tropical fruits and vegetables, produce acidic conditions in the body, including weak unhealthy blood. Meanwhile, balanced foods such as whole grains, beans and bean products, vegetables, and sea vegetables produce alkaline conditions in the body, including strong and healthy blood.

5. The Way of Life for Humanity

> "Nothing is so strong as gentleness, nothing so gentle as real strength."
>
> —St. Francis

Practicing a Natural Way of Life

Physical and Spiritual Food: As a manifestation of the infinite Order of the Universe, living within boundless space and time, human beings are capable of eating everything. First, according to our biological nature, we eat the minerals of the earth, the waters of the earth, and all biological life, including plants and animals. Second, we consume air and the atmosphere surrounding the earth by breathing through both the respiratory system and the entire surface of the skin. Third, we take in various sorts of vibrations, ranging from long waves to short waves, from low frequency to high frequency, through our sensory receptions and the entire surface of the body. The sense of touch deals with vibrations that manifest as solid matter; the sense of taste deals with vibrations that manifest in liquid form; the sense of smell deals with vibrations that manifest in gaseous form; the auditory sense receives vibrations of sound transmitted through the atmosphere; and the visual sense further interprets light waves. The nourishment from these sources may be classified as sensory foods.

Beyond sensory food, we receive nourishment from waves and radiation in our environment. These include nearby impulses and vibrations, such as the energy of grain ripening in the fields, and far distant influences, such as cosmic rays and galactic waves coming from hundreds of billions of light years away. These vibrations are absorbed into the surface of our body, and we transmute some of them into electromagnetic waves that are circulated through the Energy Channel and system of meridians. They charge our body's organs, glands, and trillions of cells. By this charge, we move, digest our food, breathe, think, and act.

As a species, we eat both visible food—minerals, water, vegetables, animals, and air—as well as invisible food—vibration, waves, radiation, and various rays (see Figure 41). We may call the former physical food and the latter spiritual food. Physical food we ingest primarily through the digestive and respiratory systems on the front or surface of the body, while spiritual food is ingested primarily through the nervous system and the network of meridians on the back or deep inside of the body. We eat physical food only at intervals, but we eat spiritual food continuously. Physical food is taken in limited volume, but spiritual food is taken without limit.

Figure 41. Food and Cosmology

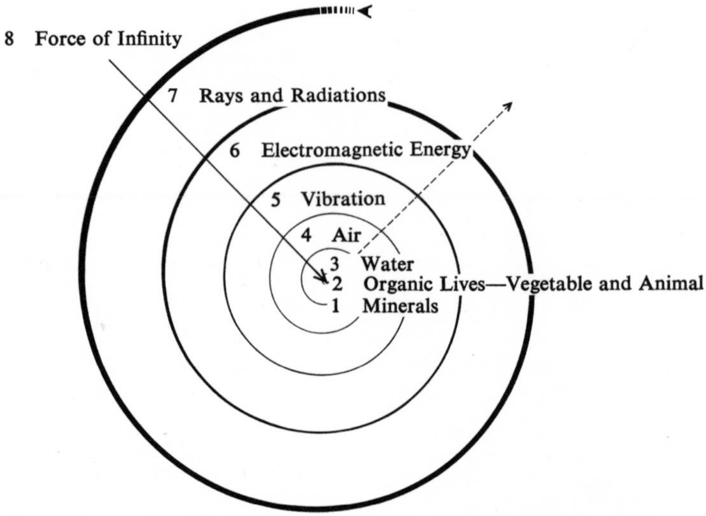

Environments 1 through 4 are physical and material food. Environments 5 through 8 are unphysicalized spiritual food. The physical and material foods are eaten through the nose and mouth and descend to the lungs and intestines, while spiritual food is taken in through the nervous system and meridians, ascending toward the midbrain. Both nourish the whole body.

Between physical and spiritual food, or material food and nonmaterial food, however, there is an antagonistic and complementary relationship in the quality and volume consumed. First, the more material food we eat, the less nonmaterial food we eat. The less material food we eat, the more spiritual food we eat. Second, the more we eat animal-quality material food, the more long waves and less short waves we take in from our environment. The consumption of animal food tends to limit our perception to the immediate environment and inhibit our awareness and receptivity to the unlimited scope of infinite time and space. Third, the more we eat vegetable-quality material food, the more short waves and the less long waves we receive. The consumption of vegetable-quality food tends to broaden our mental and spiritual view and lessen our concern for small matters of the relative world.

Though we eat both physical and spiritual, material and nonmaterial food, we are unable to directly manage and control the quality and quantity of spiritual, nonmaterial food we take in. However, spiritual and nonmaterial food is controlled by regulating the consumption of physical and material food. Over this kind of food, we have almost total control. We have almost complete freedom to plant, grow, harvest, process, combine, cook, and serve the physical foods we consume. We have control over the type of cooking fire we use, the quality and type of salt, oil, and other seasonings, how much volume of food is consumed, and how often meals are prepared. Therefore, by controlling our daily food, we can change and determine the quality of mental and spiritual awareness that we develop.

Each person exercises freedom in what she or he eats and drinks. Since each of us eats slightly differently, each of us is different. No two people eat exactly the same foods or chew exactly the same way. However, people who eat the same general type of diet think and act in similar ways. The similarities and variations in the way we eat account for the rich tapestry of human experience. Some people are slower in their actions, and others are faster. Some people are more sentimental, others are more intellectual. Some people are more conservative, others are more liberal. Everyone has unique characteristics and habits (see Figure 42).

In order to balance our physical, mental, and spiritual activities through our daily life, it is essential to eat a proper diet. When we include a larger amount of animal food than we really require, our mental activities tend to become more egocentric and aggressive toward the outer world. On the other hand, if we use vegetable food almost exclusively, especially a large volume of fruits, we tend to exclusivity and a defensive attitude toward any strong stimulus coming from our surroundings. A large volume of extreme yang foods—such as meat, eggs, cheese, and poultry—and a large volume of extreme yin foods—such as milk, salad, fruits, hot spices, and alcohol—produce fear and exclusivity, sometimes expressed similarly but often in combination with

Figure 42. Yin and Yang of Birth Month

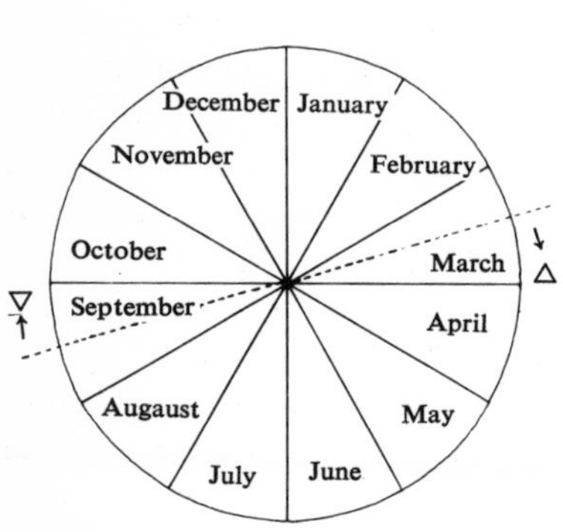

A person who was born between March and September in the northern hemisphere has a yang constitution because she or he spent her embryonic period mostly in the colder season, eating her mother's more yang quality of blood, which was nourished by more cooked winter food, including a larger consumption of animal food. Accordingly, a person who was born between September and March has the opposite, more yin constitution. A person who has a yang constitution is generally more active in society, while a person who has a yin constitution tends to be more mental and spiritual. However, they respectively seek their opposite and are attracted to their complement, throughout their lifetimes.

each other: the more yang category of food produces a more aggressive and offensive attitude, while the more yin food produces a more defensive and self-excusing tendency. The former contributes more toward a materialistic view of life, the latter a more otherworldly view. Both these ways of thinking and acting are imbalanced, ultimately leading to sickness and unhappiness. By avoiding excessive yang and yin qualities of food, our health and judgment remain strong and clear. By eating primarily whole grains and vegetables, with small supplemental amounts of other types of food, and observing the seasonal order and other principles of environmental balance, we remain in the middle. The macrobiotic dietary approach produces both physical strength and vitality as well as mental and spiritual balance.

Natural Way of Eating: Traditionally, it was recognized that mental and spiritual teachings and exercises were ineffective without proper practice of dietary balance. The macrobiotic way of life respects food as the essence of life, including the physical and spiritual environment, and regards food as a spiritual manifestation of the universe as well as recognizing its physical value. However, the way we eat is as important as what we eat. Observing the following practices will improve our health and happiness.

• We should treat every tiny grain, every slice of vegetable, and every seed, root, stem, leaf, and fruit as a spiritual manifestation. We should never waste food in the process of farming, shopping, cooking, and eating.

• Before and after we eat, we should dedicate our heartfelt gratitude for the food that has come from the infinite universe, materializing in the form of a meal, and we should dedicate our endless thanks to nature and the universe, as well as to society, which has made our existence possible at this moment. Further, we should dedicate our deep appreciation to the people who have prepared the meal, beginning from cultivation through transportation and processing, to the final stage of the cooking and serving of the food. We should be grateful to the plants and animals who have given their lives that we may live. This may take any comfortable form, such as grace, a moment of silent prayer or meditation, or chanting.

• While we are eating, we should chew thoroughly in order to both physicalize and spiritualize what we are eating, maintaining in our mind constant self-reflection whether we are worthy to consume the meal. We should reflect on the physical and spiritual activity that shall come from this food, for the benefit of society and all people, and for the harmony with nature and the universe.

• When we finish eating, we should be clearly aware that what we have shared with friends and family—eating together, drinking together—is now producing a similar quality of blood, body, thought, and movement. We should extend this consciousness to every person living in our society and in our world, thinking of them all as one family upon the earth and in the universe.

• During the meal, we should never leave any food remaining on our plate or dishes. After the meal we should wash our own dishes and utensils and keep them in beautiful order with silent thanks for their efficient service in making it possible for us to enjoy the meal.

Spiritual practice and understanding is inseparable from biological nourishment. By eating whole foods in a spirit of modesty and humility, and in a graceful and beautiful manner, all other aspects of life will proceed harmoniously.

Natural Clothing: When we eat macrobiotically, we begin to recover our natural sensitivity and start to avoid synthetic clothing and artificial fabrics, especially those that come in direct contact with the surface of the body. Vegetable-quality materials such as cotton and jute, as well as silk and other natural fabrics, are much more comfortable and allow the natural electromagnetic energy in the environment to flow smoothly throughout the body. Natural materials also permit smooth breathing and proper exchange of heat and water through the skin. Synthetic fibers, in contrast, can impede this energy flow and disrupt normal metabolism. Our taste in colors and ornaments also changes toward those that are more gentle and graceful. We appreciate simple, natural beauty and are less attracted to adornments and extreme colors or patterns. We often prefer to make our own clothes and furnishings, including quilts and *futons*, rather than purchase ready-made apparel and accessories. Furthermore, as our condition improves and we decrease our consumption of excessive calories, fat, and liquid, our garments can be kept for a longer period. Health and beauty become radiant through simple, natural clothing and graceful design.

Natural Dwellings: As we grow closer to nature, we begin to appreciate wood, stone, and other natural materials for our homes and shelters more than metal and concrete. The former tends to make the atmosphere softer and quieter, while the latter creates a harder and more oppressive feeling. A peaceful mind, deep reflection, and clear ideas are nourished by the presence of peaceful materials in our dwellings. For our furniture, desks, cabinets, closets, and other objects, materials derived from plants are preferred over animal and synthetic quality materials. The color of walls and curtains should also be more subdued and plain rather than vivid and complex. If we wish to keep our happiness, we must arrange our homes more in contact with nature.

Traditional Japanese homes, for example, maintain a clear distinction between the inside and outside of the house. The floor of the house is elevated and constructed from wood, paper, and bamboo with the aid of some earth plaster. The use of these materials contributes to the family's tranquility. Also, *tatami* mats, made from weeds and straw, cover the floor. Taking off the shoes at the entrance of the house and sitting on these mats traditionally harmonizes the mind and body with nature. *Shoji* screens and *fusuma* sliding doors, made of paper and wood, are used to divide rooms. By moving the screens or sliding the doors, room space is easily adjusted, contributing further to the flexibility and harmony of the household.

Natural Furnishings: In other parts of the world, as well as Japan, people traditionally built their houses in harmony with the surrounding environment. The doors and windows of traditional homes are usually far larger than those in modern buildings and are readily adjustable according to the change of season or weather. Traditional people invited more natural light into their homes, and they often brought plants and soil into the rooms in the form of flower arrangements, potted plants, *bonsai* displays (miniature trees and plants), and *bonkei* arrangements (miniature natural scenes). Houses were traditionally heated to maintain natural comfort and were not kept at unnecessarily high or artificially low temperatures. Modern central heating and air conditioning became popular in recent years as people eating the modern diet began to lose their natural ability to adjust to their surroundings. A sedentary lifestyle further contributed to an insulation from the natural environment and an inability to harmonize with changing weather conditions. As we eat macrobiotically, our natural defense mechanism is restored, and our bodies adjust more easily to extremes of hot and cold, necessitating less dependence on central heating in winter and air conditioning in summer. Further, we are able to balance these factors naturally with slight modifications in our diet and physical activity.

Natural Technology: The discoveries and inventions of modern science and industry have contributed substantial convenience and efficiency to our daily life. However, at the same time, many technological applications are hazardous to our health and spiritual well-being. Artificial electromagnetic energy in our environment changes the atmospheric charge surrounding us, producing various effects on our physical and mental condition. Often we may notice a general fatigue, mental irritability, and unnatural metabolism as the result of high voltage lines, electrical appliances, and other communications equipment in our vicinity. Cooking on an electric range or in a microwave oven or using irradiated (picowaved) food especially contributes to undesirable effects on the molecular structure of food, as well as on our digestion and nourishment, and should preferably be avoided. Synthetic home furnishings and artificial building materials may prevent healthy relaxation. When we start to change our blood to a healthy quality by eating a more centrally balanced diet, we naturally begin to reduce our reliance upon technological comforts in our environment. We appreciate, value, and continue to use some of the technological advances of modern civilization. However, we should reduce our reliance on the use of excessive mechanical or electronic conveniences that may hinder the smooth exchange of energy between ourselves and the natural environment. We especially try to avoid those features of modern life that may contribute to the development of sickness or make the recovery from sickness more difficult.

Natural Personal Care: The use of natural quality goods and methods in the care of our personal needs is also beneficial to our health and development. When we brush our teeth, we should avoid the use of any chemicalized or synthetic toothpaste or toothpowder. Instead we may use more natural materials such as sea salt, dentie tooth powder, clay, and natural vegetable chlorophyll paste or powder. Similarly, when we wash and bathe our face and body, instead of using chemically colored and perfumed soap, we can use more naturally processed soap, including those of clay bases or with other plant materials. To care for the hair and skin, as well as lips and nails, we should also avoid any cosmetics and conditioners that been processed with chemical and synthetic additives. We should use more natural quality materials as were commonly and traditionally used before modern society developed. In Asia, sea vegetables were used to care for hair; in Europe plant juices were used to color the lips, cheeks, and nails. In caring for our skin, instead of using chemically produced hand creams and skin lotions, we can use natural sesame oil or olive oil or natural lotions containing these oils, with excellent results. Also for cleaning our clothing and for washing our dishes, soaps and detergents made from natural ingredients are preferred to artificially made products.

Since our human nature has evolved as part of the natural environment, we should maintain contact with nature as much as possible. Appreciating the earth as our mother and the heavens as our father, and nature as a whole as the source of our life, is central to all traditional cultures and civilizations. When we respect and love our natural surroundings, our health and spirit blossom. The earth, the sun, the stars, and the infinite universe have created and nourished our life and growth. By becoming one with nature in our daily life, our life becomes endlessly fulfilling and happy.

Respect for Ancestors and Love for Offspring

Without the infinite universe and its endless order, no celestial or terrestial phenomena would have appeared. Without the order of nature, biological life would not have developed. Without ancestors, human life would not have existed. Everyone has parents—father and mother. Every father and mother has parents. All grandparents have parents. For hundreds and thousands of years, human life and culture has been transmitted from generation to generation. Modern humanity is the end product of a long process of tradition—biological, psychological, and spiritual—spanning thousands of lifetimes.

Respect for parents is the foundation of every human culture and civilization. No one who respects and loves his or her parents can substantially depart from harmonious personal behavior and social relations. During the period we developed in embryo, infancy, and childhood, our parents showered love and care upon us. Their love for their children was unconditional, and they treated us as their own life. They were worried when we suffered with sickness. They could not sleep for many days and weeks while we were struggling with various physical, mental, and social ills. When adults become parents, their view of life starts to form around the development of their children. Many parents work harder than ever to take care of their offspring and provide them with the best opportunities in life. Even when parents use harsh expressions and discipline their children, they seldom do so to punish or neglect them; rather they hope that the children may grow stronger experiencing difficult situations.

While growing up, we often do not see the love extended to us by our parents. When we begin to have our own children, we start to understand how much love and care we received. However, at that time, we often are unable to extend our thanks to our parents because we are occupied in caring for our own children or involved in various social activities. When we reach the age when we are able to think back and understand the past care and protection bestowed on us by our parents and wish to express our gratitude to them, many parents have already passed away. Parents love and care for their children unconditionally. Similarly, children, when they grow up, should respect and care for their parents unconditionally. It is a natural, universal principle of human conduct. If we do not practice parental love, however great we are in fame, position, property, and social influence, we are worthless in the eyes of the Order of the Universe.

Love and Care of Parents: Respect and care for parents includes the following considerations:

- When living with our parents, we should extend our daily greetings to them every morning after we get up and every evening before going to sleep. When we live apart from our parents, we should communicate with them regularly as often as possible, informing them of what we are doing. We should try not to worry them about ourselves. From time to time, we should send them monetary and material assistance, however small, or other symbols of our appreciation.

• When parents are ill or in any difficulty, whether emotional, financial, or social, we should extend our unconditional assistance and support. Even if we have to sacrifice our own development, comfort, and prosperity, we should unconditionally help to relieve them from suffering.

• When living together with our parents, we should arrange every day if possible, or as often as possible, the opportunity to be together sharing meals. At that time, we should serve our parents and should wait to eat until they have started to eat. Their seats should be arranged at the most comfortable place at the head of the table. During mealtime, we can report on our activities, ask what can be done for our parents, and exchange general conversation.

• We should seek our parents' advice and opinions about life in general and receive their inspiration and guidance. We should also ask as much as possible to hear about their experiences in life in past years, as well as stories about grandparents and ancestors. We should find out where our family originated and lived in past generations, how and what they were doing, and with what dream and spirit our ancestors conducted their lives.

• We should first report happy and joyous news to our parents, before anyone else. Conversely, we should try to avoid letting them know of any sadness we experience. However, the happiness and joy of our parents should be treated as our own happiness and joy, and their sadness and misery felt as our own unhappiness.

In modern society, aged parents often live out the end of their lives in nursing homes, retirement centers, or other institutions reserved for the elderly, even though their children are healthy and prosperous. This is one of the saddest aspects of present day civilization. So long as they are alive, we should make every effort to help our parents and, if necessary, arrange for them to live out their days in our own homes, cooking and taking care of them if they are ill. Respect for parents is not merely a monetary and material question but a more emotional and spiritual question, and we should express our love to them limitlessly and unconditionally.

Through respect for our parents, we learn about our ancestors. The spirit of our forebears is living biologically, psychologically, and spiritually within us. From our parents, we receive our biological and psychological constitution, carrying forward the influence of our grandparents, and, further, the influences of great-grandparents upon them. Practically, seven generations are manifested within our physical, mental, and spiritual constitution very clearly, and theoretically, an unlimited number of generations is represented in our existence. By learning about our family's historical roots and heritage, we extend our appreciation to past generations of ancestors, whose dream we embody. If it is not possible to physically trace their past, we can connect with them spiritually through self-reflection, prayer, and meditation.

We should set a time every morning and/or evening, if possible, to extend our prayers to them, to report what we are doing and to wish spiritual happiness to our ancestors, together with our dedication of endless gratitude to them for the hardships and difficulties they endured. If daily prayers are not practical, then every month or at least every year, a regular date should be selected to pray on their behalf. We may offer special meals on such occasions, and such meals should not contain animal-quality food. Minimally, such offerings should consist of whole grains, water, and unrefined sea salt. When we dedicate our prayers with a food offering to the ancestral spirits, it is traditional to use the most central or unspoiled part of the cooked food before serving to the family and dinner guests.

In the Far East, a small shrine or altar is traditionally set up in the quietest room of the house for this purpose. There the names of ancestors or symbols of ancestral spirits are inscribed, and on important occasions, family and relatives gather and confer in front of this sacred spot. Furthermore, on the memorial anniversaries of family members who have passed away and of cherished ancestors, family, relatives, and friends gather for special ceremonies of remembrance, either in the home or in a community shrine or temple.

We should keep alive any memory, or retain any objects or keepsakes, which our ancestors especially appreciated and enjoyed, and regard these as our family treasures. We should preserve them faithfully and pass them on to the next generation. We should also tell our children and grandchildren about their ancestors: their dream, their spirit, their work, and their understanding, and let them be aware of the stream of life and tradition coming down through countless generations.

Respect for ancestors, however, should not be limited to only several generations or even several hundred generations back. Respect for family and tradition should not be limited to only direct forebears and descendants or the particular culture, civilization, or religion in which we grew up. Whether we are Chinese, Jewish, or Scandinavian, our respect for ancestors and the past should go back far beyond the beginning of written history. It should extend back to the common ancestors of all humankind, all races, all ethnic backgrounds, and eventually reach our common origin: nature, earth, the universe, and one infinity or God. Respect for ancestors and parents is inseparable from respect for the Order of the Universe, the source and origin of all life. From our immediate family, our respect and love expands to all people and beings, in a spirit of brotherhood and sisterhood. In this way we come to realize our common origin and destiny with all of life.

Love and Care of Children: Parents love and care for their children intuitively, just as many biological species instinctively protect their offspring. However, in the case of human parents, such love and care should not be governed only by biological instinct but also be directed more by an intellectual and spiritual understanding of the future of the children and their relation to human society.

Often, especially in modern society, parents' love and care for their children takes a sentimental orientation. Children are protected from all hardships including cold weather, material poverty, social misery, and various other difficulties. Such artificial separation from life's adversities tends to spoil children's development of self-discipline, endurance, vitality, and understanding. Wise parents often arrange for their children to experience various hardships, accompanied by the wish that they may grow into strong personalities. Sentimental parents also often try to nourish their children more than is really necessary. Material wealth, advanced education, a comfortable household, and sweet words are not essential requirements for bringing children to mature adulthood. During their lifetime, children will naturally encounter various vicissitudes, from which they must develop their happiness. Therefore, wise parents first teach their children how to keep their health; second, how to judge various problems; third, how to manage by themselves the necessities of daily life, including cooking, housekeeping, and sewing; and fourth, how to behave with other people and how to love nature and the universe. Children who are brought up to observe the macrobiotic way of life are able to adapt to their natural and social environment without complaining. They also display maximum endurance and patience in any difficult situation and reflect on changing themselves rather than try to change others. They also display great courage and ambition in solving any problem that may arise, always seeking to turn difficulties into opportunities and new hope. Children who have not been brought up macrobiotically tend to resist unfamiliar circumstances, complain about an uncomfortable environment, accuse other people, and retreat from—or try to impose themselves upon—situations beyond their immediate control.

In caring for and loving their children, parents should not expect any personal reward or emotional satisfaction. Often parents insist that their children undergo certain experiences, study a certain subject or go to a certain college, or enter a certain occupation, based upon their own personal desire. True love and care for children is expressed by guiding their development and helping them to realize their potential through free exercise of their own abilities and aspirations, whether or not it conforms to the parents' ideals. Accordingly, parental education should be aimed at providing children a biological and psychological foundation, to maintain their health and judgment, along with an understanding of their ancestors, their community, nature, and the universe. Parental love and care should enable children to grow as people who are able to make their best contribution to society according to their own dream.

To this end, parents should strive to cultivate in the depths of their children's minds a spirit of unconditional appreciation toward everyone and everything. Parents must act as models for their children by offering their own gratitude to all beings and all experiences as they arise. For the future happiness of their children, parents must also guide them to be honest and never lie. The example of honesty and humility excercised by parents in relations with neighbors, friends, and other people automatically guides children toward the development of wholesome personalities. Parents should never be angry toward their children and at the same time should not display anger toward anyone else in their children's presence. Anger is a manifestation of sickness, especially if parents are angry or upset about the attitudes of their children; a faulty attitude in children indicates that the way of life, including the way of eating, that the parents have arranged for their children, is seriously imbalanced. This imbalance is due to the ignorance or faulty practice of the parents themselves, and the children are nothing but a natural reflection of the parents' thought and conduct.

When parents and children share together the same food, properly selected, prepared, and served, their blood quality remains the same and both enjoy health and vitality, physically and spiritually. Parents and children who eat the same way share the same mind and spirit. They are able to understand each other without words as one family. On the other hand, parents and children who eat in different ways and in a chaotic manner, as most modern families are doing at the present time, become separated and estranged through the influence of their declining blood quality on their physical and spiritual condition. Such families experience unexpected physical illnesses, mental illnesses, and emotional and intellectual conflicts, and criticize each other's view of life. The generation gap and the collapse of the family unit evolved from individual family members eating different foods and eating separately from each other. Children and offspring lose the spirit of their ancestors and traditions, and they become orphans isolated from the love and care of their own family and nature as well.

Unless dietary traditions are maintained, in a balanced but flexible macrobiotic way, through many generations over hundreds of centuries, the spirit and tradition, the love and dream that our ancestors have passed down continuously from an unknown ancient time shall perish from the earth. Unless we live in harmony with nature and eat according to natural order, our family and our children's families will decline and human evolution on this planet will end. Therefore, it is up to us to devote ourselves—as both parents and children—to care for and love each other unconditionally and keep alive the human spirit and dream to be passed on to generations without end.

Man and Woman

Traditionally, it is said that man represents heaven and woman represents earth. Consequently, the male body structure tends to be oriented by yang centripetal force, which comes from the distant galaxies and solar system to the outer periphery of the atmosphere and spirals in toward the center of the earth. In man, this force passes through the spiritual channel of electromagnetic energy, which runs from the central hair spiral on top of the head toward the penis. In the female body structure, centrifugal force expanding from the center of the earth passes upward from the uterus and ovaries to the hair spiral on the head. Of course, both sexes receive both centripetal and centrifugal force, but in different degrees (see Figure 43). In men, the predominance of heaven's force produces a tall extended body, small breasts, sexual organs that are external and downward, and facial hair. In women, the expanding earth's force passing through the body meets the incoming strong contractive force of heaven, producing a short body, expanded breasts, sexual organs that are inward and upward, and abundant hair on the top of the head. Psychologically, man is oriented to realizing his conceptual image upon the relative world of the earth, while woman is oriented to making order in her surroundings and cultivating the development of beauty and perfection.

Accordingly, the male character is developed by taking slightly more

Figure 43. Heaven and Earth Forces in Man and Woman

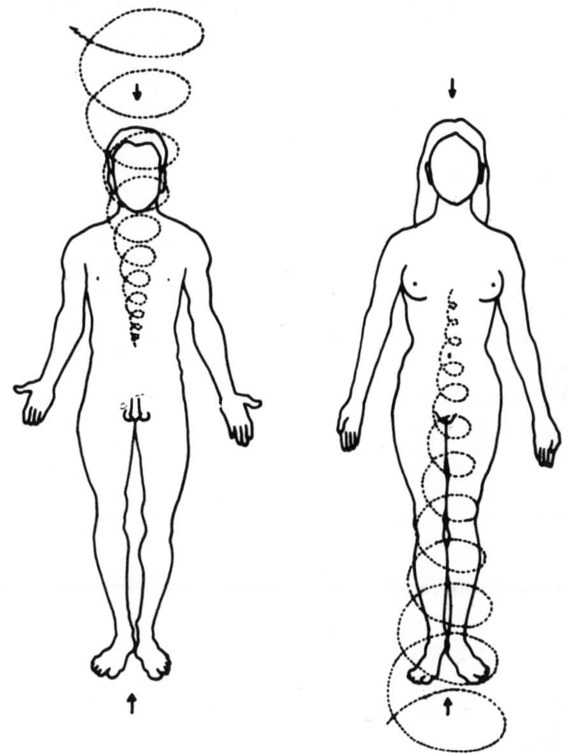

Though both sexes receive incoming *ki* or electromagnetic energy from heaven and earth, in man, heaven's energy predominates, coming in counterclockwise through the spiral at the top of the head. In woman, earth's energy is stronger, spiralling in through the uterus.

yang food than woman, including more grains, vegetables, beans, sea vegetables, salt and other minerals, and occasional animal food. The female character is benefited by taking slightly less of these items, with less seasoning and lighter cooking, and taking slightly more salads, fruit, desserts, and other yin food. Man manifests his character in physical strength, conceptual intellect, social activity, courage and ambition, and the spirit of being willing to die for his dream. On the other hand, woman manifests her character in mental understanding, emotional senstitivity, artistic gracefulness, beautifying her surroundings, gentle affection, tender care, and a spirit of being willing to die for love.

As complemental manifestations of yin and yang, man and woman share their lives together in harmony. In marriage, man and woman live together, creating and sharing balance at all levels. It was noted earlier that when a pendulum is held over a man's head, it usually spirals in a counterclockwise direction, while above a woman it moves clockwise. Interestingly, when man and woman join hands, the pendulum remains still, showing the deep unity of the forces of heaven and earth.

Sharing Food: To develop and maintain harmony, physically, mentally, and spiritually, man and woman should share the same quality of food, with slight variations suitable for each sex. About seven-eighths of the food they share should be the same, and about one-eighth can be different to maintain the uniqueness of each character. For example, in macrobiotic dietary practice, the main food—whole grains, as well as most side dishes which usually consist of cooked vegetables, beans, and sea vegetables—can be the same for man and woman. But an occasional addition of a special dish may be called for: in the case of man, this may consist of fish or seafood or else more strongly cooked vegetables, and in the case of woman, the addition of very lightly cooked leafy green vegetables or fruits in small volume. Generally speaking, in temperate and warmer climates, woman can be satisfactorily nourished by all vegetable-quality food, while man may have occasionally a supplement of animal food if he requires it.

Sharing such a diet, man and woman develop similar physical and mental conditions, while still maintaining their unique male and female characteristics and tendencies. Through such similarities and differences, they can establish the most harmonious physical relationship as well as mental understanding and become one biologically, psychologically, and spiritually.

Sharing Physical Relations: Based upon common dietary practice, physical relations between the sexes become more harmonious—in attraction, in expression, and in sensory and emotional fulfillment. Sexual intercourse is, very simply, the biological process of combining heaven's centripetal force with earth's centrifugal force, passing through both connected bodies in the form of strong waves and sparks. In such a relationship, the physical qualities of each person should be equally healthy and sensitive to the extent that they can maximize the conductivity of these forces. When we eat different food, our emotional and physical quality differ in conductivity, resulting in sexual disharmony.

In physical relationships, man is generally the initiator, taking the more active part, while woman is generally more receptive, elevating the feeling of oneness through her harmonizing approach. Man and woman may choose their home together, but their bedroom should be furnished and decorated by the woman, who is more sensitive to her surroundings and can make it prettier and more comfortable.

Sharing of Economy: When man and woman maintain separate arrangements in their monetary and material affairs, their marriage is incomplete. Home economy, except for business and public affairs, should be kept either by both or by one party, with unconditional trust. Larger events related to social activities may be managed by either party who is more involved in such affairs, but most of the home economy should be managed by woman, who is usually at the center of the household. The wise husband gives all of his personal income to his trusted wife, and she manages it, including giving her husband a daily allowance for his necessities. Man should develop full trust in woman's management of the home, and woman, responding to such trust, should manage carefully the household expenditures. Man should be generous and embracing in his attitude toward woman and all circumstances arising between them, and woman should be modest and sympathetic in her relation with man.

Sharing Families, Relatives, and Friends: Upon marriage, man and woman should consider the partner's parents as his or her own parents, the partner's brothers and sisters as his or her own brothers and sisters, and the partner's relatives as his or her own relatives. In the same manner that one extends love and respect to his or her own family, one should extend love and respect to the partner's family.

This involves learning the family history and background and having a good understanding of the traditions of the partner's family. Second, it involves learning from the partner's parents about the babyhood and childhood of the partner and having an understanding of the partner's character, personality, habits, and way of thinking. Third, it involves keeping close relations through frequent visits or correspondence with the partner's family and having an understanding of what is going on among them, being ready to extend any assistance necessary for them, and taking an active part in the partner's family gatherings. Fourth, any unhappy events in the partner's family should be fully sympathized with and attended to wholeheartedly, sharing in the family's sadness. During happy occasions in the partner's family, their joy should be shared from the heart and congratulations should be extended to the partner's family.

Fifth, any important occasion, such as pregnancy, delivery, sickness, success and failure in social activities, and others, should be reported to the partner's family—conflicts in married life that may arise are not to be excepted. One's own parents or family should not only be consulted but also the partner's family and relatives.

Similarly, all friends of the partner should be considered as one's own friends, and as the partner treats them, he or she should also treat them. In any gathering with those friends that the partner may join, he or she should also feel free to participate. The friendship and understanding of each other's friends should be cultivated. The partner's elderly associates should be respected as if they were one's own seniors, and the partner's younger associates should also be loved and cared for as if they were one's own juniors.

Sharing a Common Dream: Everyone has a direction in his or her life. Every married man and woman should share the same dream together. The way to approach the dream and the way to realize it may differ due to the different nature of man and woman. However, each approach and method should complement and support each other: man from his way and woman from her way. Man and woman should continuously expand their dream. Dreams limited to the sensory and sentimental level of satisfaction—including having a sweet home only for themselves, offering the best opportunities for their children, accumulating material wealth, and seeking social power and status—are often exhausted. When dreams such as these are reached, the meaning of togetherness is lost and the man and woman's common bond reaches a dead end. Through their own experiences, own learning, and constant seeking, man and woman should continuously evolve their dream to higher intellectual and philosophical levels of fulfillment, and further, toward the endless dream we all share in common of a peaceful society and world. As a man and woman develop such a dream together, their relationship will take on new life and energy continuously. They will never become tired, mentally and spiritually, and their marriage will continue until the end of their lives. When they first begin to live together, many modern men and women dream only of sensory and emotional satisfaction, but after marriage actually starts, they have an endless possibility of future development, as they represent heaven and earth. By developing their dream together, they naturally evolve toward endless spiritual realization.

The Biological Superiority of Woman: Biologically, woman is superior to man. Her superiority is demonstrated in the following points. First, with less animal-quality food and more vegetable-quality food, woman can maintain her health. This capacity reflects her more advanced capacity for biological transmutation. Second, women are able to live longer than men, three to four years on the average in most parts of the world. This shows her superior ability to adapt to the environment. Third, woman usually requires less volume and variety of food, demonstrating her more effective utilization of nutrients and energy. Fourth, woman has less body hair than man. In the biological world, more body hair indicates less biological development as a general principle. Fifth, women are able to transmute their food into their body and reproductive cells, the ova, out of which they further are able to develop babies in their uterus, while men are unable to change their food into babies beyond the stage of their reproductive cells, the sperm.

These unique characteristics, in addition to many others, demonstrate woman's biological superiority to man. Accordingly, due to her greater development, woman has traditionally supervised the biological care of the human species. The creation of life, not only that of her own babies but also that of her family and children, through preparation of daily food has traditionally been under woman's direction. Because of her higher judgment, woman is able to prepare daily dishes combining various environmental factors and offer them to her partner, children, and friends. The harmonious food that she prepares produces their day to day health, energy, thought and activity, mind and spirit, and ultimately culture and civilization as a whole.

In the event woman does not practice her central role in the creation of biological destiny, the family and society, the country and the world, would inevitably decline. Many families would decompose, children would scatter, and societies would degenerate from physical and mental illness. The world would fall into chaos and misery, and humanity as a whole would move toward extinction. On the other hand, when woman continues to prepare food in an orderly and balanced manner, families would become healthier in body and spirit, and society would continue to develop and prosper.

In contrast to woman, man is generally more idealistic, using his intellectual, conceptual thinking and organizing ability, as well as his physical vitality and spirit of adventure, to shape the world in his own image. In some sense, man is much more of a dreamer than woman, who is more practical in many ways. Men are often very curious, inventive, and ambitious. Man begins with his idea and dream and ends by realizing it in society. Without man's spirit of adventure, society and the world would not develop. Men are the more visible promoters and actors on the world stage, performing many dramatic roles, while women are more invisible, directing the unfolding human tale from behind the scenes. Peace and war, prosperity and decline, progress and retreat, challenge and response, and many other vicissitudes of life are conducted largely by man. But however great a man's action is, or however small his role is, all actors in the theater of life are produced and directed by their mothers, wives, and partners who create their biological and psychological qualities through the daily preparation of their meals, as well as through their offering of love and care.

To realize our endless dream, man should prepare for woman the most suitable environment where she can perform her unique ability as the center of biological development, without limitation, and man should completely surrender to whatever she prepares for him. Woman, in turn, should create, artistically and gracefully, the most harmonious meal for man, along with her love and care. Through this, man will continue to develop his dream limitlessly and work tirelessly to create a more peaceful world.

Love and Marriage

For successful relationships, patience is one of the most important manifestations of love. Another is endurance, the ability to adapt to circumstances and remain flexible in the face of change or adversity. Business may collapse, unemployment may come, the children may be sick and die, and long-time separation on account of war or other social conditions may occur. In life partnerships, it is essential to persevere and together overcome whatever difficulties may arise. In the modern world, there is a convenient expression, "I've changed my mind." This comes from the couple's lack of a common goal, dream, or direction.

Day to day understanding comes from eating home-cooked food together often, from physical contact, including touch, especially for women, and from talking together regularly. It is important for man and woman to let each other know what they are doing and thinking. They need not be too talkative. As time goes, without talking they will understand each other and become one. Only a few words will be enough. But in the beginning, good verbal communication is important.

To become part of someone else or for them to become part of you takes time. Many modern marriages collapse after only a few years. Two to three years is not enough time to really know each other. Man and woman need to take responsibility for each other. For woman, this means not discouraging her partner, especially his goal in life. If he becomes discouraged about his dream, he may leave the family in frustration. Man should encourage woman and respect her cooking and the environment she creates. Man and woman are a continual mystery to each other. Only after about age sixty, after many years living together and overcoming many difficulties, does one really begin to understand one's partner and the opposite sex. Without respecting each other's differences, a couple cannot help each other. That's why men and women seek each other out.

True love has no expectations. Whether sick, poor, or ugly, love sets no conditions. This contrasts with modern calculating love which lasts only so long as health, wealth, and physical beauty are present. Man and woman can never be happy together if there are conditions attached to their love. From time to time, it is necessary for each partner to praise the other: "You are great," "You are wonderful," "You are so lovely." Secondly, couples should apologize to each other now and then: "Forgive me for all the troubles I've caused you," "I'm sorry, I couldn't do what I intended," "I failed and will do better next time." By not having any rigid, set expectations, endless possibilities for husband, wife, and their offspring open up.

Sex and Relationships

The principles of yin and yang are helpful to understand the underlying cause for failed relationships. Traditionally, man became too yang and woman became too yin, and they could no longer harmonize smoothly. Usually the man worked very hard, endured cold weather, and ate too much animal food. As a result, his sexual appetite increased and found outlets outside the home. Conversely, the woman was expected to do little work in the home and none outside it, was sheltered from the elements, and ate too much raw food, sweets, and beverages. As a result, her basic vitality and sexual appetite decreased. This pattern is still very widespread in modern society today (see Figure 44).

However, because of the conveniences of modern society and the chaotic way of eating that prevails in most families today, man very often becomes too yin from lack of difficulties, hard work, and cold weather and the intake of too much milk, ice cream, sugar, fruits, juices, drugs, and alcohol. Meanwhile, woman becomes too yang from eating meat, eggs, chicken, and other animal food regularly, from too much salt or too longtime cooking, and from too much housekeeping or too much work outside the home.

Figure 44. Difficulties Between Partners

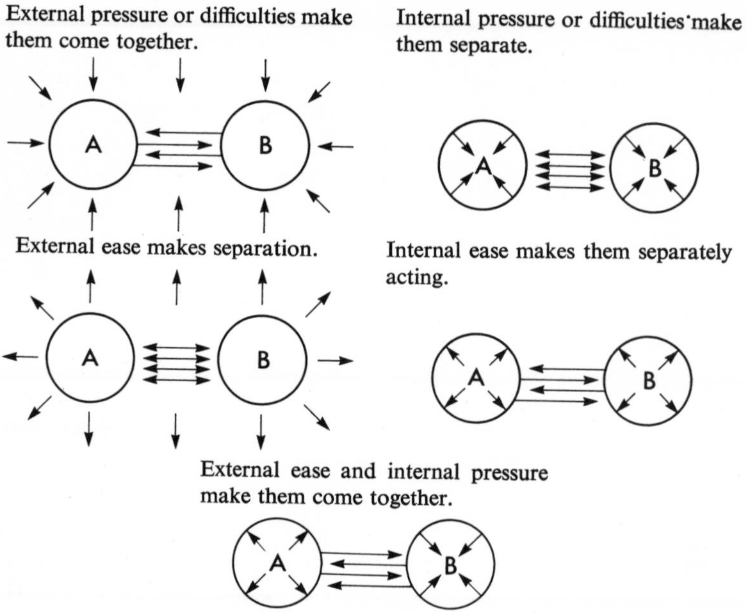

External pressure or difficulties make them come together.

Internal pressure or difficulties make them separate.

External ease makes separation.

Internal ease makes them separately acting.

External ease and internal pressure make them come together.

Though sex is only a small part of a permanent relationship, it is often the immediate cause of separation. Chaotic sexual appetite is usually the direct result of improper food consumption. Meat, eggs, poultry, and to a lesser extent fish and seafood elevate sexual desire, but the quality of sex is usually very rough and unsatisfying. Extreme yin foods, including sugar, coffee, and dairy foods reduce sexual appetite, often contributing to infertility or impotency. Foods that make the body colder, including ice cream, cold icy beverages, and fruit juice, can lead to frigidity in woman or lack of desire in man. Tropical foods (eaten in a temperate climate) such as figs and avocado, too much fruit, and too much liquids can also lead to the inability to conceive. The increase of pornography, prostitution, and unusual sexual techniques is not so much a moral problem as a biological one. After years of eating the modern diet, the body becomes stagnated, and natural sexual energy becomes blocked. People then seek out extreme methods to stimulate dulled nervous systems and become aroused. Stimulants and drugs are one way to temporarily enhance sexual abilities, but ultimately the effect wears off and successively larger doses are required in the future.

On a diet centered around grains and vegetables, sexual relations are usually very smooth and harmonious. Though less tempestuous than relations arising out of the consumption of meat and sugar, they are longer lasting and more deeply fulfilling. However, even macrobiotic couples can grow apart by becoming too imbalanced in one way or the other. Too much soymilk, raw tofu, white somen, desserts and sweets, and too much overeating in general are often associated with lack of sexual vitality.

In considering a relationship, the following questions can be asked:

• Do you seek a permanent relationship? Seeking only sensory pleasure or temporary gratification is not contributing to overall physical, mental, and spiritual growth and development. Marriage is unification at all levels.

• Woman, do you know what man's dream is? Whether it is small or big, practical or idealistic, realistic or impossible, can you support his goal? Man, do you know woman has a very busy life? Both sides work hard. Do you know how to be gentle and sweet? The home should be open and relaxed, not a battlefield or dominated by outside work or activities.

• Is the home pleasant and enjoyable, and are children loved unconditionally? Many men as well as women seek a very sweet home. Both sides must make the home very refined and orderly. With children, the home is busier than an office. When children come, they become the center of the family, and parents work for them. However, mother and father should not give up their dream for their children. Rather the children should be included in their parents' dream. Parenthood should not be "planned," and modern artificial birth control techniques are unnecessary. The universe decides who is to be born and when and will provide the necessary material support for each child as it comes along. So long as they are eating well, parents need have no worries about the size or support of their family.

• Do you criticize your partner from a personal or family perspective? For man, it is all right to criticize woman's cooking for reasons of health, for the family's health, or for balancing the next day's activities. But he should not criticize it from a sensory or sentimental place: "It doesn't taste good," "It's not attractive," "I prefer this or that." The same holds true for woman. She should scold the husband only if it pertains to the health of a family member or the family as a whole, not if it only concerns her personal likes or dislikes.

• Can you openly discuss sexual health? For a lasting relationship, it is important to freely talk about feeling and desire and understand what the partner wants. Unfortunately, in modern society there is still a notion that sex is dirty. That way of thinking and the guilt that accompanies it must be overcome. The whole universe is sex, attraction and repulsion, yin and yang. By that universal process life is continuing. Sex is a wonderful thing, a way to celebrate our aliveness and unity with one another. All forms of relationships are fine so long as the people involved truly love and care for each other.

By knowing the principles of the Order of the Universe, we can build a health, happy, and peaceful relationship that will endure across the years.

Society and Nature

When we eat, transforming part of our environment into our body, mind, and spirit, we start to shape society through our image, along with the images of other people. Society is a reflection of what we think and what we eat. Society is our product, and nature is our origin. Creating and maintaining a harmonious society is the natural result of respecting nature as our common parent.

After journeying for millions and billions of years through the infinite universe, we have appeared together as members of society at this time and place. As planetary brothers and sisters, we all share the same origin—infinity—and the same parents—the natural environment. We share also a common destiny, for we all return to nature and the infinite universe—our parents and our origin. If we adapt flexibly to the changing environment, especially through daily food preparation, unconditional love and respect will develop among all members of society. By eating together similar foods that are commonly and traditionally prepared in our region according to macrobiotic dietary principles, we develop a similar quality of blood and health, mind and thought, spirit and dream. We are able to understand each other without difficulty, and we are able to communicate whatever we think without hesitation. Such a society is, in a real sense, a free society. By following natural order, social harmony and peace will automatically be maintained.

In a free society, elders should be accorded natural recognition by virtue of their experience and wisdom. In turn, elders—including grandparents, parents, uncles and aunts—should extend their love and care to all younger persons impartially. They should consider all children of the community as their own children and all younger adults as their own younger brothers and sisters. They should extend their encouragement to the younger generation to develop and realize their dreams. They should extend consolation to the younger generation when they are in need and in despair. They should inspire the younger generation toward an understanding of life and the attainment of happiness. They should offer assistance to the younger generation when it is needed for their progress. They should serve as guides for the younger generation in the pursuit of their freedom. The elders should especially watch over the health of the younger generation and lead them toward the development of an endless dream.

Meanwhile, the younger generation should respect their elders, listening to their advice, learning from their experiences and difficulties, receiving their inspiration, understanding their background, and trying to continue to realize their ongoing dream. Even someone who is only one year older than we are should be respected as an elder. When the elders become very old, as they cared for their juniors, the younger generation should care for the elders as if they were their own parents. They should offer both spiritual support and material assistance as well as help in maintaining their health and longevity as much as possible.

Our human relations, in both private and public affairs, should be based upon mutual understanding. Public education based upon love and respect for everyone in the community is essential for our social development. Such understanding cannot be taught conceptually. It is nourished naturally through the biological and biochemical improvement of our consciousness as our way of eating improves. As our health returns and our judgment rises, we begin to regard all people, including those living far away as well as those living near by, as our brothers and sisters. A spirit of mutual respect, love, and care develops, and regardless of the situation we make no complaints or accusations against others. Our daily lives are guided by a spirit of gratitude for whatever we receive, material and spiritual, and a spirit of apology for whatever we may do that affects others through our thought and conduct.

If there is only one person in a community who understands the Order of the Universe and practices the macrobiotic way of life, his or her community will become better. If there is no such person, the community will eventually become chaotic, with people complaining to others, accusing each other, defending themselves against any other person and event. If we use others for the purpose of personal profit-making, especially in the material world, we shall attract others who will use us for the same purpose. If we put the happiness of others before our own happiness, others will be moved to put our happiness before their own.

Harmonious relations with others depend upon our own understanding and practice of life according to the Order of the Universe. Unless we maintain our physical and mental condition in accord with natural environmental cycles, we cannot enjoy peaceful relations with others. Therefore, beyond anything else, we should feel that nature and the universe are our parents. Adapting to the changing natural environment is the root of our respect for traditions and elders, our love for other people and for the younger generation, and our care of everyone and everything.

Every day it is important that we endlessly marvel at the immeasurable beauty and perpetual order of nature and the cosmos. Let us constantly marvel about how we have come from the infinite universe, physicalizing ourselves upon this earth at this time as members of the human family. Let us keep a spirit of endless appreciation for nature and the universe, including all natural phenomena and for the countless lives that have lived, are presently living, and shall live, with us. Let us be grateful for mountains and rivers, land and ocean, trees and flowers, birds and fishes, animals and vegetables, the sky and the stars.

When we experience misery of any kind let us remember that nature and the universe are still constantly cycling, and our distress is caused only by our lack of harmony.

Let us admire the wonders of nature and the universe, including all beings within them, visible and invisible, and devote our prayers and joy in their existence through occasional events, festivities, and ceremonies, as well as through self-reflection deep within our mind.

Let us keep nature around us—the forests and soil, hills and rivers, air and lakes, ocean and land—as plentiful, prosperous, beautiful, and clean as they have been in times past. When we use a part of our natural surroundings, we should devote our prayers and appreciation to the part we have used and use it modestly. Afterwards, we should restore the used portion to its original condition.

In many traditional cultures throughout the world, a variety of festivals and ceremonies dedicated to nature or the spirit of nature were observed. Ancient calendars set the days for these events, such as the day for the sun, the day for the moon, the day for the stars, and others. In the United States, events for the appreciation of nature include May Day, Arbor Day, Thanksgiving Day, and many regional festivals. In many European countries, there are also traditional days of natural celebration. In Japan such days include the Day of Prayer for the Sun (January 1), Peace Flower Day (March 3), the Cherry Blossom Festival (late March to April), Peony Day (May 5), Star Night Festival (July 7), the Lunar Festival (September 9), and the Chrysanthemum Festival (November 11), as well as spring and autumn thanksgiving ceremonies held on the equinoxes dedicated to rice and other foods.

Traditional societies also symbolized, in the image of gods and spirits, various phenomena of nature as we see in the mythology of ancient Africa, Sumeria, Greece, Rome, India, China, Japan, Scandinavia, Ireland and Britain, and North and South America. Such appreciation for nature and natural phenomena is one of the most universal human traditions and practices, extending back and unifying the human family for untold generations. In the modern age, especially since scientific, analytical observations began around the 16th Century, society's appreciation of nature has declined rapidly. The desire to use the natural environment for purely human benefit or profit-making has overruled the traditional spirit of harmonizing with nature. The modern mentality of subduing and conquering nature—our parent—has produced chemically depleted soil, contaminated water, and a polluted atmosphere. Large-scale industrial production has brought material prosperity to society by spoiling our natural resources and impoverishing the environment. This, in turn, is destroying the foundation of our biological life and the very existence of humanity itself. The macrobiotic way of life is devoted to reversing this trend and unifying society and nature. In order to restore human health, happiness, and peace and ensure the continued existence of our species on this earth, we need to self-reflect deeply about our own thought and conduct as well as the whole orientation of modern civilization.

The Spirit of Macrobiotics

When we understand our origin and our future—how we have come from One Infinity to this relative world and how we are starting to return to Infinity again and marvel at this infinite order of life—we start to wonder why we have come to this earth as human beings and for what purpose. Our dream in life depends upon the memory of our origin. Without memory there is no dream; without dream there is no life. Because we live always within an unnameable, undifferentiated, and undetermined infinite ocean of memory, we are able to image, dream, will, judge, and think.

Our life on this small planet is one infinitesimal manifestation in the endless stream of eternal life, a geometrical point in the boundless space of the infinite universe. Our life arises, changes, moves, declines, and disappears according to laws and principles of perpetual order. Our life in this space and time is a faint wave governed by the Order of the Universe, yin and yang. Macrobiotics is simply the interpretation and application of this order to human life. The spirit of macrobiotics embraces the following qualities:

Unconditional Faith in the Order of the Universe: In our daily life, our sensory, emotional, intellectual, and social consciousness often lead us to an illusory view of the world. We tend to think that we are able to live forever, that our society will continue to develop forever, and that our love and friendships will last forever. We also tend to think that something is absolutely right, something else is absolutely wrong, that this is good and that is bad, this is beautiful and that is ugly, and that this is difficult and that is easy. However, all of these relative judgments are due to our limited consciousness, which is unable to see endless change. Relative value, whether expressed in money, matter, praise, position, fame, or glory, fades away very quickly. We should not let our emotions and our senses govern our destiny. Beyond the vicissitudes of life, we need to develop infinite faith in the Order of the Universe which is eternally unchanging. During our stay in this ephemeral world, let us lead our life by developing and harmonizing our natural intuition with the natural order.

Non-Credo: The relative world, especially human society, is full of fallacies, delusions, and mysteries. We tend to believe, without experience and understanding, whatever is conceived and interpreted by our physical senses. Education, promotion, and advertising are constantly encouraging us to believe what we really do not know ourselves. Science, religion, and modern social, economic, and political systems are also realms of faith, often requiring blind obedience. We should not adopt theories and assumptions that others have developed or imitate their thinking and behavior. In a spirit of non-credo, let us seek endlessly through our own experience and understanding to realize the real, the true, the infinite.

Be Our Own Master: As human beings, we have come to this planet to develop and exercise our own judgment in all that we do. We have chosen this place and time by ourselves, and we are totally responsible for everything that we do as a mature person. When we are sick, we reflect that it is caused by our ignorance of how to behave according to the laws of nature—eating imbalanced food, thinking in a rigid or unfocused way, or acting in an extreme or chaotic manner. When we are unhappy, we reflect that it was caused by our own lack of judgment or insight, which may also arise from a way of life out of harmony with the environment. Sickness, accident, misery, and any other difficulties can be turned into health, well-being, and happiness through changing our own thought and conduct. No one else can change them in our behalf. We must initiate changes ourselves. We may receive advice, suggestions, and guidance from others—and it is usually wise to do so. But ultimately it is we ourselves who must come to a decision, make changes in our life, and accept responsibility as the master of our own destiny.

We Are Ignorant: When we reflect upon what we truly know, we realize that we are ignorant. We are ignorant of life, ourselves, others, nature—everything. Most of us do not even know what will happen to us tomorrow, how our destiny will change in the year to come, or when we will die. We do not know how to keep our health, how to be joyous, and how to become happy. We do not even know what we should eat, how we should breathe, what we should think, and how we should speak. We do not know whether what we think is real is true and whether what we think good is truly good. It is an endless dilemma and constant disappointment when we know what we seek to achieve and produce the opposite result. We do not know why we came to this world or what we should do in our life. We are always ignorant, and the more we learn, the greater our ignorance. To know that we are ignorant is the beginning of our awareness of what life is and the beginning of our understanding of what we are. The way of life that guides us toward true happiness comes from reflecting deeply on our ignorance. Because we are ignorant, we have to surrender unconditionally to the Order of the Universe. Because we are ignorant, we have to accept whatever happens around us as our responsibility. Because we are ignorant, we have to adapt to our surroundings and environment. Being humble and modest, by making ourselves the last rather than the first, even to the extent that we are nothing, is the shortest way to have complete freedom of life.

We Are What We Eat: When we know that we are ignorant and submit ourselves to the hand of nature and the Order of the Universe, we start to understand that whatever we take in the form of food, as well as any other environmental factors—water, air, vibrations, radiations, and cosmic rays—is changing and transforming us. We are what we eat. We are an image of what we take in. We are a transformation of our environment, a manifestation of this universe. We eat, therefore we exist. We eat, therefore we think. We eat, therefore we move. We eat, therefore we live. The systems, organs, tissues, cells, molecules, and atoms within our body have all come from our external world. Without food, that is, without our environment, all of our living phenomena would not continue. By changing what we take in, we change ourselves—body, mind, and spirit, and even society, culture, and civilization. When we have difficulties, we should seek the cause in what we eat. When we experience happiness, we understand that its origin is in our food. Those who know this become masters of their life and destiny. Those who know this are free, and those who do not are enslaved.

Be Grateful for Difficulties: The world and life within it proceed and change paradoxically. We seek comfort; comfort produces ease; ease produces weakness; weakness produces poverty; and poverty produces difficulty. Thus seeking comfort ends in creating difficulty. When our difficulties end, we start to seek comfort again. Therefore, comfort weakens us, and difficulties strengthen us. Poverty and cold, sickness and misery, hunger and war are all strengthening us physically, mentally, and spiritually. Whenever there is no difficulty, there is no development. If we avoid such difficulties, we eventually become weaker and decline after momentary comfort. Let us welcome at any time any sort of difficulties. Let us appreciate them as our teachers.

When we climb a mountain, the more we experience hardship, the greater joy we feel when we reach the top. When we are involved in war, the more misery we experience around us, the greater appreciation we have when peace comes. When we suffer with illness, the more serious the illness, the greater spirit of appreciation we have when we restore our health. Difficulties are truly the cause of happiness, and avoiding them is really the cause of our unhappiness. In order to be happy all the time, we should continue to put ourselves in endless difficulties.

Our Enemy Is Our Friend: There are a great variety of people in the world; they are all our brothers and sisters sharing the same dream, the same future, and the same earth. Among them we like some people and do not like some others. We love some people and hate others. Some are our friends and some our enemies. When we are with those whom we prefer as our friends, we experience comfort and pleasure, and when we are with those who are our enemies, we experience tension and hardship. We consider people who offer us sweet words of consolation and loving support to be our friends. But if we live only in their company we become weaker, like a plant in a greenhouse. When the snows and the storms come, we wither and die. On the other hand, the enemy who accuses and attacks us makes us cautious in our actions, deliberate in our thoughts, and stronger in our abilities. We develop strength of body and mind thanks to our enemies. We should be grateful to them. Because they are antagonistic, they are complementary to us. They see what we cannot see. They have what we do not have. They know what we do not know. Therefore, let us make our enemy as our best friend. If we change our enemy into our friend, we can realize our happiness as well as our enemy's happiness.

The Last Becomes the First, the First Becomes the Last: The endless movement of the universe, including our relative world, brings constant change from one state to another, and a return always to the previous state. Yin changes into yang, yang changes into yin. Yin produces yang, yang produces yin. The cycle of each day brings a repeating alternation of light and darkness; the cycle of each year brings an alternation of warm seasons and cold seasons. Cycles of celestial change include the cycles of solar activity, the cycle of the wobbling motion of the earth, and the cycle of the motion of the solar system within the Milky Way galaxy. A society begins; then it ends; then it begins again. Life begins with birth and ends at death; but from death, new life begins. Every phenomenon expanding outward eventually contracts toward the center, and when it contracts it begins to expand again. Therefore, the beginning is the end, and the end is the beginning: the first is the last, and the last is the first. Alpha is omega, omega is alpha.

When we are at the foot of the mountain, we are able to reach the top. When we are at the bottom of society, we will eventually attain the highest level. When we reach the summit, we must inevitably decline toward the bottom. The rich become the poor, the poor become the rich; the wise become the foolish, the foolish become the wise. Sickness produces health, and health produces sickness. War changes into peace; peace changes into war. The taller the tree is, the stronger is the wind that blows through its high branches. The lower the grass is, the gentler the breeze that touches it. Therefore, if we stay behind other people, we never receive any strong attack or opposition, and if we stay at a low level we never experience falling down. Therefore, if we become higher, we should bow to more people and, at that time, continuing to live in the spirit of modesty and humbleness, we harmonize our destiny: the last becomes first, the first becomes last. When we become lower, we should keep our ambitious and adventurous spirit, which is making harmony in our life and guiding us through the ups and downs of the relative world.

One Grain, Ten Thousand Grains: Nature and the universe produce constantly within themselves two out of one, three or four out of two, and many out of three or four. Perpetual differentiation as well as perpetual gathering is the Order of the Universe. The universe in which we live is expanding constantly, as we know through our modern knowledge. One seed produces hundreds of seeds; hundreds of seeds produce thousands of seeds; thousands of seeds produce millions of seeds. "One grain, ten thousand grains" is the natural order and work of life.

When we receive one piece of bread or one bowl of rice, we ourselves produce thousands of pieces of bread, thousands of bowls of rice, and return them to those who nourished us as well as many thousands of other people. When we learn any useful thing, we naturally distribute it to everyone around else. Give, give, and endlessly give is the most important principle of life. By giving, we make ourselves happy and bring happiness to thousands of other people. When we eat, we must distribute whatever we take in. If we do not do this, we cannot eat any further. Life is receiving and giving; and the more we give, the more we receive. When we keep ourselves busy from morning to evening, day and night, with the practice of the spirit of "one grain, ten thousand grains," we are living together with the expanding universe. Keeping this spirit is the essential way to realize our endless happiness.

6. Human Diseases: Cause and Recovery

> "Let food be thy medicine, and thy medicine be food."
>
> —Hippocrates

Cause of Difficulties

After physicalizing and materializing ourselves upon this earth as human beings, we shall continue our endless journey through dephysicalization and spiritualization and return to our origin, the infinite universe. During our sojourn on this planet, the basic, natural state of existence is one of health and well-being. Because we are a part of the environment and we change according to environmental changes, we can naturally adapt to any circumstances and live our lives without any difficulties. However, almost everyone, over the course of human existence, has experienced difficulties, including the struggle for survival and the continuation of life itself. Humanity has experienced difficulties arising not only through natural catastrophes and geological change but also difficulties arising from human behavior. Physical, mental, and spiritual sicknesses, as well as social and ideological confusion, are prevalent throughout the world. Modern civilization itself is in a state of chronic biological degeneration, from which it may not survive. Why are human beings suffering from so much sickness? Why are we constantly struggling with various difficulties? What can we do to overcome them?

All of the difficulties we face are due to our ignorance of who we are, what life is, and our relationship with the environment and the Order of the Universe. Sciences have developed, technologies have prospered, doctrines have prevailed; theories, assumptions, hypotheses, and discoveries have been mounting for many centuries. Yet we do not know what life is. We may have obtained the fruit of the Tree of Knowledge but we have not obtained the fruit of the Tree of Life. As far as the problems of life are concerned, we are all hopelessly ignorant. In our search for happiness, have we not looked in the wrong direction? Are our modern methods by which we try to solve the problems of life reaching a dead end? We are proud of our level of education, which is higher than that of previous civilizations. We are proud of our material wealth surpassing the wealth of ancient people. We are proud of our organized society that is more universal than in olden times, and we are proud of our knowledge which is more far-reaching than in the prehistoric age. And yet, every one of us is full of fear and anxiety, worry and depression, and surrounded with sickness and violence, greed and hatred, prejudice and insecurity. What is the cause of all this suffering? What is the origin of these troubles? How can we solve these difficulties and how are we to approach this confusion?

To deal with these problems, we have developed a comprehensive system of modern education. We have developed a remarkable governmental apparatus serving people everywhere. We have built an impressive medical and welfare system covering nearly every person in modern society. Hundreds of billions of dollars are spent, and millions of people are working for these systems to meet the difficulties we face at the present time. Are these methods adequate, proper, and really effective to build our physical, mental, and spiritual health? Are these systems really solving problems or are they creating new ones? Is there any other method that is simple and practical enough that everyone can practice it in his or her daily life without strain? If there is such a method, what is it? Let's begin by looking at a new model of health and well-being.

Health is not the state of being without sickness; it is a more positive and creative state of physical, mental, and spiritual life. Health is not something to be secured by defending and preserving ourselves from suffering with disease; rather, it is a state of actively harmonizing with our environment, of enjoying life with many other people, and of ceaseless creation and development. We are healthy, if we meet the following seven conditions:

Never Be Tired: In day-to-day life, we should not feel any fatigue if we are healthy. After a day's work, we should not complain, "I am tired." Whatever hardship we may encounter, we should be able to adapt to it with an energetic desire to work it out harmoniously. From time to time we may feel exhausted from our work, but we should recover from it after a short rest or a night's sleep. We should not feel tired mentally either. If we frequently change our mind, including our ideas and plans, our occupation and address, our partner and friends, we are in an unhealthy state. Under any circumstances, at any time, we should maintain a state of physical and mental balance that is stable, yet flexible enough to respond immediately to changing circumstances, and able to approach the new environment with a spirit of adventure.

Have a Good Appetite: In our daily life, and throughout our life, we should always have a good appetite for whatever we may encounter: appetite for food, appetite for sex, appetite for activity, appetite for knowledge, appetite for work, appetite for experience, and appetite for health, freedom, and happiness. Endless appetite is a manifestation of health, and limited appetite is a manifestation of sickness. The bigger our appetite is, the richer our life. Without appetite, there is no progress, no development, and no enjoyment. However, in order to keep a large appetite, we should avoid overindulgence. When we are hungry, we should eat so as to satisfy only 80 percent of our hunger, leaving a portion of the stomach unfilled. Oversatisfaction reduces our appetite and gradually slows down our metabolism, thinking, activity, and thirst for life. Therefore, we should keep ourselves always hungry, and as soon as we take in, we should distribute whatever we have received. Keeping emptiness within ourselves is the secret to developing an endless appreciation for life.

Have a Good Sleep: Good sleep is not sleeping for a long time but sleeping deeply for a short time. Good sleep is a result of energetic activity—physical and mental—during the time we are awake. While we are sleeping, we should usually not dream. If we remember a dream after we awake, it is because our sleep is not deep enough. Nightmares, cloudy dreams, and fragmental dreams are all signs of physical and mental unrest. To see these dreams frequently is an indication of developing mental illness. Suppose we are frequently frightened with the horrors of nightmares. We are seeing "daymares" through our same physical and mental quality while we are awake. When we are awake we surround ourselves with groundless suspicions, illusory enemies, and other delusions that turn our life into a battlefield. If we eat macrobiotically and develop our health, we will never suffer such rootless dreams—day or night—of any kind. From time to time, however, we may see a dream that comes true. A true dream is one that also happens in reality—for example, showing us a new invention, communicating with the spirits of ancestors, or alerting us to impending natural catastrophe. Thus when we see no dream or see only a true dream during our sleep, we are seeing real circumstances; and whatever we dream as true corresponds to our activities and occurrences during the daytime.

Have a Good Memory: Memory is the mother of our judgment. Without memory of what we have experienced, we would have no judgment or ability to evaluate the changing circumstances. Good memory is the foundation of all sound mental activities; they all come out of memory and return to memory. There are various kinds of memory: mechanical memory, such as the remembrance of names and numbers; memory of images, such as remembrance of scenery and events; and spiritual memory, such as remembrance of where we have come from and how we have realized ourselves in this world at this time. Among these varieties of memory, the most important is the last, the memory of spiritual destiny, by which we can understand the significance of our life, know the meaning of the present, and develop an endless appreciation of the past and a limitless aspiration toward the future. Good memory is essential to a meaningful life. All other memories, including mechanical memory and memory of images, are actually part of this memory of our spiritual origin and destiny. As we continue to live macrobiotically, we begin to recover not only memory of past occurrences and present daily events but also memory of our spiritual destiny.

People sharing the same food also understand each other better. As our health improves, we find that it is very easy to understand, agree with, and work with other people eating the same way, even though they may have been born in different places and brought up and educated in different ways. The reason they can understand each other is that they share a common, universal memory of infinite oneness, whether or not they are aware of it.

Never Be Angry: If we are in good health, throughout our lifetime we should never be angry. Since we are living within the infinite universe and we are all living in harmony with our environment, there is no reason to be angry. We know that everyone, everything, and every phenomenon—including difficulties, sicknesses, and enemies—are complementary to one another. Being angry shows our limitation, our inability to understand and embrace, our lack of patience and perseverance. In Far Eastern countries, the ideograph for anger describes anger as the mind of a slave. Another word for anger means acute sickness of the liver. In Oriental medicine, anger is correlated with liver malfunction, as other major mental and emotional reactions are correlated with disorders of other major organs. Those who do not know how to cope with changing circumstances often become very excited, while those who know how to adapt do not feel any anger. Health is the capacity to accept all circumstances with a smile, change difficulties into opportunities, and turn enemies into friends.

Be Joyous and Alert: In order to live an active and productive life, it is necessary to respond immediately to the constantly changing environment. Life is a continuous progression of such responses. We should be accurate in our expression, swift in our motion, orderly in our behavior, and clear in our thinking. Moment to moment responses such as these should be full of joy and humor. Our countenance should be bright, cheerful, and optimistic, and merry thoughts should radiate to everyone around us. Greetings should be exchanged actively to everyone we meet, morning and evening. "Good morning," "good evening," "how are you," and "thank you," are constantly exchanged, along with a smile. Like the sun that radiates its light and warmth to everyone, our presence should give joy and happiness to all beings. Joyousness is a natural result of good health and eating well day to day.

Have Endless Appreciation: As manifestations of the infinite Order of the Universe, we should know that all people and all beings are brothers and sisters accompanying one another in the journey of eternal life. We should clearly understand that there is nothing really opposing us. We should clearly know that if we experience difficulties, it is because of some underlying disharmony in our way of life; however, this condition can be changed and transformed into its opposite peacefully without any conflict or suffering. When we are healthy, we become endlessly appreciative of the Order of the Universe and all its manifestations. We are healthy when we are able to receive and embrace everything gratefully and when we are able to give of ourselves without hesitation—our ideals, our materials, our activity, our energy, and even our life itself—to all from whom and from which we have received. Even when we are physically sick, we are healthy if we are aware that we are the cause of our own sickness, thankful for the opportunity to learn, and surrender our destiny to nature in a spirit of endless appreciation. Conversely, we may be without any physical or mental symptoms of disease, but unless a deep gratitude permeates our whole life we are not truly healthy and whole.

Development of Sickness

All physical, mental, and spiritual sicknesses are closely interrelated and undergo a similar progressive development—as from a single root, many branches and leaves grow (see Figure 45). There is no disease that originates or develops independently from all other diseases and conditions of imbalance. However numerous and different the symptoms may appear, they are all connected and related with one another, and their underlying causes are practically the same. What modern medicine considers the cause of a certain sickness is often only a symptom that develops into a sickness, and not the real cause. To relieve disease, we must search for the origin and basic causes, not just suppress symptoms and other surface manifestations of disorder.

Figure 45. The Tree of Sickness

Symptoms—Various symptoms of disorders manifesting physically and mentally.

Conditions — General disharmony of cells, tissues, organs, and systems.

Cause—Improper dietary habits and degraded quality of blood and body fluids.

Origin—Lack of understanding of the Order of the Universe; imbalanced way of life, out of harmony with nature.

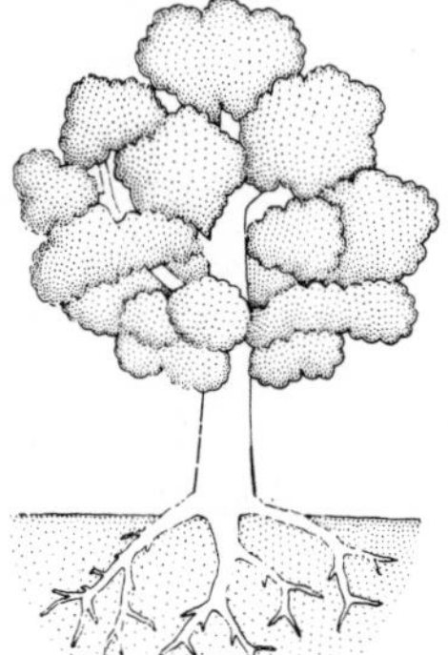

Symptoms — Appearances of leaves and stems, including their color, texture, size, and activities. (This level approached by symptomatic medicine.)

Conditions — Structure and quality of tissues and cells as well as their functioning. (Approached by adjustment of physical and psychological conditions.)

Cause — Fluid streaming within the tree, including quality and volume of water, minerals, and other nutrients. (Approached by dietary modification.)

Origin — Environment, including climate, weather, water, soil, and other natural conditions. (Approached by environmental medicine, way of life changes, and self-reflection.)

For example, in the case of high blood pressure, it is well known that the arteries and smaller blood vessels become constricted and the heart muscle becomes enlarged, causing the heart to pump under higher pressure. However, these manifestations are nothing but physical symptoms of high blood pressure, not causes. High blood pressure can be controlled to some extent medically by drugs, medication, and other symptomatic means, but so long as the way of life, including the day-to-day way of eating and thinking, does not change, it cannot be fundamentally cured and sooner or later returns in a more serious form. Let us look at another example: physical and mental fatigue caused by an anemic condition due to a lack of iron, other minerals, or certain vitamins. The symptomatic approach to this sickness tries to supply the missing minerals and vitamins in the form of capsules, injections, special food supplements, and similar measures. This approach would relieve the symptoms of anemia temporarily, but it would not prevent the recurrence of the symptoms unless there were a basic change in daily diet and orientation of consciousness.

All sicknesses—physical, mental, and spiritual—have four factors in their development:

Symptoms: Symptoms are what we usually think of or call sickness and disease. They appear as uncomfortable, abnormal bodily reactions such as pain, itching, fever, coughing, vomiting, etc.

Conditions: The various symptoms are produced by underlying conditions. For example, as discussed above, high blood pressure is produced by the underlying condition of the enlargement of the heart muscle and the constriction of the blood vessels and capillaries.

Cause: Every condition has an underlying cause, which is found in various aspects of our physical and mental tendencies, especially the general quality of our blood.

Origin: The causes of sickness—our general physical and mental tendencies, particularly our blood quality—originate in our daily habits, including dietary practice, physical exercise, mental activity, and our general view of life. In other words, all sicknesses have their origin in our life viewed as a whole.

Accordingly, there are three approaches to medicine:

• *Symptomatic and Conditional Medicine:* This type has been commonly practiced in modern Western medicine and includes trying to eliminate symptoms or change conditions by use of various invasive technical measures such as surgery, radiation therapy, chemotherapy, and the use of pharmaceutical medications. This category also includes acupuncture, moxibustion, and traditional Oriental medical techniques aimed at relieving a particular illness or condition by direct intervention into bodily processes or manipulation of electromagnetic energy (*ki*) flow.

• *Energetic Medicine:* This type deals mainly with the problem of blood and electromagnetic energy (*ki*) exchange through a change of what we consume in the form of food and drink, including various kinds of dietary practices with vitamin and mineral supplements, herbal remedies, and various physical and mental adjustments and exercises. It is mainly preventive in orientation but can be modified or adjusted to relieve particular sicknesses or conditions.

• *Medicine for Humanity:* This type deals with the way of life as a whole and is more philosophical and educational in orientation rather than technical or energetic. This approach attempts to recover the proper way of life based upon self-reflection, through an understanding of the relation between humanity and the environment, as well as the order of nature and of the universe.

The Progressive Development of Disease

Generally speaking, our sicknesses take the following progressive pattern in their development:

1st Stage: General Fatigue: A feeling of physical and mental tiredness is the beginning of sickness. This condition is often accompanied by muscular tension and hardening, frequent urination and sweating, temporary constipation or diarrhea, and short periods of feeling cold or hot. Mentally, we start to lose our clarity of thought, active perception, and accurate responses. To recover from this stage, it usually takes a short period—from a few hours to a few days—of adequate rest, a good night's sleep, proper food and drink, or sufficient exercise.

2nd Stage: Aches and Pains: When a feeling of general fatigue prevails, we begin to experience occasional pains and aches. Muscular pain, headache, cramps, and various other sorts of pains and aches appear from time to time. Temporary shortness of breath, irregular heartbeat, fever and chills, and difficulty of motion also appear in this stage. Mentally, we may experience occasional depression, worry, and a general feeling of insecurity. To restore ourselves to health from this stage usually takes from a few days to a few weeks, with proper dietary practice, active exercise, or necessary rest.

3rd Stage: Blood Disease: If our dietary practice continues to be out of balance with our environment, our quality of blood, including red-blood cells, white-blood cells, and blood plasma, becomes unsuited for maintaining harmony with our natural surroundings (see Figure 46). The quality of our blood determines the quality of our body's cells and tissues, organs, and systems. Blood disorders create various abnormal conditions in our body from which symptoms of sickness then arise. Acidosis, high and low blood pressure, anemia, purpura, leukemia, scurvy, and other diseases belong to this stage, including asthma, epilepsy, and skin diseases. Mentally, this stage appears as nervousness, hypersensitivity, continuous depression, timidity, and loss of general direction in life. To recover from blood disorders may take between ten days and three to four months, depending upon the individual condition. Once again, proper dietary practices, as well as suitable exercise and rest, need to be implemented. Simple home cares to promote active circulation of the blood may also be required in some cases.

Figure 46. The Digestive Process

Alternating yin (▽) and yang (△) secretions help digest the foods we eat.

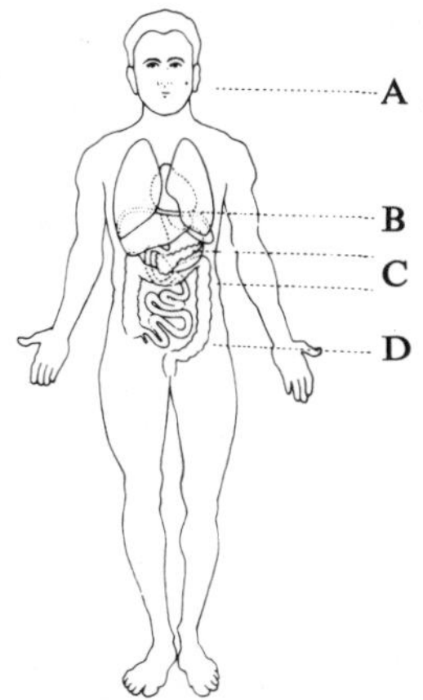

A. *Saliva*—Saliva is an alkaline liquid (△), which mainly digests and decomposes carbohydrates.
B. *Stomach Juice*—Gastric juice is acid (▽), digesting and decomposing mainly fat and protein.
C. *Liver and Gallbladder Bile and Pancreatic Juice*—These digestive liquids are alkaline (△), mainly decomposing fat, protein, and carbohydrate.
D. *Intestinal Juice*—This juice is acid (▽), digesting and decomposing all remaining carbohydrate, protein, and fat. These decomposed food molecules are absorbed into the bloodstream, which is weak alkaline (△).

4th Stage: Emotional Disorder: If an improper quality of blood circulates for a prolonged period, various emotional disorders start to appear. Short temper, excitement, anger, frustration, and a general feeling of despair are experienced frequently in daily life. A gentle approach to a problem with clear, balanced understanding is no longer possible. A general feeling of fear prevails toward new situations and surroundings, and our daily behavior and way of thinking become extremely defensive or offensive. Our physical movements become more rigid and we gradually lose flexibility in both body and mind. It requires between one month and several months to overcome these emotional and physical disorders. Dietary change toward more balanced food is essential, along with physical and mental relaxation.

5th Stage: Organ Disease: An imbalanced quality of blood circulating for a prolonged period further produces gradual changes in the quality and function of our organs and glands. Structural change, malfunction, and degeneration start to arise. Atherosclerosis, diabetes, stone formation in the kidneys or gallbladder, various types of cancer, multiple sclerosis, and many other chronic sicknesses fall in this category. Mentally, chronic stubbornness, prejudice, narrow-mindedness, and general rigidity with a delusional view of life become more apparent. To recover from this level of disease usually takes a longer period, several months to one year or more, through continuous practice of proper diet and reorientation of the way of life, including deep self-reflection.

6th Stage: Nervous Disorder: From the stage of organ and gland disease, the degenerative tendency progresses toward various nervous disorders including physical paralysis and toward mental illness including schizophrenia and paranoia. Physical and mental coordination of various functions gradually diminishes. A negative view begins to dominate daily life, and suicidal or destructive tendencies frequently manifest. It takes six months to a few years to recover completely from this stage and to regain self-assurance and trust as well as a positive view of life. The way of life has to be changed completely, including dietary practice, more harmonious relationship with the environment, and active physical exercise, together with loving care by family and friends.

7th Stage: Arrogance: An improper way of life that has been practiced for many years finally reaches the highest level of sickness—arrogance—though some of the previous stages may not have been clearly experienced. Arrogance is the most developed sickness and also the one that most universally affects people's lives today. Selfishness, egocentricity, vanity, self-pride, exclusivity, and self-justification are some of the common symptoms. Arrogance is the last stage of sickness and, at the same time, it is the cause of all previous stages. Because of the arrogance that has prevailed among many populations, the entire world is full of sickness, misery, and unhappiness, not only physically and mentally, but also socially and ideologically. To cure arrogance takes from a few years to an indefinite length of time of proper practice in a more appreciative and natural way of life. However, arrogance can also be cured instantaneously through strong emotional or spiritual experiences, especially in the face of great difficulties and failure. The cure of arrogance immediately produces a spirit of humility and modesty. It restores also the spirit of appreciation through the recognition of our ignorance. When arrogance is dissolved, a new way of life in harmony with the environment automatically begins.

Every physical, mental, and spiritual sickness belongs to one of the seven levels outlined above. All sicknesses are interdependent and interconnected with one another; they are symptoms branching out from the same root—improper way of life. As human beings we are a natural manifestation that appeared on the earth according to the evolving Order of the Universe. Thus, it is a simple matter to remain in that state of natural order and harmony. It is more difficult and complicated to get sick and suffer. Modern people, however, are suffering with many sicknesses and experiencing a rising epidemic of degenerative diseases. We take it for granted today that the ordinary person and family will suffer with some sort of serious illness and that most of us will die from heart disease, cancer, or other chronic disorder. This universal belief in modern society is contrary to our real nature and the experience of humanity over thousands and thousands of past generations. As long as we follow and live according to the laws of nature and the Order of the Universe, as our ancestors have done from the beginning, we shall enjoy health, happiness, and longevity, rarely suffering from any form of sickness.

Kinds of Human Death

As human beings we have a potentially free consciousness and free ability to change ourselves, through adapting to our natural environment. Whether we are aware of it or not, we are creating our own destinies. When, how, and where we are going to die are being determined by the convergence of various factors—physical and mental, spiritual and social—that we are causing ourselves to experience through our own way of life. Let us consider the various modes of death:

Biological Death: If our daily lives, including our dietary practices, are out of harmony with the changing natural environment, our physical and mental condition becomes unsuitable for the continuation of our life. When harmonious change no longer becomes possible, we dissolve the situation by dying. This sort of death comes through various physical and mental sicknesses. In modern society, the majority of deaths belong to this category.

Psychological Death: As a result of the continuous practice of an improper way of life, our mentality—which normally appreciates and finds joy in our surroundings, natural and social—becomes incapable of seeing a bright and happy future. We start to live in a world of fantasy or illusion. Eventually, when we can no longer adjust to the environment, we take our own lives. This death appears as committing suicide or as simply giving up the will to live and usually comes during a period of mounting difficulties and pressures. This kind of death is seen in modern society less frequently than biological death but is on the increase around the world, especially among young people.

Social Death: Modern societies are generally organized according to a conceptual image, often unconnected with real natural conditions of growth and harmony. Modern education teaches us to serve and give our lives for social causes of various kinds, such as the maintenance of certain political and economic systems, religious faiths, or racial groupings. Because of such ideological training, we participate in groups that kill and are killed on the battlefields of civil or foreign wars. Often, millions of human lives are involved in massive destruction or preparation for future warfare. Tens of millions of deaths are recorded as a result of social conflict every century.

Accidental Death: Deaths caused by accidents are also on the increase in the modern world. It is now commonly believed that accidents are unavoidable and that unexpected misfortune is a normal part of life. However, accidents are not random or purposeless. Accidents occur when our physical, mental, and spiritual conditions become unclear as a result of an unhealthy way of life. Our lack of foresight and sensitivity, our carelessness and overexcitability, and our lack of clear judgment are the major causes of accidents and accidental deaths. Whether we are the active creator of an accident or the passive recipient, it is our inadequate ability to harmonize our life that is the underlying cause of such death. If we are in harmony with our environment, we will not attract danger, and our intuition will naturally protect us under all circumstances.

Philosophical Death: There are some people who purposely terminate their lives with clear and stable minds. This kind of death is a meaningful measure, to express deep apologies, taking responsibility for what we have done to others or to the general public. In some cases, death is initiated to encourage and inspire the remaining people and the younger generations. In other cases, we continue to pursue our dream, although we know that we shall have to meet unnatural death in the course of such pursuit. Historical examples include Buddhist monks in Vietnam who peacefully immolated themselves in an attempt to inspire deep reflection in their countrymen and some Japanese *samurai* who ended their own lives to take responsibility for their conduct or to honor their land, laws, or traditions.

Natural Death: Except when natural catastrophes arise and when human beings or other species interfere, wild animals generally experience natural death. They know the time of their death before it comes. It is well known that wild elephants travel to the depths of the jungle toward their natural cemeteries when they feel that death is coming. Even among domesticated animals this instinct remains. Cats and dogs hide their bodies when they are going to die, if circumstances allow. Rats that live aboard ships often escape while the boats are in port, knowing that the coming voyage may meet with severe storm or fire. Such instinct is natural to all species.

When as human beings we live according to the order of nature, with continuous practice of proper diet and active physical and mental relations with society and other people, our lives become more prolonged than the average. We die as trees that wither in a change of climate. We feel clearly when and how our death will come. Such death arises very naturally without any particular suffering, and clarity of consciousness remains until the actual death takes place. This kind of natural death was often experienced by older people, even two and three generations ago. Traditionally, elders were healthy, sound in judgment, and wise, guiding many young people. They often chose the way, time, and place of their death, and after they passed away, their families or other intimate friends would often find arrangements that they had made in preparation for their death. The dying elders considered death a natural process, with deep appreciation for life itself.

Spiritual Death: On rare occasions, death as a means of further evolution from this life to the next life is experienced among spiritually-developed people. Often such death is self-initiated, and such a person often disappears by his or her own will, perhaps to the mountains or to the wilderness where life is ended. In other cases, the person may dissolve their body in front of friends or elevate themselves toward the atmospheric vibrational world. Examples of spiritual death include Lao Tzu, who set forth his understanding of the Order of the Universe in the *Tao Te Ching* and then disappeared riding a water buffalo out of China, and Elijah, a prophet in ancient Israel, who is said to have ascended to heaven in a whirlwind.

With the exception of massive death arising from earthquakes, floods, volcanoes, and other natural catastrophes, all human deaths belong to one of the above categories. Among modern people, death is most often of the biological, psychological, social, and accidental varieties rather than philosophical, natural, and spiritual. The former are kinds of death resulting from physical, mental, and spiritual sicknesses—and may all be classified as suicide, or self-caused. The latter deaths are from a healthy life conducted according to the natural order. The macrobiotic way of life leads not only to improving our physical and mental health and well-being but also to developing our spiritual ability to die naturally and be born harmoniously in the next world of vibration and spirit.

Yin and Yang in Physical and Mental Sicknesses

All physical and mental sicknesses can be classified according to their symptoms and causes into three major categories: 1) those caused by excessive yin—centrifugal and expansive tendencies—or deficient yang—centripetal and contractive tendencies; 2) those caused by excessive yang tendencies or deficient yin tendencies; and 3) those caused by both excessive yang and excessive yin tendencies or by both deficient yang and deficient yin tendencies.

The accompanying tables (see Tables 14–23) list selected symptoms and diseases, arranged according to these three major categories.

Table 14. Disorders of the Skin and Hair

Yin (▽)	Yang (△)	Yin (▽) and Yang (△) Combined
Representative Symptoms:		
Increased redness	Bluish or yellowish (jaundiced) appearance	Hardening and thickening of the skin
Inflammation, swelling	Constriction of capillaries	Tumor with pus discharge
Watery discharge	Dryness of surface skin	
Disintegration of tissue		
Diseases:		
Allergy	Asphyxiation	
Infection	Pallor	Pigmentation, as in Addison's disease
Fever	Cyanosis by incomplete oxygenation of blood	
Hyperemia		Warts, moles
Baldness—peripheral regions of head	Baldness—central regions of head	Baldness—complete
Freckles	Grey hair	White patches
Extreme moisture resulting from hyperthyroidism	Extreme dryness as in heat stroke	Elephantitis
Skin cancer		Malignant melanoma
Kaposiś sarcoma		

Table 15. Disorders of the Muscular System

Yin (▽)	Yang (△)	Yin (▽) and Yang (△) Combined
Representative Symptoms:		
Sudden paralysis	Gradual paralysis	Immobility
Swelling	Constriction	Constriction
Inflammation	Hardening	Inflammation
General weakness		General weakness
Pains		
Tension	Immobility	
Diseases:		
Tetany	Tetanus (lockjaw)	Stiffness of neck and shoulder
Cramp		
"Charley-horse"	Sprain	Torticollis (wryneck)
Hernia		
Spasm		
Progressive muscular dystrophy	Myotonia	Muscular atrophy
		Myositis
		Myasthenia gravis

Table 16. Disorders in Blood and Body Fluids and the Circulatory System

Yin (▽)	Yang (△)	Yin (▽) and Yang (△) Combined
Representative Symptoms:		
Lack of vitality	General fatigue	General fatigue
General fatigue		
Dilation, swelling, inflammation	Constriction of circulatory vessels	Hardening
Reduction of red blood cells	Reduction of white blood cells, in some cases	Imbalance among blood cell number
Bleeding	Thickening of blood	Higher cholesterol and fatty content in blood
Weakening of arterial and venous walls	Bleeding	
Diseases:		
Nutritional anemia	Scurvy	Pernicious anemia
Hemophilia		
Leukemia		
Hodgkins' disease		
Lymphoma		
Purpura		
Cushing's syndrome	Systolic hypertension	Diastolic hypertension
	Eclampsia hypertension	Renal hypertension
Some low blood pressure	Some low blood pressure	Arteriosclerosis
Some cerebral thrombosis	Coronary heart disease	Some cerebral thrombosis
Cerebral hemmorrage	Angina pectoris	Prinzmetal angina
Fibrillation	Heart attack	Atherosclerosis
Tachycardia	Bradycardia	Irregular heart beats
Some heart failure	Some heart failure	Rheumatic heart disease
Valve disorders		Infectious heart disease
Pulmonary heart disease		Peripheral heart disease
Congenital heart defects		Acute thrombosis or embolism
Raynaud's phenomenon	Buerger's disease	Aneurysm
		Varicose veins
		Phlebitis
		Cardiomyopathy

Table 17. Disorders of the Bones and Joints

Yin (▽)	Yang (△)	Yin (▽) and Yang (△) Combined
Representative Symptoms:		
Swelling	Consolidation of joints	Swelling
Inflammation	Abnormal inward curve and deformation	Inflammation
Softening or deformation		Stiffness and deformation
Infectious conditions	Immobility	Hardening
Diseases:		
Infectious arthritis	Metabolic arthritis—(gout)	Rheumatoid arthritis
Osteoarthritis		Bursitis
Osteomyelitis	Osteitis fibrosa	
Osteomalacia		
Bunion		
Flat foot	Club foot	
Acromegaly	Hunchback	
Frequent dislocation		
Rickets		Paget's disease
Pott's disease		
Scoliosis	Bone cancer	Malignant melanoma

Table 18. Disorders of the Digestive System

Yin (▽)	Yang (△)	Yin (▽) and Yang (△) Combined
Representative Symptoms:		
Swelling	Constriction; sometimes swelling	Swelling
Inflammation	Inflammation	Inflammation
Looseness of tissue	Hardening	
Enlargement of organs	Formation of pus and tumors	Production of pus and tumors
Spasmic pains		Lack of metabolic coordination
Slowness of metabolism	Fever	
Diseases:		
Tooth decay	Tooth erosion	
Inflammation of gums		
Chronic constipation and diarrhea	Temporary constipation	Obesity
Vomiting		
Mumps	Appendicitis	Hemorrhoids
Adenoids	Cholecystitis	
Tonsilitis		
Colitis		

(*Continued*)

Yin (▽)	Yang (△)	Yin (▽) and Yang (△) Combined
Gastric pancreatitis		
Stomach ulcers	Duodenal ulcers	
Cirrhosis	Jaundice	Hepatitis
Dysentery		Cholera
Candidas		Hypoglycemia
Diabetes		Typhoid fever
Harelip		Gallstones
Upper stomach cancer		Lower stomach cancer
Esophageal cancer	Colon cancer	Spleen cancer
	Rectum cancer	
	Pancreatic cancer	Liver cancer

Table 19. Disorders of the Respiratory System

Yin (▽)	Yang (△)	Yin (▽) and Yang (△) Combined
Representative Symptoms:		
Dilation of organs and tissues	Constriction of respiratory system	Expansion or constriction in respiratory organs
Difficulty in breathing	Difficulty in breathing	Difficulty in breathing
Inflammation; swelling	Inflammation in some cases	Inflammation in some cases
Infectious conditions	Shortness of breath	Some coughing
Sneezing, hiccoughing	Choking	Gutteral voice
Yawning, snoring	Some coughing	
Sighing, crying, sobbing		
Some coughing		
Stuttering		
Diseases:		
Asthma		Pneumonia
Bronchitis		
Croup		Mucus—fat accumulation in lungs
Diphtheria		
Emphysema		Empyema
Hay fever		
Pleurisy		
Tonsilitis		
Adenoids		
Tuberculosis		
Whooping cough		
Some conditions of cyanosis	Some conditions of cyanosis	
Collapsed lung		Consolidation
Mouth cancer		Lung cancer
Throat cancer		Tongue cancer

Table 20. Disorders of the Nervous System

Yin (▽)	Yang (△)	Yin (▽) and Yang (△) Combined
Representative Symptoms:		
Swelling	Constriction and hardening of nervous system	Some expansion and some constriction of nervous system
Inflammation		
Nervousness	Inflammation in some cases	
Trembling		
Numbness	Cold body temperature	
Pain	Sweating	
Watery discharge	Rigidity	Imbalance and instability
Less movement	Greater movement	Accumulation of mucus and fat
Vertigo, dizziness		
Sensation of fatigue	Sensation of hunger	
Loss of memory		
Insomnia		
Fragmented dreams	Sleepwalking	Nightmares
Fear	Paranoia	
Worry	Short temper; anger	
Some frustration	Some frustration	General frustration
Some excitability	Some excitability	
Hypersensitivity	Hate; stubbornness	Resentment
	Narrow view	
Diseases:		
Mental depression	Mental depression	Insecurity
Schizophrenia	Psychosis	Emotional imbalance
Detachment of retina glaucoma		Astigmatism
Myopia (nearsightedness)	Short-sightedness	
Stye		Cataract
Conjunctivitis		
Some color blindness	Some color blindness	
Crossed eyes—outward	Crossed eyes—inward	
Bloodshot eyes		
Transmission and peripheral deafness		Central deafness
Loss of equilibrium		Loss of equilibrium
Some headache—front and more peripheral regions of head	Some headache—deep and at more central and back regions of head	Cauliflower ear
Some Parkinson's disease—small trembling	Some Parkinson's disease—greater shaking	
Some multiple sclerosis	Some multiple sclerosis	
Epilepsy	Grinding teeth	
Meningitis		
Outer brain cancer	Inner brain cancer	

Table 21. Disorders of the Urinary System

Yin (▽)	Yang (△)	Yin (▽) and Yang (△) Combined
Representative Symptoms:		
Swelling	Swelling, especially joints	Swelling
Water intoxication	Water retention	
Sweating	Sweating	Sweating
Colorless urine	Dark urine	
Expansion of urinary systems	Constriction of urinary passages	Constriction or expansion of urinary system
General fatigue	Urination difficulty	Accumulation of mucus and fat in organs
Frequent urination		
Pains and inflammation in some cases		
Diseases:		
Cystitis	Oliguria	Uremia
Enuresis	Dysuria	
Pyelitis		Nephritis
Movable kidney		
Some retention	Some retention	Edema
Some anuria	Some stricture	Some anuria
Movable kidney		Kidney stone
Incontinence		Bladder cancer
		Kidney cancer

Table 22. Disorders of the Endocrine System

Yin (▽)	Yang (△)	Yin (▽) and Yang (△) Combined
Representative Symptoms:		
Hypersecretion of yin hormones, and	Hyposecretion of yin hormones, and	Irregular and unbalanced secretion of yin and yang hormones
Hyposecretion of yang hormones	Hypersecretion of yang hormones	
Expansion in growth	Constriction in growth	Unbalanced growth
General fatigue	General irritability	General frustration
Diseases:		
Exothaermic goiter (Graves' disease)	Simple goiter	Unbalanced and complex yin and yang symptoms combined
Toxic goiter		
Acromegaly	Myxedema (Gull's disease)	Irregular growth
Gigantism	Dwarfism	
Pituitary basophilism	Pituitary cachexia (Simmond's disease)	

Yin (▽)	Yang (△)	Yin (▽) and Yang (△) Combined
Diabetes mellitus	Diabetes insipidus	Hypoglycemia
Tetany	Hyperinsulinism	
Addison's disease	Osteitis fibrosa	
	Cushing's syndrome	
	Adrenogenital syndrome	
Hyposecretion of the testes	Sexual precocity	Irregular menstruation
	Virilism	
Hypogonadism	Lack of sexual libido	Frequent change of sexual and physical vitalities
Some menstrual disorders, irregularity	Some menstrual disorders, irregularity	

Table 23. Disorders of the Reproductive System

Yin (▽)	Yang (△)	Yin (▽) and Yang (△) Combined
Representative Symptoms:		
Disorder and malfunction mainly in male organs	Disorder and malfunction mainly in female organs	
Inflammation, excessive moisture, swelling	More dryness, inflammation and swelling in some cases	Inflammation and swelling in some cases
Loss of sexual libido	Excessive sexual libido	Irregular sexual libido
Diseases:		
Hydrocele	Anorchidism	Breast cysts
Prostatic hypertrophy	Cryptorchidism	
	Monorchidism	Chancroid
Some urethral stricture	Some urethral stricture	
Vesculitis	Phimosis	
Retroversion of uterus	Anteversion of uterus	
Prolapsed uterus		Syphilis
Gonorrhea	Vaginismus	Vaginal discharge
Longer menstrual cycle	Shorter menstrual cycle	Irregular menstrual cycle
Breast cancer	Ovarian cancer	Uterine cancer
	Vaginal cancer	Fibroid tumors
	Prostate cancer	Dermoid tumors
	Testicular cancer	
Candidas		
Herpes		
Aids		

General Approach: When the symptoms manifested are generally caused by excess yin (or a deficiency of yang), the approach to the sickness should be to balance the condition toward more yang. For convenience, we may call this a yin disease or disorder for which a more yang approach is required.

Likewise, when the symptoms manifested are more yang (or caused by a deficiency of yin), the person's condition should be changed toward more yin. We may call this a yang disease or disorder for which a more yin approach is required.

When the symptoms manifested are caused by both excessive yin and yang (or a deficiency of both), the approach should be to bring the condition to a middle state, by harmonizing both forces. We may call this a disease or disorder caused by both yin and yang combined for which a more moderate or standard approach is required.

To restore harmony with the environment, various adjustments in daily life may need to be made in the following areas (see Table 24):

Table 24. Adjustment of Environment and Activity

For Yin (▽) Disease	For Yang (△) Disease	For Disease Caused by Both Yin (▽) and Yang (△) Combined
Atmospheric Condition Should Be:		
Drier	More moist	
Sunnier	Less sunny	General, standard conditions
Brighter light	Dimmer light	
Fresh, cool air	Less air circulation	
Activity Should Be:		
More active, physical exercise	Less active physically	Average activity
Less mental activity	More mental activity	
Climate Should Be:		
Warmer	Colder	Average
Sunnier regions	More northern regions	Normal regions

Atmospheric Adjustments: For yin diseases, it is generally advisable to keep the humidity of the surrounding air lower than in the case of other diseases and to have more sunshine and brightness, as well as smooth circulation of air in the room. For yang diseases, it is often advisable to keep the surroundings slightly more moist, dimmer, and with less circulation of air. If the conditions of the disease include a combination of yin and yang, the surroundings should generally be kept in a moderate condition, neither too dry nor humid, neither too sunny nor shady, nor too breezy or still.

Activity Level Adjustments: For yin diseases, more active physical exercise is generally advisable, except in cases of pains, fever, fatigue, and exhaustion, all of which require rest. For yang disease, on the other hand, it is generally advisable to actively exercise less often. For diseases of both yin and yang combined, average activity is advisable. Also, for chronic yin diseases, more physical activity in general is recommended, and for chronic yang diseases, more mental activity is advisable.

Climatic Adjustments: For a yin disease arising in a colder region or in the winter season, it is often useful to move to a warmer, sunnier climate, while for a yang disease arising in a warmer region or in the summertime, it is often helpful to move to a colder and more northern region. When we change our place of living, we naturally change our dietary habits in the new climate. For this reason, a change in residence is often effective. Whether the change is temporary or permanent will depend on the individual case. In most instances, once general health is restored, the person can safely return to their previous environment and, by modifying their diet, continue to stay well and active.

Dietary Adjustments: Dietary practices should be changed according to the nature of the causes and symptoms of the sickness. The selection, preparation, and manner of eating of the foods should be carefully modified and adjusted according to principles of yin and yang in order to restore harmony with the environment. Modern medicine makes chemical analyses of the leaves, roots, and vitamin and mineral content of various plants and organic compounds in order to isolate the active ingredient or synthesize them in the laboratory. This approach does not work because it does not take into account the underlying energetic nature of health and disease.

In nourishing the various organs, we need to know the type of *ki* (natural electromagnetic energy) that governs their growth and development. Earth's ascending force makes expanding structures such as leaves and fruits, while heaven's descending force makes for contractive structures such as stems and roots. Thus organs with yin structures are governed by earth's force, and organs with yang structures are created by heaven's force. However, the function or flow of electromagnetic energy (*ki*) in the organs or their meridians is opposite to their structure. Though expanded in structure, fruits are small and condensed. Though contracted in structure, roots spread or expand underground. Table 25 shows these relationships.

Table 25. Antagonistic-Complementary Relations Among Major Organs

Governed by Earth's Force	*Governed by Heaven's Force*
Yin Structure *Yang Function*	*Yang Structure* *Yin Function*
Lungs	Colon
Liver	Gallbladder
Kidney	Bladder
Heart	Small Intestine
Spleen-Pancreas	Stomach
Brain	Uterus/Prostate

For example, in terms of function, the lungs are more yang and their structure is more yin, while the function of the colon is more yin and its structure is yang. For conditions of ordinary good health, we nourish the respective organs with the type of food that governs their energy flow. Thus we eat carrots (more yang) to stimulate the lungs (more yang) and carrot tops (more yin) to activate the colon (more yin). However, in cases of imbalance, such as cancer, we temporarily offset the excess accumulation of energy in the affected organ by emphasizing the complementary opposite factor. Thus for lung (functionally more yang) tumors, proportionately more carrot greens (more yin) are advised, while for colon (functionally more yin) tumors slightly more carrot roots (more yang) are taken.

To take another example, the brain's small compact cells are governed primarily by earth's force and thus need to be nourished by predominantly vegetable-quality food, especially whole cereal grains which they resemble. Different foods influence different sides of the brain. The spring harvest influences the left side (more yin), while the autumn harvest influences the right (more yang). Thus we might take lighter, more quickly prepared foods such as leafy green vegetables to stimulate the left side of the brain which governs complex and creative thinking. Heavier and longer cooked foods such as hearty stews and root vegetables influence the right side of the brain which governs simple and basic behavior, expression, and consciousness.

The prostate gland in men and the uterus in women are naturally influenced by yang energy, but excess yang easily accumulates there, so in case of sickness lighter vegetable-quality food is recommended. To dissolve meat, chicken, or other animal food that often accumulates in these regions, for the time being upward leafy green vegetables such as scallions can be given. Once stagnation and blockages have been dissolved, then proportionately more root vegetables and other good-quality yang foods can be taken to strengthen the prostate or uterus and make a sound, healthy condition.

In the temperate climates of the world, the following general guidelines may be observed for physical, mental, and spiritual disorders (see Table 26):

Table 26. General Guidelines for Dietary Adjustments*

Kind of Food	*More Yin* (▽) *Condition*	*Excess Yin* (▽) *and Yang* (△) *Condition*	*More Yang* (△) *Condition*
General cooking	Slightly more salty, stronger cooking	Moderate cooking	Less salty, lighter cooking
Grains (50 to 60% of daily volume)	Brown rice, barley, corn, whole wheat, millet, buckwheat, regularly; oats, rye, occasionally; baked flour products occasionally; noodles/pasta occasionally	Brown rice, barley, whole wheat, corn, regularly; millet, buckwheat, oats, rye, occasionally; bread and baked flour products minimize; noodles/pasta occasionally	Brown rice, barley, corn, whole wheat, regularly; oats, rye, occasionally; millet, buckwheat, minimize; bread and baked flour products minimize; noodles/pasta occasionally
Soup (1 to 2 cups or bowls daily)	Slightly stronger flavor (slightly more miso, tamari soy sauce, or sea salt)	Moderate flavor	Milder flavor (less miso, tamari soy sauce, or sea salt)
Vegetables (25 to 30% daily volume)	All temperate-climate types daily but emphasize more root varieties, moderate amount of round ones, and less leafy greens; avoid raw salad;	All temperate-climate types daily but emphasize more round varieties; minimize raw salad; frequent boiled or pressed salad	All temperate-climate types daily but emphasize more leafy greens, round ones; less root ones; occasional raw salad; frequent boiled or

Kind of Food	*More Yin* (▽) *Condition*	*Excess Yin* (▽) *and Yang* (△) *Condition*	*More Yang* (△) *Condition*
	occasional boiled or pressed salad		pressed salad
Beans and bean products (5% daily)	A little more strongly seasoned, use less regularly	Moderately seasoned and moderate volume	Lightly seasoned, use more regularly
Sea vegetables (5% daily volume)	Longer cooking, slightly thicker taste	Moderate cooking, medium taste	Quicker cooking, lighter taste
Pickles (small volume daily)	More long-time, stronger pickles	Either type in moderation	More short-time, lighter pickles
Condiments (tiny volume daily)	Stronger use	Moderate use	Lighter use
Animal food	Occasional small volume of white-meat fish or seafood	Minimize fish or seafood	Avoid or minimize fish or seafood
Oil	Occasional use, dark sesame only; apply with brush as little as possible; consume no raw oil	Occasional use, dark sesame or corn oil only; apply with brush as little as possible; consume no raw oil	Regular use, sesame or corn oil only in moderation, consume no raw oil
Fruit/Dessert	Avoid or minimize; a few raisins or other dried and cooked fruit if cravings arise	Small amount of dried or cooked fruit (locally grown and seasonal) if craved or naturally sweetened dessert	Occasional dried, cooked, or raw fruit and naturally sweetened dessert
Seeds and nuts	Occasional lightly roasted seeds; limit nuts and nut butters	Occasional lightly roasted seeds; a few nuts and nut butters	Occasional lightly roasted seeds; a few nuts and nut butters
Beverages	Longer cooked, thicker-tasting bancha or other traditional tea	Medium cooked, medium-tasting bancha or other traditional tea	Shorter cooked, lighter-tasting bancha or other traditional tea

*These guidelines are only for the initial period until the condition improves, approximately 1 to 2 months, depending upon the individual case.

Although the above guidelines are effective for all sicknesses and disorders, several points require careful consideration:

• *Cooking:* If the way of cooking is not proper, the expected results will not be produced, even though natural and organic quality food is prepared. Over- or underheating, excessive or insufficient use of water, too much or too little salt, oil, and other seasonings, too long or too short time of cooking, as well as the use of improper cooking utensils, diminish the beneficial effects of the food. The art of cooking is one of the most important aspects in the healing of various sicknesses. It requires not only an understanding of the proper techniques but also a loving spirit on the part of the cook and a grateful mind on the part of the person who eats. Introductory cooking classes from experienced macrobiotic cooking instructors are recommended for everyone. Even though we are proficient in some other style of cooking, until we have actually seen and tasted food prepared according to macrobiotic principles, we will not have a standard against which to measure our own cooking.

• *Volume:* However good the food and the cooking are, their effectiveness can be reduced by overeating. It is an important practice to avoid overeating and to stop eating when the appetite is about 80 percent satisfied.

• *Chewing:* Regardless of the circumstances, good chewing is one of the most important practices in the way of eating. The more we chew, the more we are able to utilize the energy and nutrients of the food. To maintain a normal, healthy condition, chewing each mouthful at least fifty times or more is advisable. In the event of sickness, chewing seventy to one hundred times is usually required. If the sickness is more serious, the amount of chewing may be increased to 150 times or more per mouthful. Completely mixing the food with saliva, until it is liquid in form, is the key to the smooth operation of all digestive functions, and this, in turn, directly serves for the smooth production of healthy blood. In the event that chewing is not possible due to very serious illness, physical or mental weakness, or defective teeth, food can be served in mashed form so that it may be mixed slowly with saliva. Also, it is traditional in many cultures for someone who is unable to eat solid food to be nourished back to health with food thoroughly chewed (but not swallowed) by other family members.

• *Changing the Diet:* When we start macrobiotics, it may be difficult to eliminate completely and immediately all previous types of food regularly eaten, including meat, eggs, dairy food, sugar and other artificial sweets, and refined and mass-produced chemicalized foods and beverages. If that is the case, it is recommended to gradually reduce the amount of undesirable foods and beverages and to gradually increase the amount of proper food and beverages.

Moreover, when we have been taking drugs (licit or illicit) or medications, it is especially necessary to reduce them gradually, in most cases taking a few weeks to several months depending upon the type of drugs or medication and the extent to which they have been taken. In the case of life-supporting drugs or medication, this process of withdrawal may take several years, or the medication may need to be continued indefinitely. In such cases, a medical doctor's supervision is advised. The greater the volume of undesirable food or drugs taken in the past, the slower the rate of change should be. However, if we have not taken such substances, the previous diet can be changed almost immediately and macrobiotic dietary guidelines can be adopted.

Control of Recovery Rate: There is a complementary relationship between principal food—whole cereal grains and their products—and all other foods in the standard macrobiotic diet—soup, beans, vegetables, sea vegetables, seeds and nuts, fruit, animal food, dessert, and beverages. If we wish to accelerate our recovery, generally speaking, we should increase the proportion of principal food and decrease all other side dishes proportionately. On the other hand, if we wish a more gradual recovery, particularly if we have been taking some sort of medication, it is recommended to decrease the amount of principal food and increase all other supplemental foods proportionately. However, the principal food should not be less than 50 percent by volume of each meal.

Often, in traditional societies, only grains and their products were eaten with almost no side dishes for a period of up to ten days in order to restore physical and mental equilibrium. A small volume of soup, seasonings and condiments, and beverages accompanied the rice, barley, millet, or other grains. The 100 percent cereal grain diet is also beneficial for spiritual development, for periods of three to seven or ten days. However, because of its strong effects, it is not a regular daily diet and should not be continued more than ten days, or imbalance can develop. Ideally everyone who adopts this practice should be under the supervision of an experienced macrobiotic guide.

In normal daily life, principal food can fluctuate between 30 and 70 percent of each meal, and supplemental food can be adjusted accordingly, depending upon our daily activities and social environment.

However, generally, the more we eat in the higher range (50 to 60 percent), the more balance we achieve in our physical, mental, and spiritual activities.

Transition and Discharge

When beginning the practice of proper diet to recover our health, we may experience some physical and mental reactions during a short transition period, usually lasting from three to ten days, and in some cases up to four months until the quality of the blood fully changes. If our native constitution is strong and well structured, these reactions are usually negligible. However, if our embryonic and childhood development suffered from chaotic dietary habits (see Figure 47), if we have ingested many chemicals, drugs, or medications, or if we have had surgery or an abortion, these discharge reactions will be more pronounced.

Figure 47. The Changing Ear

Traditional balanced ear

Modern ears are losing the earlobe; instead, we see ears attached directly to the head. The long earlobe has been known as a sign of happiness as well as of balanced physical and mental conditions. The earlobe is developed by proper mineral intake while the absence of an earlobe is due to a lack of minerals and overconsumption of animal protein. These shapes are formed during embryonic development through the nourishment coming from the placenta. When the mother's nourishment is proper, the baby is born with good earlobes. For further examples of how our health is reflected in features of the face and body, see Michio Kushi's *How to See Your Health: The Book of Oriental Diagnosis* (Japan Publications, 1980).

Modern, unbalanced ear

Whatever the case may be, we should not worry if these reactions occur. They are part of the natural healing process and signify that our systems are regenerating themselves, dislodging and throwing off the excess that has accumulated over many years. These reactions may be generally classified as follows:

General Fatigue: A feeling of general fatigue may arise among people who have been eating an excessive amount of animal protein and fat. The energetic activity that they may have previously experienced was the result of the vigorous caloric discharge of these excessive foods rather than a more healthy, balanced, and peaceful way of activity. Often these people initially experience physical tiredness and slight mental depression until the new diet starts to serve as an energy supply for activity. Such a period of fatigue usually ends within a month.

Pains and Aches: Pains and aches may sometimes be experienced, especially by people who have been taking excessive liquid, sugar, fruits, or any other extremely yin quality of food and beverages. These pains and aches—such as headaches and pains in the area of the intestines, kidneys, and chest—occur because of the gradual contraction of abnormally expanded tissues and nerve cells. These aches and pains disappear—either gradually or suddenly—as soon as these abnormally expanded areas return to a normal condition. This usually takes between three and fourteen days, depending upon the previous condition.

Fever, Chills, and Coughing: As the new diet starts to form a more sound quality of blood, previous excessive substances—excessive volume of liquid, fat, and many other things—begin to be discharged. If at this time the functions of the kidneys, urinary system, and respiratory system have not yet returned to normal, this discharge sometimes takes the form of fever, chills, or coughing. These are temporary and disappear in several days without any special treatment.

Abnormal Sweating and Frequent Urination: As in the symptoms described above, unusual sweating may be experienced by some people from time to time, for a period of several months, and other people may experience unusually frequent urination. In their previous diets, these people have been taking excessive liquid in the form of water, various beverages, alcohol, fruits, fruit juices, milk or other dairy food. By reducing these excessive liquids and fats accumulated in the form of liquid, the body returns to a normal, balanced, healthy condition. When metabolic balance has been gradually restored, these discharges will cease.

Skin Discharge and Unusual Body Odors: Among the forms of elimination is the discharge of unusual odors from the entire body surface, through breathing, urination, or bowel movements and often, in the case of women, through vaginal discharges. This usually occurs among people who were previously taking excessive volumes of animal fat, dairy food, and sugar. In addition, some people experience—for only short periods—skin rashes, reddish swelling at the tips of the fingers and toes, and boils. These types of elimination arise especially among people who have taken animal fat, dairy food, sugar, spices, chemicals, drugs, and among those who have had chronic malfunctions of the intestines, kidneys, and liver. However, these eliminations naturally heal and usually disappear within a few months without any special attention.

Diarrhea or Constipation: People who have had chronically disturbed intestinal conditions, caused by previous improper dietary habits, may temporarily experience either diarrhea (usually for several days) or constipation (for a period lasting up to twenty days). In this case, diarrhea is a form of discharge of accumulated stagnated matter in the intestines, including unabsorbed food, fat, mucus, and liquid. Constipation is the result of a process of contraction of the intestinal tube, which was abnormally expanded due to the previous diet. As this contraction restores normal elasticity to the intestinal tube, the elimination of bowel movements resume.

Decrease of Sexual Desire and Vitality: There are some people who may feel a weakening of sexual vitality or appetite, not necessarily accompanied by a feeling of fatigue. The reason for such a decline is that the body functions are working to eliminate imbalanced factors from all parts of the body and excessive vitality is not available to be used for sexual activity. Also, in some cases, the sexual organs are being actively healed by the new quality of blood and are not yet prepared to resume normal activity. These conditions, however, last only for a short period, usually a few weeks and, at most, a few months. As soon as this recovery period is over healthy vitality and desire for sexual activity return.

Temporary Cessation of Menstruation: In a few women, there may be a temporary cessation of menstruation. The reason for this cessation is that in the healing of the entire body, once again the vital organs need to receive energy first. Less vital functions, including reproductive activities, are healed later. The period of cessation of menstruation varies with the individual. However, when menstruation begins anew, it is healthy and natural, and begins to adjust to the normal twenty-eight-day lunar cycle and presents no discomfort, as was previously often the case. Mental clarity and emotional calm are strengthened as well as physical flexibility.

Mental Irritability: Some people who have been taking stimulants, drugs, and medications for long periods experience emotional irritability after changing their dietary practices. This irritability reflects adjustments taking place in the blood and various body functions, following the change to the different quality of food, and generally passes within one week to several weeks, depending upon how deeply affected the body systems were by the previous habitual use of such drugs and medications. The consumption of sugar, coffee, and alcohol for long periods, as well as longtime smoking, also produces temporary emotional irritability when the new diet is initially practiced.

Other Possible Transitory Experiences: In addition to the above conditions, some people may experience other manifestations of adjustment, such as hair loss, bad dreams at night, or a feeling of coldness, as well as temporary changes in perception and sensitivity, including the sense of touch, taste, smell, hearing, and vision. These too will pass.

In many instances, the discharge process is so gradual that none of these more visible temporary conditions arises. However, when they do appear, the symptoms vary from person to person, depending upon their inherited constitution and physical condition, and usually require no special treatment, naturally ceasing as the whole body readjusts to normal functioning. In the possible event that the symptoms are severe or uncomfortable, the discharge process can be slowed down by modifying the new diet to include continuous consumption of some previous food in small volume—about 10 to 30 percent of the meal—until balance is restored. The important thing is to understand that the discharge mechanism is part of the normal healing process and these symptoms are not to be suppressed by taking drugs or medications, resorting to vitamin or mineral supplements, or going off the diet altogether in the mistaken belief that it is ineffective, deficient, or creating allergic reactions. If there is any uncertainty or question about proper practice that arises during this transition period, a qualified macrobiotic educator or medical professional should be contacted.

During the transitional period, there will be times when we crave the taste, texture, odor, and other characteristics of previous foods and drinks, especially those we had in childhood. Often, when eating such foods, we suffer from feelings of guilt. These feelings should be put aside and a more relaxed attitude developed. Instead of feeling as if we have committed a sin, we should reflect and try to understand why such cravings arose. Usually, during the first weeks or months of the new diet, these cravings reflect a natural discharge process. As our condition improves, the toxins and mucus that have accumulated in our bloodstream and internal organs are eliminated from the body through the bowels, urination, perspiration, and other excretory functions. As they leave the body, the discharged food particles often impress themselves in our consciousness and we experience them as cravings. At other times, after our condition has stabilized, these occasional cravings signify that our diet is imbalanced in the opposite yin or yang direction from the food which we are attracted. Thus, if we are attracted to fruit juice or ice cream, our diet is probably too salty, overcooked, and generally too yang. If we are attracted to fish, eggs, or other animal products, we are consuming too many sweets, liquids, and other strong yin foods. These promptings are one of the body's ways of alerting us to a disequilibrium in our way of eating.

Rather than suppress these natural urges, it is better to acknowledge them and take a tiny volume of the previous type of food from time to time until such cravings lessen and finally go away, as they ultimately will. During the transition period, the following table may serve as a guide in substituting better-quality foods for the previous items that we miss (see Table 27).

Table 27. Making the Transition to Macrobiotics

Cravings	Replacement	Goal
Meat	Fish, seafood	Whole grains, beans, seitan, tofu, tempeh
Sugar, molasses, chocolate, carob, and other highly refined sweeteners	Maple syrup, honey	Rice syrup, barley malt, and ultimately natural sweeteners from grains and vegetables
Dairy food, cheese, milk, cream, butter	Organic dairy food, in small volume; nuts and nut butters; soy milk	Miso, natto, tofu, tempeh; seeds and seed butters, in small volume
Tropical and subtropical fruits and juices; artificial juices and beverages	Organic fruits and juices	Organic temperate-climate fruit (fresh, dried, and cooked) and cider or juice in season and in small volume
Coffee, black tea, soft drinks, diet drinks	Herbal teas, green tea, mineral water	Bancha twig tea, grain coffee, and other traditional nonstimulant, nonaromatic beverages

Medicinal Use of Common Food

In addition to the adjustments noted above, there may sometimes be a need for some traditional natural applications to hasten improvement. These methods can be called home cares, home remedies, or folk treatments. Each one has been developed through the actual experiences of people for many centuries. They are simple and practical enough for anyone to use under most normal circumstances. They are also sufficiently useful and effective that constant medical attention is usually not required. The materials used for such treatments are, in most cases, common daily food items and usual household supplies, easily obtainable at any time. All traditional cultures and civilizations have relied upon natural ways of healing, and some of these methods are more effective than modern medicine, without producing any side effects. They are also much more economical than the modern way of treatment.

Some examples of the medicinal use of common foods that have been used traditionally for many centuries in Far Eastern countries are as follows:

Lotus Root Tea: Helps relieve coughing and dissolves excess mucus in the body. Grate one-half cup fresh lotus root, squeeze the juice into a pot, and add a small amount of water. Cook for 5 to 8 minutes, add a pinch of sea salt or tamari soy sauce, and drink hot.

Shiitake Mushroom Tea: Used to relax an overly tense, stressful condition and to help dissolve excess animal fats. Soak a dried black shiitake mushroom cut in quarters. Cook in 2 cups of water for 20 minutes with a pinch of sea salt or 1 teaspoon of tamari soy sauce. Drink only one-half cup at a time.

Tamari Bancha Tea: Neutralizes an acidic blood condition, promotes blood circulation, and relieves fatigue. Pour 1 cup of hot bancha twig tea over 1 to 2 teaspoons tamari soy sauce. Stir and drink hot.

For a comprehensive guide to medicinal foods and home cares, including the ginger compress and taro potato plaster, please see Michio Kushi's *Macrobiotic Home Remedies*, edited by Marc Van Cauwenberghe, M.D. (Tokyo • New York: Japan Publications, 1985).

In some cases, supplementary forms of healing such as acupuncture, moxibustion, and shiatsu massage are helpful in releasing blockages and either stimulating or dispersing energy. For example, in the case of acupuncture, the needles act like antennae, attracting energy from the atmosphere and charging different areas. The same thing occurs with moxa. Fire is used to gently initiate energy flow in stagnant areas.

In the case of people who have had surgery, drug therapy, hormonal therapy, or previous nutritional counseling, the macrobiotic dietary guidelines may need further modification to balance the effects of the medical treatment as well as those of the underlying condition. Therefore, it is advisable for such a patient to consult a medical doctor, nutritional consultant, or other appropriate professional on how to adjust the macrobiotic diet to his or her unique medical situation and nutritional needs. Together with proper food preparation and cooking, it may be necessary to continue periodic medical checkups to monitor the person's changing condition as these adjustments, which may include increased total food consumption, especially of protein, complex carbohydrates, minerals, vitamins, or saturated vegetable or animal fat, are implemented. In other cases, regular medical treatment may be required, especially in emergencies or immediate life-threatening circumstances.

The Five Stages of Transformations

The laws of yin and yang are our basic compass to understand movement and relationships. However, the process of change can be further refined into five stages of transformation (see Figure 48). The electromagnetic energy or vibration generated between poles of outward and upward moving centrifugal (yin) force and inward and downward moving centripetal (yang) force can be classified into five basic types:

1. **Upward Energy:** Light, upward movement arises and starts to become active.

2. **Active Energy:** Expansion reaches a peak, diffusing actively in all directions.

3. **Downward Energy:** At its extreme, yin turns to yang and the contractive half of the cycle begins. Solidification or condensation begins.

4. **Gathering Energy:** The contractive tendency reaches its most compact, crystalized state. This tendency can be called gathering-like.

Figure 48. Five Stages of Energy Transformation

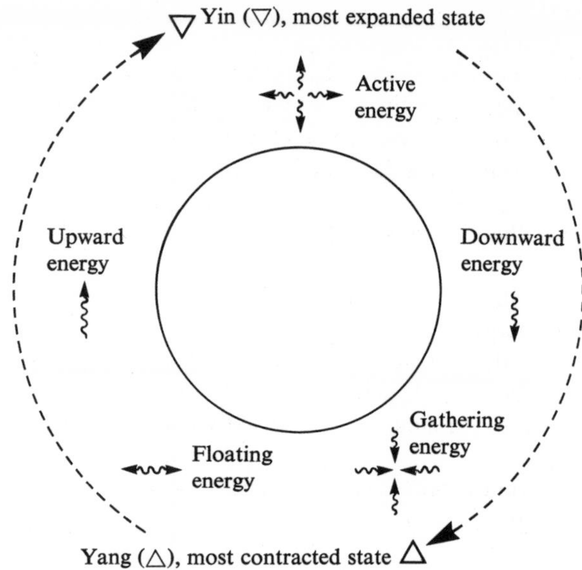

5. **Floating Energy:** At this stage, yang turns back to yin. Solidification starts to dissolve, and expansion arises.

Traditionally the terms Tree, Fire, Soil, Metal, and Water were associated with the five transformations. However, they were used only to illustrate the transitory phases in this moving, dynamic process. They should not be taken literally. It is generally preferable to look at the five stages from an energetic or atmospheric point of view, using the terms Upward, Active, Downward, Gathering, and Floating rather than the five elements. Also, like the atmosphere or the seasons, there are many inbetween tendencies among the various stages, overlapping tendencies, and multiple tendencies. Because there are so many cycles within cycles in nature, all five phases are actually present to some degree within all phenomena.

Some people may have the impression that the concept of the five transformations originated and was practiced only in the Far East. Actually, since the process described by the five transformations is universal, this understanding was common throughout the ancient world. The fivefold process is alluded to in the Gospel of Luke and other parts of the New Testament, as well as in the newly recovered *Gospel Accord-*

ing to Thomas. In Thomas's account Jesus refers to these universal stages as "five trees in paradise" and says that whoever understands them will know eternal life.

The understanding of this universal process also underlies the practice of acupuncture and other forms of traditional medicine, as it was understood that the energy within the human body and throughout nature flows in accord with this cycle. For example, atmospheric energy changes throughout the course of a day can be classified as follows:

- *Morning:* the sun rises, and the day's activities begin; expansive, upward energy
- *Noon:* the sun reaches a peak overhead and activity is at its height; diffuse, active energy
- *Afternoon:* the sun starts to reverse direction; activity diminishes; the atmosphere becomes heavier; downward energy
- *Evening:* the sun sinks and eventually sets; condensed, gathering energy
- *Night:* darkness prevails; the atmosphere feels suspended; melting or floating energy

The seasons of the year can also be classified into five stages (see Figure 49):

- *Spring:* rising, expansive, upward energy
- *Summer:* very active, outward energy
- *Indian summer:* stabilized, falling, downward energy
- *Autumn:* solidified, gathering energy
- *Winter:* frozen, dissolving, floating energy

The types of mind or awareness can be divided into five categories:

- Idealistic, aspiring, romantic, hopeful mind; upward energy
- Bright, expanded, radiant mind; active energy
- Thoughtful, considerate, balanced mind; downward energy
- Inward, self-reflective, analytical, orderly mind; gathering energy
- Flexible, adaptable, meditating, observing mind; floating energy

There are countless other cycles within nature that reflect this universal order, including the origin and development of the universe and solar system, the rise of subatomic particles and elements, the biological evolution of plants and animals, the organs and systems of the body, the tastes and properties of foods, and personal and social character and destiny.

Figure 49. Daily and Seasonal Cycles

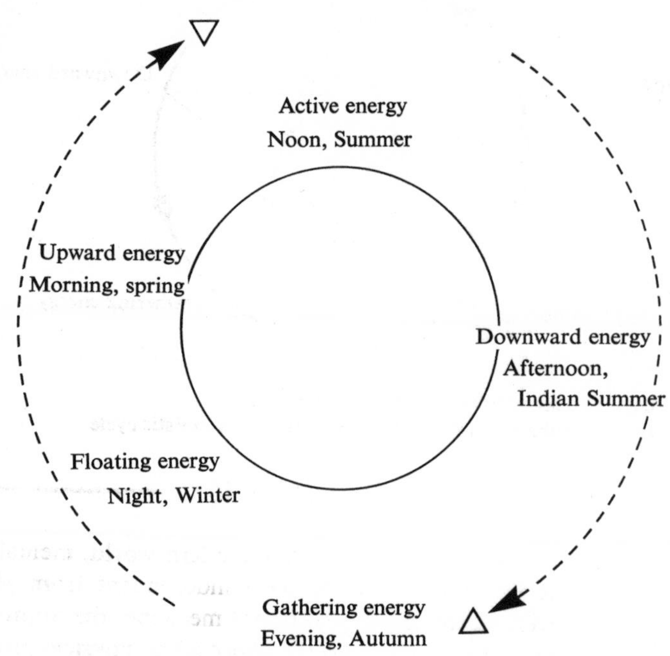

The cycle of energy flow among the five stages of change exhibits two basic tendencies. The first is nourishing or stimulating, and the second is complementary/antagonistic or conflicting.

The nourishing tendency proceeds around the spiral in a clockwise direction. Thus upward energy stimulates active energy. Active energy nourishes downward energy. Downward energy supports gathering energy. Gathering energy encourages floating energy. Floating energy nurtures upward energy.

The complementary/antagonistic tendency produces strain or conflict between every other stage (see Figure 50). Thus upward energy inhibits downward energy; downward energy dominates floating energy; floating energy controls active energy; active energy restricts gathering energy; and gathering energy limits upward energy.

Figure 50. Complementary and Antagonistic Cycles

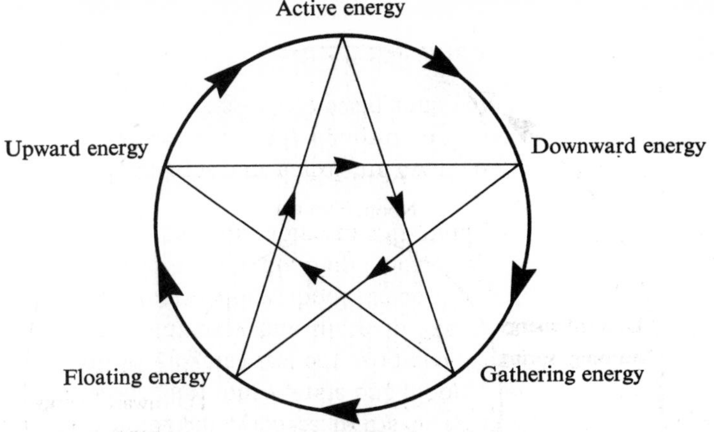

Outer clockwise direction = Nourishing cycle
Inner starlike direction = Complementary/antagonistic cycle

Mental Disorders: Cause and Approach

Relation Between Mind and Body: In the modern world, mental problems are approached as though they were independent from physical problems. However, as we see in traditional medicine, the approach to mental problems is not separate from the approach to physical problems. Physical sicknesses are immediate causes of mental disturbances, and mental troubles immediately affect the physical condition. Both mental and physical problems are two different manifestations arising from the same root: a disorderly way of life, including the habitual practice of improper diet, and a lack of balance in mental and physical activities.

It has been traditionally known that each major organ in the body is connected with mental, emotional, and spiritual manifestations (see Figure 51). These manifestations have been understood as progressive developments, taking place according to the five transformative stages of interaction between centrifugal (yin) and centripetal (yang) tendencies:

- Healthy conditions of the liver and gallbladder are connected with patience and endurance, while unhealthy conditions produce short temper and anger.
- Healthy conditions of the heart and small intestine are connected with gentleness, tranquility, intuitive comprehension, spiritual oneness,

Figure 51. Five Stages of Physical and Mental Transformation

In Sickness:

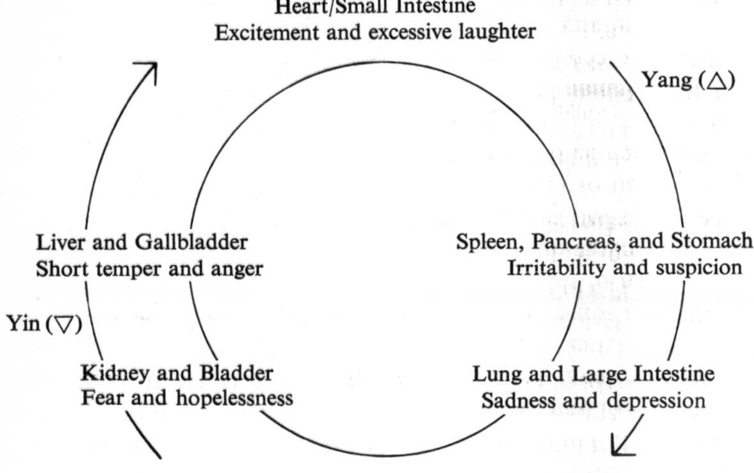

In Health:

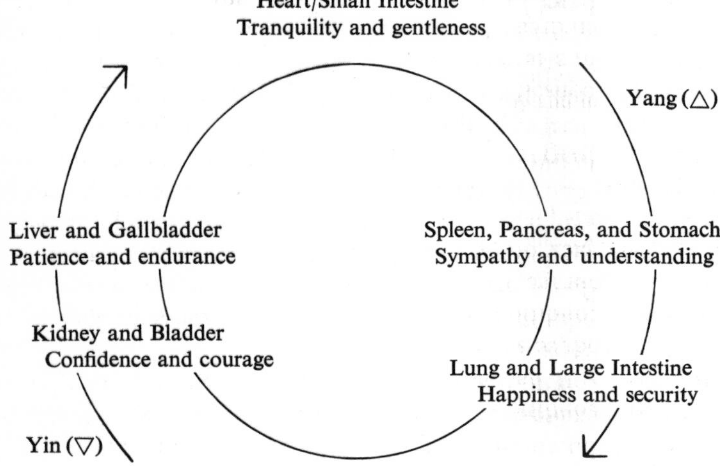

and a merry, humorous expression, while unhealthy conditions produce separateness, excitement, and excessive laughter.

• Healthy conditions of the spleen, pancreas, and stomach are connected with sympathy, wisdom, consideration, and understanding, while unhealthy conditions produce irritability, skepticism, criticism, and worry.

• Healthy conditions of the lungs and large intestine are connected with a feeling of happiness, security, and wholeness, while unhealthy conditions produce sadness, depression, and melancholy.

• Healthy conditions of the kidneys and bladder are connected with confidence, courage, and inspiration, while their unhealthy conditions produce fear, lack of self-esteem, and hopelessness.

Understanding Dreams

Often we are conscious of the kinds of dreams we see at night, and we remember them after we awake. As we saw earlier, there is a direct connection between dreaming at night and the realization of our life's dream during the day. Food and its vibration create our dreams. If our food changes, our dreams also will change.

Dreams at night can generally be classified into five different categories:

Nightmares: Dreams of violence, murder, suffering, stabbing, blood, and monsters fall in this category. Such dreams result from the intake of large amounts of animal food, especially beef, pork, and other mammals' meat, but also from excessive fish and seafood, especially red-meat and other fatty varieties. The liver and gallbladder, heart and small intestine, are affected to some degree by the heavy intake of animal food, leading to the creation of these type of images. Dreams of being chased, killed, or attacked reflect disorders in the kidneys and stomach, arising from such things as too much salty food, eggs, and cheese, usually accompanied by sugar or other strong sweetener. In about two weeks, frightening images such as these generally disappear on the macrobiotic diet.

Dreams of Human Events: Dreams of meeting with people, social events, parties, ceremonies and festivities, arguments and quarrels, and other human affairs come under this heading. These dreams result from the intake of large amounts of fat and oils which may come from either animal or vegetable sources. In this case, the kidneys, bladder, spleen, pancreas, and stomach are more affected.

Dreams of Excitement and Destruction: Images of fire (such as the house burning), earthquakes, war, and many other kinds of natural and social excitement form a third category. These dreams result from the intake of large amounts of hot spices, aromatic stimulant seasonings and beverages, including alcohol and cola; also excessive intake of baked and burned food. In this case, the liver, gallbladder, spleen, pancreas, and stomach are more affected.

Dreams such as falling from high places follow the excessive eating of tree fruits or juices which cause the heart to beat irregularly. Dreams of drowning or struggling are usually proceeded by too much liquid (especially just before sleeping) or salty foods that retain liquid; the brain cells become watery and these images come out, especially when the humidity is high. Dreams of flying often follow consumption of chicken or wild game; roasted seeds; or animal food accompanied by honey, spices, sugar or other strong yin. Dandelion, some species of mushrooms, and other plants that reproduce by wind-borne seeds or spores can also give rise to this type of dream. Dreams of sexual indulgence are generally caused by the intake of excessive amounts of protein and fat, as well as oily and greasy foods of all kind.

Fragmented Dreams: Floating, misty, disconnected dreams that are easily forgotten and that make us tired upon waking make up this group of dreams. These dreams result from overeating in general or the intake of excessive amounts of sugar and other sweets, beer and other milder alcoholic beverages, excessive volume of liquid, fruit, fruit juices, and, often, drugs and medications. In this case, the lungs, large intestines, kidneys, and bladder are more affected. Repetitious dreams are caused by eating the same way day after day. These are easily ended by more variety in food selection and cooking.

Dreams of Natural Scenes: Natural scenery, including celestial phenomena such as the sun, moon, and stars, wind, rain, snow, mountains, forests, rivers, and oceans, comprise the last category of dreams. These dreams result from the intake of beans and vegetables, excessively imbalanced in proportion to principal food, whole cereal grains; and also from excessive salad, fruits, and liquid. In this case, the lungs, large intestine, heart, and small intestine are more affected.

When we dream at night, we are seeing our surroundings and interpreting them into impressions through the same cerebral activity and nervous functions that are taking place while we are awake. If our brains and nervous functions are disordered, our dreams will also be disordered. To experience life clearly and interpret our surroundings properly, without personal distortion or delusion, we must learn to lead a more natural way of life. Proper eating will eventually enable us to dream true dreams —beyond space and time—both when we are awake and when we are asleep.

The Progressive Development of Mental Disorders

When our dietary practice and our general way of life are not in accord with the change of natural conditions, we begin to develop mental disorders as our physical orientation becomes disordered. Generally, an overly yang mentality tries to override other people, while an overly yin mentality rejects other people. Mental disorders develop gradually in seven progressive stages, as the chaotic way of life continues:

Yin Mental Disorders: Overconsumption of sugar and other sweeteners, fruits, fruit juice, chemicals, most medications, drugs, alcohol, hot spices, ice cream, some vegetables of tropical and semitropical origin, excessive liquid, and other strong yin substances produce: 1) General mental fatigue, which manifests as complaining and as gradual loss of clear thinking and behavior. 2) Feelings of melancholy, gradual loss of ambition, and self-confidence; the beginning of forgetfulness and vague memory. 3) Emotional irritability and fear, prevailing depression; a defensive attitude. 4) Suspicion and skepticism, misconceptions and misinterpretations, general attitude of retreating from life. 5) Discrimination and prejudice based upon an inferiority complex. 6) Loss of self-discipline; chaos in thinking and attitude; schizophrenic symptoms. 7) Yin arrogance characterized by total inability to adapt to the environment and the creation of a world of fantasy and illusion.

Yang Mental Disorders: Overconsumption of meat, eggs, poultry, cheese and other hard dairy food, other animal quality food, salt, baked and burned food, and other extreme yang substances, as well as insufficient liquid intake, produce: 1) General mental fatigue, which manifests as frequent changing of the mind and gradual loss of steadiness in mind and attitude. 2) Beginning of rigidity, gradually developing into stubbornness and insistent attention to trivial matters. 3) Excitability, short temper, prevailing discontent, and an offensive attitude. 4) Conceptualization, leading to adherence to various "isms" and delusional beliefs.

5) Discrimination and prejudice against others based upon a superiority complex. 6) Exclusive indoctrination, egocentric thinking and attitude, and paranoid symptoms. 7) Yang arrogance characterized by total inability to accept others and self-righteous attempts to control or coerce others.

In modern society, the overwhelming majority of people fall in one or more of the above categories of yin or yang mental disorders. Modern civilization itself can be viewed as an enormous mental health clinic, with hundreds of millions of people who are mentally disordered. Political, legal, and economic systems and many other social systems in modern society are contributing to the accelerated development of mental illness by perpetuating delusional belief systems, as well as regulating people who have chaotic attitudes arising from mental imbalance. Most of modern education especially is serving both functions, alienating us from the natural order of our environment, separating us from the memory of our common origin and destiny, and dividing us from each other in building a more peaceful world.

For humanity to recover from present-day disorders—physical, mental, and spiritual—we need a more comprehensive approach to life, including a reorientation of our civilization as a whole, a change to proper dietary practices, and deep self-reflection. Otherwise, personal health may be achieved, but the human family as a whole will continue to suffer and eventually cease to exist through biological and social extinction.

To sum up, the process of healing involves four steps: 1) a gradual transition to the new way of eating and living over a period of about two to three months; 2) adjustment to the macrobiotic diet and way of life or dissolving a particular disorder in the case of illness, usually over a period of three to four months as the blood quality changes and continuing for a year or more depending on the individual case as the digestive, circulatory, and nervous systems begin to improve; 3) widening of the diet as general health returns and continued daily practice of the standard macrobiotic way of eating and a more natural lifestyle to accomplish and secure a happy, healthy, peaceful life, usually for a period of about seven years as all the cells, tissues, and organs of the body change in quality; and 4) evolution to a free, unconscious diet and lifestyle bound by no "should's," "have to's, and "ought's," arising naturally and automatically after about seven to ten years.

7. Medical and Scientific Studies

"If you drink very much from a bottle marked 'poison,' it is almost certain to disagree with you, sooner or later."

—Lewis Carroll
Alice in Wonderland

"The doctor of the future will give no medicines but will interest his or her patients in the care of the human frame, in diets and in the cause and prevention of diseases."

—Thomas Edison

This chapter summarizes some of the major medical, nutritional, anthropological, agricultural, and sociological studies, past and present, related to macrobiotics and the development of a more healthy, happy, and peaceful way of life. Sources are provided at the end of each item, and specific foods or other factors involved are noted in parentheses for easy reference.

Traditional Dietary Sources

• *The Yellow Emperor's Classic of Internal Medicine*, dating in written form to about the third century B.C., discusses the application of yin and yang to treating sickness and recommends a balanced diet to prevent and relieve serious disease. The text states that in former days people treated disease "by cereal soups to be drunk for ten days" but that medicine had degenerated and now people treated illness with herbs, acupuncture, and moxibustion. Source: *A Complete Translation of Nei Ching and Nan Ching*, translated by Dr. Henry C. Lu (Vancouver: The Academy of Oriental Heritage, 1978.) (Brown Rice and Millet, Yin and Yang)

• In the fifth Century B.C., Hippocrates, the Father of Western medicine, taught a natural healing method emphasizing environmental and dietary factors. He especially recommended barley and wheat and supplemented dietary adjustments with simple, safe compresses made of grains, vegetables, and herbs which could be prepared at home. "I know too that the body is affected differently by bread according to the manner in which it is prepared. It differs according as it is made from pure flour or meal with bran, whether it is prepared from winnowed or unwinnowed wheat, whether it is mixed with much water or little, whether well mixed or poorly mixed, overbaked or underbaked, and countless other points besides. The same is true of the preparation of barley meal. The influence of each process is considerable and each has a totally different effect from another. How can anyone who has not considered such matters and come to understand them possibly know anything of the diseases that afflict mankind? Each one of the substances of a man's diet acts upon his body and changes it in some way and upon these changes his whole life depends . . ." Source: Hippocrates, "Tradition in Medicine," *Hippocratic Writings*, G. E. R. Lloyd, editor, J. Chadwick and W. N. Mann, translators (New York: Penguin Books, 1978). (Wheat, Barley)

• During the Babylonian Captivity, King Nebuchadnezzar commanded several of the most gifted young men of Israel to be brought to court to enter the royal service. The king instructed Malasar, the master of his household, to feed Daniel and his three companions the best meat and wine from the royal table. The Israelites, however, refused the rich food and instead asked for the simple food they were used to. The steward replied that he would lose his head if the king saw Daniel and his friends undernourished in comparison to the young Babylonians their age also in training for royal service. Daniel replied: "Try, I beseech thee, thy servants for ten days, and let pulse [whole grains, lentils, seeds] be given us to eat, and water to drink. And look upon our faces, and the faces of the children that eat of the king's meat: and as thou shalt see, deal with thy servants. And when he had heard these words, he tried them for ten days. And after ten days their faces appeared fairer and fatter than all the children that ate of the king's meat. So Malasar took their portions, and the wine that they should drink: and he gave them pulse. And to these children God gave knowledge and understanding in every book, and wisdom: but to Daniel the understanding also of all visions and dreams." Source: The Book of Daniel (Old Testament) 1: 8–17. (Pulses, Grains and Vegetables)

• In 1558 Venetian-born architect and counselor Louis Cornaro wrote an essay on health and diet describing how he suffered from a terminal stomach disorder in middle-age which he overcame by adopting a grain-based diet and avoiding certain kinds of animal food, raw salads, fruit, pastries, and sweets. Stating that we cannot partake of a "more natural food" than plain dark bread, Cornaro lived to age 102 and his book became one of the most influential books on health and diet during the Renaissance. Source: Louis Cornaro, *The Art of Living Long* (Milwaukee: William F. Butler, 1935). (Whole Grain Bread, Animal Food, Sweets)

• In 1713 Japanese physician Ekiken Kaibara recommended balanced diet to protect against chronic disease. "A person should prefer light, simple meals. One must not eat a lot of heavy, greasy, rich food. One should also avoid uncooked, chilled, or hard food. . . . Of everything one eats and drinks, the most important thing is rice, which must be eaten in ample amounts to ensure proper nutrition. . . . Bean paste has a soft quality and is good for the stomach and intestines." Source: Ekiken Kaibara, *Yōjōkun: Japanese Secret of Good Health* (Tokyo: Tokuma Shoten, 1974). (Brown Rice, Miso)

• Christoph W. Hufeland, M.D., an 18th Century macrobiotic philosopher, professor of medicine, and physician to Goethe, recommended a simple grain and vegetable diet, warned of the health hazards of meat and sugar, and promoted breastfeeding, exercise, and self-healing. "The more a man follows Nature, and is obedient to her laws, the longer he will live; the further he deviates from these the shorter will be his existence . . . . The healing power of nature must, above all things, be supported from the beginning, because it is the principal means which lies in ourselves for rendering the causes of disease ineffectual. This may be done chiefly by not accustoming the body at first too much to artificial assistance; otherwise Nature will be so used that she will depend on foreign aid, and at length lose altogether the power of assisting herself." Source: Christoph Hufeland, M.D., *Macrobiotics or the Art of Prolonging Life*, (English translation, London: John Churchill, 1853). (Whole Grains and Vegetables, Breastfeeding)

• At the end of the 19th Century, Japanese physician and macrobiotic philosopher Sagen Ishizuka, M.D. published the results of many years' research and study, outlining a broad theory of human physiology, food, health, sickness and medicine based on the dynamic balance between sodium and potassium in the environment and diet. On the basis of his own work as a military doctor in China and general practitioner in Japan, as well as readings in anthropology, he concluded that whole cereal grains contained the ideal balance of nutrients and should form the foundation of the human diet, supplemented with beans, vegetables, seeds and nuts, and a small amount of fish or game depending on the climate, region, and season of the year. Sources: Sagen Ishizuka, *Kagakuteki Shoku-Yō* ("A Chemical Nutritional Theory of Long Life"), 1897 (Tokyo: Nippon C.I., 1975), and *Shokumotsu Yōjōhō: Ichimei Kagakuteki Shoku-Yō Tai Shin Ron* ("A Method for Nourishing Life Through Food: A Unique Chemical Food-Nourishment Theory of Body and Mind"), 1898 (Tokyo: Nippon C.I., 1974). (Whole Grains, Sodium and Potassium)

Modern Nutritional Studies

• From 1904 to 1911 British surgeon Robert McCarrison traveled in the Hunza, a remote Himalayan kingdom in the then Northwest Territory of India. There he was astonished to discover a completely healthy culture in which the infectious and degenerative diseases of modern civilization, including colonial India, were unknown. "I never saw a case of asthenic dyspepsia, of gastric or duodenal ulcer, of appendicitis, of mucous colitis, or of cancer," he informed his medical colleagues. McCarrison theorized that the unusual health and longevity of the Hunza people were due primarily to their daily diet of whole-wheat chapatis, barley, and maize, supplemented by leafy green vegetables, beans and legumes, apricots, and a small amount of animal food. The Hunzas did not eat refined white rice, sugar, black tea, or spices as did most of the Indian population. In 1927 as Director of Nutritional Research in India, Dr. McCarrison discovered that rats fed the modern, refined diet of Bengal and Madras contracted cysts, abscesses, heart disease, and cancer of the stomach, while those fed the Hunza whole-grain diet remained healthy and free of all disease. Sources: Robert McCarrison, M.D., "Faulty Food in Relation to Gastro-Intestinal Disorder," *Journal of the American Medical Association* 78: 1–8, 1922 and G. T. Wrench, M.D., *The Wheel of Health* (London: O. W. Daniel, 1938). (Whole Grains and Vegetables, White Rice, Sugar, Refined Foods)

• During World War I, Mikkel Hindhede, M.D., Superintendent of the State Institute of Food Research, persuaded the Danish government to shift its agricultural priorities from raising grain for livestock to grain for direct human consumption. Accordingly, in the face of a foreign blockade, the Danes ate primarily barley, whole-rye bread, green vegetables, potatoes, milk, and some butter. In the nation's capital, the death rate from all causes, including cancer, fell 34 percent during 1917 to 1918. "It was a low protein experiment on a large scale, about 3 million subjects being available," Hindhede reported to his medical colleagues. ". . . People entered no complaints; there were no digestive troubles, but we are accustomed to the use of whole bread and we knew how to make such bread of good quality." Source: M. Hindhede, "The Effects of Food Restriction During War on Mortality in Copenhagen," *Journal of the American Medical Association* 74: 381–82, 1920. (Whole Grains and Vegetables, Animal Food, Protein)

• In 1913, Yukikazu Sakurazawa, later known as George Ohsawa, cured himself of terminal tuberculosis after reading a book on health and diet by Sagen Ishizuka, the founder of macrobiotics in Japan. Over the next fifty years, Ohsawa devoted his life to spreading macrobiotics and guiding thousands of people to health and happiness. Among the many medical and scientific experiments he conducted, in 1941 he oversaw the treatment of twenty-three sick and wounded soldiers at a military recuperation center in Tokyo. All medications were stopped, and the soldiers were fed brown rice and vegetables. Wounds and infections were treated with salt water only. After one month, all the men had made progress physically and their morale was higher. Source: Yukikazu Sakurazawa, *Hitotsu no Hōkoku: Aru Byōin ni okeru Jikken no Hōkoku* ("A Report: A Report of a Hospital Experiment") 1941 (Tokyo: Nippon C.I., 1976). (Brown Rice, Vegetables, Salt)

• During World War II, rates of cancer, heart disease, and other degenerative illnesses declined as a result of wartime restrictions on articles in the modern diet. For example, in England and Wales, breast cancer mortality markedly fell as consumption of sugar, meat, and fat declined and consumption of grains and vegetables increased. By 1954, consumption of these foodstuffs returned to prewar levels, and breast cancer levels eventually climbed to previous levels as well. Source: D. M. Ingram, "Trends in Diet and Breast Cancer Mortality in England and Wales, 1928–1977," *Nutrition and Cancer* 3 (2): 75–80, 1982. (Grains and Vegetables, Animal Food)

• For many years dental surgeon Weston Price performed field work among the Indians of North America, the Eskimo, the Polynesians, and the Australian Aborigines and reported no trace of cancer, heart disease, and other degenerative illnesses among those cultures and communities following traditional ways of eating. He noted that the diseases of modern civilization appeared only following the introduction of white flour, white rice, sugar, canned food, and other articles of modern diet. Source: Weston Price, D.D.S., *Nutrition and Physical Degeneration* (Santa Monica: Price-Pottenger Nutritional Foundation, 1945). (Whole Foods, Refined Food)

• In 1965 investigators at Johns Hopkins School of Medicine first observed that 15 percent of all whites and 70 percent of all blacks tested were unable to digest lactose, the sugar in milk. Since then it was found that the vast majority of the world's population is lactose intolerant, or allergic to dairy foods, except for mother's milk. Summing up a growing body of evidence, a medical doctor concluded, "The drinking of cow milk has been linked to iron-deficiency anemia in infants and children; it has been named as the cause of cramps and diarrhea in much of the world's population, and the cause of multiple forms of allergy as well; and the possibility has been raised that it may play a central role in the origins of atherosclerosis and heart attacks." Source: Frank A. Oski, M.D., and John D. Bell, *Don't Drink Your Milk* (Wyden Books, 1977). (Milk, Dairy)

• In 1975 nutritionists at the University of Rhode Island tested fifty young adults eating macrobiotically in the Boston area and found that they fell within the normal range for weight, skinfold thickness, and other anthropometric values and that foods common to their dietary practice met all nutritional requirements, though in some cases nutrient intakes were below the norm. The researchers noted that calcium and energy intakes for the ten macrobiotic children examined were low; however, subsequent medical studies have shown that animal protein inhibits the absorption of calcium and thus modern society's calcium norms are probably too high. Source: P. T. Brown and J. G. Bergan, Ph.D., "The Dietary Status of 'New' Vegetarians," *Journal of The American Dietetic Association* 67: 455–59. (Calcium, Protein)

• In 1977 a study of seventy-eight former U.S. Navy prisoners of war in Vietnam showed that they had less endocrine, nutritional, and metabolic diseases, as well as less circulatory, nervous system, genito-urinary, and musculoskeletal diseases, than other Navy pilots. The researchers cited the Vietnamese diet—high in rice and vegetables and low in dietary cholesterol and fat—as a major factor in their better physical health. "In contrast to the life of the POWs during confinement, control group members usually had access to an abundant diet—high in animal fat—to tobacco, to alcohol, and experienced the stresses of their jobs where only excellent performance was rewarded by promotions." Source: John A. Plag, Ph.D., "American POWs from Vietnam: Follow-Up Studies of the Subsequent Health and Adjustment of the Men and Their Families" (San Diego: Naval Health Research Center, 1977). (Rice, Animal Food)

• In 1980 researchers at the University of Rhode Island studied seventy-six macrobiotic people and reported they generally met currently acceptable medical and nutritional guidelines, including mean values for hemoglobin, hematocrit, serum iron, and transferrin saturation, serum ascorbic acid, vitamin A, beta-carotene, riboflavin, vitamin B_{12}, and folate. Source: J. G. Bergan and P. T. Brown, "Nutritional Status of 'New' Vegetarians," *Journal of The American Dietetic Association* 76: 151–55. (Blood Quality, Vitamin B_{12})

• In 1984 a Congressional Subcommittee, chaired by Congressman Claude Pepper, investigating holistic health care practices, concluded that the "macrobiotic diet appears to be nutritionally adequate. . . . The diet would also be consistent with the recently released dietary guidelines of the National Academy of Sciences and the American Cancer Society in regard to possible reduction of cancer risks." Source: *A Report by the Chairman of the Subcommittee on Health and Long-Term Care of the Select Committee on Aging*, House of Representatives, May 31, 1984, p. 67. (Cancer)

• In 1985 a physician at Mass General Hospital in Boston recommended that her colleagues educate themselves about common-sense models of health and disease, including macrobiotics. "The macrobiotic literature . . . contains a clearly enunciated set of principles concerning the biology of disease. Health, in accordance with traditional Chinese medicine, is viewed as the result of maintaining a dynamic balance between yin and yang in daily life." Source: Muriel R. Gillick, M.D., "Common-Sense Models of Health and Disease," *New England Journal of Medicine*, 313: 700–03. (Yin and Yang)

Infant and Childhood Nutrition

• A 1968 study showed that only 11 percent of American mothers attempted to breastfeed their children, and of these, over two-thirds gave up within 30 to 40 days. Mother's milk contains many antibodies that resist the growth of undesirable bacteria and viruses, protecting against a wide variety of childhood illnesses including rickettsia (which can cause Rocky Mountain spotted fever and typhus), salmonella, polio, influenza, intestinal infections, strep infections, staph infections, and others. Source: D. B. and E. F. P. Jeliffe, ed., "The Uniqueness of Human Milk," *American Journal of Clinical Nutrition* (August 1971). (Breastfeeding, Milk)

• In a 1977 study of vegetarian preschool children, researchers at New England Medical Center Hospital in Boston found that the growth of macrobiotic youngsters did not significantly differ from those of nonmacrobiotics before age two. After age two, macrobiotic children tended to put on weight more quickly than the children brought up on yoga diets, Seventh-Day Adventist diets, or other vegetarian regimes. Nearly all the children had been breastfed, and it was found that macrobiotics who had been weaned did not differ in caloric intake from nonmacrobiotics. Source: M. W. Shull, M. Ed., et al., "Velocities of Growth in Vegetarian Preschool Children," *Pediatrics* 60: 410–17. (Growth and Development, Breastfeeding)

• In a 1978 study of 119 vegetarian and macrobiotic children with a mean age of about two years, Boston nutritionists reported they were generally smaller, leaner, and lighter than nonvegetarian children. Despite varying degrees of avoidance of meat and other animal foods, consumption of protein, carbohydrate, and fat in the diets of those children age one year or older who were no longer being breastfed fell within normal levels. Source: J. T. Dwyer et al., "Preschoolers on Alternate Life-Style Diets," *Journal of The American Dietetic Association* 72: 264–70. (Growth and Development, Breastfeeding)

• In a 1980 study of mental development and I.Q., macrobiotic and vegetarian children were significantly brighter and more intelligent than ordinary youngsters their age. The test group consisted of twenty-eight children in the Boston area between two and eight years old, with a mean age of four years old. The mean I.Q. was 116 for the group as a whole, or 16 percent above average. The children's mean mental age was found to exceed their mean chronologic age by approximately a year. The macrobiotic children's I.Q.'s and mental ages were higher than the other vegetarians, though not statistically significant. "In the judgments of both the pediatrician and psychologic technician, the children as a group were bright," the researchers stated. "It was puzzling, however, that the results of developmental testing were so much superior to those which would be expected among an unselected group of children." Source: T. Dwyer et al., "Mental Age and I.Q. of Predominantly Vegetarian Children," *Journal of The American Dietetic Association* 76: 142–47. (I.Q., Mental Age)

• A British nutritionist found that a macrobiotic day-care center in London not only "supported normal growth" in nursery schoolchildren but could be used as a model to implement national dietary guidelines. Comparing the nutritional adequacy of macrobiotic meals provided preschool children by the Community Health Foundation with ordinary meals at a nursery in Notting Hill, the investigator found that the macrobiotic food consisting of brown rice and other whole grains, miso soup, vegetables, beans, sea vegetables, and other supplemental foods met current U.K.-R.D.I. dietary, energy, and nutrient standards and that the children's anthropometric measurements including weight, height, and skinfold thicknesses were normal. In contrast, the ordinary nursery school diet was high in dairy food, lard, and other saturated fats that have been associated with the development of atherosclerosis beginning in childhood. "The diet composition of children in Group I [standard nursery] could be made more desirable by a reduction in the amount of full-cream milk and meat and an increase in the amount of cereal foods. . . ," the researcher concluded. "The total diet of Group II [macrobiotic nursery] met the U.S. Dietary Goals for fat, sugar, and carbohydrate content, although the home diets of the children were similar to that of the general population. This illustrates the power and potential of nursery meals to contribute to the adoption of a nutritionally sound and beneficial national diet." Source: Valerie Ventura, "A Comparative Study of the Meals Provided for Pre-School Children by Two Day Nurseries" (London: Department of Nutrition, Queen Elizabeth College, 1980). (Whole Grains and Vegetables, Milk, Fat)

Heart Disease

• In 1972 Japanese researchers reported that wakame, a common sea vegetable eaten in Asia, suppressed the reabsorption of cholesterol in the liver and intestine in laboratory experiments. Other studies showed that hijiki, another sea vegetable, and shiitake mushroom also lowered serum cholesterol and improved fat metabolism. Source: N. Iritani and S. Nogi, "Effects of Spinach and Wakame on Cholesterol Turnover in the Rat," *Atherosclerosis* 15: 87–92. (Sea Vegetables, Shiitake Mushrooms)

• In 1974 Harvard Medical School researchers reported a direct relation between blood pressure levels and articles of diet, especially the consumption of animal food. From Nov. 1972 through Feb. 1973, 210 men and women from many different backgrounds eating macrobiotically in Boston study houses were subjected to a wide range of medical tests. Overall, the researchers found that the men had mean systolic blood pressures of 109.7 mm Hg and diastolic pressures of 60.9. The women had slightly lower readings, 100.9 and 58.2 respectively. Both of these measurements fell well within the normal blood pressure category and approached the systolic level of 100 under which Framingham Heart Study researchers theorized there would develop virtually no coronary heart disease. Meanwhile, those in the group who ate fish or seafood regularly as a supplement to grains and vegetables had significantly higher blood pressure than those who ate no animal food. The addition of sea salt at the table was not associated with changes in blood pressure in those examined, and those individuals who abstained from coffee or cigarette smoking had lower systolic but not diastolic pressures. Married persons also had lower systolic pressures, as did those who meditated. The unexpectedly low blood pressure of the macrobiotic group was considered all the more remarkable because of the relatively short time the participants in the study had been on the new diet. "The generally short duration (less than 2 years) of adherence in half suggests that dietary effects on BP [blood pressure] become established relatively earlier. Perhaps of greater interest is that the declared intake of food from animal sources is significantly associated with higher pressures in individuals and there is significant clustering of systolic BP among the members of communal households, a phenomenon hitherto observed only in relation to first-degree relatives of an individual and with varying degrees of association for spouses." The implications of these findings for a pluralistic society composed of many different racial and ethnic backgrounds were far-reaching. Source: F. M. Sacks, Bernard Rosner, and Edward H. Kass, "Blood Pressure in Vegetarians," *American Journal of Epidemiology* 100: 390–98. (Whole Grains, Fish, Salt, Meditation)

• In 1975 Harvard Medical School researchers reported that Boston-area macrobiotic people eating a diet of whole grains, beans, fresh vegetables, sea vegetables, and fermented soy products had significantly lower cholesterol and triglyceride levels and lower blood pressure than a control group from the Framingham Heart Study eating the standard American diet of meat, sugar, dairy foods, potatoes and tomatoes, and highly processed, chemicalized foods. The average serum cholesterol in the macrobiotic group was 126 milligrams per deciliter versus 184 for controls. Analysis further showed that consumption of dairy foods and eggs significantly raised cholesterol and fat levels in those eating macrobiotically, although fish was consumed as much as dairy and eggs combined. "The low plasma lipid levels in the vegetarians," the researchers concluded, "resemble those reported for populations in nonindustrialized societies" where heart disease, cancer, and other degenerative illnesses are uncommon. Source: F. M. Sacks et al., "Plasma Lipids and Lipoproteins in Vegetarians and Controls," *New England Journal of Medicine* 292: 1148–51. (Whole Grains, Dairy Food, Eggs)

• In 1978 an internationally noted heart disease and cancer researcher concluded that animal-quality protein is a major factor in the development of heart disease. "Epidemiological data derived from human populations show that the positive correlation between animal protein in the diet and mortality from coronary heart disease is at least as strong as that between dietary fat and heart disease. . . . The trend toward increasing mortality from coronary heart disease in the United States during this century coincides with a doubling in the ratio of animal protein to vegetable protein in the diet. . . ." Source: K. K. Carroll, "Dietary Protein in Relation to Plasma Cholesterol Levels and Atherosclerosis," *Nutrition Reviews* 36: 1–5. (Protein)

• In a 1981 study of twenty-one macrobiotic persons, Harvard Medical School researchers reported that the addition of 250 grams of beef per day for four weeks to their regular diet of whole grains and vegetables raised serum cholesterol levels 19 percent. Systolic blood pressure also rose significantly. After returning to a low-fat diet, cholesterol and blood pressure values returned to previous levels. Source: F. M. Sacks et al., "Effects of Ingestion of Meat on Plasma Cholesterol of Vegetarians," *Journal of the American Medical Association* 246: 640–44. (Whole Grains and Vegetables, Beef)

• Dr. William Castelli, director of the Framingham Heart Study, the nation's oldest and largest cardiovascular research project, and a participant in research on macrobiotic people at Harvard Medical School, noted that macrobiotic people have healthier hearts and circulatory systems than conditioned athletes, "The macrobiotic vegetarians we studied, incidentally, had a [total cholesterol to HDL cholesterol] ratio of 2.5. Boston marathon runners were at 3.4. These are ratios at which we rarely, if ever, see coronary heart disease." Dr. Castelli also contrasted the healthfulness of the macrobiotic food program at Boston's Shattuck Hospital with ordinary hospital food. "Dr. Robert Wissler, the professor and chairman of the Department of Pathology of the University of Chicago fed the usual house diet of the Billings Hospital (the University of Chicago Medical School's major university hospital) to his baboons and they all lost their legs from atherosclerosis. How our patients are supposed to get well from this is beyond my imagination." Sources: William P. Castelli, M.D., "Lessons from the Framingham Heart Study," in Michio Kushi, *Cancer and Heart Disease* (Tokyo • New York: Japan Publications, 1982), pp. 101–05 and Michio Kushi with Ed Esko, Tom Igelhart and Eric Zutrau, *Crime and Diet* (Tokyo • New York: Japan Publications, 1987). (Grains and Vegetables, Diet and Exercise)

• In 1982 scientists at the University of Western Ontario reported that the addition of soy protein in a person's diet could reduce serum cholesterol levels irrespective of other dietary considerations. In addition to animal studies, the researchers compared human volunteers who drank either cow's milk or soy milk and reported that "both cholesterol and triglyceride values dropped substantially during the soy period." Source: *Journal of the American Medical Association* 247: 3045–46. (Soyfoods)

• In 1983, Dutch heart researchers reported that macrobiotic men and boys had the most ideal cholesterol and other blood values in studies of groups of nonvegetarian, semi-lactovegetarian, lactovegetarian, and macrobiotic men aged thirty to thirty-nine years and boys aged six to eleven years old. The report was funded by the Netherlands Heart Foundation. Source: J. T. Knuiman and C. E. West, "The Concentration of Cholesterol in Serum and in Various Serum Lipoproteins in Macrobiotic, Vegetarian, and Non-vegetarian Men and Boys," *Atherosclerosis* 43: 71–82. (Blood Quality)

• In 1983, researchers at the Academic Hospital of the Ghent University in Belgium evaluated the blood values of twenty men working at Lima Natural Foods Factory who had an average age of thirty-six and had been macrobiotic for about eight years. According to the tests, all the men were very healthy. Their blood pressure and body weights were low, their hormone levels favorable, and they had normal values for proteins, vitamins, and minerals. Overall, however, their cholesterol values were superior to ordinary people. J. P. Deslypere, M.D., one of the researchers, concluded, "[In] the field of cardiovascular and cancer risk factors this kind of blood is very favorable. It's ideal, we couldn't do better, that's what we're dreaming of. It's really fantastic, like children, whose blood vessels are still completely open and whole. This is a very important matter, deserving our full attention." Source: Rik Vermuyten, *MacroMuse* (Fall/Metal 1984), p. 39. (Blood Quality)

• In 1984, physicians at Columbia Presbyterian Hospital in New York City reported that patients with angina pectoris, a form of coronary heart disease, showed significantly improved blood pressure values and lowered coronary risk factors after ten weeks on a macrobiotic diet and treatment with biofeedback. The chief researcher, Dr. Kenneth Greenspan of the hospital's Laboratory and Center for Stress Related Disorders, reported that cholesterol levels dropped from an average 300 to 220, levels of blood pressure also dropped, patients could walk about 20 percent farther in stress tests, and three patients with severe angina showed no symptoms at the end of the study. The participants, mostly businessmen, and their wives learned how to cook and ate together at the Natural Gourmet Cookery School under the direction of longtime macrobiotic and natural foods cook Annemarie Colbin. Dr. Greenspan reported that there was "tremendous enthusiasm and adherence" to the new diet. The study was funded and monitored by the New York Cardiac Center. Source: Michio Kushi and Alex Jack, *Diet for a Strong Heart*

(New York: St. Martin's Press, 1985), p. 131. (Whole Grains and Vegetables, Exercise, Stress)

• In 1984 Harvard researchers reported that the amount of vegetable-quality protein consumed in the diet did not significantly affect blood pressure levels. In a six-week experiment, eighteen macrobiotic students and associates of the Kushi Institute were divided into two groups that received, respectively, a high protein supplement and a low protein control supplement in opposite sequence of 6-week periods. The high protein supplement consisted of a patty weighing 58 grams of a 60 : 40 soy protein/wheat protein mixture, while the low protein supplement considered of a brown rice patty. No difference in blood pressure during the two periods was observed. Source: F. M. Sacks, M.D., P. G. Wood, and E. H. Kass, M.D., Ph.D., "Stability of Blood Pressure in Vegetarians Receiving Dietary Protein Supplements," *Hypertension* 6 (2): 199–201. (Protein, Brown Rice)

• In 1985 Harvard researchers presented results of an epidemiological study comparing diet and mortality from coronary heart disease among groups of men born and living in Ireland, men born in Ireland who had emigrated to Boston, and men born in the Boston area of Irish immigrants. In respect to blood pressure, they found that vegetable-quality foods may operate at least in part through reducing blood pressure and other factors to modify risk of coronary heart disease. Though only suggestive, these results tended to parallel several other more conclusive studies showing that eating a diet high in fiber, especially cereal grain fiber, decreases both systolic and diastolic blood pressure. "While risk of coronary heart disease has been reported to be related to intake of dietary lipids, an equally consistent finding has been the [inverse] relationship with starch and complex carbohydrates." Source: Lawrence Kushi, Sc. D. et al., "Diet and 20-Year Mortality from Coronary Heart Disease: The Ireland-Boston Diet-Heart Study," *New England Journal of Medicine* 312: 811–18. (Fiber, Grains)

Cancer

• Looking back over four decades of medical work in French Equatorial Africa, Dr. Albert Schweitzer reported that he had never had any cancer cases in his hospital and that its occurrence among the African people was very rare. He attributed the rise of degenerative diseases to the importation of European foods including condensed milk, canned butter, meat and fish preserves, white bread, and especially refined salt.

"It is obvious to connect the fact of increase of cancer with the increased use of salt by the natives. In former years there was only available the little salt extracted from the ocean." Source: Albert Schweitzer, M.D., *Briefe aus dem Lambarenespital*, 1954. (Animal Food, Refined Food, Salt)

• In 1968 a major epidemiological study indicated that dietary habits and environmental influences are the chief determinants of the world's varying cancer rates and not genetic factors. Data showed that in the course of three generations, Japanese migrants in the United States contracted colon cancer at the same rates as the general American population. In contrast, the regular colon cancer rate in Japan remained about one fourth the American incidence. Source: W. Haenszel and M. Kurihara, "Studies of Japanese Migrants," *Journal of the National Cancer Institute* 40: 43–68. (Diet vs. Genetic Factors)

• In 1970 Japanese scientists at the National Cancer Center Research Institute reported that shiitake mushrooms had a strong anti-tumor effect. In experiments with mice, polysaccharide preparations from various natural sources, including the shiitake mushroom commonly available in Tokyo markets, markedly inhibited the growth of induced sarcomas resulting in "almost complete regression of tumors . . . with no sign of toxicity." Source: G. Chihara, et al., "Fractionation and Purification of the Polysaccharides with Marked Antitumor Activity, Especially Lentinan, from *Lentinus edodes* (Berk.) Sing. (An Edible Mushroom), *Cancer Research* 30: 2776–81. (Shiitake Mushrooms)

• In 1971 a Japanese cancer researcher reported that people who regularly ate tofu were at less risk for stomach cancer than those who did not. Source: T. Hirayama, "Epidemiology of Stomach Cancer," in T. Murakami (ed.), *Early Gastric Cancer. Gann Monograph on Cancer Research, 11* (Tokyo: University of Tokyo Press, pp. 3–19). (Tofu)

• In 1972 a Japanese scientist reported that leukemia in chickens could be reversed by feeding them a mixture of whole grains and salt. The experiment was conducted by Keiichi Morishita, M.D., technical chief for the Tokyo Red Cross Blood Center and vice president of the New Blood Association. Source: K. Morishita, M.D., *The Hidden Truth of Cancer* (San Francisco: George Ohsawa Macrobiotic Foundation, 1972). (Whole Grains, Salt)

• In 1974 Japanese scientists reported that several varieties of kombu and mojaban, common sea vegetables eaten in Asia and traditionally used as a decoction for cancer in Chinese herbal medicine, were effective in the treatment of tumors in laboratory experiments. In three of four samples tested, inhibition rates in mice with implanted sarcomas ranged from 89 to 95 percent. The researchers reported that "the tumor underwent complete regression in more than half of the mice of each treated group." Similar experiments on mice with leukemia showed promising results. Source: I. Yamamoto et al., "Antitumor Effect of Seaweeds," *Japanese Journal of Experimental Medicine* 44: 543–46. (Sea Vegetables)

• A 1975 study in the Caspian littoral region of Iran, an area of high esophageal cancer, associated this disease with lower intake of lentils and other pulses, cooked green vegetables, and other whole foods. Source: H. Hormozdiari et al., "Dietary Factors and Esophageal Cancer in the Caspian Littoral of Iran," *Cancer Research* 35: 3493–98. (Lentils, Vegetables)

• Persons who regularly eat cereal grains, pulses, vegetables, seeds, and nuts are less likely to get lymphoma or Hodgkin's disease than persons who do not usually eat these foods, according to a 1976 epidemiological survey based on World Health Organization data from sixteen countries. Source: A. S. Cunningham, "Lymphomas and Animal-Protein Consumption," *The Lancet* 2: 1184–86. (Whole Grains, Pulses, Vegetables, Seeds, Nuts)

• In 1977 an Indian cancer researcher concluded that thorough chewing seemed to lower the risk of cancer. "The proper chewing of meals ensuring that mucous-rich saliva mixed with the food seemed to be protective factors." Cancer also appeared to more prevalent in south India where white rice and considerably more fat, oil, and spices are used in cooking than in north India where whole-grain chapatis and thick dal made with lentils are the staple. Source: S. L. Malhotra, "Dietary Factors in a Study of Cancer Colon from Cancer Registry, with Special Reference to the Role of Saliva, Milk and Fermented Milk Products, and Vegetable Fibre," *Medical Hypotheses* 3: 122–26. (Chewing, Whole Grains, Lentils)

• In 1978 epidemiologists reported that cancer of the lung, breast, and colon increased two to three times among Japanese women between 1950 and 1975. During that period, milk consumption increased 15 times; meat, eggs, and poultry climbed 7.5 times; and rice consumption dropped 70 percent. In Okinawa, with the highest proportion of centenarians, longevity was associated with lowered sugar and salt intake and higher intake of protein and green-yellow vegetables. Source: Y. Kagawa, "Impact of Westernization on the Nutrition of Japan," *Preventive Medicine* 7: 205–17. (Animal Food, Rice, Sugar, Salt)

• In 1980 scientists reported that a diet high in soybeans reduced the incidence of breast cancer in laboratory experiments. The active ingredient in the soybeans was identified as protease inhibitors, also found in certain other beans and seeds. Source: W. Troll, "Blocking of Tumor Promotion by Protease Inhibitors," in J. H. Burchenal and H. F. Oettgen (eds.), *Cancer: Achievements, Challenges, and Prospects for the 1980s, Vol. 1*, (New York: Grune and Stratton, pp. 549–55). (Soyfoods, Seeds)

• In 1981 Japan's National Cancer Center reported that people who eat miso soup daily are 33 percent less likely to contract stomach cancer and have 19 percent less cancer at other sites than those who never eat miso soup. The thirteen-year study, involving about 265,000 men and women over forty, also found that those who never ate miso soup had a 43 percent higher death rate from coronary heart disease than those who consumed miso soup daily. Those who abstained from miso also had 29 percent more fatal strokes, 3.5 times more deaths resulting from high blood pressure, and higher mortality from all other causes. Source: T. Hirayama, "Relationship of Soybean Paste Soup Intake to Gastric Cancer Risk," *Nutrition and Cancer* 3: 223–33. (Miso Soup)

• A 1981 Chicago study found that regular consumption of foods containing carotene, a precursor to vitamin A, protected against lung cancer. Over a period of nineteen years, a group of 1,954 men at a Western Electric plant were monitored, and those who regularly consumed carrots, dark green lettuce, spinach, broccoli, kale, Chinese cabbage, peaches, apricots, and other carotene-rich foods had significantly lower lung cancer rates than controls. Source: R. B. Shekelle et al., "Dietary Vitamin A and Risk of Cancer in the Western Electric Study," *The Lancet* 2: 1185–90. (Carotene, Yellow and Dark Green Vegetables)

• Vegetarian women are less likely to develop breast cancer, researchers at New England Medical Center in Boston reported in 1981. The scientists found that vegetarian women process estrogen differently from other women and eliminate it more quickly from their body. The study involved forty-five pre- and postmenopausal women, about half of whom were vegetarian and half nonvegetarian. The women consumed about the same number of total calories. Although the vegetarian women took in only one third as much animal protein and animal fat, they excreted two to three times as much estrogen. High levels of estrogen have been associated with the development of breast cancer. "The difference in estrogen metabolism may explain the lower incidence of breast cancer in vegetarian women," the study concluded. Source: B. R. Goldin et al., "Effect of Diet on Excretion of Estrogens in Pre- and Postmenopausal Incidence of Breast Cancer in Vegetarian Women," *Cancer Research* 41: 3771–73. (Diet and Estrogen)

• A 1981 epidemiological study found that populations with a low risk of esophageal cancer in Africa and Asia consume more millet, cassava, yams, peanuts, and other foods high in fiber or starch than high-risk groups. Source: S. J. van Rensburg, "Epidemiologic and Dietary Evidence for a Specific Nutritional Predisposition to Esophageal Cancer," *Journal of the National Cancer Institute* 67: 243–51. (Millet, Fiber)

• In 1983, researchers at the Tulane School of Public Health and Tropical Medicine made plans to study the effectiveness of the macrobiotic diet on cancer patients in the New Orleans area. Source: Michio Kushi and Alex Jack, *The Cancer-Prevention Diet* (New York: St. Martin's Press, 1983), p. 121.

• In 1984, a team of researchers at medical schools and hospitals in Boston, headed up by Dr. Robert Lerman, director of Clinical Nutrition at University Hospital, announced plans to evaluate about 700 cancer patients who had seen Michio Kushi for dietary and way of life counseling and match them up with controls from the Eastern Cooperative Oncology Group tumor registry at the Dana-Farber Cancer Institute in Boston. Source: Michio Kushi and Alex Jack, *The Cancer-Prevention Diet* (New York: St. Martin's Press, revised edition, 1985), p. vii.

• In a 1984 experiment at the Harvard School of Public Health, laboratory animals fed a control diet with 5 percent Halies (kombu), a brown sea vegetable, developed induced mammary cancer later than animals not fed seaweed. "Seaweed has shown consistent antitumor activity in several *in vivo* animal tests," the researcher concluded. "In extrapolating these results to the Japanese population, seaweed may be an important factor in explaining the low rates of certain cancers in Japan. Breast cancer shows a 3-fold-lower rate among premenopausal Japanese women and a 9-fold-lower rate among postmenopausal women in Japan than reported for women in the United States. Since low levels of exposure to some toxic substances have been shown to be carcinogenic, then it may be that low levels of daily intake of food with antitumor properties may reduce cancer incidence." Source: J. Teas, M. L. Harbison, and R. S. Gelman. "Dietary Seaweed [Laminaria] and Mammary Carcinogenesis in Rats," *Cancer Research* 44: 2758–61. (Sea Vegetables)

• In 1985 the National Cancer Institute reported that radiation therapy and chemotherapy were ineffective and in some cases produced toxic side-effects as follow-ups to surgery in the treatment of cancer. "Except possibly in selected patients with cancer of the stomach, there has been no demonstrated improvement in the survival of patients with the 10 most common cancers when radiation therapy, chemotherapy, or both have been added to surgical resection." The ten most common cancers include lung, colorectum, breast, prostate, uterus, bladder, pancreas, stomach, skin, and kidney. Shortly after the report was published, the author, Dr.

Steven A. Rosenberg, the N.C.I.'s chief of surgery, operated on President Ronald Reagan's colon cancer and instead of chemotherapy or radiation treatment put him on a modified whole grain diet. Source: Steven A. Rosenberg, M.D., Ph.D., "Combined-Modality Therapy of Cancer," *New England Journal of Medicine* 312: 1512–14. (Radiation, Chemotherapy)

• In 1986, medical researchers reported that the war on cancer was being lost and that despite advances in diagnosis and treatment from 1950 to 1982 cancer incidence and mortality had steadily risen. Overall, between 1960 and 1982 the age-adjusted mortality rate increased 8.7 percent (unadjusted rise was 56 percent) and incidence increased 8.5 percent. "A shift in research emphasis, from research on treatment to research on prevention, seems necessary if substantial progress against cancer is to be forthcoming," the investigators concluded. Source: John C. Bailar III and Elaine M. Smith, "Progress Against Cancer," *New England Journal of Medicine* 314: 1226–32.

Radiation and Fallout

• In August 1945, at the time of the atomic bombing of Japan, Tatsuichiro Akizuki, M.D., was director of the Department of Internal Medicine at St. Francis's Hospital in Nagasaki. Most patients in the hospital, located one mile from the center of the blast, survived the initial effects of the bomb, but soon after came down with symptoms of radiation sickness from the fallout that had been released. Dr. Akizuki fed his staff and patients a strict macrobiotic diet of brown rice, miso and tamari soy sauce soup, wakame and other seaweed, Hokkaido pumpkin, and sea salt and prohibited the consumption of sugar and sweets. As a result, he saved everyone in his hospital, while many other survivors in the city perished from radiation sickness. Source: Tatsuichiro Akizuki, M.D., *Nagasaki 1945*, London: Quartet Books, 1981. (Brown Rice, Miso, Sea Vegetables, Salt)

• In 1964 scientists at the Gastro-Intestinal Research Laboratory at McGill University in Montreal, Canada, reported that a substance derived from the sea vegetable kelp could reduce by 50 to 80 percent the amount of radioactive strontium absorbed through the intestine. Stanley Skoryna, M.D. said that in animal experiments sodium alginate obtained from brown algae permitted calcium to be normally absorbed through the intestinal wall while binding most of the strontium. The sodium alginate and strontium were subsequently excreted from the body. The experiments were designed to devise a method to counteract the effects of nuclear fallout and radiation. Source: S. C. Skoryna et al., "Studies on Inhibition of Intestinal Absorption of Radioactive Strontium," *Canadian Medical Association Journal* 91: 285–88. (Sea Vegetables)

• In 1968 Canadian researchers reported that sea vegetables contained a polysaccharide substance that selectively bound radioactive strontium and helped eliminate it from the body. In laboratory experiments, sodium alginate prepared from kelp, kombu, and other brown seaweeds off the Atlantic and Pacific coasts was introduced along with strontium and calcium into rats. The reduction of radioactive particles in bone uptake, measured in the femur, reached as high as 80 percent, with little interference with calcium absorption. "The evaluation of biological activity of different marine algae is important because of their practical significance in preventing absorption of radioactive products of atomic fission as well as in their use as possible natural decontaminators." Source: Y. Tanaka et al., "Studies on Inhibition of Intestinal Absorption of Radio-Active Strontium," *Canadian Medical Association Journal* 99: 169–75. (Sea Vegetables)

Arthritis

• The regular consumption of tomatoes, potatoes, eggplants, and other solanaceous plants that originated in South America or other tropical regions of the world is believed to be a contributing factor in the loss of natural immunity in temperate climates and may lead to a wide range of sicknesses ranging from colds and flu to skin rashes and itches, loss of sexual vitality, polio, and others. Dr. Norman Childers, a professor of horticulture at Cook College in New Jersey who has worked with solanaceous plants all his life, reported that regular consumption of tomatoes, potatoes, and eggplants is a primary cause of arthritis. He noted that in arthritic patients symptoms of this potentially crippling disease go away usually in a period of several weeks to several months when they stop eating these foods. Source: Norman Childers, *The Nightshades and Health*, Somerville, N. J.: Horticultural Publications, 1977.

Diabetes

• In an Oregon study, six borderline diabetics were put on a macrobiotic diet for thirty days. Excluding the one obese subject, the researchers reported a significant drop in cholesterol levels from a mean of 140 to 110. The subjects were primarily lacto-ovo-vegetarians, accounting for their low cholesterol levels to begin with. A control group of ten macrobiotic subjects showed average cholesterol levels consistent with the Harvard Medical School findings in the mid-1970s. Source: Mark Mead, "In Search of the Sweet Life: A Dietary Approach to Diabetes Mellitus," Reed College Biology Thesis, in cooperation with the Oregon Health Sciences University, 1984. (Blood Quality)

AIDS

• In 1983 a group of men in New York City with AIDS (Acquired Immunity Deficiency Syndrome) began macrobiotics. They hoped to change their blood quality, recover their natural immunity, and survive this otherwise always fatal illness. In 1984 immunologists in New York and Boston began to monitor the blood samples and immune functions of ten men with Kaposi's sarcoma (a usual symptom of AIDS). Preliminary results indicated that most of the men were stabilizing on the diet. "Survival in these men who have received little or no medical treatment appears to compare very favorably with that of KS patients in general. We suggest that physicians and scientists can feel comfortable in allowing patients, particularly those with minimal disease, to go untreated as part of a larger [dietary] study or because non-treatment is the patient's choice." Source: "Patients with Kaposi Sarcoma Who Opt for No Treatment" (letter), *The Lancet*, 2: 223, July 27, 1985. (Blood Quality, Immune Functions)

• In 1986, AIDS researchers reported that patients with moderately intact immune systems seem to be responsive to macrobiotics and were stabilizing on the diet. Investigators from Boston University Medical School announced that T4 positive cells and lymphocyte numbers appeared to be increasing in the first two years after diagnosis in the majority of men with Kaposi's sarcoma who were macrobiotic and that average survival time—31 months—had already surpassed any previous AIDS group under study. Source: John Beldeka, Ph.D. and Elinor Levy, Ph.D., International AIDS Conference, Paris, France, June, 1986.

• In 1979, Frank Kern, assistant director at Tidewater Detention Center in Chesapeake, Virgina, a state facility for juvenile offenders, decided to initiate some dietary reforms in a macrobiotic direction. He arranged an experiment in which sugar was taken out of the meals and snacks of twenty-four inmates. The boys, aged twelve to eighteen, were jailed for offenses that ranged from disorderly conduct, larceny, and burglary to alcohol and narcotics violations. Coke machines were removed from the premises and fruit juice substituted in vending machines for soft drinks, while honey and other milder sweeteners were substituted for refined sugar. The three-month trial was designed as a double-blind case-control study so that neither the detention center personnel nor the inmates knew that they were being tested. At the end of the trial period, the regular staff records on inmates' behavior were checked against a control group of 34 youngsters who had been institutionalized previously. Researchers found that the youngsters on the modified diet exhibited a 45 percent lower incidence of formal disciplinary actions and antisocial behavior than the control group. Follow-up studies over the next year showed that after limiting sugar there was "an 82 percent reduction in assaults, 77 percent reduction in thefts, 65 percent reduction in horseplay, and 55 percent reduction in refusal to obey orders." The researchers also found that "the people most likely to show improvement were those who had committed violent acts on the outside." Source: Stephen S. Schoenthaler, Ph.D., "The Effect of Sugar on the Treatment and Control of Antisocial Behavior," *International Journal of Biosocial Research* 3, no. 1 (1982): pp. 1–9. (Sugar, Soft Drinks, Diet and Crime)

• In 1979 several inmates at Linho prison in Lisbon, Portugal, began eating macrobiotically and attending lectures on Oriental philosophy and medicine, shiatsu massage, and visual diagnosis by Chico Varatojo, a Kushi Institute graduate and teacher from Lisbon. Soon thirty prisoners had become macrobiotic, and prison officials allowed them to use a large kitchen where they cooked and ate together several times a week. Linho, a maximum security institution, housed Portugal's most dangerous criminals, including Antonio (To Zé) José Aréal, mastermind of a gang of armed robbers and kidnappers that had been the object of a nation-wide manhunt. As a result of attitude and behavioral changes on the macrobiotic diet, To Zé and most of the other prisoners attending classes received commutations and were released early. "The food can change people," stated Senhor Alfonso, a prison administrator. To Zé went on to study at the Kushi Institute in Boston and taught macrobiotics in New Bedford, Massachusetts, site of a large Portuguese speaking population, before returning to teach and help other prisoners in Portugal. Source: Meg Seaker, "Fighting Crime with Diet: Report from a Portuguese Prison," *East West Journal*, July, 1982, pp. 26–34. (Diet and Crime)

• In 1980, a macrobiotic lunch program was started at the Lemuel Shattuck Hospital in Boston for doctors, nurses, and staff. Overall response was favorable and improved noticeably after the macrobiotic food line was integrated with the regular cafeteria line. By the second year, half of the food served each day in the cafeteria was prepared macrobiotically. Regular attendance increased from about 60 to 120 to 200 persons each day. At lunch, from 70 to 90 percent of all meals served included at least one item from the macrobiotic menu. Source: Michio Kushi with Edward Esko,Tom Igelhart and Eric Zutrau, *Crime and Diet Psychology* (Tokyo • New York: Japan Publications, 1987).

• In 1982, Dr. Jonathan Lieff, Chief of Psychiatry and Geriatric Services at the Lemuel Shattuck Hospital in Boston and doctors at Tufts University School of Nutrition, designed an experiment to test the effect of macrobiotic food vs. regular institutional food on long-term psychiatric and geriatric patients. The patients had been diagnosed with psychosis, dementia, bipolar disorder, and depression, and some of them had been confined in the Shattuck Hospital for most of their life. In a double-blind study in which neither the ordinary hospital staff nor patients knew they were participating, macrobiotic meals designed to look and taste like regular foods were introduced to two wards of patients over an eight-week period. Altogether 187 food items on the macrobiotic menu were prepared, as well as chicken, coffee, and butter which were difficult to simulate. "The results showed a significant decrease in manifest psychosis and irritability in the experimental group," the researchers concluded. "This pilot study suggests that diet could have a real impact upon mental illness, but because of the multiple variables it is impossible to tell which variables are important." Elimination of sugar, food preservatives, dairy products, and processed food were mentioned as possible factors as well as the introduction of whole grains and vegetables. Source: Jonathan D. Lieff, M.D., et al., "A Double Blind Study of the Effect of Diet on Behavior in a Geriatric Psychiatric Ward" (Boston: Lemuel Shattack Hospital, 1984). (Psychiatric and Geriatric Patients)

• The traditional diet of humanity consisted of whole cereal grains and other foods of primarily vegetable quality rather than meat and other animal food as popularly believed. "Recent investigations into the dietary habits of prehistoric peoples and their primate predecessors suggest that heavy meat-eating by modern affluent societies may be exceeding the biological capacities evolution built into the human body. The result may be a host of diet-related health problems, such as diabetes, obesity, high blood pressure, coronary heart disease, and some cancers. The studies challenge the notion that human beings evolved as aggressive hunting animals who depended primarily upon meat for survival. The new view—coming from findings in such fields as archaeology, anthropology, primatology, and comparative anatomy—instead portrays early humans and their forebears more as herbivores than carnivores. According to these studies, the prehistoric table for at least the last million and a half years was probably set with three times more plant than animal foods, the reverse of what the average American currently eats." Source: Jane E. Brody, "Research Yields Surprises About Early Human Diets," *New York Times*, Science Section, May 15, 1979. (Plant vs. Animal Food)

• The few Stone Age cultures remaining in the world today consume primarily vegetable-quality food. Scientists who studied fifty-eight contemporary hunter-gatherer societies found that their diets contained from 50 to 70 percent complex carbohydrates from plant sources. Animal food comprised 25 to 30 percent of the total volume, and none of the tribes consumed milk, sugar, alcohol, or salt added at the meal. Source: H. C. Trowell and D. P. Burkitt, *Western Diseases: Their Emergence and Prevention* (Cambridge, Mass.: Harvard University Press, 1981), p. 15. (Plant vs. Animal Food)

• In 1985 anthropologists reported that the traditional diet of paleolithic times, including wild grains, roots, beans, nuts, tubers, and fruits, as well as wild game, appeared to be protective against cancer, heart disease, and other degenerative diseases. "Differences between the dietary patterns of our remote ancestors and the patterns now prevalent in industrialized countries appear to have important implications for health, and the specific pattern of nutritional disease is a function of the stage of civilization." Although some ancient societies ate more animal food than today, the amount and type of fat consumed was very different. Modern domesticated animals contain about eight to ten times more fat than their wild counterparts, and wild game contains over five times more polyunsaturated fat per gram than is found in domestic livestock which is highly saturated in quality. "The diet of our remote ancestors may be a reference standard for modern human nutrition and a model for defense against certain 'diseases of civilization,'" the researchers concluded. Source: S. B. Eaton, M. D. and M. Konner, Ph.D., "Paleolithic Nutrition," *New England Journal of Medicine* 313: 283–89. (Animal Food, Fat)

Agriculture and Energy

• In 1971, Frances Moore Lappé compiled information showing that there was enough food to end world hunger but from 50 to 90 percent of the world's grain was fed to livestock rather than people. To get one pound of beef, it takes 18 pounds of grain and soybeans; pork, 6 pounds; turkey, 4 pounds; eggs, 3 pounds; chicken, 3 pounds. Meanwhile, pounds of usable protein per acre were tabulated as follows: 356 pounds from soybeans; 260 pounds from rice; 211 pounds from corn; 192 pounds from other legumes; 138 pounds from wheat; 82 pounds from milk; 75 pounds from eggs; 45 pounds from meat of all kinds; and 20 pounds from beef. Source: Frances Moore Lappé, *Diet for a Small Planet* (New York: Ballantine, 1971). (Rice, Plant vs. Animal Food)

• A 1974 study found that despite improvements in transportation, the establishment of the modern supermarket, and the introduction of ready-to-eat and convenience foods, housewives today were spending more time shopping for food and preparing meals than their mothers or grandmothers. In 1968, the average nonworking American housewife spent 18 hours a week on food preparation versus 23 hours per week in 1926, while shopping hours rose from 4 to 8 per week over the same period. Source: J. Vanek, "Time Spent in Housework," *Scientific-American* 231: 116–20, 1974.

• In 1978, a researcher reported that the modern food and agriculture system uses vast amounts of oil and other fossil fuels. This includes the energy used in the manufacture of heavy farm equipment, chemical fertilizers and pesticides, and in processing and refining. The major users of energy are the meat and meat products industry and the sugar industry followed by the beverage and soft drink industry. Altogether, per capita use of energy for modern food production and processing comes to the equivalent of 375.4 gallons of oil per year, or about 1 gallon of gasoline a day. Source: Maurice Green, *Eating Oil: Energy Use in Food Production* (Boulder, Co.: Westview Press, 1978). (Chemicals, Meat and Sugar)

• In a 1980 report on organic farming, the U.S. Department of Agriculture reported that its researchers were "impressed by the ability of organic farmers to control weeds in crops such as corn, soybeans, and cereals without the use (or with only minimal use) of herbicides. Their success here is attributed to timely tillage and cultivation, delayed planting, and crop rotations. They have also been relatively successful in controlling insect pests." The investigators also found that organic practices contributed to controlling soil erosion, minimizing water pollution, and conserving energy; could result in substantial energy savings over chemical farming; and overall were generally competitive with nonorganic methods. "Certainly, much can be learned from a holistic research effort to investigate the organic system of farming, its mechanisms, interactions, principles, and potential benefits to agriculture at home and abroad," the report concluded. Source: *Report and Recommendations on Organic Farming* (Washington, D.C.: U.S. Department of Agriculture, Government Printing Office, 1980). (Organic Farming)

• In 1982 physicians at the Department of Family and Preventive Medicine at the University of Southern California School of Medicine warned their colleagues of an increased risk of leukemia for persons whose occupations expose them to electrical and magnetic fields. These occupations included electronic technicians, electricians, power linemen, welders and flame cutters, and electrical engineers. "Although we know of no tumour induction in animals from exposure to this spectrum on non-ionizing electromagnetic energy, radiowaves and microwaves have been shown to affect the number and type of white cells in the peripheral blood of animals and to affect immunoglobulin and endocrine function in animals." Source: W. E. Wright, J. M. Peters, and T. M. Mack, "Leukemia in Workers Exposed to Electrical and Magnetic Fields" (letter), *The Lancet* 2: 1160.

• In 1984 researchers at Rutgers University reported that non-organic produce had as little as 25 percent as much mineral content as organic produce. The scientists compared beans, cabbage, lettuce, tomatoes, and spinach purchased at a supermarket and an organic natural foods store and found substantially higher levels of phosphorous, calcium, magnesium, pottasium, sodium, boron, manganese, iron, copper, and cobalt and other minerals and trace elements in the organically grown vegetables. Source: Firman E. Baer, "Variations in Mineral Content in Vegetables" (New Brunswick, N.J.: Rutgers University), 1984. (Organic vs. Chemically Grown Food)

Biological Transmutation

• In 1959 French scientist Louis Kervran started publishing his discoveries in the field of biological transmutation—the synthesis of necessary but unavailable chemical elements out of simpler, available ones. Based on the theories of George Ohsawa that elements can be transmuted into one another peacefully without smashing the atom, Kervran showed that in living biological systems sodium could change into potassium, manganese could be obtained from iron, silica from calcium, and phosphorous from sulfur. Kervran's work began in Algeria when he was consulted to explain how workers could remain unshaded in the hot sun all day drilling wells. According to conventional science, the men should have died of hyperthermia. For six months, everything they ingested and excreted was carefully monitored. It was found that the men ingested large amounts of salt that were not secreted and excreted large amounts of potassium that were not ingested. "I came to the conclusion that it was sodium which, disappearing to become potassium, created an endothermal reaction (thus causing heat to be absorbed). Hence by instinct one consumes more salt in a dry and hot country. This is why salt is so important in Africa, the Middle East, etc., where caravans travel up to 1,000 kilometers to bring back salt." The macrobiotic theory of biological transmutation has wide industrial, scientific, and social applications. For example, Kervran suggested that biological transmutations could be applied to rendering harmless nuclear wastes, toxic spills, and other chronic environmental hazards. Source: Louis C. Kervran, *Biological Transmutations* (Brooklyn: Swan House, 1972), pp. 27–29. (Energy)

• In 1978 U.S. military scientists tested the theory of biological transmutations and verified the transmutation of matter from cell to cell and atom to atom. "The works of Kervran, Komaki, and others were surveyed; and it was concluded that, granted the existence of such transmutations (Na to Mg, K to Ca, and Mn to Fe), then a net surplus of energy was also produced. A proposed mechanism was described in which Mg adenosine triphosphate, located in the mitochondrion of the cell, played a double role as an energy producer. In addition to the widely accepted biochemical role of MgATP in which it produces energy as it disintegrates part by part, MgATP can also be considered to be a cyclotron on a molecular scale. The MgATP when placed in layers one atop the other has all the attributes of a cyclotron in accordance with the requirements set forth by E. O. Lawrence, inventor of the cyclotron. It was concluded that elemental transmutations were indeed occurring in life organisms and were probably accompanied by a net energy gain. . . .

The relatively available huge supplies of the elements which have been reported to have been transmuted and the probable large accompanying energy surplus indicate a new source of energy may be in the offing—one whose supply would be unlimited." Source: Solomon Goldfein, "Energy Development from Elemental Transmutations in Biological Systems," Report 2247, Ft. Belvoir, Va.: U.S. Army Mobility Equipment Research and Development Command, 1978. (Energy)

Exercise and Sports

• The Tarahumara Indians are the healthiest native community in North America. The Tarahumaras live in the Sierra Madré Occidental Mountains in north central Mexico and eat a traditional diet of corn, beans, and squash. Meat is seldom eaten, and eggs are taken only occasionally. The 50,000 Tarahumaras use no mechanical energy in farming, travel only by foot, and engage in marathon kickball competitions. Community members have also represented Mexico as marathon runners in the Olympics. Researchers who have studied this native culture report that high blood pressure and obesity are absent and death from cardiac and circulatory complications, as well as other degenerative diseases, is unknown. Source: William E. Connor et al., "The Plasma Lipids, Lipoproteins, and Diet of the Tarahumara Indians of Mexico," *American Journal of Clinical Nutrition* 31 (1978): 1131–42. (Kickball, Corn)

• In 1983 a Japanese professional baseball team climbed from last place to first place by switching to a macrobiotic diet. After taking over the last place Seibu Lions in October, 1981, as manager, Tatsuro Hirooka initiated a dietary experiment. Restricting the players' intake of meat, sugar, and white rice, he instructed them to eat brown rice, tofu, vegetables, and soybean products. He told the men that animal food increases an athlete's susceptibility to injuries. Conversely, natural foods, they were told, protect the body from sprains and dislocations and keep the mind clear and focused. During the 1982 season, the Lions were ridiculed by their archrivals, the Nippon Ham-Fighters, a team sponsored by a major meat company. However, the Lions defeated the Ham-Fighters for the Pacific League crown and continued to the Japan World Series and beat the Chunichi Dragons. The Lions won the championship again the following year as well. Source: "The Veggie Baseball Team," *Parade Magazine*, April 15, 1984. (Baseball, Brown Rice, Tofu)

8. One Peaceful World

"The destiny of nations depends upon what and how they eat."

—Brillat-Savarin
The Physiology of Taste

The Biological Revolution of Humanity

Modern humanity is facing a biological crisis. The most critical problem confronting us today is not political, economic, religious, or ideological; it is the question of whether the human race can continue to survive and develop on this planet, or whether it will continue to rapidly degenerate and eventually become extinct. A biological Noah's Flood now prevails everywhere throughout modern societies. Village to village, town to town, country to country, continent to continent, people everywhere are suffering from an epidemic of heart disease, cancer, diabetes, mental illness, infertility, AIDS, and other degenerative and immune-deficiency diseases.

No one who lives within modern civilization is exempt from this worldwide current of biological degeneration. From the newborn to the aged, housewives to businessmen, workers to national leaders, beggers to millionaires—whether black or white, Oriental or Occidental, Christian or Buddhist, capitalist or communist, rich or poor, man or woman—everyone is on trial at this critical time. Governmental policies, religious teachings, educational programs, and social systems all appear unable to meet this universal crisis. The best solution modern society can come up with is biotechnological—organ transplants, artificial organ implants, and eventually genetic engineering leading to the creation of an artificial species.

If we wish to maintain our human quality and spirit and continue our natural evolution on this earth, it is necessary to devote our heartfelt efforts toward the reconstruction of humanity on all levels—individual, family, community, national, and international. When the course of degeneration is reversed, a new world will begin based on a sound biological foundation with new social, ideological, and spiritual orientations. Otherwise, there shall be no peace in the world and no hope for the future of our species.

Reorientation of the Individual

In order to recover and develop our physical, mental, and spiritual health, we need to reorient our way of life in the following ways:

- We should reflect upon our own daily life, whether we are pursuing only sensory pleasure and emotional comfort, forgetting our native potential for greater happiness and higher freedom.
- We should reflect further upon our daily food and drink and consider whether our meals are really balanced to produce the best quality of blood and cells as well as to secure the best mental and spiritual conditions.
- We should also reflect upon our thought and behavior, toward our parents, family, friends, and other people and consider whether our respect and love are really dedicated from the heart and whether our behavior toward them is really serving for their health and happiness.
- We should also reflect upon our direction as a society and consider whether we are building cultures and civilizations in harmony with the order of nature or ignoring the natural environment.
- We should reflect, finally, upon our understanding of the cosmos: do we really know where we have come from and where we are going in this infinite universe?

The beginning of self-recovery from all personal unhappiness, including physical and mental disorders, is our understanding of the perpetual order of yin and yang, their dialectical and dynamic change governing every phenomenon. The compass of yin and yang will help us recover our native and intuitive memory and understanding of the infinite Order of the Universe, its mechanism of change, and its manifestation in our human life and daily activities.

In order to release ourselves from all physical and mental disorders, changing our degenerative tendencies toward health and happiness, we must first apply our understanding of yin and yang to our daily dietary practice—how to choose, prepare, and take our food and drink. Through proper eating, our blood and body will become sound and whole. Mental and spiritual well-being will naturally follow. Without any special preventive measures other than diet, we are able to maintain our physical health, suffering no serious sickness or disability. Without any other special mental or psychological training, we are able to establish a sound mentality, experiencing no delusions or other mental disorders. Without any special efforts other than the simple compass of yin and yang, we are able to understand with ease any subject that we desire to learn. Without any special education, we are naturally able to develop a spirit of love for other people and of harmony with our environment. Without imposing upon ourselves any special restrictions, we do not harbor any thoughts of destruction and violence. Without any special experience, we are naturally inspired with the spirit of perseverance and endless aspiration, enduring any hardship with gratitude. Without any other training, we are able to experience our oneness with every being and all phenomena surrounding us.

Food is creating us. If the nourishment we receive is proper, we are naturally more energetic physically, more comfortable emotionally, and more elevated spiritually than when our way of eating is imbalanced and disorderly. If our daily food is improper, our health declines, our emotions are disturbed, and our spirit becomes chaotic. Personal feelings, social relations, and our approach to any problems are influenced by what we eat. When we feel any frustration and disturbance, when we meet any difficulty and hardship, we should first reflect upon what we have been eating. Our physical and mental habits, as well as tendencies in our thinking and capacities of our consciousness, all depend upon what we have been eating for a long period, from the embryonic stage through childhood up to the present. To change our food is to wholly change ourselves. Through food, consciously or unconsciously, we shape our destiny.

There are three stages of personal eating:

Eating to Recover from Physical and Mental Disorders: At this stage, the way of eating—including the selection, preparation, and manner of eating of our food—should be strictly observed according to individual dietary recommendations made for the particular person or condition. Along with developing an understanding of yin and yang and principles of balance, this more disciplined way of eating should be followed until the condition stabilizes and harmony with the environment is restored. For many people in modern society, this is the beginning stage of eating according to natural order. When usual good health is achieved, we naturally move on to the next level.

Eating to Maintain Health and Energetic Activities: At this level, our food should be wider in variety and manner of preparation. It may fluctuate within a reasonable scope of balance, depending upon personal activities and social requirements. Principal food—whole cereal grains and their products—should continue to serve as the center of daily meals, with all other dishes as supplements. Sensitivity to the changing seasons, atmospheric conditions, daily weather patterns, and other environmental factors becomes more refined as our ability to adapt to our surroundings grows and develops.

Eating to Develop and Realize Our Dream: At this level, a natural continuation of the second stage, our way of eating becomes more intuitive. We adjust freely the kinds, volume, preparation, and time of eating of our foods according to the dream that we wish to realize in life. Each food and way of preparation has certain physical and mental effects. Knowing these characteristics, we freely manage our daily eating to maintain the highest levels of health and judgment, to understand our purpose in life, and to realize our dream. This way of eating is truly making use of our freedom and is the highest art with which we can liberate ourselves in all domains of life. For example:

• To be religious and spiritual, eat vegetable-quality food including whole cereal grains, beans, vegetables, and fruits with the minimum possible amount of animal food.

• To be social and businesslike, eat mostly vegetable-quality foods including grains and beans, cooked in a standard way, in a wider variety of methods with the addition of a small volume of animal food.

• To perform heavy physical labor, eat more volume of food, including whole cereal grains, beans, vegetables, and animal food, richly cooked, as well as a larger volume of liquid.

• To be more intellectual, eat whole grains, beans, and vegetables with the occasional addition of a small volume of animal food and fruits.

• To be more sensitive and aesthetic, eat mostly vegetable-quality food, including raw salad. Fruits may be added, as well as a little more liquid and a small volume of animal food if desired.

• To be physically active, eat regularly. To be mentally active, eat less volume.

• To be violent and warlike, eat more animal food and sugar, with a variety of food prepared in a disorderly manner.

When we are physically or emotionally ill, we are unable to enjoy our life on this earth. We all need to recover our health as soon as possible and begin to pursue our common dream—the creation of one peaceful world—with many other people who are also healthy. Life is nothing but endlessly realizing our endless dream. If we are not doing so, we are seriously ill and separated from the deepest yearnings of our own heart.

Reorientation of the Family and Community

A healthy family is the greatest blessing. A sick family is the greatest tragedy. When one person becomes sick, the whole family suffers; and when one family suffers, the whole community becomes unstable. A family that has a sick person has been imbalanced for some time. A community that has many sick families has been disordered for a long period.

Sicknesses—physical and mental—never arise without cause, and the underlying cause, in all instances, is our own disorderly way of life. Sicknesses are a warning from our intuition (or, we may say, the voice of God) telling us that our way of life has been in disharmony. A person suffering from sickness should reflect deeply, apologizing to him- or herself, family, community, and universe. Sentimental consolations, including the presentation of flowers, fruits, or candies, to a sick person are not helpful at all. Sick people need our deep concern and warm care to guide them toward the proper understanding of why they are suffering. They also need us to guide and inspire them toward the proper food and nourishment that will end their suffering without any further complications and serve as a basis for the way of life which they need to follow from now on.

Beyond anything else, the orientation of family and community should be directed toward maintaining the best health of their members. To keep a family in healthy physical, mental, and spiritual condition, it is not necessary to have regular consultations or to receive any special treatment from a family doctor. The best traditional method is the common practice of gathering the family together regularly to eat meals that are prepared according to natural order and in a loving spirit. Usually, the center of the household is the mother, who is most mindful of everyone's daily health and well-being, though anyone who is mature physically and mentally can serve as the daily cook. Through her love and skill in the kitchen, the family is able to derive limitless benefits.

At the table, everyone's physical and mental conditions are periodically observed and discussed in a light, humorous spirit, and meals can be adjusted according to everyone's personal requirements with condiments, garnishes, and seasonings. Special dishes may even be prepared for certain members of the family. During the meal, each member of the family exchanges daily thoughts and experiences in harmonious conversation, creating a spirit of fellowship and mutual respect. Naturally, as the family eats the same food together, a similar quality of blood and consequently thinking develops. Over time, the family becomes one, with all members sharing the same dream and destiny in life.

Without eating whole balanced meals together, there can be no biological, psychological, and social unity, which is the essence of the family. The home becomes only an impersonal living place. When family members eat in separate ways and at separate times, dissatisfaction and division spread. Personalities and opinions begin to differ and clash, eventually causing a lack of understanding and sympathy. Though there may be other contributing factors, the fundamental reason for the increase of conflicts, arguments, separation, and divorce among married people and the disintegration of the modern family is a decline of the home-cooked family meal.

Similarly, in community life, if the majority of people do not eat a well balanced diet, social disorder prevails. In such a community, the number of sick people suffering physically and mentally increases. Together with the decomposition of family life, many people become unable to support themselves, which results in constant expansion of public welfare systems, including unemployment benefits, social security, and other retirement and pension programs. Medical facilities as well as public and private insurance systems must continuously expand their scope. Psychological and behavioral disorders rise, requiring the construction of larger mental health centers, remedial educational programs, and prisons and correctional facilities, as well as more extensive legal systems and powerful bureaucracies to administrate these systems.

The structure and operation of modern societies is based upon fear and suspicion, insecurity and anxiety. Human relations become laden with distrust as people suffer from false, self-imposed delusions. Greed and selfishness prevail in community life as every member of society becomes defensive and protective of his or her private interests and benefits. To control the excesses of this way of life, the community must produce educational, political, economic, religious, and military systems that regulate and restrict daily life through rules and ethics, laws and taxes, force and punishment. Training is geared toward standardization: everyone is taught the same concepts to meet the uniform set of requirements. Individual freedom and creative self-expression are sacrificed in the process. Greater community sickness only leads to greater social organization and greater control over our lives. At the same time, spreading physical and mental degeneration causes the rapid internal weakening of society itself. Finally, replete with sick people, sick families, and sick communities, economically unable to support itself, and politically unable to govern because of leaders who are sick or lacking in vision and judgment, the civilization collapses.

Biological Revolution: In the 20th Century, modern societies are rapidly declining from such basic biological causes. Modern preventive and protective measures are constantly on the increase but have proved ineffective. Religious teachings are losing their influence on people; ethical and moral codes and centuries-old traditions are no longer adaptable, with the result that there are no common principles, philosophies, or values by which people may live. Modern education has lost the spirit of respect for teachers and teachings, and love for the students, and no longer instills in the students the understanding of life. Medical establishments are suffering from higher expenses, ineffective treatments, and an ever-increasing number of patients. Families are decomposing rapidly; individual and social crimes are mounting.

In this modern crisis, all historical measures to change society have proved obsolete, including spiritual and religious teachings, social and educational programs, philosophical and scientific approaches, and political and economic systems. Humanist philosophies such as those which developed during the Renaissance, declarations of independence and freedom as we see in the history of the United States, revolutions like that in France in the 18th Century, reformations such as those within Protestantism and Buddhism, ideologies such as Communism, and technological advances such as space travel and computers—all these social movements or expressions are unable to save modern people from their rapid degeneration.

During past crises, humanity self-reflected and purified itself. Abraham made purification with oil. Baptism with water was done by John on the River Jordan, and salvation with the Holy Spirit was practiced by Jesus and the early Christians. Now is the time for the last and most fundamental method of purifying humanity and changing our destiny—biological renewal of our blood and organs, our tissues and brain cells.

The biological transformation of humanity is an entirely peaceful revolution, requiring no laws or doctrines, violence or mass movements. It is also the most universal revolution, able to prevail throughout the world, crossing over national, racial, ideological, religious, and cultural boundaries. It spreads from person to person, home to home, community to community, and country to country, beginning in every kitchen and ending in the realization of one peaceful world.

At the social level, the purpose of macrobiotics is to reverse the course of biological degeneration, achieve one peaceful world, and secure the endless development of humanity. The new course will develop naturally in a series of interrelated steps. First, we will regain our commonsense understanding of humanity, our origin and our future, our place and relation with the Order of the Universe, and its practical application to our daily lives. Second, we will recover the wholesome quality of food through change toward a more natural and organic agriculture system and traditional food processing methods. Third, worldwide distribution of these food products and their preparation according to macrobiotic principles will begin. Fourth, the spread of proper food and cooking methods will speed the recovery of the physical and mental health of every person, family, and community through the above practices. Fifth, the creation of a healthy biological foundation will lead to the development of a new orientation of society including education, medicine, economics, politics, and spirituality. Sixth, the development of a society in harmony with the natural environment will lead to the dissolution of unnecessary and destructive defensive and protective measures through a gradual and natural elevation of consciousness from the basic stages of fear and insecurity. Seventh, one world society will be established within which everyone is able to enjoy health, happiness, and freedom by the gradual elimination of all unnatural and artificial boundaries.

World Federal Government

Historical Review: From the beginning of recorded history, the human race has continuously sought to create a peaceful society. This desire has been felt not only among people who love peace and abstain from war but also among those who have engaged in war to achieve peace. Even Alexander the Great, Genghis Khan, Napoleon, and other military conquerors dreamed of establishing a peaceful worldwide empire. Plato's *Republic* (370 B.C.), Augustine's *The City of God* (A.D. 413), Thomas More's *Utopia* (1516), Campanella's *The City of the Sun* (1623), Hobbe's *Leviathan* (1651), Kant's *Discourse on Perpetual Peace* (1795), and numerous other portraits of ideal and peaceful societies have been presented throughout history.

When World War I (1914–1918) ended with great suffering and

misery, the League of Nations was formed to avoid future destruction and warfare. When the League collapsed and World War II (1939–1945) brought greater destruction throughout the world, the United Nations was formed to maintain international peace and security. In addition to these political efforts, there have been many international efforts to realize peace through religious, humanitarian, economic, and cultural cooperation. The world has definitely been moving toward a globally organized society. Cooperative systems of mutual assistance have helped unify different nations and races, traditions and customs, cultures and ideologies. International cooperation now encompasses almost all domains, including communication, transportation, space exploration, the use of energy, financial investment, economic development, and problems of health and welfare.

However, despite the trend toward the creation of a world society, several important problems remain to be solved to truly realize one peaceful world. Political conflicts between liberal and communistic countries, economic conflicts between developed and developing countries, religious conflicts between Catholics and Protestants, Christians and Moslems, old doctrines and new beliefs, cultural conflicts between theoretical sciences and aesthetic understanding, traditional conflicts between Western and Eastern customs, and many other such conflicts are still causing difficulties and divisive thinking in the world today. Since 1945 serious attempts have been made to overcome these various divisions, especially those involving national interests, by forming a world federal government. Among those who have contributed to this cause are Thomas Mann, Upton Sinclair, Norman Cousins, Albert Einstein, Robert Hutchins, Henry Osborne, and Edgar Gavaert among Western thinkers and Mohandas Gandhi, Jawaharlal Nehru, Toyohiko Kagawa, George Ohsawa, and others among Eastern thinkers. During the postwar period, proposals to establish a world federal government have been presented in the congresses and parliaments of many countries. Many legislatures, judicial bodies, and executive administrators have urged the adoption of this goal as an objective of their international policies.

Between 1945 and 1955, movements to establish world federal government consisted of two major currents: 1) to amend the United Nations charter to develop a world federal government by limiting national sovereignty, and 2) to form a world congress with representatives chosen by the citizens of each country. During the same period, more than fifty drafts of world constitutions were proposed by individuals, organizations, research groups, and other associations. The University of

Chicago's special committee to draft a world constitution published its "Preliminary Draft of a World Constitution." The world federal governments viewed by such proposals would be organized with political constitutions similar to that of the United States. The proposed world congress would have two houses: one house representing the national governments of the world and the other house composed of representatives elected by the people. For example, one representative would be selected for every 1 million or 5 million people.

Limitations of World Federal Government: A long-cherished dream of humankind has been the establishment of one world, whether expressed as one world community, world commonwealth, or world federation. However, even if such a world government were formed as a political and social structure unifying the current countries and blocs of countries, it could not ensure humanity's ultimate happiness. A world community with a central government would be able to halt worldwide destruction and warfare, especially if the central government were powerful enough to control all major destructive measures, including nuclear power. However, even with the formation of world government, many problems related to human safety and well-being would remain unsolved.

Halting warfare does not necessarily eliminate the cause of warfare. It would serve as a valuable symptomatic treatment to temporarily ease world conflict, but unless the underlying cause of war was remedied, conflict sooner or later would erupt again with greater intensity. Peace is not merely the absence of war; it is a state in which no cause for war exists. Such a state is possible when all parties and interests regard each other as complements of a larger whole and when no one thinks of violence as a possible solution to human problems. Such a mentality is gained not through modern education or social training but through the biological and psychological improvement of humanity. Simply speaking, when everyone reaches a physical and mental condition free of nightmares and delusions, peace in society will naturally follow. Any structural social changes, including the establishment of world government, will not serve to realize true peace unless there are corresponding efforts to elevate humanity biologically and psychologically.

Meanwhile, in the absence of a sound biological foundation, even if world government were established and existing political, economic, and social systems were unified, numerous physical and mental disorders would continue to exist. Modern humanity would continue to decline from the spread of heart disease, cancer, mental illness, loss of reproductive ability, AIDS and other degenerative and immune-deficiency diseases, and eventually the internal structure of such a world community would decompose through the weakening of human health and consciousness. In the event the world government adopted the same shortsighted policies of present-day national governments—leading to environmental pollution, food contamination, and the energy crisis, as well as family dissolution and human distrust—humanity's unhappiness and degeneration would accelerate on a worldwide scale.

Standardization and uniformity of thought, expression, and behavior are other drawbacks to the establishment of one world community. For example, if the world government adopted a system of world education, all the children of the world would grow up according to the same regulated forms and concepts, hindering individual ingenuity and creativity. If uniform legal structures were created, human relations could become dominated by concepts and laws instead of by love, sympathy, and understanding. If modern nutritional standards and uniform dietary recommendations were imposed not taking into account differing climates, seasons, and personal needs, humanity's connection with ancestral tradition and millions of years of evolutionary development could be severed. Nature thrives on diversity. Unless, the wonderful richness and variety of different human qualities and values are respected, the new world order would rapidly decline. Hybrid seeds produce spectacular yields in the short run but over time become weaker than the hardy native strains they have displaced. In the same way, a standardized human society would be unable to adapt to changing environmental circumstances and quickly perish.

Without understanding the order of nature and the laws of the infinite universe, including proper dietary practices modified and adjusted for different regions and personal needs, any structural changes in society and world order could eventually prove harmful. The more powerful international systems become, the greater the danger.

The dream of one peaceful world, or of one world government, is imperishable. But it can be achieved only through humanity's biological, psychological, and spiritual development. First, we must restore the health of each individual and family, thereby eliminating the physical and mental disorders that are crippling modern society and are the real cause of conflict and war. Second, we must free our consciousness from all nightmares and delusions through a more natural way of life, including a more balanced way of eating. Third, we must develop universal love and understanding among people, transcending all differences of nationality and race, tradition and culture, belief and ideology, recognizing everyone as brothers and sisters of one planetary family. Through these three steps, a united world, established on a solid biological, psychological, and spiritual foundation, will be realized in the course of society's natural growth and development.

Beyond National Boundaries: When we fly over the land, we see mountains, rivers, forests, and fields, and we see no borderlines. When we voyage on the ocean, we see skies and clouds, water and waves, but we see no boundaries. All animal species spread across the land and ocean freely. Why do we—humanity, particularly modern humanity—create limitations and live within certain artificial boundaries and borders? If we saw this planet from a distance, far away in space, like the astronauts who went to the moon, we would laugh at our folly in establishing national boundaries and in threating to destroy our beautiful planet in the name of national sovereignty.

What is a nation? A nation does not exist in nature and on this earth. A nation exists only in the imagination. A nation is a concept that we have come to believe through modern education, and we behave according to what we have learned. While other species require no identification to travel, we must carry a passport and visa, as well as other permits and identification papers. Our freedom of travel, choice of residence, and behavior are severely restricted. Before we are a citizen of any modern nation, we are citizens of the human race. Before our country is one of the nations drawn on the map, our country is the earth, the solar system, and the universe. National borderlines that have been designed for political reasons during the course of history should be gradually replaced by more natural territorial arrangements reflecting differences in climatic and geographical conditions as well as in available food and dietary practices. Because of these factors, natural differences in people's physical and mental conditions arise, and many varieties of cultural and social expression appear. Based on these differences, natural territorial arrangements would become self-evident. The future structure of the nation and its cultural, social, and spiritual heritage should spring from its biological nature and should not be imposed for any other reasons. Real sovereignty should not belong to any political and economic power claiming national or international autonomy; rather it lies in the physical and mental health of individuals and families. We all naturally love the land where we were born, where our parents and ancestors lived and died, and where our daily foods are grown. But our spirit and consciousness must grow and embrace the earth as a whole. Our ultimate allegiance is owed to the sovereignty of nature and the Order of the Universe, which is indivisible and imperishable.

The Future World Community

The future world community will reflect a universal understanding that all human beings are brothers and sisters of one great planetary family. The modern orientation of national governments is political. The orientation of the world federal governmental organization, however, should be one of education and service, not control and enforcement. In the transition period, all national governments should expand their educational and service functions, gradually reducing their legal, political, and military jurisdictions.

World Fundamental Education: International organizations should help the people of the world gain an understanding of the laws of nature and the Order of the Universe and their relation to human society and its development. All persons should understand their natural origin and destiny and orient their life according to their dream and ability.

On the most elementary level, all people, beginning in early childhood, should learn how to keep their health and know what to do when they become sick. They should have a knowledge of their daily food and should learn the effectiveness of appropriate dietary practices for their physical, mental, and spiritual development. They should also learn that they are primarily responsible for their own health and destiny.

On the secondary level, children should learn the basic way of living, including cooking, sewing, housekeeping, gardening, and basic repairing. On this level, they should also understand how to take care of other people when they are sick and should learn the spirit of love and care for other people.

At this level, everyone should also master the primary ways of communication, including speaking, writing, calculating, and other expressions of our theoretical and aesthetic natures. They should read widely in all subjects and in many styles, including stories and poetry. They should experience physically and mentally through actual participation in the making of crafts, the creative and fine arts, gardening and housekeeping.

At the third level, children should learn the spirit of respect for elders, including parents and ancestors. The history of humanity also should begin to be presented, including specific personal family and community histories. Everyone's health should be maintained through active physical exercise, preferably interwoven with the daily life. Basic farming, including the cultivation of essential foods, as well as all basic knowledge and techniques for life, should be learned.

At this same level, children should be encouraged to observe and experience various natural phenomena, to know how they are changing in an orderly fashion according to the laws of balance and harmony. The antagonistic and complemental constitution of the endless universe should be revealed in simple and practical ways. The spirit of marveling at nature and the cosmos should be encouraged to grow. Knowledge should not be given, but rather everyone should be guided to discover for themselves. Yin and yang is the universal compass to understand and solve various questions and riddles of life that we all experience such as: Why is the sky blue? Why is the grass green? Why do we have two eyes and one mouth? Why are snowflakes six-sided? Artistic expression should be encouraged, with everyone's originality and ability respected.

In the fourth level, pre-adolescent or early teenage education should be designed for both boys' and girls' common interests. However, separate classes should also be arranged for their different interests. Boys should be given more physical and social training with emphasis on developing their courage and ambition, while girls should be encouraged to develop more their sensitivity and understanding. Proper relations between man and woman should be well understood, with the aid of reasonable guidance. Both boys and girls, of course, should continuously be encouraged to explore and learn about human affairs and social events, as well as natural phenomena, including the biological, psychological, and spiritual realms, along with an understanding of the earth, the solar system, and the celestial order.

Active life experiences, including the learning of technological skills, as well as involvement in social life and human relations, should be arranged, in addition to intellectual and aesthetic studies. Common sense, based upon the universal consciousness of the brotherhood and sisterhood of all humanity, should be developed on this level.

From the fifth level, falling during the latter period of adolescence, everyone should be given the opportunity of starting to choose their major path of learning according to their own interests. From this level on, some people would follow a more academic direction, some a more technical training, and others a more professional orientation. However, everyone should be continuously encouraged to make their own inventive discoveries and creations and to find answers to their own questions. At this level, everyone should begin to experience the profound realization that the order that is working in their own body and mind is also working in human relations and in society, and the very same order is also working in all phenomena throughout the universe. At this level also, respect for the universality of human culture and civilization, including deep appreciation for all past generations and sense of responsibility for all future generations, should begin to be felt.

From the next, sixth, level—post-adolescence and the late teenage years—everyone should be free to pursue their own interests regardless of subject and of whether they learn through intellectual studies or through actual experience. Throughout this period, they should be guided to reflect for themselves, to judge themselves, and to discover who they are, what dream they should pursue, and how they should play throughout their lives. Not only the physical, material world, but also the spiritual and invisible world, should be understood through their own study and experience.

At the seventh stage, everyone should be encouraged to express their own discoveries, inventions, and assumptions to the public, either in writing or in speech, and to demonstrate the experience they have acquired in public in any manner they wish to choose. The imitation or copying of previously existing ideas and thoughts should be discouraged. Education may be considered to be completed when such original creations, expressed in any manner, are performed well. There should be no definite time of graduation, and there should be no requirement to remain in the educational system after the fourth level.

To sum up, the comprehensive principles of world education are: 1) Everyone is free to orient their life according to their own dream. 2) Everyone should be creative and inventive, in their own search for health, happiness, truth, and freedom. 3) Everyone should understand that all people are related as family members sharing the same planet and that all phenomena in the universe are manifestations of one infinity. 4) A spirit of harmony, respect, and love is the essence of individual health, family unity, and the development of humanity as a whole.

World Public Service

Another function of world government or organization, besides world education, is world public service. World public service consists of three main aspects: 1) public utility service, 2) public health service, and 3) natural agriculture.

World Public Utility Service: The public utility service would handle all basic social conveniences necessary for healthy, natural living, including world communications, transportation, construction of worldwide utility systems, and distribution of natural resources and other necessary materials. The public utility service would be subdivided into continental, territorial, and possibly bioregional divisions, assuming primary responsibility for providing local services and functions. However, worldwide services would be offered equally to everyone.

World Public Health Service: The public health service would be responsible not only for maintaining and protecting the general public from physical and mental disorders but also restoring criminals to society and a responsible life through proper dietary guidance and a more natural way of living. All crimes are the manifestation of physical and mental sickness. Current legal and penal systems, based on confinement and punishment, do not solve the underlying cause of violent and destructive behavior, and it is universally agreed that almost no modern offenders are rehabilitated. In the future, the biological and psychological origin of crime and other socially undesirable behavior will be more widely known. The public health service would replace present-day methods of incarceration with proper nutritional care and education of the way of life according to the Order of the Universe.

The need for medical care and facilities in the future world would naturally diminish as people regained their health and judgment. Overall, medicine would become more preventive in orientation. However, for some cases such as accidents or emergencies, medical intervention and technology would be readily available. At the same time, proper dietary practices would bring a decrease in psychological disorders, resulting in the substantial reduction of violence, hatred, prejudice, and greed throughout society. Society would automatically become more peaceful and, at the same time, more energized in the pursuit of constructive programs. Pharmaceutical care and the insurance industry would naturally lose their value. Together with world education, the world health service would become the most important force in maintaining a peaceful world.

Natural Agriculture

The physical, mental, and spiritual health of the world's people depends mostly upon their daily practice of proper diet according to natural order. Return to a more natural way of farming is essential for the realization of one healthy, peaceful world.

In the future world, as macrobiotic principles and understanding spread, agriculture would become less international and national, and more regional and local. In the case of continents that have relatively little geographic and climatic variety, as in North America, the food that we eat should ideally be produced within approximately a 500-mile radius. In the case of continents or areas such as Europe and India, which have more geographic and climatic variety, this radius should be decreased to about 200 miles or in proportion to the degree of variety. In the case of islands, such as the Far Eastern and Northern European isles, this radius should be further decreased, possibly to 100 miles, because of the richness in the variety of geographic and climatic conditions.

Agriculture should be conducted according to the practices of natural, organic cultivation, avoiding the use of chemically produced fertilizers, pesticides, and insecticides. During the process of human evolution over millions of years, chemicals were not applied in the production of food—until only a short time ago, the early part of the 20th Century. Because of the use of thousands of varieties of chemicals, which are mostly extremely expansive (yin) in quality, agricultural products have become larger in appearance and volume. However, they have lost their strength, vitality, and rich taste, as well as their compact organic structure—all contracted (yang) qualities. By eating those products, modern men and women have been rapidly degenerating and developing extreme yin tendencies. For example, they are taller, weaker, have shorter memories, and have larger mouths, noses, and other features than their parents, grandparents, and ancestors. The abundant use of chemical fertilizer further depletes one of our most important natural resources—the elements in the soil—and adversely affects the life of the microorganisms in the soil that are serving for the healthy growth of plants.

We should return as soon as possible to the natural, organic methods of cultivation that have been traditionally practiced throughout the world for many centuries. However, in order not only to maintain and protect our health but also to evolve and develop as a strong human species, our agriculture should be further developed from natural, organic cultivation to an even more natural agriculture. The objective of this natural agriculture is to restore domesticated whole grains, beans, and vegetables to their original, free, wild character.

This natural agriculture is based upon the understanding that humanity has evolved through natural processes out of the surrounding environment, including the vegetable world. We are a manifestation of our environment, and it is not our purpose to reform that environment. When we start to think that we should regulate our food by changing the quality of the plants, this egocentric view creates an unnatural separation between us and the natural world. By allowing the food to return from its present cultivated quality to its more natural and wild state, we would also restore our true humanity. Our own health and consciousness would reach new heights, and our ability to adapt to the environment would greatly improve.

Natural agriculture requires the gradual decrease of human participation in the cultivation of food, finally reaching a state in which the less we participate the better the crops are. Natural agriculture includes the following practical principles:

Non-Weeding: Weeds and vegetable plants naturally occur together. The practice of weeding reduces the natural tilling of the soil that is accomplished by the roots of weeds, as well as decreases the microorganisms that normally thrive in those roots. The healthy growth of weeds is beneficial to the flourishing of various crops. In farming and gardening, however, smaller, shorter, and softer weeds such as clover are more desirable, and it may be necessary to replace the larger, taller, and harder varieties with these kinds.

Non-Tilling: If weeds are removed, the soil is not tilled by the usual natural process and human labor for tilling becomes necessary. When such tilled soil receives rainfall, it tends to become harder, requiring even further labor for tilling. On the other hand, if we leave the desirable weeds in the field, thereby accomplishing natural tilling, these weeds also help to hold water from the rainfalls and keep the soil suitably moist. Conventionally tilled soil cannot keep moisture for a long period and usually requires artificial irrigation or watering.

Non-Fertilizing: Because of weeding and tilling, the soil produces only those vegetables that are planted, and large spaces are left open between plants. Fertilizers must be brought in from outside and applied to the land in order to maintain the nutrients in the topsoil. However, if weeds are allowed to grow naturally on the land, they replenish the soil when they die, securing rich humus and other soil conditions for the coming year. Furthermore, if we return the unused portion of harvested plants to the land in the form of compost, the soil will be further enriched and ready to use the following year.

Non-Spraying: If we cultivate only a single species of plant in an area, it is often invaded by insects, worms, and animals that are attracted to that particular species. Of course, this is mainly due to the practice of weeding and to monocultivation. However, if we keep the land covered with weeds or grow various species of plants together—for example, root vegetables and green leafy vegetables—such invasions are minimized. In nature, there is no place where only a single species of plant grows; there are always several different species growing together. Changing from monocultivation to polycultivation is essential for natural agriculture.

Non-Seeding: At harvest time, we should not take all the products of the land; we should leave 10 to 20 percent unharvested. These remaining plants will produce seeds that eventually scatter over the land, and from these seeds new plants will start to grow. When we repeat this process over several years, seeding by human labor becomes unnecessary. Labor will only by needed to thin out excessive growth. In the case of cereal grains, this method may not be applicable, particularly in smaller fields; but other plants, including most garden vegetables, can be left to their own natural cycles of growth.

Non-Pruning: To ensure the natural growth and development of any plant, especially trees producing fruits and flowers, we should avoid artificial pruning. The branches and leaves of all plants grow according to spirallic laws of nature. When we interfere by artificial trimming, cutting, and pruning, the plants can no longer maintain their natural quality. Of course, this results in the production of an unnatural quality of fruits and flowers. To our human eyes, pruned trees may appear more beautiful or symmetrical, but they are actually deformed and imbalanced in the eyes of nature. A natural quality of plant produces a natural, strong humanity, and an unnatural quality of plant produces an unnatural, weak humanity.

Generally speaking, natural agriculture is a powerful method to help reverse the modern trend toward biological degeneration. When our daily food is naturally strong, our physical health, psychological well-being, and spiritual development advance without limit. Our consciousness, including our capacities for insight, foresight, imagination, telepathy, and other extrasensory perception, begins to develop as the quality of our food improves. Our awareness is also heightened as our cooking improves and as we discover the modest volume of food we really need. As balance is restored, we begin to truly appreciate the natural taste and richness of whole, unprocessed foods; the use of artificial flavoring becomes unnecessary, and only a small amount of unrefined sea salt and unrefined vegetable quality oil in cooking satisfies our desire. Natural agriculture is the gateway to the garden of paradise which we lost long before our written history began.

Principles of Natural Economy

When we observe all species of animals other than modern human beings, we see that they are always playing—running in the fields, flying in the sky, or swimming in the waters. They do not work. When we reflect how the human race began on this earth some millions of years ago, we wonder whether it is really necessary for our evolutionary development to continue working in such an artificially regulated manner. Nowadays it is universally agreed that we must work to make a living, but do we really need to work? Why is work necessary for modern humanity but not other species? If we do not really need to work and can enjoy our freedom, what is wrong with the orientation of modern society?

When we were born as infants, did we expect that the greater part of our adult life would be dedicated to working for our livelihood and not doing what we really wanted to do? Have we come from the infinite universe to this earth, manifesting as human beings, in order to learn how to work, to engage every day in regulated activities from 9 to 5, and to retire at age sixty or sixty-five, followed soon after by our death? How many people in the modern world are really enjoying their lives and doing what they want to do? Were we born to work, or were we born to play? What is the purpose of our life? If we are not enjoying wholehearted play from morning to night, is it really worthwhile to continue living, even for a few years? One of the essential problems all modern men and women face is whether every day we are doing what we really want to do.

The principles of natural economy are found in the common understanding of what we are and what the universe is and are applicable to all human beings. They include:

One Grain, Ten Thousand Grains: The universe is constantly expanding as modern astronomy has revealed. Infinite expansion is the fundamental nature of the universe itself. Within the cosmos, therefore, every phenomenon tends to expand, differentiate, and reproduce endlessly. The law of natural production is constant creation. One grain, if it falls on proper soil, produces hundreds of grains. They, in turn, produce hundreds of thousands of grains, and they further produce hundreds of millions of grains.

Our daily household and social economy should reflect this principle of endless production and endless distribution. In administration and operation, we should use natural methods as much as possible and minimize artificial ones. When we apply our human technology to accelerate and multiply natural powers and forces, we disturb natural cycles of balance and harmony. This results in the destruction of our health and, if carried to an extreme, can lead to the end of human existence or even the earth itself.

Health—the Source of Our Capital and Labor: The fundamental resource of our economy is neither financial power (capital), material wealth (land, natural resources), nor the productive ability of machinery and equipment (including human labor). These are secondary factors—the means to operate production and distribution. The real source of our capital and labor is: 1) the physical, mental, and spiritual health of all the individual people of the world and 2) the natural forces and environmental conditions, including the earth, solar system, and the universe. Present-day economic systems are in reality anti-economical. They are working against the principles of natural economy by contributing to the deterioration of human health and the destruction of the natural environment.

Before anything else, humanity requires sound health and judgment, for which macrobiotic principles, including the practice of proper diet, need to be applied everywhere around the world. A return to individual and social health will secure the fundamental capital and labor necessary for all kinds of economic operations. At the same time, sources of energy should not be directed exclusively to resources deposited in the earth, which are limited and therefore exhaustible. We should seek energy and power among the forces that have created and are maintaining the earth, including solar energy, the electromagnetic power of the solar system, and various vibrations, waves, and rays streaming in to our planet almost limitlessly from outer space.

Principles of Operation: The operation of any economic enterprise—from a household to a corporation—should be conducted consciously with an understanding of yin and yang, the laws of balance and harmony. Balance and harmony should be maintained between the universe and the earth; biological life and the environment; all animal and vegetable life, and the human species; world human production and territorial needs; and material wealth and individual well-being. These five major areas of balance and harmony should be considered in the design and operation of all economic enterprises. At present, the driving force of modern economy is mainly the pursuit of material wealth, convenience, and comfort. Because of this narrow, limited orientation, human well-being, including physical and mental health, is in danger despite economic prosperity. Environmental conditions, the survival of all other biological species, and the existence of the earth itself are approaching a critical stage.

The supply of food and basic living necessities should be arranged within each territory or natural region according to principles of self-support, self-sufficiency, and harmonious adaptation to the natural environment. All other materials and facilities can be traded widely and freely throughout the world with a view to sharing intellectual understanding and aesthetic experience, as well as the benefits of world civilization.

The economic principles that have guided the world in past ages are now under review. The ideas of Adam Smith, Thomas Malthus, Karl Marx, Friedrich Engels, and John Maynard Keynes, as well as other theories of capitalism, socialism, and communism, are based on a very fragmented understanding of the principles of the universe and what is really needed for the health and welfare of every human being. Economic systems and structures should develop more naturally and less conceptually, As our health improves and our consciousness develops, economic systems will gradually reorient in the direction of family systems, whether on a world, territorial, or household scale. Natural economy is based upon love and respect for everyone and for all species, as well as nature, the earth, and the universe as a whole.

The modern world will end chaotically unless we proceed with biological, psychological, and spiritual revolution. With the spread of macrobiotic principles, including a balanced way of eating and thinking, the world community will become peaceful and flourish. Everyone will establish their own health and well-being, and the world will be governed by an understanding of the Order of the Universe. There will be no more need for supermarkets, drug stores, hospitals, insurance companies, welfare systems, banks, factories, courts, police forces, prisons, and armies. These and the other institutions of modern life for which we constantly work and pay taxes will naturally disappear as balance and harmony are restored. We shall be free from early morning to late at night to play tirelessly with one another as brothers and sisters living together on this beautiful planet we call the earth. It is up to us—at this turning point in history—to establish one peaceful world and preserve humanity's natural spirit and quality to be passed on to endless generations.

9. Realizing Our Endless Dream

"If the flesh has come into existence because of the spirit, it is a marvel, but if the spirit has come into existence because of the body, it is a marvel of marvels."

—Jesus in *The Gospel According to Thomas*

The World of Vibration

We have come from infinity. We have manifested ourselves, through seven stages of physicalization and materialization. At the terminus of this contractive, centripetal course, we were conceived with our parents' reproductive cells: the egg (yang) and sperm (yin). This is the beginning of our return to our origin: the infinite universe. In this returning journey, we dephysicalize and spiritualize ourselves, taking the expanding centrifugal direction (see Figure 52).

During sexual relations between our parents, the mother's *hara* attracts strong incoming energy and fusion arises. As a result of rhythmical movement, heat is generated, and at the peak, a high charge of energy is released, something like thunder and electricity.

If the woman's egg and man's sperm are sufficiently charged at the proper time, fertilization occurs. This is like an axis shift on land. A tiny form evolves in this highly energized state, and cell division begins. About seven days later, implantation starts in the fallopian tubes. From this time on, the embryo is nourished by the mother's blood, whose quality depends directly upon what she eats.

Altogether human consciousness is comprised of five spirits. 1) At the time of conception, the mother and father's spirit combine. The spirit that is created is traditionally known in the Far East as the *Sei-shi*,

Figure 52. Spiritual Development

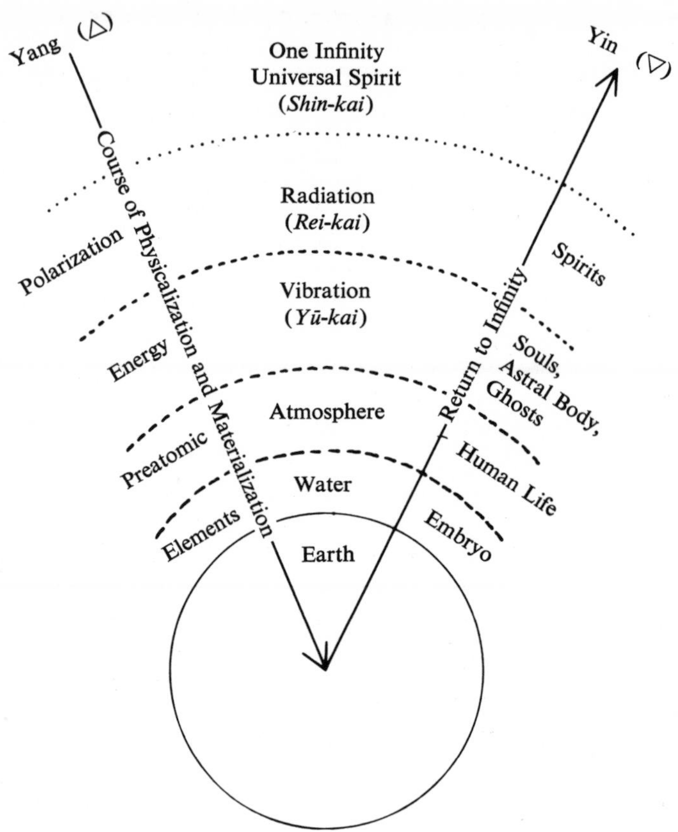

or will. 2) At implantation, the spirit of food starts to influence and shape the new organism, forming the placenta and budding organs. This is known as the *Kon*, or soul. 3) After three months, as various embryonic organs form, a charge comes and enters the fetus, causing the heart to beat and charging the energy centers, or chakras. This is known as the *Shin*, or divine spirit. It comes from heaven, and its very high energy activates certain brain rhythms, including the memory center. 4) Then the spirit of the environment enters in, including the weather, the sun, and other atmospheric and climatic cycles. This is known as *Chi*, or the spirit of desire and understanding, and includes the spirit of pregnancy—the mother's thinking—and the spirit of the birthplace—the unique conditions where the child is born. 5) Finally at birth, the baby takes a breath and the spirit of air, or *Haku*, enters in.

These five spirits, or energies, make up the human being. When we are born, one by one, they enter and charge the body, and when we die, one by one they leave it and return to their original sphere.

Our embryonic life was lived in a world of water in the mother's uterus, a small, dark world. In this world, we created our protoplasmic body, the organism composed of cells, to prepare for the next life. We emerged from the womb, discarding the placenta and umbilical cord that nourished us, into a new world surrounded with air. The far larger and brighter space within which we live our infancy, childhood, and later adult life circumscribes the entire surface of the earth. This world alternates between brightness and darkness, day and night, summer and winter. In this world, we continue to develop our protoplasmic body for a period of about twenty years.

Although our physical development usually stops at about this point, we continue to develop unceasingly our emotional, intellectual, social, ideological, and universal consciousness, together with the constant refinement of our physical qualities. We develop the energetic body—our electromagnetic constitution that deals with vibrations and waves of consciousness.

The food and energies that we ingest nourish our consciousness and spirit. Like the yolk of an egg nourishing the emerging chick, the body acts as a placenta to the growing Tree of Life within us. Our roots as human beings are in heaven, and the *ki* or electromagnetic energy that animates us comes primarily from above through the chakras before branching out to the meridians and then to trillions of cells. Each cell has spirit, nourished constantly by energy and vibration from heaven and earth. We are fully spiritualized when these cells are activated. When we talk, act, think, or touch, spiritual power radiates from us. Thus it is important to select the right kind of vibrational/spiritual energy at all times. In addition to proper food, we should seek the highest quality environment, scenery, culture, and companionship.

When our energetic body matures, in the same way that we transferred ourselves from the world of water to the world of air, we transfer our life from the world of air to the world of vibration, leaving the protoplasmic body behind us at death. The world of vibration that we enter is far greater in space and far brighter than the air world. The spatial dimension of the vibrational world covers the entire sphere of the solar system and is experienced as a single unit. There is no darkness. Consciousness is continued in this new world, which is usually called the spiritual world. Communication proceeds not only in the world of spirit but also between the vibrational world and the human world.

In the event that we nourish ourselves properly in the air world and refine our physical, mental, and spiritual vibration to a level of maturity sufficient to be born into the next, vibrational world, our death is natural and spiritual. If we are born into the next world through such spiritual death, we enjoy a large dimension of free consciousness with spiritual happiness. Furthermore, after our spiritual quality matures in the next, vibrational life, we proceed to a higher and more universal plane, dissolving the vibrational body into waves and rays. This world is far larger than the vibrational world, covering the entire dimension of the galaxy. From this stage, our life further continues to develop and eventually, through changing ourselves at infinite speed, we become one with the universal consciousness of God or infinity.

The vibrational or spiritual world spirals in an opposite way to our world, expanding rather than contracting. While on earth, we usually cannot perceive this dimension because we are limited to the five senses. Everything we experience is moving in a yang direction, and we do not have instruments for the other way. Although it surrounds and overlaps our world, we cannot perceive the larger yin realm. In that world, what is ahead of us is farther away, going faster and faster. Its expanding logarithmic speed makes it very hard to discover. Thus, except sometimes for ghosts, for true dreams, or other "extrasensory" experiences, we cannot see or feel the world of spirit.

The world of vibration is trillions of times bigger than our world, covering the entire solar system and galaxy. While our basic movement on earth is horizontal, in that world it is vertical. The world of spirit is all bright compared to the half bright/half dark world here. In this world things take time to physicalize, while in the next world they manifest instantly. There, what we think is reality. If we visualize something, its image appears immediately. Our earth world is actually part of the larger vibrational world, since air is vibration. Here, thinking is also doing, but usually we cannot see any immediate effects, so we consider it unreal.

Life in the Spiritual World

After death our consciousness proceeds to the next world, the world of spirit. Our physical body, which is yang, is a general manifestation of heaven's force although it receives both the forces of heaven and earth. It deals, primarily, with the yang, material world. The destiny of this body is to return to the earth.

Consciousness, on the other hand, is governed generally by the centrifugal or expanding force of earth. Its destiny is to ascend toward heaven. All biological life separates at death into two; one part, the physical body, decomposes back into the earth, while the more spiritual, energy body, rises. The part that continues to live, our consciousness, can be called the soul or vibrational body. It is this electromagnetic mass that carries consciousness.

After reaching physical maturity on earth, we begin our true spiritual development. This growth continues until death, which is nothing more than the birth of our vibrational body into the next world. After a period of growth in that world, we return to this life through the process of reincarnation. At this time we again combine the physical material of earth with our vibrational body and continue the development of our spiritual quality. This alternation between the two worlds continues until our consciousness is refined enough to exist on the next level of life. Our goal on earth is to mature to the point where we no longer need the experiences in the material world for development.

In the Far East, the traditional name for the next world is *Yū-Kai. Yū* means astral, ghost, or soul, and *Kai* refers to sphere or world. The physical world is called *Gen-Kai. Gen* means present, visible, sensory, or detectable. It deals basically with the five senses, while the *Yū-Kai* consists of vibrations which cannot be perceived with our physical senses. Our spiritual or vibrational body in the next world is referred to in the Orient as the *Yū-Tai.*

The physical world is composed of very condensed vibrations and is a thick form of spirit. In the next world, where energy is more yin, our lifespan is longer than on earth. We live about seventy to eighty years in this life. In the next world, the *Yū-Kai,* we live much longer. The average is about six hundred to one thousand earth years. The general ratio is 1 earth year to 7 years in the spiritual world.

While on earth we may be aware of the spiritual world, but it seems vague. When in the spiritual world, we perceive physical existence, but again, only in a general way. In the next world, although conditions are very different, we still are living and enjoy life. There are mountains and rivers and communities. The relation between the physical and the spiritual world is front and back, antagonistic and complementary. In the *Yū-Kai* we meet the people whom we knew in this life. Our parents, ancestors, and friends appear in their vibrational form. Of course, relationships are very different there, because we no longer have a physical body. Love is expressed not as sexual attraction but as sympathy, kindness, and sharing.

In this life, everyone has a body manifested by heaven's force, and all are living on the same level, physically. The next life is different. Free of this heavy physical body, our consciousness rises to the level of our development, according to the quality of our vibrations. Unlike life on earth, there is a wide range of existence in the spiritual world.

Equality is the ideal on earth because everyone is on the same general physical level. But the next world is more vertical, although horizontal differentiation also appears. In the spiritual world there are low, middle, and high planes, with many gradations in between. The quality of our *Yū-Tai*, and the level we will exist on in the *Yū-Kai*, is 90 percent determined by the development we make in this world, according to such factors as how and what we eat, the type of thoughts we have, and the overall quality of our lives. Physical life reflects, to a great extent, the quality of our development in our mother's womb. Our condition in the womb became our constitution after birth. In the same way, the quality of consciousness developed in this life determines the level we will exist on in the vibrational world. We may say that physical existence is the embryonic stage for life in the next world, and our condition in this life becomes our constitution in the next.

As we all know, if the embryonic life in the mother's uterus is not properly nourished—by food, environment, and love—a miscarriage, early birth, deformation, or retardation arises, and infants who are born with these conditions must suffer in the human world. Similarly, if our nourishment in this air world is not proper, we experience physical, mental, or spiritual deformity or retardation while we are alive and usually die unnaturally as a result of sickness, accident, or other undesirable causes. This results in an unexpected, immature birth into the next, spiritual world. A premature birth in that world may cause us to suffer in darkness even though the vibrational world is full of light. In such cases, delusions of consciousness and attachment to this world cause departed spirits to wander among human society, often manifesting as ghosts.

Our Spiritual Journey

We go through a process of physicalization when we are born. We become more yang, more condensed. As we embark on our journey of spiritualization, our return to infinity, we begin to expand or diffuse, to become lighter and more refined. We change from longer to shorter waves, until ultimately, we lose our differentiation and merge with God or the Eternal. This journey takes millions of years. We must mature through each stage or level of life before moving to the next. Until we do, we repeatedly return to the previous stage until our development on that particular level is complete.

The earth's vibrational sphere extends only partially into the spiritual world. But in the next life, the entire solar system is encompassed in the vibrational sphere, and this becomes our home. This area encompasses the sun and the planets, including perhaps several that have not as yet been discovered. The *Yū-Kai* also extends beyond, into the cometary field, which is some thousand times larger than the planetary field. It moves in a huge spiral motion. The make-up of the total dimensions and vibrations of the solar system take on the appearance of a ball. The visible, physical part is the core. It is covered by the invisible, vibrational field or aura of the solar system. Together they form a complementary, antagonistic unit.

The next solar system, Alpha Centauri, comprises another unit of physical and vibrational energy. This unit is the *Yū-Kai* of that particular solar system. If our body is refined at death, we freely and naturally enter into the next world. The entire solar system unit can be our home. Then, upon earth or another planet, we again materialize through the process of reincarnation. However, when our quality is poor, we cannot choose the place because we are still attached to the earth's vibrational field. We must return to earth until we lose our attachment to it, or, in other words, until we refine the quality of our consciousness.

In our mother's womb, we lived in darkness. On the earth we live in a world alternating between light and darkness. The *Yū-Kai* is a world of brightness. An electron is a small, preatomic particle. Vibrations are smaller and are composed of a particle and a wave. We may call them lifetrons, universons, cosmons, or cosmic building blocks. These elementary units make up the vibrational world. They sparkle and are charged with beautiful light. But if our quality is not refined at death, we will not perceive this beauty, because our perception is distorted by attachment and resistance. The vibrational body has not fully developed in this case, and just as a premature baby has a difficult time surviving in the physical world after birth, we will experience difficulties and will probably have to return to earth to continue our growth.

In traditional societies, babies were born with head down as the mother squatted. Conversely, at the end of life, people went from here to the next world sitting up, with the consciousness naturally going out the top of the head. At birth, the first breath is a breathing out, while at death it is a breathing in. The "ah, ah, ah" sound at death is directed to the energy center at the top of the head, not to the lungs. The soul comes out at the head gradually like labor contractions at birth, as the fires extinguish in the lower chakras one by one.

As the moment of death approaches, our breathing quickens. We are yinnizing ourselves with oxygen, accelerating the separation of body and spirit. At death, the consciousness floats out the top and looks down at the body from above. Our consciousness or vibrational body is attached to our physical body by a vibrational string. This cord can extend for thousands of miles. But just as at birth the umbilical cord is cut, at death this vibrational cord is severed. Our physical body is the placenta for our vibrational body, and the string connecting both exists in our physical body as the meridians of *ki* or electromagnetic energy. If the vibration is heavy, the spirit can stay attached to the air world for a time, but if it is light it floats up. Then one or two spiritual guides come and escort the spirit to the next realm. Sometimes the spirit does not realize what is happening, whether it is alive or dead, or still a human or not. Gradually it recognizes that it is living differently and does not require air to breathe, only vibration. After death, it usually takes seven days to forty-nine days to enter and settle in the next world by the earth calendar. The soul or spirit needs to be well prepared to adapt to that realm.

Unfortunately, today many people die prematurely by sickness, accident, or war. In this case their consciousness is usually not yet sufficiently developed for life in the spiritual world. They have not accomplished the things they would have liked to, and they do not yet know the meaning of life. They are frightened of death and have no knowledge of the purpose of life. This is reflected in degenerative disease, which is nothing more than a symptom of our ignorance of life. When someone dies at this stage, their birth into the next world is often full of struggle and resistance, because they are still attached to the relative life on earth. In this case the vibrational body is not very refined. It is heavy and chaotic, and in the next world the immediate experience is one of darkness and resistance as they struggle against the confinement they have created. Such people do not swim smoothly in the ocean of vibration.

However, if our life on earth develops harmoniously—if our mother ate well while pregnant, was a hard worker and a humble person; if we had a smooth, natural birth; and if we were fed mother's milk and as a child had a variety of experiences, including hardships that helped us grow strong—our physical, mental, and spiritual development will proceed smoothly. If we eat well and remain active, we will enjoy a long life and have a natural death. Our passing into the next world will be peaceful and smooth. In this case, we will know our time of death and will continue to make our consciousness peaceful as it approaches. Even though we may have made many mistakes in early life, if we continue to live macrobiotically, we will gradually become like a sage or a saint in the last stage of our human life.

Such people naturally rise to higher levels in the next world, moving beyond the earth's vibrational sphere into the solar sphere. After a lifetime in that world, they proceed to the next life, dying, discarding their vibrational body, changing into waves and being born into that world. In the Orient this level of life is called the *Rei-Kai,* meaning the spiritual sphere and our body on this level is called *Rei-Tai,* or spiritual body, although it is more like an image than a body as we know it. Physically speaking, it is a group of rays or waves.

Table 28. The Spiritual World

World	*Nourishment*	*Identity*	*Scope*
Water	Placenta	Body	Womb
Air	Food	Consciousness	Earth
Vibrational	Consciousness	Vibrational Body	Solar System
Spiritual	Soul	Spiritual Wave	Galaxy
Divine	Spirit	Divine Wave	Entire Universe
Nonmanifest	—	—	Infinity

The lower sphere of the *Rei-Kai* is the solar spiritual realm. It is surrounded by the world of waves and rays. In the Orient people speak of the spirit, called "Rei," and in the West we are concerned with the physical world. Both are the same. One refers to the physical and the other the spiritual; each is a different aspect of the same reality.

The next level of life, the *Rei-Kai,* encompasses the entire Milky Way galaxy, including its invisible vibrational world, which is much larger than the three dimensions that we usually perceive.

As our vibrational body dissolves and we enter into the galactic world, we change ourselves into rays and waves. Our consciousness exists in the form of image and thought as we begin to travel at tremendous speed through vast dimensions. If our quality is not developed for life in this world, we are reborn into the solar vibrational world, and from there, down through the solar system to this world or other planetary worlds. Reincarnation continues as we move back and forth until our vibrational body is matured to the degree necessary for life in the next world.

But, if our quality is developed, we live a natural life in the *Rei-Kai* and at its transformation progress smoothly to the next plane, the *Shin-Kai* or divine sphere. Living in the galactic spiritual world, we are able to materialize ourselves into any system within the galactic field. There are about 100 million solar systems in the Milky Way galaxy, and each system has at least several planets. There are many millions of planets, among which about 2 to 3 percent are suitable for biological life. Initially, we manifest in the vibrational form in a certain system or planet and then materialize into biological life and are ultimately born as a human being.

In the galactic world we can easily make thought reality. If we think that we want to be born in this solar system, on the third planet, as a human being, if the image is there, at that moment we are materializing on the earth as a human being. But from the perspective of this world, the process takes billions of years to unfold, because the perception of time is so different.

In the galactic world, life moves at tremendous speed, and so things happen almost instantaneously. One year there is comparable to thousands of years on earth. A thought in that world has occurred thousands of years before we experience it on this planet. For example, our birth on earth was preceded thousands of years ago by our vibrational appearance here. A thought, image, or wave in that world arises. We select our life on earth and first manifest into this solar system's vibrational sphere, in the *Yū-Tai* form. From there, we move to the earth's *Yū-Kai*, its vibrational sphere, and from there materialize upon the earth as a human being.

There is also a nonphysicalized manifestation in the form of a ray or thought. If we want to do this we distribute our thought to many planets. The inhabitants, the present-day manifestations of biological life, receive this impulse in their brains, and begin to think similar thoughts of peace and love. This can be done on one planet or many, and the inhabitants will receive our image in the same way an antenna picks up radio signals. Obviously, individuals with poor quality receiving equipment will be unable to process these waves. Often, very few individuals among the population are sensitive enough to pick up and interpret the vibrations. These people begin to teach and to act as "messengers of God." Many of the prophets and founders of the world's religions were examples of this.

We expand further into space toward the infinite universe as we leave the galactic sphere. At this time our body changes again, from ray or wave, thought or image, into infinite movement at infinite speed. At this time our consciousness extends throughout the universe and we become, or merge with, God or infinity itself. Time or space no longer exists for us. We are undifferentiated. We have realized our true self, our origin and destiny.

It was from this level that we began the process of physicalization. If our development proceeds smoothly, we go from our mother's womb to birth into the air world, to birth into the vibrational world and its various levels, to birth in the solar system's spiritual world, to birth in the galactic divine world, to God or Infinity.

But the process does not proceed this smoothly because we destroy our quality and must return again and again to certain levels. Either our physical condition is not developed enough or we still have attachments and delusions at the time of death. Our vibrational quality is still heavy and chaotic. On the average, we return to human life about three hundred times before our quality is ready for the next world.

We ourselves decide when to return, if necessary, to the air world to further our understanding of the laws of change and harmony, to develop compassion and love, and to help others. In the *Yū-Kai* we choose the proper parents, ideally those who are in excellent health, know the secret of food, and have a warm heart. A baby born to such a family is spiritually oriented and may grow up to help and teach many, many people.

Death is part of the natural evolutional process on the way to returning to our eternal origin. When we die, as when we are born, we go from one dimension to the next. It is a wonderful enlightening process. Unfortunately, modern people do not know the Tree of Life and think only material things are important such as wealth, weight, and physical gain. Eating cheese, beef, sugar, white flour, canned goods, and other improper foods leads to chaos in day-to-day life and physical, mental, and spiritual stagnation. Existence becomes a fight for money and property, for status and success, for physical pleasure and beauty. For these ephemeral things, countless lives are lost or wasted, families are broken, and wars are fought.

Because they have not paid attention to their food or environment, millions of people undergo needless suffering from heart disease, cancer, mental illness, and other degenerative diseases and to make balance have to decompose their bodies prematurely. Their last years or days are a constant struggle, with intensive care, oxygen supplies, intravenous feedings and injections, and often life support equipment leading to a lingering death and astronomical medical expenses that impose hardships on their family. It is very sad. For so many people today, life is a continual battle, from beginning to end, rather than the adventure and joyous experience it was meant to be.

Many people today die without maturing and are not ready to live in the next world. Because they have failed to develop their spiritual side and are unprepared to leave the earth, attachment arises and vibrational consciousness is very rough. In that form, such spirits often remain on earth for many years as ghosts, or they exist in a confusing state between two worlds where they create images around them of money, cursing, and battle. That we call hell.

In the world of vibration, there is no hell or punishment. That world is completely bright. However, just as many people on earth live in a delusional world populated by dangerous microorganisms, mutant cells, harmful weeds and insects, and enemies of different religions, races, and political beliefs, so some spirits on the periphery of the *Yū-Kai* are still struggling with their own dark images and cannot perceive the light around them. While a natural death is peaceful and radiant, an unnatural birth into the next world can be accompanied by suffering and inability to see the light. A smooth, calm transition is essential, and even three days eating macrobiotically before dying makes a big difference.

Meditation and Prayer

In life we face many difficulties, challenges, and disappointments. At this time, meditation can help restore direction and harmony to our lives (see Figure 53). There are two basic types of meditation: 1) yang meditation, which activates the *hara* and stabilizes the mind and body toward the center of the earth, and 2) yin meditation, which focuses on the midbrain and uplifts us toward the vibrational and spiritual worlds.

The first type of meditation fills us full of energy so that we become immovable as a mountain or rock. Our confidence grows and our spirit is indomitable. Yang meditation is accomplished by breathing down to the area of the *hara*, holding the breath for a while, and then breathing out. The body feels hotter as we continue, stressing the long out breaths. This meditation is very good for overcoming sadness, depression, and fear and to develop will and resolve.

The second type of meditation opens the body and mind up to the world of consciousness and the next life. Yin meditation is performed by focusing on the energy center between the eyebrows, holding the hands open at the side, and breathing up. Breathing in is emphasized rather than breathing out, and the body begins to lift up toward heaven. The body feels cooler, the hands become drier, and the metabolism slows down and is lower. Ultimately, experienced meditators become unconscious, and their consciousness separates and appears in distant places.

In addition to these two types, there are many other ways to meditate, self-reflect, and pray. Consciousness can be directed to developing ourselves, healing others, and assisting departed spirits, as well as tranquilizing the world as a whole.

By prayers, for example, we can help wandering spirits go to the *Yū-Kai*. Immature spirits, or ghosts, attach themselves to the immediate family or closest friends because of the same way of eating and thinking. By eating well and by brighter, higher thinking, we can help them detach. We can do this by raising our own vibrational level and praying for them a few minutes each day, explaining to them that they are no longer living in this world and thus no longer need to be attached to the earth.

Figure 53. Basic Meditation

Yang Meditation
(*Hara*)

Yin Meditation
(*Midbrain*)

Yang meditation focuses on the energy center below the abdomen, while yin meditation concentrates on the midbrain.

By projecting images of light and harmony, we can help them perceive the next world. Encouraging them to move on and develop there, we can explain that one day we will join them there. Talking like this in ordinary conversation or just thinking silently is very beneficial. When the spirits around us are released, we ourselves feel happier and uplifted.

Through meditation, self-reflection, and prayer, we can transform ourselves and the world around us. By mentally changing ourselves, our body changes, just as by changing our physical condition, our mental condition also improves. Through meditation and similar mental and spiritual exercises, we can return to our infinite source, empty our minds of our troubles, and come back to the everyday world refreshed and inspired to begin anew.

Spirit and Destiny

Our body nourishes our spirit, which goes to the next world. Modern science sees food as consisting only of protein, fat, carbohydrates, and various vitamins and minerals. It does not see or understand energy, because *ki* or natural electromagnetic force cannot be measured by mechanical and sensory means. The overriding question today is: Can modern civilization develop a food and agricultural system to really nourish high quality vibration and consciousness in order to overcome degenerative disease and the threat of war and to continue human biological and spiritual evolution?

Cereal plants grow straight up. They do not hang down at the top like fruits, which were eaten by the apes and monkeys that preceded us. By eating grains, human consciousness developed and is evolving toward the heavens. By eating predominantly vegetable-quality food, our spirit soars. In contrast, animal food contracts our awareness and narrows our intellect and understanding. It keeps us tied to the earth. We cannot experience the bright vibrations of the spiritual world if we continually eat meat, eggs, poultry, and dairy food. Thus what we eat every day is of paramount spiritual importance.

Our life is our dream, and the earth is for our training as our playground. We can choose, formulate, and create the life we wish. It is entirely up to us. The whole universe is backing us. Millions of friends today are now eating the same way and sharing the same blood quality. With them we can act and play together to realize humanity's common dream of building One Peaceful World and continuing our endless journey through the stars.

The laws of yin and yang are invisible, but everything moves according to these principles. The spiritual world is governed by the laws of change and harmony as well as our world here. Spirit, body, mind, society, nature, planets, and galaxies all move according to the same spirallic laws. The Kingdom of Heaven embraces existence as a whole, and the next life like this one is constantly changing. Something appears, then the opposite appears. This is the universal law of balance.

Our life is eternal, though our human life is ephemeral. Our dream is endless, though our human desires are finite. The purpose of life—discovering, understanding, and becoming one with the infinite Order of the Universe—is imperishable, though our human works are in vain. We play in this universe, living our eternal life, transforming ourselves constantly, manifesting ourselves into various forms. We enjoy the freedom to change ourselves to adapt to the changing environment and to continue to develop endlessly. Happiness is the endless realization of our endless dream.

Appendixes

Biological and Social Decline

The following figures give a statistical profile of the current biological and social decline of modern society, as represented by the United States, and of the global environment. They are derived from the most recent reports of the American Heart Association, the American Cancer Society, and other national medical and public health organizations as well as the United Nations, Worldwatch Institute, SIPRI (Stockholm International Peace Research Institute), and other international sources. The U.S. population is about 225 million.

Personal Decline

Aches: 73 percent of Americans suffer from occasional headaches, 50 percent from aches of the back, muscles, and joints, and 27 percent from dental pain.

AIDS: Acute symptoms of Acquired Immune-Deficiency Syndrome (AIDS) have appeared in about 19,000 people between 1979 and 1986. An estimated 2 million Americans are now infected of whom an estimated 20 percent or more will develop AIDS. The disease is doubling every year, and if current rates continue it will affect 64 million Americans by 1990. It originally affected primarily male homosexuals, intravenous drug users, hemophiliacs, and persons from certain tropical climates. However, now it is beginning to turn up in women, heterosexual men, and other groupings and has now spread to Africa, Europe, the Soviet Union, the Middle East, Asia, and Latin America. There is no current medical treatment.

Alzheimer's Disease: This degenerative disease of the brain cells affects an estimated 1 million persons, usually between the ages of 40 and 70. There is no current medical treatment.

Arthritis: 50 million Americans (about 1 in 4) are affected by arthritis. This includes 7.3 million crippling cases, mostly rheumatoid arthrities. Osteoarthritis, or degenerative joint disease, affects 97 percent of all people over 60. About 250,000 children also suffer from some form of this disease.

Birth Defects: 12.7 million Americans have birth defects. In the last 25 years, the number of children reported born with physical abnormalities, mental retardation, or learning defects has doubled, jumping from 70,000 in the late 1950s to 140,000 in 1983, including about 25,000 babies born each year with congenital heart defects. This represents a jump from 2 percent of babies born with defects to 4 percent.

Cancer: The second leading cause of death in modern society, cancer claims about 440,000 Americans each year. In addition, 850,000 new cases will develop along with another 400,000 cases of usually nonfatal skin cancer. At the turn of the century, the cancer rate was about 1 in 25 persons. By 1950 it had risen to about 1 in 8, and today it will affect nearly 1 in every 3 Americans now living. Lung cancer is rising the most rapidly, while breast cancer will develop in 1 of every 11 women. About 1.5 million biopsies are performed each year.

Cardiovascular Disease: Heart attacks, stroke, and other circulatory disorders are the No. 1 cause of death in modern society, taking 1 in every 2 lives. This has climbed from about 1 death in 9 due to heart and blood vessel disease in 1920. Today 58 million people have high blood pressure, a major risk factor. Each year about 1.5 million Americans have a heart attack, and 550,000 of them will die. Another half million will suffer a stroke, about one third of which are fatal. Surgically, 1.6 million circulatory operations and procedures are performed each year in the U.S., including 159,000 bypass grafts, 177,000 pacemaker operations, and 414,000 cardiac catheterizations.

Cerebral Palsy: An estimated 750,000 Americans have this disorder, about 1 in 300.

Diabetes: 11 million Americans currently have diabetes, about 1 in 20. Members of some Indian tribes are 7 to 10 times as likely as non-Indians to contract the disease.

Epilepsy: 2.1 million Americans have epilepsy, about 1 in 100.

Hearing Loss: About a half million Americans are totally deaf. Severe hearing loss in infants appears to have increased dramatically in the early 1980s. The number of cases of profound hearing impairment reported in babies under 18 months rose almost five times between 1982 and 1983.

Kidney Dialysis: Between 1972 and 1982 the number of kidney dialysis patients rose from 10,300 to 82,000.

Mental Illness: At any given time, 29 million Americans—nearly 1 in 5 adults—suffer psychiatric disorders ranging from mildly disabling anxiety to severe schizophrenia. About 5 million of these people seek medical treatment every six months.

Multiple Sclerosis: About half a million Americans have this disorder, about 1 in 450.

Natural Death: More than 70 percent of the population die in modern hospitals. In contrast, at the turn of the century, most people died at home.

Osteoporosis: About 25 percent of all women over 60 will break a bone, due primarily to the degenerative thinning of the bones, which makes them more susceptible to fracture.

Parkinson's Disease: About 1.5 million Americans have this disorder, about 1 in 150.

Polio: Although polio appeared to be wiped out by vaccine in the 1950s, Post-Polio Sequelae (Syndrome) is beginning to appear a generation later. 75,000 polio sufferers, representing about 25 percent of those who recovered three decades ago, are now suffering loss of strength in their arms and legs, aches, and exhaustion, and in many cases have had to return to ventilators.

Sexually Transmitted Diseases: An estimated 30 million Americans have herpes or other new S.T.D. The number is expected to increase geometrically, with no effective medical prevention and relief at the present time. Syphilis, gonorrhea, and other older venereal diseases affect slightly over 1 million people.

Surgery: In 1981, 25.6 million medical operations were performed, a 62 percent increase over the previous decade.

Transplants: Each year about 6,000 kidney transplants are performed, 200 pancreas transplants, 175 heart transplants, and 165 liver transplants.

Family Decline

Abortion: Between 1974 and 1984, the number of legal abortions doubled. Currently 1.5 million abortions are performed each year, about 1 for every 3 births.

Alcohol Abuse: An estimated 14 million Americans are alcoholics, about 1 in 10 adults. Alcohol abuse is a growing problem among young persons as well and a major cause of family troubles, violence, and decline.

Broken Homes: More than one half the children under 18 (13 million) now live in a home with one or both parents missing.

Divorce: At the turn of the century, 1 in 12 marriages ended in divorce. By 1940 the rate had increased to 1 in 6. In 1970 it was 1 in 3, and in the early 1980s it was 1 in 2.

Drug Abuse: From 1970 to 1980, there was an estimated 50 percent increase in illegal drug use and a 250 percent increase in prescriptive drugs such as tranquilizers, sedatives, and stimulants. Forty percent of men and 60 percent of women report having used one or more medications every 48 hours. Twenty million people use marijuana daily. In 1981, 1 in 6 high school seniors tried cocaine.

Family Violence: An estimated 6 million women are abused by their husbands or boyfriends every year, and from 2,000 to 4,000 die as a result of their injuries. The nation's police spend about one third of their time responding to domestic violence calls, while the leading cause of injury to women is physical assault by a spouse or partner. An estimated 280,000 men are physically assaulted by their wives or partners every year. Child abuse is also on the rise. Reported cases doubled between 1976 and 1981 to 851,000 and rose another 12 percent during 1982. Unreported cases of child abuse or neglect are estimated to be another 5 million.

Fast Foods: About 40 percent of all food dollars are spent on meals eaten away from home. Sales of fast food rose 86 percent between 1972 and 1984.

Low Sexual Desire: Psychologists report that low sexual desire or inhibited sexual desire is rapidly growing among both men and women, accounting for about 50 percent of all visits to sex clinics.

Old Age Homes: The number of people living in nursing and old age homes tripled from 470,000 in 1960 to just over 1,400,000 in 1980.

Pet Degeneration: An estimated 30 percent of all dogs, including up to 75 percent of older dogs, suffer from heart disease. Cancer in pets is also epidemic.

Reproductive Disorders: 1 out of every 5 American couples is infertile. Sperm count in men has dropped 30 to 35 percent since 1920. More than 20 percent of sexually active males are estimated to be sterile. An estimated 40 percent of women have Premenstrual Syndrome (PMS), including 3 percent with severe cases. Forty percent of women have fibroid tumors. Five of the ten most frequent operations are now performed on the female reproduction organs. These 4.2 million operations include nearly 700,000 hysterectomies and 500,000 operations to remove the ovaries, so that at by age 60 over half of American women have had their wombs or ovaries removed. Cesarean section tripled in the 1970s to about 1 in 5 births. The rate of adverse pregnancies among women working at VDTs (video display terminals) increased by 50 percent in the early 1980s.

Single Households: In the 1950s, single person households made up less than 10 percent of households. By 1984, nearly 25 percent of all households were made up of people living alone.

Sterilization: 18 percent of couples of childbearing age avoid pregnancy through voluntary sterilization of either partner, making it the most popular form of birth control. Between 1965 and 1982, female sterilization rose from 7 to 26 percent, while male sterilization rose from 5 to 15 percent.

Community Decline

Accidents: About 90,000 people die accidentally each year, and 8.8 million receive disabling injuries. An estimated 84 percent of these accidents involve human error.

Advertising: The average urban American is exposed to 1,600 commercial messages a day, including newspaper, radio, and television ads, signs and billboards, and commercial mail and telephone calls. By age 16, the typical child has seen about 80,000 commercials for highly processed and refined foods on TV.

Crime: 23 million households are touched by crime each year, representing about 27 percent of all households. About one third of these households experience violent or frightening crimes such as rape, robbery, burglary, or assault. Of the 20,000 homicides each year, about one third occur between family members, one third between friends and acquaintances, and one third between strangers.

Dependency: 65 million Americans receive some form of government aid, including 32 million on Social Security and 27 million on Medicare.

Disability: 5 million Americans are incapacitated, requiring help from family or community members in one or more basic activities such as walking, going outside, bathing, dressing, using the toilet, getting in or out of bed, or eating.

Media Violence: By age 16, the average child has seen 18,000 murders on TV, including an average of 5 to 6 violent acts per hour on prime time. About 50 percent of music videos contain violent action or suggestions of violence.

Medical Costs: In current dollars, medical and health care costs rose tenfold between the 1930s and 1970s and are expected to rise another 1,000 percent by the year 2000. In 1986, from heart disease alone, direct medical costs, home nursing expenses, and lost output due to disability were estimated at $78.6 billion. Indirect costs in lowered productivity, increased insurance premiums, and family turmoil can only be inferred. Medical costs are a primary cause of inflation, rising at a rate about twice as fast as the rest of the economy.

Prison Population: In 1985 the nation's inmate population rose to 490,000, a jump of 5 to 6 percent from the previous year.

Robots: In 1985 the total robot population in the United States reached 16,000. By the early 1990s, an estimated 50,000 new robots will be manufactured each year, eventually displacing the industrial work force, including welders, painters, machinists, toolmakers, machine operators, inspectors, and assemblers. In one Japanese plant, robots are already producing other robots.

School Violence: In a typical month, 282,000 secondary students are physically attacked, 112,000 robbed, and 2.4 million report thefts at school. Meanwhile, 125,000 teachers are threatened with physical assault or violence, and 1,000 teachers require medical attention as a result of being attacked while in school.

Environmental Decline

Air Pollution: Industrialization has produced high rises in atmospheric carbon dioxide, lead, sulphur dioxide, and other chemicals leading to widespread air pollution, smog, and acid rain. They could also create a greenhouse effect, raising global temperatures and triggering massive climatic changes and submerging seacoasts. Agriculture, food processing, and food transportation contribute directly and indirectly to this problem. For example, 65 percent of automobile pollution comes from trips to the supermarket.

Cropland Loss: Between 1945 and 1975, 30 million hectares of land in North America were lost to concrete and asphalt. Half of the land paved over was arable.

Deforestation: In 1950, 30 percent of the world's land surface was covered by forest. In 1975, tropical rain forests and woodlands declined to 12 percent and by 2000 are expected to shrink to 7 percent. Logging, mining, and cattle ranching are major causes of deforestation. 70 percent of the 2 billion people who use wood as their main fuel source lack adequate supplies.

Desertification: 28 percent of the world's land suffers from drought, and by the middle of the 21st Century one third of the remaining farmland could be lost to artificial encroachment of the desert. In Africa, monocropping, overgrazing, deforestation, and poor irrigation have resulted in chronic droughts and famines.

Energy Depletion: Petroleum accounts for 45 percent of all energy use worldwide. Known oil reserves will be depleted early in the 21st Century. The United States with 6 percent of the world's population consumes about 30 percent of total energy.

Seed Loss: By the year 2000, an estimated two thirds of all seeds will be of uniform hybrid strains. The loss of genetic diversity and monocropping will make plants further vulnerable to pests, blight, and other threats, now accounting for loss of about one third of the world's harvest.

Soil Erosion: In the United States, one third of the farmland has declined in productivity because of erosion. One inch of topsoil takes from 100 to 2,500 years to develop naturally and can be destroyed by modern farming techniques in 10 years.

Toxic Wastes: There are 4.5 million known toxic chemicals and 375,000 new chemicals are produced annually. In the U.S., chemical production increased 67 percent between 1967 and 1977. Most have never been tested or certified as safe. Pesticides, PCBs, heavy metal, and other residues accumulate in fatty tissues as they move up the food chain. By the time they reach human, their concentrations can increase a million times. Each year 1 ton of chemical wastes are produced per capita in the U.S., and most are released into the environment or disposed of illegally.

Water Depletion: 70 percent of global water use goes to irrigate new "miracle crops" produced with artificial fertilizers and sprays. Water tables are dangerously low in many parts of the country from excessive agricultural irrigation. For example, 1 pound of meat requires up to 6,000 gallons of water to produce, while 1 pound of rice requires 250 gallons and 1 pound of wheat 60 gallons.

Water Pollution: The world's oceans, lakes, and waterways are increasingly polluted from oil spills, chemical runoffs, pesticides, PCBs and industrial pollutants, heavy metals, and sewage. 90 percent of the pollutants remain in coastal waters, though ocean currents transport chemical residues worldwide so that high levels of DDT, for example, have turned up in the fat of antarctic penguins.

Wildlife Loss: One species of plant is currently vanishing each day from the spread of modern civilization. Twenty to 40 animals are dependent on each plant. At present rates, 130 species of animals will become extinct each day by the end of the century, and one quarter of all animal species now existing will disappear by the mid-21st Century.

Global Decline

Armed Forces: The U.S. and U.S.S.R. each have about 750,000 armed troops stationed abroad. Other countries in Europe, Asia, Africa, and the Middle East have another half million soldiers on foreign soil. Between 1958 and 1981, almost two thousand satellites were launched into space for purposes of military communication, reconnaissance, warning, and data gathering.

Arms Expenditures: The nations of the world spend an estimated $800 billion annually on defense and war. By comparison, the United Nations' six largest agencies spend the yearly equivalent of only one and half days of the arms race. Fifty percent of the world's engineers and physicists are directly employed in weapons development.

Chemical and Biological Weapons: The U.S. and U.S.S.R. each have an estimated several hundred tons of deadly poison gas, including nerve gas, stockpiled for military use. France has a small supply of nerve gas.

Hunger: An estimated 40 million people die each year from hunger and hunger-related diseases, half of whom are children. This is the equivalent of 300 jumbo jet crashes a day. However, there is more than enough food for everyone. The main problem is that 40 percent of the world's grain (including 90 percent of American grain) is fed to cattle or other livestock to produce meat, poultry, dairy food, or other animal products for consumption in modern societies. Also one third of the world's fish catch is used for animal-feed to fatten livestock.

Nuclear False Alarms: In a recent 18-month period the North American Defense Command reported 151 computer failures signalling a Soviet attack. The lead-time prior to missile launch is from 6 to 10 minutes.

Nuclear Proliferation: Between 1945 and 1981, six countries developed nuclear weapons and conducted 1,321 atomic explosions above and below ground. By the early 1980s, 48 countries had nuclear reactors or nuclear research reactors that could manufacture weapons-grade material. At present there is no safe storage method for nuclear waste. Plutonium-239 has a half-life of 240,000 years and uranium-238 4.5 million years, posing a lethal threat for many generations to come.

Nuclear Weapons: Together the U.S. and U.S.S.R. possess an estimated 40,000 to 50,000 nuclear weapons totalling 15,000 megatons of destructive capability. The Hiroshima bomb had a strength of .03 megaton. 15,000 of these warheads are poised for land or sea-based missile delivery. Modern nuclear submarines each carry up to 8 times the total firepower of World War II, and a single missile can be launched with ten warheads each independently targeted to destroy a single city. According to a UN report, a typical 1-megaton bomb exploded over a city with 1 million inhabitants would result in 270,000 deaths by blast and fire, 90,000 deaths by fallout, and 90,000 injured. Two thirds of the buildings would be demolished or badly damaged, roads would be erased, water and energy mains destroyed, and most of the remaining city would be obliterated in a sea of blazing rubble.

Poverty: An estimated 1 billion people live in abject material poverty. About 50 percent are small farmers and 20 to 25 percent landless laborers who are affected by modern agricultural dislocations as well as drought and famine.

War: Since World War II, there have been 160 armed conflicts between nations resulting in 16 million deaths, mostly civilians. The rate of new wars has increased from an average of 9 a year in the 1950s to 14 in the 1980s.

Dietary Goals and Recommendations

Dietary Goals for the United States

In 1977, the U.S. Senate Select Committee on Nutrition and Human Needs issued *Dietary Goals for the United States*, a landmark report on the nation's way of eating, health, and future direction. The Senate findings, also known as the McGovern Report after its chairman, George McGovern, concluded:

> During this century, the composition of the average diet in the United States has changed radically. Complex carbohydrates—fruit, vegetables, and grain products—which were the mainstay of the diet, now play a minority role. At the same time, fat and sugar consumption have risen to the point where these two dietary elements alone now comprise at least 60 percent of total calorie intake, up from 50 percent in the early 1900s.
>
> In the view of doctors and nutritionists consulted by the Select Committee, these and other changes in the diet amount to a wave of malnutrition—of both over- and under-consumption—that may be as profoundly damaging to the Nation's health as the widespread contagious diseases of the early part of this century. The over-consumption of fat, generally, and saturated fat in particular, as well as cholesterol, sugar, salt, and alcohol have been related to six of the leading causes of death: Heart disease, cancer, cerebrovascular diseases, diabetes, arteriosclerosis, and cirrhosis of the liver.

United States Dietary Goals:

1. Increase carbohydrate consumption to account for 55 to 66 percent of the energy (caloric) intake.
2. Reduce overall fat consumption from approximately 40 to 30 percent of energy intake.

3. Reduce saturated fat consumption to account for about 10 percent of total energy intake; and balance with polyunsaturated and monounsaturated fats, which should account for about 10 percent of energy intake each.

4. Reduce cholesterol consumption to about 300 mg. a day.

5. Reduce sugar consumption by almost 40 percent to account for about 15 percent of total energy intake.

6. Reduce salt consumption by about 50 to 85 percent to approximately 3 grams a day.

The goals are expressed graphically as below:

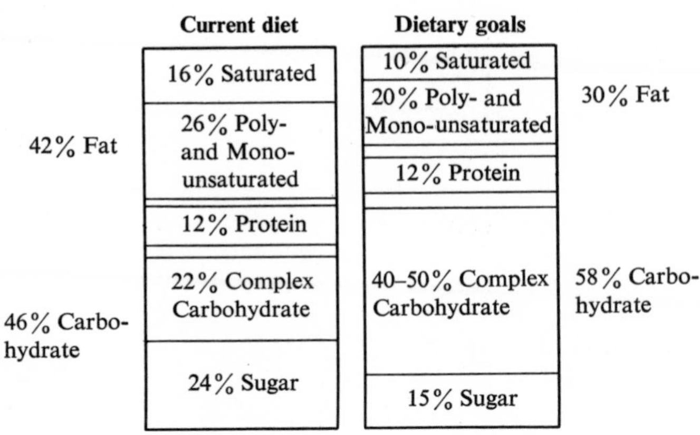

Sources for current diet: *Changes in Nutrients in the U.S. Diet Caused by Alterations in Food Intake Patterns*. B. Friend. Agricultural Research Service. U.S. Department of Agriculture, 1974. Proportions of saturated versus unsaturated fats based on unpublished Agricultural Research Service data.

The Goals Suggest the Following Changes in Food Selection and Preparation:

1. Increase consumption of fruits and vegetables and whole grains.
2. Decrease consumption of meat and increase consumption of poultry and fish.
3. Decrease consumption of foods high in fat and partially substitute polyunsaturated fat for saturated fat.
4. Substitute non-fat milk for whole milk.

5. Decrease consumption of butterfat, eggs, and other high cholesterol sources.
6. Decrease consumption of sugar and foods high in sugar content.
7. Decrease consumption of salt and foods high in salt content.

Source: *Dietary Goals for the United States*, Senate Select Committee on Nutrition and Human Needs (Washington, D.C.: Government Printing Office, 1977).

The Surgeon General's Report

In 1979 the U.S. Surgeon General issued *Healthy People*, a report on the nation's health that suggested degenerative disease could be relieved as well as prevented by dietary means and called for substantial increases in the consumption of whole grains, vegetables, and fresh fruit and reductions in meat, eggs, dairy food, sugar, and other processed foods. The report states in part:

> A good case can be made for the role of high intake of cholesterol and saturated fat, usually of animal origin, in producing high blood cholesterol levels which are associated with atherosclerosis and cardiovascular diseases.
>
> Animal studies have show that reducing serum cholesterol can slow down and even reverse the atherosclerotic process.
>
> And, in man, certain studies have shown: that people in countries where diets are low in saturated fats and cholesterol have lower average serum cholesterol levels and fewer heart attacks; and that Americans who habitually eat less fat-rich diets (vegetarians and Seventh-Day Adventists, for example) have less heart disease than other Americans. Other observations in man suggest the possibility that certain types of atherosclerosis may be reversed by cholesterol-lowering diets.

Healthy Nutrition: Individual nutritional requirement variations make exact dietary standards impossible to establish. Variations also occur in the same person at different times—during pregnancy, with aging, during acute or chronic illness, or with changes in physical activity.

But given what is already known or strongly suspected about the relationship between diet and disease, Americans would probably be healthier, as a whole, if they consumed:

• only sufficient calories to meet body needs and maintain desirable weight (fewer calories if overweight);

• less saturated fat and cholesterol;

• less salt;

• less sugar;

• relatively more complex carbohydrates such as whole grains, cereals, fruits and vegetables; and

• relatively more fish, poultry, legumes (e.g., beans, peas, peanuts) and less red meat.

. . . The processing of our food also makes a difference. The American food supply has changed so that more than half of our diet now consists of processed foods rather than fresh agricultural produce. . . . Increased attention therefore also needs to be paid to the nutritional qualities of processed food.

Source: *Healthy People: The Surgeon General's Report on Health Promotion and Disease Prevention* (Washington, D.C.: Government Printing Office, 1979).

The American Heart Association Diet

Since the 1960s, the American Heart Association has cited faulty diet as a major cause of cardiovascular disease and continually revised its dietary guidelines in the direction of more whole, unprocessed foods. A 1980 A.H.A. publication noted:

> Habitual excesses in eating habits—especially of fats, salt, and possibly sugar—are high on the list of controllable factors that have been linked to cardiovascular disease. . . . It is recommended that the proportion of fat to the total caloric intake be kept to somewhere between 30 and 35 percent, and that vegetable (polyunsaturated) fat be substituted for that from animal sources as an important means of lessening the risk of atherosclerosis and coronary disease. . . . Most people in the United States consume more protein than they need. To lessen the risk of cardiovascular diease, the balance should be shifted in favor of more complex carbohydrates, such as are found in fresh fruits and vegetables. On the other hand, overindulgence in the chemically simpler sugars, in the form of desserts, soft drinks, and snack foods, is to be avoided. . . .

The 1985 American Heart Association Diet stated that fat intake could be reduced even lower than 30 percent. The list of recommended daily foods included a wide range of vegetables and fruits, including broccoli, cabbage, mustard greens, kale, collards, carrots, pumpkins, and winter squash; breads, cereals, pasta, and starchy vegetables including whole-grain bread and brown rice; low-fat meat and poultry, fish seafood, nuts, dried beans, peas, and other meatless main entries including tofu; and vegetable-quality fats and oils. The list of foods to avoid included whole milk, most cheeses, ice cream, and other high-fat dairy products; eggs (maximum 2 per week) and foods prepared with eggs; red-meat (except for lean cuts), cured meat, and organ meats; butter and other animal-quality fats and hydrogenated fats and oils; sugary desserts, store-bought desserts and mixes, and highly processed snacks.

Source: *The American Heart Association Heartbook* (New York: Dutton, 1980), pp. 65–66 and "The American Heart Association Diet" (Dallas: American Heart Association, 1985).

The National Academy of Sciences' Report on Cancer and Diet

In 1982 the National Academy of Sciences issued *Diet, Nutrition, and Cancer*, a 472-page report to the National Cancer Institute, in which the modern diet was associated with a majority of common cancers, especially malignancies of the stomach, colon, breast, endometrium, and lung. The panel reviewed hundreds of current medical studies associating long-term eating patterns and estimated that diet is responsible for 30 percent to 40 percent of cancers in men and 60 percent of cancers in women.

Interim Dietary Guidelines: It is not now possible, and may never be possible, to specify a diet that would protect everyone against all forms of cancer. Nevertheless, the committee believes that it is possible on the basis of current evidence to formulate interim dietary guidelines that are both consistent with good nutritional practices and likely to reduce the risk of cancer. These guidelines are meant to be applied in their entirety to obtain maximal benefit.

1. There is sufficient evidence that high fat consumption is linked to increased incidence of certain cancers (notably breast and colon cancer)

and that low fat intake is associated with a lower incidence of these cancers. The committee recommends that the consumption of both saturated and unsaturated fats be reduced in the average U.S. diet. An appropriate and practical target is to reduce the intake of fat from its present level (approximately 40 percent) to 30 percent of total calories in the diet. The scientific data do not provide a strong basis for establishing fat intake at precisely 30 percent of total calories. Indeed, the data could be used to justify an even greater reduction. However, in the judgment of the committee, the suggested reduction (i.e., one-quarter of the fat intake) is a moderate and practical target, and is likely to be beneficial.

2. The committee emphasizes the importance of including fruits, vegetables, and whole grain cereal products in the daily diet. In epidemiological studies, frequent consumption of these foods has been inversely correlated with the incidence of various cancers. Results of laboratory experiments have supported these findings in tests of individual nutritive and nonnutritive constituents of fruits (especially citrus fruits) and vegetables (especially carotene-rich and cruciferous vegetables).

These recommendations apply only to foods as sources of nutrients—not to dietary supplements of individual nutrients. The vast literature examined in this report focuses on the relationship between the consumption of foods and the incidence of cancer in human populations. In contrast, there is very little information of the effects of various levels of individual nutrients on the risk of cancer in humans. Therefore, the committee is unable to predict the health effects of high and potentially toxic doses of isolated nutrients consumed in the form of supplements.

3. In some parts of the world, especially China, Japan, and Iceland, populations that frequently consumed salt-cured (including salt-pickled) or smoked foods have a greater incidence of cancers at some sites, especially the esophagus and the stomach. In addition, some methods of smoking and pickling foods seem to produce higher levels of polycyclic aromatic hydrocarbons and *N*-nitroso compounds. These compounds cause mutations in bacteria and cancer in animals and are suspected of being carcinogenic in humans. Therefore, the committee recommends that the consumption of food preserved by salt-curing (including salt-pickling) or smoking be minimized.

4. Certain non-nutritive constituents of foods, whether naturally occurring or introduced inadvertently (as contaminants) during production, processsing, and storage, pose a potential risk of cancer to humans. The committee recommends that efforts continue to be made to mini-

mize contamination of foods with carcinogens from any source. Where such contaminants are unavoidable, permissible levels should continue to be established and the food supply monitored to assure that such levels are not exceeded. Furthermore, intentional additives (direct and indirect) should continue to be evaluated for carcinogenic activity before they are approved for use in the food supply.

5. The committee suggests that further efforts be made to identify mutagens in food and to expedite testing for their carcinogenicity. Where feasible and prudent, mutagens should be removed or their concentration minimized when this can be accomplished without jeopardizing the nutritive value of foods or introducing other potentially hazardous substances into the diet.

6. Excessive consumption of alcoholic beverages, particularly combined with cigarette smoking, has been associated with an increased risk of cancer of the upper gastroinestinal and respiratory tracts. Consumption of alcohol is also associated with other adverse health effects. Thus, the committee recommends that if alcoholic beverages are consumed, it be done in moderation.

Further Excerpts: Just as it was once difficult for investigators to recognize that a symptom complex could be caused by the lack of a nutrient, so until recently has it been difficult for scientists to recognize that certain pathological conditions might result from an abundant and apparently normal diet. . . .

Technological advances in recent years have led to changes in the methods of food processing, a greater assortment of food products, and, as a result, changes in the consumption patterns of the U.S. population. The impact of these modifications on human health, especially the potential adverse effects of food additives and contaminants, has drawn considerable attention from the news media and the public. Advances in technology have resulted in an increased use of industrial chemicals, thereby increasing the potential for chemical contamination of drinking water and food supplies. The use of processed foods and, consequently, of additives, has also increased substantially during the past four decades . . . More than 55 percent of the food consumed in the United States today has been processed to some degree before distribution to the consumer. . . .

The dietary changes now under way appear to be reducing our dependence on foods from animal sources. It is likely that there will be continued reduction in fats from animal sources and an increasing dependence on vegetable and other plant products for protein supplies.

Hence, diets may contain increasing amounts of vegetables products, some of which may be protective against cancer. . . .

Source: *Diet, Nutrition, and Cancer* (Washington, D.C.: National Academy of Sciences, 1982).

American Cancer Society Dietary Guidelines

In 1984, the American Cancer Society issued dietary guidelines for the first time in respect to the cause and prevention of cancer.

> . . . There is now good reason to suspect that dietary habits contribute to human cancer, but it is important to understand that the interpretation of both human population (epidemiologic) and laboratory data is very complex, and as yet does not allow clear-cut conclusions . . . Foods may have constituents that cause or promote cancer on the one hand or protect against it on the other. No concrete dietary advice can be given that will guarantee prevention of any specific human cancer. The American Cancer Society nonetheless believes that there is sufficient inferential information to make a series of interim recommendations about nutrition that, in the judgment of experts, are likely to provide some measure of reducing cancer risk. . . .

Recommendations:

1. Avoid obesity.
2. Cut down on total fat intake.
3. Eat more high fiber foods, such as whole grain cereals, fruits and vegetables.
4. Include foods rich in vitamins A and C in the daily diet.
5. Include cruciferous vegetables, such as cabbage, broccoli, Brussels sprouts, kohlrabi, and cauliflower in the diet.
6. Be moderate in consumption of alcoholic beverages.
7. Be moderate in consumption of salt-cured, smoked, and nitrite-cured foods.

Source: *Nutrition and Cancer: Cause and Prevention* (New York: American Cancer Society, 1984).

American Diabetes Society Dietary Guidelines

In 1979 the American Diabetes Association revised its dietary recommendations, stating that "carbohydrate intake should usually account for 50 to 60 percent of total energy intake," with "glucose and glucose containing disaccharides (sucrose, lactose) . . . restricted." In addition, the guidelines recommended that "whenever acceptable to the patient, natural foods containing unrefined carbohydrate with fiber should be substituted for highly refined carbohydrates, which are low in fiber" and "dietary sources of fat that are high in saturated fatty acids and foods containing cholesterol should be restricted."

Source: "Principles of Nutrition and Dietary Recommendations for Individuals with Diabetes Mellitus: 1979," *Journal of the American Dietetic Association* 75: 527–30.

Canadian Dietary Guidelines

In 1977 the Canadian Department of National Health and Welfare issued dietary recommendations as follows:

- The consumption of a nutritionally adequate diet, as outlined in Canada's Food guide.
- A reduction in the proportion of fat in the diet to 35 percent of the total energy intake. A source of polyunsaturated fatty acid (linoleic acid) should be included in the diet.
- The consumption of a diet that emphasizes whole-grain products and fruits and vegetables and minimizes alcohol, salt, and refined sugars.
- The prevention and control of obesity through a reduction in excess consumption of food and an increase in physical activity. Precautions should be taken that no deficiency of vitamins and minerals occurs when the total energy intake is reduced.

Source: "Nutrition Recommendations for Canadians," *Canadian Medical Association Journal* 120 (10): 1241–42 (May 19, 1979).

British Dietary Guidelines

In 1983 the National Advisory Committee on Nutritional Education (N.A.C.N.E.) presented dietary goals for the United Kingdom. *The Lancet*, Britain's chief medical journal, summarized the goals as follows:

> The long-term dietary goals set out in the report of the N.A. C.N.E. working party propose substantial reductions in the national consumption of fat (25 percent for total and 40 percent for saturated fat), sugar (50 percent), and salt (25 percent), and a rise in consumption of dietary fibre (50 percent). A reduction in alcohol consumption is also recommended. . . .
>
> The British diet, in common with nearly all national diets, is constantly changing. Until about 200 years ago, sucrose was eaten in very small amounts and only by the affluent. The intake proposed by the NACNE working party corresponds to that in 1870–74. For the mass of the population, total fat consumption was below 30 percent of total energy until well into this century. Those who doubt the practicality of change may overlook the substantial changes in the British diet since 1945 and even in the past 10 or 15 years, towards a higher level of processing and the introduction of many new foods of which a large number are not British in origin (e.g., hamburgers, yoghourt, pasta).

Source: "Implementing the N.A.C.N.E. Report," *The Lancet* 2: 1151–56 (Dec. 10, 1983).

American Association for the Advancement of Sciences' Symposium on the Impact of *Dietary Goals*

In 1981 a panel of the American Association for the Advancement of Science met to evaluate the national impact of implementing *Dietary Goals for the United States*. Beyond an improvement in public health, the symposium found that dietary changes would have far-reaching social and economic benefits. The scientists concluded that adoption of a diet centered on whole cereal grains rather than meat, poultry, and other animal foods would have significant effects on everything from land, water, fuel, and mineral use to the cost of living, employment rates, and the balance of international trade. Based on government and industry figures, the panel summarized its findings as follows:

Land: production of animal foods uses 85 percent (340/400 million acres) of all cropland, and 95 percent (1,230/1,300 million acres) of all agricultural land in the United States, and it is largely responsible for the extensive abuse of rangeland and forestland and for the loss of soil productivity through erosion and mineral depletion.

Water: production of animal foods uses nearly 80 percent of all piped water in the United States, and it is chiefly responsible for pollution of two-thirds of U.S. basins and for generating over half of the pollution burden entering the nation's lakes and streams.

Wildlife: production of animal foods is responsible for extensive destruction of wildlife through conversion and preemption of forest and rangeland habitats and through massive poisoning and trapping of "predators."

Energy: production, processing, and preparation of animal foods consumes approximately 14 percent of the national energy budget, which is roughly equivalent to the fuel needed to power all our automobiles, only a little less than our total oil imports, and more than twice the energy supplied by all our nuclear power plants.

Materials: processing and packaging of animal foods uses large amounts of strategically important and critically scarce raw materials including aluminum, copper, iron and steel, tin, zinc, potassium, rubber, wood, and petroleum products.

Food resources: 90 percent of our grains and legumes and approximately one half of the fish catch is fed to livestock, while 800 million people are going hungry.

Cost of living: meats generally cost five to six times as much as foods containing an equivalent amount of vegetable protein, and consumption of animal foods adds approximately $4,000 to an average household's annual budget, including the cost of increased medical care.

Employment: production and processing of animal food has led to the centralization and automation of this industry, idling thousands of farm and food workers and small farmers.

International trade: the value of imports of meat and other animal foods, farm machinery, fertilizers, and petroleum for production of animal foods is approximately equivalent to our national trade deficit of $40 billion.

Source: Alex Hershaft, Ph.D., "Introductory Statement," A Symposium on the National Impacts of Recommended Dietary Changes (Toronto: American Association for the Advancement of Science, January 4, 1981).

Chronology of Macrobiotics in North America and Abroad

1949: Thanksgiving: Michio Kushi arrives in the United States after completing graduate studies at Tokyo University and inspired by George Ohsawa.

1950: Kushi pursues studies at Columbia University and begins to contact famous thinkers about the way to peace and harmony. He sends articles back to Ohsawa's World Government newspaper in Tokyo. Ohsawa translates *The Meeting of East and West* by F.S.C. Northrop into Japanese.

1951: Aveline Tomoko Yokoyama, champion seller of Ohsawa's World Government newspaper, arrives in the United States and settles in New York with Michio Kushi.

1952: The Kushis visit London, Paris, and Belgium in connection with world government activities. Herman Aihara, a student of Ohsawa's, arrives in the United States. In Japan, Ohsawa writes a biography of Benjamin Franklin.

1953: George and Lima Ohsawa leave Japan for India to teach the unique principle.

1954: Kushis begin weekly lectures on Oriental philosophy and medicine and natural foods cooking in New York.

1955 July: The Ohsawas leave India by ship and arrive in Africa. Oct.: The Ohsawas visit Dr. Schweitzer's hospital in Lambarene. Chiiko

(Cornellia) Yokota comes to the United States and settles in New York with Herman Aihara.

1956 January: Ohsawa suffers from tropical ulcers and recovers with the help of a food package from the Kushis in New York. Feb.: the Ohsawas arrive in Paris and lecture in Belgium, Switzerland, Germany, Sweden, Italy, and England. In New York, the Kushis and Aiharas engage in several small business enterprises, including Azuma, a Japanese gift shop which is the first store to sell macrobiotic food in the United States.

1957: Ohsawa starts publication of *Yin and Yang* in France.

1959: Dr. Clifford W. Hesseltine, chief of the Fermentation Lab at the USDA Northern Regional Research Center in Peoria, Ill. begins research on miso and tempeh. Dec.: Ohsawa visits New York. Edgar and Pierre Gevaert start Lima Foods in St. Martin-Laten, Belgium.

1960 January: Ohsawa Foundation starts in New York. George Ohsawa begins a ten-day lecture series at the Buddhist Academy in New York. A mimeographed edition of Ohsawa's *Zen Macrobiotics* is distributed. July-Aug.: The Kushis, Aiharas, and Ohsawa lead the first American macrobiotic summer camp at Southampton, Long Island. *Macrobiotic News* starts in New York. In Greenwich Village, Alcan Yamaguchi starts the Zen Teahouse and in mid-town Manhattan near Carnegie Hall Michio Kushi and Mr. Sato help organize Musubi, the first macrobiotic restaurants in the United States. Junsei Yamazaki, a Japanese macrobiotic farmer and food producer, makes the first rice cakes by hand at Musubi.

1961: Ohsawa publishes *The Book of Judgment* in English and discusses biological transmutation with French scientist Louis Kervran. Rachel Carson's *Silent Spring* comes out, inspiring the modern ecology movement. Dr. Frederick Stare, chairman of the department of nutrition at Harvard University, attacks Carson and defends the use of DDT and other agricultural chemicals. July-Aug.: The Kushis, Aiharas, and Ohsawas lead the second American macrobiotic summer camp in the Catskill Mountains near Wortzboro, N.Y. Aug.: Following the Berlin Crisis, a caravan of 13 macrobiotic families led by Robert Kennedy, Lou Oles, and Herman Aihara leave New York and drive across country to Chico, California where radioactive fallout is believed to be minimal in case of war.

1962 March: The Chico community founds Chico-San and begins importing miso and traditional foods from Japan. Summer: The first West Coast macrobiotic summer camp is held. Ohsawa publishes *The Atomic Age and the Philosophy of the Far East* in French. The Paradox macrobiotic restaurant opens in New York's Greenwich Village.

1963: Michel Abehsera, a French Moroccan Jew arrives in New York from Paris, and establishes a macrobiotic restaurant called l'Epicerie. Aug. 18: In a *New York Herald Tribune* article by Tom Wolfe, Ohsawa predicts that President Kennedy will experience great danger because of *sanpaku* (upward turning) eyes, which signify an accident or early death in Oriental diagnosis. Nov.: Michio opens the Genpei Restaurant in New York. Ohsawa visits the East and West Coasts. In Boston, Ohsawa and Kushi give the first lecture on macrobiotics at the Matson Academy of Karate in the Back Bay.

1964: Ohsawa contacts the Japanese Diet and Sony and Toshiba about his discoveries in transmuting elements but receives no reply. Summer: George Ohsawa joins the Kushis at the first Massachusetts summer camp at Gay Head on Martha's Vineyard and lectures at Big Sur Summer Camp. Sept.: The Kushis settle in Cambridge, Mass., giving classes at Harvard and opening an East West Institute in their home. *Zen Cookery* is compiled by Cornellia Aihara. Chico-San starts commercial production of rice cakes. Junsei Yamazaki comes to Chico and starts commercial miso production. Scientists at McGill University start a series of experiments over the next several decades indicating that sea vegetables can absorb and eliminate strontium-90 and other radioactive elements from the body.

1965 May: Ohsawa visits Vietnam and predicts the Viet Cong will defeat the United States because they have a healthier diet of rice and vegetables. Ohsawa organizes a Spiritual Olympics in Japan. Author and journalist Bill Dufty, who met Ohsawa in Paris, writes *You Are All Sanpaku.* Ohsawa's *Cancer and the Philosophy of the Far East* comes out in French. The Ohsawas visit Cambridge and several other places on a European and American tour. The FDA raids and closes down the Ohsawa Foundation in New York for selling food as a remedy for illness. A national media campaign starts against macrobiotics led by a vociferous group of doctors, nutritionists, and lobbyists for the food processing industry. Dec.: The Kushis are forced to leave Cambridge and move to Wellesley and start an Aikido Dojo with Mr. Tamura where they teach and distribute macrobiotic foods.

1966 April: The Kushis moves to Brookline and Aveline Kushi opens Erewhon, a small macrobiotic food shop with the help of Evan Root, Ron Kotzsch, Bruce MacDonald, and others. April 23: George Ohsawa dies in Japan. Michio Kushi, who has been teaching to a handful of students in the back of Erewhon, begins twice weekly lectures at the Arlington St. Church in Boston. First issue of *The Order of the Universe* magazine appears with Kushi seminars edited by Jim Leadbetter. July-Aug.: The Spiritual Olympics is attended by 100 macrobiotic people from around the world in Japan. Herman Aihara renames his magazine *The Macrobiotic* and it appears monthly through the early 1980s. Tao Books under Tom Hatch begins to spread macrobiotic information.

1967: Dr. Akizuki writes a book in Japanese telling how he saved his patients in Nagasaki from atomic radiation with miso soup and other macrobiotic foods. Shizuko Yamamoto, a student of George Ohsawa's, settles in the United States and begins to teach shiatsu. Summer: Peak of the hippy subculture, centered in the Haight-Ashbury district of San Francisco, and the movement for peace in Vietnam. Brown rice, miso soup, and seaweed are dispensed at street kitchens and the natural foods movement booms across the country. As macrobiotic activity expands in Boston, the first Study House opens on University Road in Brookline. In Tokyo, Mitoku opens to supply North America and Europe with good quality miso, shoyu, and other macrobiotic foods.

1968: Sanae, the first macrobiotic restaurant in Boston, opens on Newbury Street, managed by Evan Root and with Carolyn Heidenry and Peggy Taylor as first waitresses. Erewhon moves to a new retail store on Newbury St. and opens a wholesale division and warehouse on the Boston Wharf under the direction of Paul Hawken and Bill Tara. Erewhon becomes a pioneer and trend setter for the whole natural foods industry as new retail outlets open across New England, New York, and the mid-Atlantic. Summer: Aveline opens a study house in Los Angeles and a West Coast Erewhon. The Lundberg brothers in Richvale, California, start producing organically grown brown rice. Abehsera's *Zen Macrobiotic Cooking* is published.

1969: The Aiharas hold the first annual ten-day summer camp in French Meadows in the Sierra Mountains.

1970: Aihara establishes the George Ohsawa Macrobiotic Foundation (G.O.M.F.) in San Francisco. Duncan and Susan Sims start Still Mountain Farm, a macrobiotic community in British Columbia. Abehsera's *Cooking for Life* is published. Muso Shokuhin in Osaka begins to export macrobiotic foods. In Arkansas Carl Garrich of Lone Pine Rice and Bean Farm begins producing organic brown rice. Nov.: Japanese scientists report that shiitake mushrooms have an anti-tumor effect.

1971 January: *East West Journal* is founded by students of the Kushis, including Ron Dobrin, Rebecca Greenwood, and Jack Garvy, and publishes its first issue as a small 12-page biweekly. In addition to lecture materials, recipes, and news of macrobiotics around the world, *EWJ* in its early issues reports on the Hopi prophecy, which warns of "a gourd of ashes" that will fall from the sky and destroy the North American continent unless nature is respected, and on the views of Edwin Reischauer, former US Ambassador to Japan. The Seventh Inn Restaurant with help of Leonard Jacobs and other students of the Kushis opens off the Boston Public Gardens. Dr. Frederick Stare of Harvard attacks macrobiotics in a *Ladies Home Journal* article, "The Diet That's Killing Our Children." In a cover story in *EWJ*, Kushi diagnoses Richard Nixon's health and notes the president is "rapidly approach[ing] the danger point" and unless he changes his way of eating faces losing "his clear judging ability." The White House physician dismisses the warning. Frances Moore Lappé writes *Diet for a Small Planet*. Journalist James Reston's acupuncture treatment in China focuses attention on Oriental medicine.

1972: The East West Foundation (EWF), a nonprofit educational organization, for the teaching of all aspects of the macrobiotic way of life, philosophy, culture, Oriental medicine, and various traditional arts, is established in Boston with Michio Kushi serving as President. Aveline Kushi establishes Kita Noh Gaku Institute for the cultural arts, which sponsors masters from Japan. *Chico-San Cookbook* is published. Prof. Kervran's *Biological Transmutations* appears in English. Japanese heart disease researchers report that wakame, hijiki, and shiitake mushrooms inhibit cholesterol buildup in the body. Drs. Frank Sacks and Edward Kass of Harvard Medical School begin first of many medical research experiments on macrobiotic people in the Boston area.

1973: Lima Ohsawa visits Boston with fifty Japanese macrobiotic friends and an international conference on One Peaceful World is held.

An EWF booklet edited by Edward Esko presents an overview of Kushi activities and future plans. Feb.: *EWJ* publishes interview with Yōko Ono about her and John Lennon's interest in macrobiotics. Noboru Muramoto, a Japanese macrobiotic herbalist, writes *Healing Ourselves*. Under editor Robert Hargrove *EWJ* becomes the voice of alternative lifestyles, foreign and home-grown gurus, and new age communities. Over the next two years the colorful 48-page tabloid runs regular features by or about Alan Watts, Swami Satchidananda, Chogyam Trungpa, Isabel Hickey, William Irwin Thompson, and Werner Erhard as well as profiles of The Farm, Lindifarne, New Alchemy Institute, and Findhorn. Macrobiotic activity begins in Uruguay under leadership of Enrique Kersevich, Jan van Toorn, and Mauricio Waroquiers.

1974: EWF begins organized seminars and programs in Boston, coordinated by Edward and Wendy Esko and Olivia Oredson. The first in a series of Kushi Oriental Medical Seminars for medical professionals is held at the Statler Hilton Hotel in Boston. May–June: The Kushis lecture in Japan and Taiwan. The Aiharas start the Vega Institute in Oroville. Lima Ohsawa's *The Art of Just Cooking* is published. In London, Bill Tara and Peter Bradford set up Sunwheel Foods. The first macrobiotic study by Harvard researchers appears in the *American Journal of Epidemiology*. Japanese cancer researchers report that kombu is protective against tumors in laboratory experiments. Sherman Goldman becomes editor of *East West Journal*.

1975: EWF begins publication of *Macrobiotic Case Histories*. Michio Kushi begins to lecture on the macrobiotic approach to cancer. The *New England Journal of Medicine* publishes a study showing that macrobiotic people have ideal cholesterol and blood pressure levels and that blood pressure is affected by the consumption of animal food. Suzanna Sarué brings macrobiotics to Lebanon. June: The Kushis hold first International Seminars in Europe, speaking in London and Paris. August: EWF holds first Amherst College Summer Residential Program. EWF organizes ongoing macrobiotic study programs at the University of Massachusetts and sponsors a Natural Foods Symposium at Boston University at which Michio Kushi and Frances Moore Lappé address over a thousand people. Jacques and Yvette de Langre set up Happiness Press in Magalia, Calif. and disseminate information on the production of unrefined sea salt and naturally fermented bread. Oct: The Kushis give seminars in Amsterdam, Lisbon, Rome, Milan, Ghent, and Paris. Baldwin Hill Bakery is started by Hy Lerner and Paul Petrofsky in Phillipston, Mass., making organic sourdough bread widely available. Bill Dufty writes *Sugar Blues* and the Shurtleffs write *The Book of Tofu.*

1976: EWF publishes *A Dietary Approach to Cancer According to the Principles of Macrobiotics*, which is distributed to several hundred leading cancer researchers and institutes around the world. Under Sherman Goldman, *EWJ* begins focusing public attention on the relationship between diet and degenerative disease with articles by Ivan Illich, Dr. Robert Mendelsohn, and LaLeché founder Marian Tompson on the limits of modern medicine and investigative reports by Peter Chowka on the failure of the National Cancer Institute, the American Cancer Society, and the American Heart Association to promote dietary research. Bill Tara organizes the Community Health Foundation in London. March: On their first Latin American visit, the Kushis lecture in Caracas, Venezuela, and during the year also give seminars in Bologna, Paris, Ghent, Barcelona, Madrid, Lisbon, London, Entrevaux, Amsterdam, and Rome. During the mid-70s, the Kushis' students begin to open East West centers and offer cooking classes and way of life counseling around the country: Denny and Judy Waxman in Philadelphia, Murray Snyder in Baltimore, Michael Rossoff in Washington, D.C., Roy Steevensz and Cecile Levin in Los Angeles, Sandy and Rebecca Greenwood in Boulder, Blake Larkin in Seattle, Bill Spear in Middletown, Conn., Joseph Palumbo and Dr. Keith Block in Chicago, Kezio Schulberg and Annemarie Colbin in New York, Sandy Pukel in Miami, and Francine and Claude Paiement in Montreal. Prof. Jean Kohler heals himself of pancreatic cancer and submits his case history to leading magazines. August: *EWJ* publishes interview with poet Robert Bly on "Gurus, Grounding Yourself in the Western Tradition, and Thinking for Yourself" which is hailed by one literary magazine "as the most important article since Ezra Pound spoke out on the responsibility of the artist early in the century." Sept.: *The Book of Miso* by Bill Shurtleff and Akiko Aoyagi appears. Noboru Muramoto sets up the Asunaro Institute near Glen Ellen, California, to make miso, shoyu, and other traditional foods. A macrobiotic delegation, headed by Michio Kushi, presents evidence of the link of diet to degenerative disease to the staff of the Senate Select Committee on Nutrition and Human Needs headed by George McGovern. Nov.: Kushi speaks in Vancouver at the World Symposium on Humanity.

1977 January: The Senate's Report, *Dietary Goals for the United States,* is published, linking the nation's rising consumption of meat, sugar, refined foods, and dairy products with six of the leading causes of death, including heart disease and cancer, sending shock waves through the American food industry and medical profession. February: The Kushis lecture in Costa Rica, Rio de Janeiro, Sao Paulo, and Caracas. February: Kushi's *The Book of Macrobiotics* is published. March: EWF holds the first of five annual Cancer and Diet conferences at Pine Manor College, Chestnut Hill, Mass. and publishes *A Nutritional Approach to Cancer*. April: *EWJ* switches from large format to regular magazine size and in the summer runs a three-part interview with poet Gary Snyder. April: EWF establishes the International Medical-Scientific Advisory Board. June: The Kushis lecture in Switzerland, France, Portugal, and Holland. September: Kushi visits the White House and presents "Food Policy Recommendations for the United States." Oct.: *Pediatrics* reports on the general health of macrobiotic infants. Kushi begins appearances on the Harvard School of Public Health television for area medical schools and universities. In Holland, Adelbert and Wieke Nelissen start Manna Foods, which becomes one of the largest macrobiotic natural foods companies in Europe. Dec. 4: Michio Kushi appears on the cover of the *Boston Globe Sunday Magazine*. The first Kushi Institute opens in London.

1978 February: Kushi lectures at the United Nations. March: New England Medical Center Hospital reports on the normal health of macrobiotic babies and infants. EWF publishes Kushi's *The Macrobiotic Way of Natural Healing* and Wendy Esko's *An Introduction to Macrobiotic Cooking*. May: U.S. Army scientists confirm Prof. Kervran's work on biological transmutations. July: The Kushis visit Gstaad, Switzerland; Woumen, Belgium; Bologna; Lisbon; and London. July 19: *New York Times* quotes Dr. Stare, whose credibility evaporated when consumer groups uncovered his connection as a paid consultant to Kellogg's, Continental Can, and the Sugar Association, "The macrobiotic diet, as we've known it for the past three or four years, is a healthy diet." The Kushis attend the Macrobiotic and Natural Food Fair in Belgium and the First European Congress of Macrobiotics held in London, to be held in varying locations every year thereafter. Kushi's *Oriental Diagnosis* comes out. August: Dr. Anthony Sattilaro, president of the Methodist Hospital in Philadelphia and suffering from terminal cancer, starts macrobiotics after picking up two hitchikers, Sean McLean and Bill Bachbracher, and attending classes with Denny and Judy Waxman at the EWF in Philadelphia. The first American Kushi Institute is established in Brookline with an entering class of 17 students, all but a handful of whom are from Europe and South America. Olivia Oredson and Carolyn Heidenry are the K.I.'s first directors. First macrobiotic center and agricultural project is established in Lebanon. Masanobu Fukuoka's *One-Straw Revolution* is published.

1979: Jean Kohler's *Healing Miracles Through Macrobiotics* is published. Japan Publications brings out Kushi's *Natural Healing Through Macrobiotics*, Aveline's *How to Cook with Miso*, and Wendy Esko's *Introducing Macrobiotic Cooking*. The U.S. Surgeon-General's Report, *Healthy People*, cites macrobiotic studies that show whole foods can not only prevent but also relieve degenerative disease. The American Diabetes Association calls for increased consumption of complex carbohydrates and natural food. Feb.: Kushi lectures at the United Nations. April: Kushi speaks at the World Symposium of Humanity in Toronto. May: The Kushis visit Japan with Gloria Swanson and Bill Dufty. July: The Kushis attend the first international macrobiotic summer camp at Lausanne, Switzerland. Yogi Amrit Desai's Kripalu Ashram in Summertown, Pennsylvania, becomes macrobiotic. March: Thom Leonard and Richard Kluding found the Ohio Miso Co., the first non-Oriental miso company in North America. Aug. 18–24: Poet Robert Bly and natural farmer Masanobu Fukuoka speak at the Amherst Summer Camp. Aug. 28: Dr. Robert Mendelsohn, Dr. Anthony Sattilaro, Marian Tompson, and Dr. Norman Ralston speak at the EWF Cancer and Diet Conference in Boston. Aug. 29: The Kushis host the First North American Macrobiotic Congress, attended by about 100 delegates in Brookline, Mass. Nov.: Alex Jack takes over the helm of *EWJ* and over the next three years focuses the magazine on a macrobiotic approach to social issues, including world hunger, the association of diet and crime, the nuclear arms race and world peace. Chico Varatojo of UNIMAVE starts macrobiotic lectures in Linho prison in Portugal. Michio Kushi's *The Book of Do-In*, Shizuko Yamamoto's *Barefoot Shiatsu*, and Dr. Mendelsohn's *Confessions of a Medical Heretic* come out. Rev. Jyomo Tanaka comes to the United States and begins to teach Esoteric Buddhism and macrobiotics.

1980: Kushi's *Oriental Diagnosis* comes out. Jean Kohler appears twice on the nationally syndicated *Evening Magazine* TV show and generates wide public interest in macrobiotics. *EWJ* begins monthly column on visual diagnosis examining the health of world leaders including Jimmy Carter, Ayatollah Komeini, Prime Minister Gandhi, Margaret Thatcher, Reagan and Kennedy, Brezinski and Kissinger, Pope John Paul II and the Dalai Lama. Feb.: Univ. of Rhode Island researchers report on the nutritional adequacy of the macrobiotic diet. The *Journal of the American Dietetic Association* reports that macrobiotic children have higher IQ's than ordinary youngsters. March: *EWJ* publishes first article on Dr. Sattilaro. May–June: Alex Jack visits China and organizes a macrobiotic banquet for Chinese religious leaders at the Zen temple in Peking featuring American-grown organic brown rice and miso. Sept.: *Saturday Evening Post* reprints the *EWJ* article about Dr. Sattilaro and EWF receives 35,000 inquires. Sept. 14: Jean Kohler dies of liver infection and autopsy confirms that he has healed his cancer. Open Sesame Restaurant opens in Brookline Village. EWF publishes *Cancer and Diet: A Nutritional Approach to Degenerative Disease.* Kushi Institute opens in Amsterdam. Michio Kushi delivers lecture on possibility of nuclear war in the 1980s and focuses macrobiotic activity in a social direction. Michio Kushi's *New Era of Humanity* and *How to See Your Health: Book of Oriental Diagnosis*, Herman Aihara's *Learning from Salmon and Other Essays*, and Edward and Wendy Esko's *Macrobiotic Cooking for Everyone* come out. Shattuck Hospital macrobiotic food project initiated by Eric Zutrau and Tom Igelhart. USDA issues *Report and Recommendations on Organic Farming* citing environmental and energy benefits.

1981 January: An American Association for the Advancement of Science panel reports that a whole grain diet can have beneficial effects on all aspects of society including land, water, energy, wildlife, trade, employment, and health. The Kushi Foundation is established to coordinate macrobiotic educational and research activities. Bill Tara becomes director of the Kushi Institute in Boston and the K.I. begins a program of teacher certification. Frank Kern initiatesa macrobiotic food experiment at Tidewater Detention Center in Chesapeake, Virginia. March: *New York Times* publishes an article about macrobiotic activities of composer John Cage and dancer Maurice Cunningham. July: On a European tour, the Kushis visit Sicily and Padua and 700 people attend an all-European macrobiotic conference in Innsbruck, Austria. Kushi Institute opens in Antwerp. August: The *Journal of the American Medical Association* publishes a macrobiotic study showing that meat significantly raises blood pressure. The Japan National Cancer Center reports that people who eat miso soup regularly have less cancer and heart disease than others. Oct.: Singer John Denver holds a benefit concert for the Kushi Institute in Boston. Erewhon is sold and reorganized under Nature Food Centers. Oct.: John and Jan Belleme found the American Miso Company in Rutherfordton, N.C. Dec.: *EWJ* awards the first John Lennon Memorial Peace Award for the most imaginative essay on how all nuclear weapons were dismantled and peace came to earth. EWF presents a symposium, "Macrobiotics and Preventive Health Care," at Boston University featuring Michio Kushi and Dr. William Castelli, director of the Framingham Heart Study. The Soycrafters Association of North America, a natural foods trade group of 1,200 individual members, reports that there are 154 tofu companies, 32 tempeh companies, and 10 miso companies in the United States and Canada.

1982: A European Macrobiotic Assembly is formed with a secretariat in Antwerp and guided by Rik Vermuyten, Jon Sandifer, and other European teachers. Spring: On a European tour, the Kushis visit José Joaquim, Antonio José Aréal, and other prisoners in Portugal. After his sentence is commuted, Aréal later studies in Boston and establishes a macrobiotic center in a Portuguese-speaking area of New Bedford, Mass. April: Staff of Life, a macrobiotic food relief service organized by yoga instructor Karin Stephan and *EWJ* editor Alex Jack, holds a benefit concert with pianist Enrico Arias in Boston. Spring: Researchers at the Shattuck Hospital in Boston initiate macrobiotic project with geriatric and psychiatric patients. EWF's *Cancer and Heart Disease* appears with a chapter on the value of macrobiotics in preventing heart disease by Dr. William Castelli, director of the Framingham Study. June: The National Academy of Sciences issues *Diet, Nutrition, and Cancer*, with interim dietary guidelines moving in a macrobiotic direction. August: *Life Magazine* publishes an article on Dr. Sattilaro and macrobiotics. Sept.: Sattilaro's book, *Recalled by Life*, written with Tom Monte, appears and makes a tremendous impact. The Kushi Institute outgrows its facilities in Brookline and the Kushis purchase a 600-acre estate in Becket in the Berkshire Mountains as a future campus. Steve Minkin becomes *EWJ* editor. Oct.: Christian and Gaella Elwell start South River Miso Co. in Conway, Mass. Dec.: The Kushis give lectures on a macrobiotic approach to world government in Costa Rica. A symposium on "World Hunger and Macrobiotics" is held at Colby College in Maine sponsored by Rev. John Ineson and the Macrobiotic Way of Life Center. A macrobiotic community headed by Bill Tims, Tom Monte, Frank Head, and Joel Wollner starts in Fayettesville, Arkansas, and later founds Mountain Ark Trading Company. *MacroMuse* magazine starts in Washington, D.C. under the guidance of Michael and

Peggy Rossoff. Steve Acuff and other macrobiotic teachers begin lectures and bring information to Eastern Europe. Sherman Goldman arrives in Israel to teach.

1983: Dutch heart researchers report that macrobiotic men and boys tested best in comparison to nonvegetarians, semilactovegetarians, and lactovegetarians. Tulane University nutritionists announce plans for a long-term case-control study of the macrobiotic approach to cancer. Donna Cowan becomes Michio Kushi's personal secretary and begins to organize the Kushi Office. April 5: Gloria Swanson dies. June 1: *The Cancer-Prevention Diet* by Michio Kushi and Alex Jack is published. September: Kushi and macrobiotic counselors start meeting with AIDS sufferers in New York. Sept.: The American Cancer Society issues dietary guidelines for the first time. Oct.: United Nations International Macrobiotics Society opens in New York under the leadership of Katsuhide Kitatani. Nov.: Haruo Kushi is invited to speak at the American Heart Association annual meetings in Anaheim, Calif. Kushi Institute opens in Florence under Ferro Ledvinka. In Japan, the Seibu Lions win the Japan World Series after becoming macrobiotic. Under publisher Leonard Jacobs and editor Mark Mayell, *EWJ* focuses on natural living and health. *People Magazine* runs article about actor Dirk Benedict relieving prostate cancer with macrobiotics.

1984: EWF begins active public education in New England, establishing a network of fifteen centers and holding public events and media presentations in Massachusetts, Rhode Island, Maine, Vermont, and New Hampshire. Jan.: World citizen Garry Davis, a folk hero among Ohsawa's students thirty years earlier, lectures at the Kushi Institute in Boston and names Michio Kushi as World Health Commissioner for the World Service Agency. March: cancer patient Neil Scott is paroled from a Texas prison after a nationwide campaign for his release by *EWJ* readers. May: Rep. Claude Pepper's Subcommittee on Health and Long-Term Care dismisses attacks on macrobiotics and reports that its dietary recommendations are similar to the National Cancer Institute and other medical bodies. May: A team of Boston medical researchers headed by Robert Lerman at University Hospital announces plans for a preliminary study of the macrobiotic approach to cancer. Macrobiotic food is given to angina patients in a clinical study at Columbia Presbyterian Hospital in New York. June: The Kushis lecture at Le Linge Bleu (The Blue Line), an association of cancer patients, in Paris and at the World Health Organization in Geneva. Summer: 500 people attend the international summer camp in Lenk, Switzerland. EWF presents first macrobiotic children's gathering at Becket. July: A Harvard researcher reports that kombu helps prevent breast cancer in laboratory experiments. Aug.: The Kushis and Aiharas lead 500 people in an EWF summer camp in Becket. Aug.: the Sixth North American Macrobiotic Congress meets in Becket. September: Kushi is elected president of the World Federation of Natural Alternative Medicine in Madrid, Spain. Oct.: The Kushis lecture at UNESCO in Paris. Sept.: Gov. Michael Dukakis proclaims Holistic Health and Nutritional Awareness Month in Massachusetts. Oct.–Nov.: 400 people attend the European Macrobiotic Assembly and Teacher's Seminar in Florence. Nov.: A new New York Macrobiotic Center opens. December: The first Caribbean Macrobiotic Congress is held in Miami and the first Middle Eastern Congress in Tel Aviv, Israel. Radio station WKVT in Brattleboro, Vermont, begins regular broadcasts of the "Macrobiotic Minute" public service spots. The Kushi Institute Review Board reports that 330 macrobiotic teachers, counselors, and graduates are certified in North America and Europe. Kushi Institute opens in Lisbon. Carolyn Heidenry's *An Introduction to Macrobiotics* comes out. Michio Kushi starts Spiritual Training Seminars in Becket. *Macrobiotics Today* succeeds *The Macrobiotic*, and macrobiotic centers on the West Coast form a Pacific Macrobiotic Community. The Macrobiotic Learning Center opens in Brookline under the direction of Lauren Spector.

1985: Citizens for Dietary Responsibility, under the leadership of Helaine Honig, Steve Levine, and David Biggers, mobilizes support to defeat legislation in Massachusetts and elsewhere sponsored by the American Dietetic Association to monopolize nutritional counseling. Phiya Kushi reorganizes EWF in Boston. A galaxy of new macrobiotic books appears including Michio Kushi and Alex Jack's *Diet for a Strong Heart*, the Kushis' and Eskos' *Macrobiotic Pregnancy and Care of the Newborn*, Kushi and Dr. Marc Van Cauwenberghe's *Macrobiotic Home Remedies*, Aveline Kushi and Wendy Esko's *Changing Seasons Cookbook*, Virginia Brown and Susan Stayman's *Macrobiotic Miracle: How a Vermont Family Overcame Cancer*, Aveline Kushi and Alex Jack's *Aveline Kushi's Complete Guide to Macrobiotic Cooking*, the Kushis' and Alex Jack's *Macrobiotic Diet*, Ron Kotzsch's *Macrobiotics: Yesterday and Today*, Bill Tara's *Macrobiotics and Human Behavior* and the first volumes in the Macrobiotic Health Education Series and the Macrobiotic Food and Cooking Series on *Allergies* by the Kushis and Mark Mead and *Diabetes and Hypoglycemia* by the Kushis and John Mann. Rice Dream, a macrobiotic ice cream made with amazake, comes out. April: Michio Kushi profiled in *Interview Magazine*. Rev. John Ineson and Edward Esko record macrobiotic songs of peace at the Maine Spring Camp, including "One Peaceful World" and "Planetary Family." June: The National Cancer Institute reports that radiation and chemotherapy are ineffective and in some cases life-threatening as a follow-up to surgery in the case of nine out of the ten most common cancers. July: Alex Jack and Gale Beith give a seminar on a macrobiotic approach to President Reagan's cancer in Dallas. July: In a letter in the *Lancet*, medical researchers report preliminarily that AIDS patients on the macrobiotic diet seem to be stabilizing. The Kushi Institute establishes a center in Bern, Switzerland, managed by Mario Binetti. July–Aug.: Macrobiotic food program begins with prisoners at Powhatan State Prison in Virginia. Oct.: A Macrobiotic World Peace Symposium is organized by the Lilienthal family in Frankfurt, Germany. Dec.: The Brookline Board of Education honors Michio Kushi in a distinguished citizen's lecture. Chico-San is sold to the Heinz Food Company and Ohsawa Japan is formed. Gingha Japanese Macrobiotic Restaurant opens in Stockbridge, Mass. Former *EWJ* associate editor Stevie Daniels becomes editor of *Rodale's Organic Gardening*.

1986: EWF begins public education in the Berkshires. April: Kushis visit Japan and make plans to open a Kushi Institute in Tokyo. American Cancer Society's annual door-to-door fund drive distributes pamphlets "Eating to Live: What Food May Help You Reduce Your Cancer Risk?" emphasizing whole, unprocessed foods. May 17: Michio Kushi's 60th birthday party and reunion attended by about 300 people in Becket. Formation of One Peaceful World Society announced. An EWF symposium on AIDS and Diet features the Kushis; Anthony Muto and Jim Farrat, macrobiotic AIDS liasons from New York; Ken Alan Hadden, member of the Holistic Therapies Team, AIDS Action Committee, Boston; Linda Sacred Thorn Hamelin and Janet Jagodzinski, lesbian and gay community organizers and macrobiotic associates, Boston; Drs. Elinor Levy and John Beldekas of the Boston University medical team monitoring the macrobiotic AIDS group. June: Japan Publication brings out Elaine Nussbaum's *Recovery: From Cancer to Health through Macrobiotics* and Rev. John Ineson's *The Way of Life: Macrobiotics and the Spirit of Christianity*. Michio Kushi lectures at the American Holistic Medical Association annual meetings in St. Louis. At the international AIDs conference in Paris, Drs. Levy and Beldekas report that about 50 percent of the macrobiotics AIDS patients are generally stabilizing and have survived longer than any other group under study.

Food Composition Tables

(Numbers in parentheses denote values imputed—usually from another form of the food or from a similar food. Zero in parentheses indicates that the amount of a constituent probably is none or is too small to measure. Dashes denote lack of reliable data for a constituent believed to be present in measurable amount. Asterisk (*) indicates information unavailable. Calculated values, as those based on a recipe, are not in parentheses. Brackets indicate retinol equivalents.) (Sources: U.S. Department of Agriculture Handbook #8 (1975), Japan Nutritionist Association *Food Composition Tables* (1964, 1984), German *Food Composition and Nutrition Tables* (1981–82), *Food Composition Tables for Use in the Middle East* (1970), and data supplied by trade associations and producers.)

(Composition of Foods, 100 grams, Edible Portion)

Food and Description	Water	Food energy	Protein	Fat	Carbohydrates Total	Carbohydrates Fiber	Ash	Calcium	Phosphorous	Iron	Sodium	Potassium	Vit. A	Vit. B_1 (Thiamin)	Vit. B_2 (Riboflavin)	Niacin (Nicotinic Acid)	Vit. C (Ascorbic Acid)
	%	*Cal.*	*Grams*	*Grams*	*Grams*	*Grams*	*Grams*	*Mg.*	*Mg.*	*Mg.*	*Mg.*	*Mg.*	*I.U.*	*Mg.*	*Mg.*	*Mg.*	*Mg.*
1. GRAINS																	
Amaranth	9.4	391	15.3	7.1	63.1	2.9	2.6	490	455	3.9	2	—	0	0.14	0.32	1.0	3
Barley, pearled	11.1	349	8.2	1.0	78.8	0.5	0.9	16	189	2.0	3	160	(0)	0.12	0.05	3.1	(0)
Barley, whole	14.0	335	10.0	1.9	71.7	5.2	2.4	40	320	4.5	4	—	(0)	—	—	—	(0)
Buckwheat, whole grain	11.0	335	11.7	2.4	72.9	9.9	2.0	114	282	3.1	—	448	(0)	0.6	—	4.4	(0)
Corn, white and yellow	72.7	96	3.5	1.0	22.1	0.7	0.7	3	111	0.7	Trace	280	400	0.15	0.12	1.7	12
Cornmeal	12.0	355	9.2	3.9	73.7	1.6	1.2	20	256	2.4	(1)	(284)	510	0.38	0.11	2.0	(0)
Couscous	12.0	354	11.3	0.8	75.0	0.2	0.7	48	128	1.0	31	220	0	0.07	0.06	1.2	0
Fu	—	365	28.5	—	—	—	0.5	33	130	3.3	30	—	0	0.15	0.05	1.0	0
Millet, whole grain	11.8	327	9.9	2.9	72.9	3.2	2.5	20	311	6.8	—	430	(0)	0.73	0.38	2.3	(0)
Noodles:																	
Soba	13.5	360	10.8	1.8	73.0	0.4	0.9	30	210	5.0	700	*	0	0.20	0.08	1.2	0
Somen	14.0	341	8.4	1.3	71.8	0.3	4.5	24	110	1.8	1,200	*	0	0.12	0.04	1.0	0
Udon	72.0	116	2.6	0.3	24.9	0.1	0.2	5	25	0.3	120	*	0	0.04	0.01	0.2	0
Oats, whole grain	12.5	313	13.0	5.4	66.1	10.6	3.0	55	320	4.6	10	*	0	0.30	0.10	1.5	0
Oatmeal or rolled oats (Dried form)	8.3	390	14.2	7.4	68.2	1.2	1.9	53	405	4.5	2	352	(0)	0.60	0.14	1.0	(0)

Quinoa	11.4	—	16.2	6.9	63.9	3.5	3.3	141	449	6.6	—	—		—	—	—	
Rice, brown, whole grain	12.0	360	7.5	1.9	77.4	0.9	1.2	32	221	1.6	9	214	(0)	0.34	0.05	4.7	(0)
Brown rice *mochi*	15.5	336	7.6	2.3	73.2	1.2	1.4	10	290	1.1	3	*	0	0.36	0.10	4.5	(0)
Rice, white	15.5	351	6.2	0.8	76.9	0.3	0.6	6	150	0.4	2	*	0	0.09	0.03	1.4	0
White rice *mochi*	40.0	249	4.5	0.4	54.8	0.3	0.3	4	60	0.3	2	*	0	0.04	0.02	1.0	0
Rice Cakes	—	235	3.7	1.2	52.8	0.47	0.6	32	164	1.9	3.3	135	0	0.04	0.03	2.8	0
Rice Flour	—	366	6.4	1.8	80.4	0.3	0.6	24	135	1.9	5	241	0	0.10	0.05	2.1	0
Rice *Koji*	—	334	6.0	0.7	73.4	—	0.4	—	—	—	—	—	—	—	—	—	
Rye, whole grain	11.0	357	9.4	1.0	77.9	0.4	0.7	22	185	1.1	(1)	156	(0)	0.15	0.07	0.6	(0)
Seitan, fresh	—	118	18.0	—	—	0.1	0.2	19	44	3.6	—	38	0	0.03	0.02	0.8	0
Sorghum	11.0	332	11.0	3.3	73.0	1.7	1.7	28	287	4.4	—	350	0	0.38	0.15	3.9	0
Sweet Rice	—	360	7.4	2.1	77.1	0.8	1.3	21	243	3.4	11	288	0	0.30	0.12	5.0	0
Sweet Rice Flour	—	372	6.6	0.4	82.7	0.3	1.5	12	148	0.8	4	84	0	0.10	0.02	1.7	0
Wild Rice	8.5	353	14.1	0.7	75.3	1.0	1.4	19	339	4.2	7	220	0	0.45	0.63	6.2	0
Wheat, whole grain (Hard, red spring)	13.0	330	14.0	2.2	69.1	2.3	1.7	36	383	3.1	(3)	370	(0)	0.59	0.12	4.3	(0)
Wheat flour (Whole, from hard wheat)	12.0	333	13.3	2.0	71.0	2.3	1.7	41	372	3.3	3	370	(0)	0.55	0.12	4.3	(0)
2. BEANS (Uncooked)																	
Azuki	15.5	326	21.5	1.6	58.4	4.3	3.0	75	350	4.8	7	*	6	0.50	0.10	2.5	0
Black Beans	11.2	339	22.3	1.5	61.2	4.4	3.8	135	420	7.9	25	1,038	30	0.55	0.20	2.2	—
Chickpeas (Garbanzos)	10.7	360	20.5	4.8	61.0	5.0	3.0	150	331	6.9	26	797	50	0.31	0.15	2.0	—
Falafel	28.6	195	5.8	12.0	49.3	0.3	4.0	40	186	4.9	—	—	[7]	0.06	0.05	8	—
Lentils, whole	11.1	340	24.7	1.1	60.1	3.9	3.0	79	377	6.8	30	790	60	0.37	0.22	2.0	—
Lima Beans	10.3	345	20.4	1.6	64.0	4.3	3.7	72	385	7.8	4	1,529	Trace	0.48	0.17	1.9	—
Mung beans, sprouted	88.8	35	3.8	0.2	6.6	0.7	0.6	19	64	1.3	5	223	20	0.13	0.13	0.8	19
Navy Beans	10.9	340	22.3	1.6	61.3	4.3	3.9	144	425	7.8	19	1,196	0	0.65	0.22	2.4	—
Peas:																	
Whole	11.7	340	24.1	1.3	60.3	4.9	2.6	64	340	5.1	35	1,005	120	0.74	0.29	3.0	—
Split	9.3	348	24.2	1.0	62.7	1.2	2.8	33	268	5.1	40	895	120	0.74	0.29	3.0	—
Pinto, calico, and Mexican	8.3	349	22.9	1.2	63.7	4.3	3.9	135	457	6.4	10	984	—	0.84	0.21	2.2	—
Soybeans, raw	10.0	403	34.1	17.7	33.5	4.9	4.7	226	554	8.4	5	1,677	80	1.10	0.31	2.2	—
Kinako (Roasted soy flour)	5.0	426	38.4	19.2	32.4	2.9	5.0	190	500	9.0	4	*	5	0.40	0.15	2.0	—

Food and Description	Water	Food energy	Protein	Fat	Carbohydrates		Ash	Calcium	Phosphorous	Iron	Sodium	Potassium	Vit. A	Vit. B_1 (Thiamin)	Vit. B_2 (Riboflavin)	Niacin (Nicotinic Acid)	Vit. C (Ascorbic Acid)
					Total	Fiber											
	%	*Cal.*	*Grams*	*Grams*	*Grams*	*Grams*	*Grams*	*Mg.*	*Mg.*	*Mg.*	*Mg.*	*Mg.*	*I.U.*	*Mg.*	*Mg.*	*Mg.*	*Mg.*
Miso:																	
Barley	48	154	12.8	5.0	21.0	1.9	14.9	116	190	3.5	4,600	*	0	0.04	0.10	1.5	0
Hatcho	40	224	21.0	10.2	12.0	1.8	16.8	154	264	7.1	4,100	*	0	0.04	0.13	1.3	0
Red	50	153	13.5	5.8	19.1	1.9	14.8	115	190	4.0	4,600	*	0	0.03	0.10	1.5	0
White, mellow	57	215	12.3	1.4	27.5	1.3	4.9	31	138	1.3	3,200	*	0	0.03	0.10	1.5	0
Yellow, light	49	155	13.5	4.6	19.6	1.8	12.8	90	160	4.0	4,100	*	0	0.03	0.10	1.5	0
Natto (Fermented soybeans)	62.7	167	16.9	7.4	11.5	3.2	1.5	103	182	3.7	—	249	0	0.07	0.50	1.1	0
Okara	84.5	65	3.5	1.9	9.2	2.3	0.9	76	43	1.4	4	*	0	0.07	0.56	1.1	0
Soy Flour	—	292	20.3	12.0	27.1	3.8	4.8	189	540	7.5	—	—	[90]	0.40	0.16	2.0	0
Soy Milk	90.8	42	3.6	2.0	2.9	0.02	0.5	15	49	1.2	2	58	[30]	0.03	0.02	0.5	0
Tempeh	60.4	157	19.5	7.5	11.3	1.4	1.3	142	240	5.0	—	—	[18]	0.28	0.05	2.5	0
Tofu:																	
Fresh	84.9	72	7.8	4.3	2.3	0	0.7	146	105	1.7	6	42	0	0.02	0.02	0.5	0
Dried	10.4	436	53.4	26.4	7.2	0.2	2.6	590	710	9.4	18	*	0	0.05	0.04	0.6	0
Fried	44.0	346	18.6	31.4	4.6	0.1	1.4	300	230	4.2	20	*	0	0.02	0.02	0.5	0
Yuba	8.7	432	52.3	24.1	11.9	0	3.0	270	590	11.0	80	*	20	0.20	0.08	2.0	0
Soybean sprouts	86.3	46	6.2	1.4	5.3	0.8	0.8	48	67	1.0	—	—	80	0.23	0.20	0.8	13
3. POTATO and STARCHES																	
Arrowroot	—	342	0.4	0.1	84.5	—	0.3	9.9	31	1.7	—	—	0	0.06	0	0	—
Cornstarch	92.8	21	2.0	0.4	3.6	0.8	1.2	—	—	—	—	—	—	—	—	—	—
Jinenjo	68.0	121	3.5	0.1	27.5	0.9	0.9	21	46	0.7	7	*	0	0.08	0.02	1.0	5
Kuzu:																	
Dried	13.6	—	13.3	2.2	321	31.4	7.4	—	—	—	—	—	—	—	—	—	—
Powder	16.5	336	0.2	0.1	83.1	0	0.1	17	10	2.0	2	*	0	0	0	0	0
Potato, white	79.8	76	2.1	0.1	17.1	0.5	0.9	7	53	0.6	3	407	Trace	0.10	0.04	1.5	20
Sweet Potato	70.6	114	1.7	0.4	26.3	0.7	1.0	32	47	0.7	10	243	8,800	0.10	0.06	0.6	21
Taro Potato	73.0	98	1.9	0.2	23.7	0.8	1.2	28	61	1.0	7	514	20	0.13	0.04	1.1	4

4. SUGAR and SWEETENERS																	
Barley Malt	3.2	367	6.0	Trace	89.2	Trace	1.6	48	294	8.7	80	230	—	0.36	0.45	9.8	—
Chocolate Syrup	31.6	245	2.3	2.0	62.7	0.6	1.0	17	92	1.6	52	282	Trace	0.02	0.07	0.4	0
Honey	17.2	304	0.3	0	82.3	—	0.2	5	6	0.5	5	51	0	Trace	0.04	0.3	1
Maple Syrup	8.0	348	—	—	90.0	—	0.9	143	11	1.4	14	242	—	—	—	—	0
Molasses	24.0	232	—	—	60.0	—	8.5	290	69	6.0	37	1,063	—	—	0.12	1.2	—
Raw Sugar (brown)	2.1	373	0	0	96.4	0	1.5	85	19	3.4	30	344	0	0.01	0.03	0.2	0
Rice Syrup	17.0	321	0	0	83.0	0	0	2	1	0.1	1	*	0	0	0	0	0
White Sugar	0.5	385	0	0	99.5	0	Trace	0	0	0.1	1	3	0	0	0	0	0
5. OIL and FATS																	
Butter	15.5	716	0.6	81.0	0.4	0	2.5	20	16	0	987	23	3,300	—	—	—	0
Corn Oil	—	930	—	100.0	—	—	—	15.0		1.3	1.0	1.0	[0.14]	—	—	—	—
Lard	0	902	0	100	0	0	0	0	0	0	0	0	0	0	0	0	0
Margarine	15.5	720	0.6	81.0	0.4	0	2.5	20	16	0	987	23	3,300	—	—	—	0
Olive Oil	0.2	926	—	99.6	0.2	—	—	—	—	—	1.0	—	0.12	—	—	—	—
Safflower Oil	—	925	—	99.5	—	—	—	—	—	—	—	—	—	—	—	—	—
Sesame Oil	—	879	22.0	100.0	0	0	0	1.3	0.66	0.01	26	2.6	0	Trace	Trace	0.01	0
Soybean Oil	—	917	—	98.6	—	—	—	—	—	—	—	—	[3.5]	—	—	—	—
Sunflower Oil	0.2	928	—	99.8	—	—	—	—	—	0.3	—	—	[0.03]	—	—	—	—
6. SEEDS and NUTS																	
Almonds	4.7	598	18.6	54.2	19.5	2.6	3.0	234	504	4.7	4	773	0	0.24	0.92	3.5	Trace
Brazil nuts	4.6	654	14.3	66.9	10.9	3.1	3.3	186	693	3.4	1	715	Trace	0.96	0.12	1.6	—
Cashews	5.2	561	17.2	45.7	29.3	1.4	2.6	38	373	3.8	15	464	100	0.43	0.25	1.8	—
Chestnuts:																	
Fresh	52.5	194	2.9	1.5	42.1	1.1	1.0	27	88	1.7	6	454	—	0.22	0.22	0.6	—
Dried	8.4	377	6.7	4.1	78.6	2.5	2.2	52	162	3.3	12	875	—	0.32	0.38	1.2	—
Filberts (hazelnuts)	5.8	634	12.6	62.4	16.7	3.0	2.5	209	337	3.4	2	704	—	0.46	—	0.9	Trace
Peanuts	5.6	564	26.0	47.5	18.6	2.4	2.3	69	401	2.1	5	674	—	1.14	0.13	17.2	0
Peanut Butter	1.8	581	27.8	49.4	17.2	1.9	3.8	63	407	2.0	607	670	—	0.13	0.13	15.7	0
Pecans	3.4	687	9.2	71.2	14.6	2.3	1.6	73	289	2.4	Trace	603	130	0.86	0.13	0.9	2
Pine nuts	5.6	552	31.1	47.4	11.6	0.9	4.3	—	—	—	—	—	—	0.62	—	—	—
Pumpkin Seeds	4.4	553	29.0	46.7	15.0	1.9	4.9	51	1,144	11.2	—	—	70	0.24	0.19	2.4	—

Food and Description	Water	Food energy	Protein	Fat	Carbohydrates Total	Carbohydrates Fiber	Ash	Calcium	Phosphorous	Iron	Sodium	Potassium	Vit. A	Vit. B_1 (Thiamin)	Vit. B_2 (Riboflavin)	Niacin (Nicotinic Acid)	Vit. C (Ascorbic Acid)
	%	*Cal.*	*Grams*	*Grams*	*Grams*	*Grams*	*Grams*	*Mg.*	*Mg.*	*Mg.*	*Mg.*	*Mg.*	*I.U.*	*Mg.*	*Mg.*	*Mg.*	*Mg.*
Sesame Butter	—	448	17.9	38.8	14.9	0.38	0.31	52.4	43	0.84	3.4	35.5	[1.05]	0.05	0.01	0.36	0
Sesame Seeds	5.4	563	18.6	49.1	21.6	6.3	5.3	1,160	616	10.5	60	725	30	0.98	0.24	5.4	0
Sunflower Seeds	4.8	560	24.0	47.3	19.9	3.8	4.0	120	837	7.1	30	920	50	1.96	0.23	5.4	—
Tahini	2.5	692	21.5	62.0	10.2	1.0	2.8	100	840	9.0	—	—	0	1.08	0.17	4.5	0
Walnuts (English)	3.5	651	14.8	64.0	15.8	2.1	1.9	99	380	3.1	2	450	30	0.33	0.13	0.9	2
7. FISH and SHELLFISH																	
FISH:																	
Bass, striped	77.7	105	18.9	2.7	0	0	1.2	—	212	—	—	—	—	—	—	—	—
Bluefish	75.4	117	20.5	5.3	0	0	1.2	23	243	0.6	74	—	—	0.12	0.09	1.9	—
Bonito	67.6	168	24.0	7.3	0	0	1.4	—	—	—	—	—	—	—	—	—	—
Carp	77.8	115	18.0	4.2	0	0	1.1	50	253	0.9	50	286	170	0.01	0.04	1.5	1
Codfish	81.2	78	17.6	0.3	0	0	1.2	10	194	0.4	70	382	0	0.06	0.07	2.2	2
Eel	64.6	233	15.9	18.3	0	0	1.0	18	202	0.7	—	—	1,610	0.22	0.36	1.4	—
Flounder	81.3	79	16.7	0.8	0	0	1.2	12	195	0.8	78	342	—	0.05	0.05	1.7	—
Haddock	80.5	79	18.3	0.1	0	0	1.4	23	197	0.7	61	304	—	0.04	0.07	3.0	—
Herring	69.0	176	17.3	11.3	0	0	2.1	—	256	1.1	—	—	110	0.02	0.15	3.6	—
Iriko	—	327	68.2	4.0	0	0	14.4	2,062	1,377	20.3	885	1,154	—	0.04	0.20	14.2	—
Mackerel	67.2	191	19.0	12.2	0	0	1.6	5	239	1.0	—	—	[450]	0.15	0.33	8.2	—
Salmon	63.6	217	22.5	13.4	0	0	1.4	79	186	0.9	—	—	—	—	0.08	7.2	9
Sardine	61.8	203	24.0	11.1	—	—	3.1	437	499	2.9	823	590	220	0.03	0.20	5.4	—
Smelt	79.0	98	18.6	2.1	0	0	1.1	—	272	0.4	—	—	—	0.01	0.12	1.4	—
Snapper	78.5	93	19.8	0.9	0	0	1.3	16	214	0.8	67	323	—	0.17	0.02	—	—
Trout, rainbow	66.3	195	21.5	11.4	0	0	1.3	—	—	—	—	—	—	0.08	0.20	8.4	—
Tuna	70.5	145	25.2	4.1	0	0	1.3	—	—	1.3	—	—	—	—	—	—	—
Whitefish, lake	71.7	155	18.9	8.2	0	0	1.2	—	270	0.4	52	299	2,260	0.14	0.12	3.0	—
SHELLFISH:																	
Abalone	75.8	98	18.7	0.5	3.4	0	1.6	37	191	2.4	—	—	—	0.18	0.14	—	—
Clams	85.8	54	8.6	1.0	2.0	—	2.6	—	208	—	—	—	—	—	—	—	—
Shortnecked clam	85.4	63	10.6	1.3	1.5	0	1.2	80	180	7	200	*	180	0.04	0.15	1.5	10

King crab	78.5	93	17.3	1.9	0.5	—	1.8	43	175	0.8	—	—	2,170	0.16	0.08	2.8	2
Octopus	82.2	73	15.3	0.8	0	0	1.5	29	173	—	—	—	—	0.02	0.06	1.8	—
Oyster	84.6	66	8.4	1.8	3.4	—	1.8	94	143	5.5	73	121	310	0.14	0.18	2.5	—
Shrimp	78.2	91	18.1	0.8	1.5	—	1.4	63	166	1.6	140	220	—	0.02	0.03	3.2	—
Squid	80.2	84	16.4	0.9	1.5	—	1.0	12	119	0.5	—	—	—	0.02	0.12	—	—
8. MEAT and POULTRY																	
Beef, sirloin	55.7	313	16.9	26.7	0	0	0.8	10	155	2.5	65	355	50	0.07	0.15	4.1	—
Hamburger—ground beef	60.2	268	17.9	21.2	0	0	0.7	10	156	2.7	—	236	40	0.08	0.16	4.3	—
Chicken	63.0	239	18.2	17.9	0	0	0.9	10	176	1.6	—	—	920	0.08	0.19	6.7	—
Duck	54.3	326	16.0	28.6	0	0	1.0	(10)	(176)	(1.6)	—	—	—	(0.08)	(0.19)	(6.7)	—
EGGS:																	
Whole	73.7	163	12.9	11.5	0.9	0	1.0	54	205	2.3	122	129	1,180	0.11	0.30	0.1	0
Yolk	51.1	348	16.0	30.6	0.6	0	0.7	9	15	0.1	146	139	0	Trace	0.27	0.1	0
White	87.6	51	10.9	Trace	0.8	0	0.7	9	15	0.1	146	139	0	Trace	0.27	0.1	0
Frankfurters	55.6	309	12.5	27.6	1.8	—	2.5	7	133	1.9	1,100	220	—	0.16	0.20	2.7	—
Goat Meat	74.2	123	20.6	3.8	0.1	0	1.3	8	—	2	90	*	0	0.15	0.08	4.0	0
Ham	54.3	327	15.2	29.1	0	0	0.8	9	170	2.3	70	285	0	0.74	0.18	4.0	—
Horsemeat	73.6	125	20.5	3.7	1.0	0	1.2	4	200	2	100	*	20	0.10	0.10	3.5	0
Lamb	60.8	262	16.9	21.0	0	0	1.3	10	152	1.3	75	295	—	0.15	0.21	4.9	—
Pheasant	69.2	151	24.3	5.2	0	0	1.2	—	—	—	—	—	—	—	—	—	—
Pork	54.8	323	16.4	28.0	0	0	0.8	9	185	2.5	70	285	0	0.80	0.19	4.2	—
9. DAIRY FOOD																	
CHEESE:																	
Cheddar (American)	37.0	398	25.0	32.2	2.1	0	3.7	750	478	1.0	700	82	[1,310]	0.03	0.46	0.1	(0)
Cottage	78.3	106	13.6	4.2	2.9	0	1.0	94	152	0.3	229	85	[170]	0.03	0.25	0.1	(0)
Edam	33.8	389	31.7	28.4	1.0	0	5.1	850	640	0.6	1,300	*	1,100	0.04	0.50	0.3	0
Cream, raw	71.5	211	3.0	20.6	4.3	0	0.6	102	80	Trace	43	122	840	0.03	0.15	0.1	1
Ice Cream	63.2	193	4.5	10.6	20.8	0	0.9	146	115	0.1	63	181	440	0.04	0.21	0.1	1
MILK:																	
Condensed Milk	27.1	321	8.1	8.7	54.3	0	1.8	262	206	0.1	112	314	360	0.08	0.38	0.2	1
Dry Milk (Powder)	2.0	502	26.4	27.5	38.2	0	5.9	909	708	0.5	405	1,330	1,130	0.29	1.46	0.7	6

Food and Description	Water	Food energy	Protein	Fat	Carbohydrates		Ash	Calcium	Phosphorous	Iron	Sodium	Potassium	Vit. A	Vit. B_1 (Thiamin)	Vit. B_2 (Riboflavin)	Niacin (Nicotinic Acid)	Vit. C (Ascorbic Acid)
					Total	Fiber											
	%	*Cal.*	*Grams*	*Grams*	*Grams*	*Grams*	*Grams*	*Mg.*	*Mg.*	*Mg.*	*Mg.*	*Mg.*	*I.U.*	*Mg.*	*Mg.*	*Mg.*	*Mg.*
Goat's Milk	87.5	67	3.2	4.0	4.6	0	0.7	129	106	0.1	34	180	[160]	0.04	0.11	0.3	1
Human Milk	88.2	61	1.4	3.1	7.1	0	0.2	35	25	0.2	15	*	120	0.02	0.03	0.2	5
Skim Milk	90.5	36	3.6	1	5.1	0	0.7	121	95	Trace	52	145	Trace	0.04	0.18	0.1	1
Whole Milk	87.4	65	3.5	3.5	4.9	0	0.7	118	93	Trace	50	144	140	0.03	0.17	0.1	1
Sherbet	67.0	134	0.9	1.2	30.8	0	0.1	16	13	Trace	10	22	60	0.01	0.03	Trace	2
Yogurt	89.0	50	3.4	1.7	5.2	0	0.7	120	94	Trace	51	143	74	0.04	0.18	0.1	1
10. VEGETABLES (Uncooked)																	
Asparagus	91.7	26	2.5	0.2	5.0	0.7	0.6	22	62	1.0	2	278	900	0.18	0.20	1.5	33
Bamboo Shoot	91.0	27	2.6	0.3	5.2	0.7	0.9	13	59	0.5	—	533	20	0.15	0.07	0.6	4
Beets	87.3	43	1.6	0.1	9.9	0.8	1.1	16	33	0.7	60	335	20	0.03	0.05	0.4	10
Beet Greens	90.9	24	2.2	0.3	4.6	1.3	2.0	119	40	3.3	130	570	6,100	0.10	0.22	0.4	30
Broad Beans	72.3	105	8.4	0.4	17.8	2.2	1.1	27	157	2.2	4	471	220	0.28	0.17	1.6	30
Broccoli	89.1	32	3.6	0.3	5.9	1.5	1.1	103	78	1.1	15	382	2,500	0.10	0.23	0.9	113
Brussels Sprouts	85.2	45	4.9	0.4	8.3	1.6	1.2	36	80	1.5	14	390	550	0.10	0.16	0.9	102
Burdock	78.8	75	4.1	0.1	16.3	1.5	0.7	47	71	0.8	45	*	0	0.30	0.05	0	2
Cabbage, common	92.4	24	1.3	0.2	5.4	0.8	0.7	49	29	0.4	20	233	130	0.05	0.05	0.3	47
Cabbage, Chinese	95.0	14	1.2	0.1	3.0	0.6	0.7	43	40	0.6	23	253	150	0.05	0.04	0.6	25
Carrots	83.2	42	1.1	0.2	9.7	1.0	0.8	37	36	0.7	47	341	11,000	0.06	0.05	0.6	8
Cauliflower	91.0	27	2.7	0.2	5.2	1.0	0.9	25	56	1.1	13	295	60	0.11	0.10	0.7	78
Celery	94.1	17	0.9	0.1	3.9	0.6	1.0	39	28	0.3	126	341	240	0.03	0.03	0.3	9
Collard Greens	86.9	40	3.6	0.7	7.2	0.9	1.6	203	63	1.0	43	401	6,500	0.20	(0.31)	(1.7)	92
Cucumber	95.1	15	0.9	0.1	3.4	0.6	0.5	25	27	1.1	6	160	250	0.03	0.04	0.2	11
Daikon (Long radish)	94.1	19	0.9	0.1	4.2	0.7	0.7	35	26	0.6	—	180	10	0.03	0.02	0.4	32
Daikon Leaves	83.5	49	5.2	0.7	8.5	1.4	2.1	190	30	1.4	100	*	3,000	0.10	0.30	0.5	90
Dandelion Greens	85.6	45	2.7	0.7	9.2	1.6	1.8	187	66	3.1	76	397	14,000	0.19	0.26	—	35
Eggplant	92.4	25	1.2	0.2	5.6	0.9	0.6	12	26	0.7	2	214	10	0.05	0.05	0.6	5
Endive	93.1	20	1.7	0.1	4.1	0.9	1.0	81	54	1.7	14	294	3,300	0.07	0.14	0.5	10
Garlic	61.3	137	6.2	0.2	30.8	1.5	1.5	29	202	1.5	1.9	529	Trace	0.25	0.08	0.5	15
Gingerroot, fresh	87.0	49	1.4	1.0	9.5	1.1	1.1	23	36	2.1	6	264	10	0.20	0.04	0.7	4

Grape Leaves	75.5	97	3.8	1.0	15.6	2.6	1.5	392	44	3.9	55	370	[1,566]	0.26	0.08	1.5	120
Green Beans	90.1	32	1.9	0.2	7.1	1.0	0.7	56	44	0.8	7	243	600	0.08	0.11	0.5	19
Green Peas	78.0	84	6.3	0.4	14.4	2.0	0.9	26	116	1.9	2	316	640	0.35	0.14	2.9	27
Kale	87.5	38	4.2	0.8	6.0	1.3	1.5	179	73	2.2	75	378	8,900	—	—	—	125
Kohlrabi	90.3	29	2.0	0.1	6.6	1.0	1.0	41	51	0.5	8	372	20	0.06	0.04	0.3	66
Leeks	85.4	52	2.2	0.3	11.2	1.3	0.9	52	50	1.1	5	347	40	0.11	0.06	0.5	17
Lettuce (Iceberg)	95.5	13	0.9	0.1	2.9	0.5	0.6	20	22	0.5	9	175	330	0.06	0.06	0.3	6
Lotus	82.6	62	2.4	0.1	14.3	0.9	0.6	20	80	0.5	30	*	0	0.05	0.03	0.5	20
Mushrooms:																	
Common varieties	90.4	28	2.7	0.3	4.4	0.8	0.9	6	116	0.8	15	414	Trace	0.10	0.46	4.2	3
Shiitake	15.8	—	12.5	1.6	65.5	5.5	4.6	16	240	0.39	—	*	0	0.32	0.74	10.0	0
Mustard greens	89.5	31	3.0	0.5	5.6	1.1	1.4	183	50	3.0	32	377	7,000	0.11	0.22	0.8	97
Okra	88.9	36	2.4	0.3	7.6	1.0	0.8	92	51	0.6	3	249	520	(0.17)	(0.21)	(1.0)	31
Onions	89.1	38	1.5	0.1	8.7	0.6	0.6	27	36	0.5	10	157	40	0.03	0.04	0.2	10
Parsley	85.1	44	3.6	0.6	8.5	1.5	2.2	203	63	6.2	45	727	8,500	0.12	0.26	1.2	172
Parsnips	79.1	76	1.7	0.5	17.5	2.0	1.2	50	77	0.7	12	541	30	0.08	0.09	0.2	16
Peppers:																	
Red	74.3	93	3.7	2.3	18.1	9.0	1.6	29	78	1.2	—	—	21,600	0.22	0.36	4.4	369
Sweet	93.4	22	1.2	0.2	4.8	1.4	0.4	9	22	0.7	13	213	420	0.08	0.08	0.5	128
Pumpkin	91.6	26	1.0	0.1	6.5	1.1	0.8	21	44	0.8	1	340	1,600	0.05	0.11	0.6	9
Rutabaga	87.0	46	1.1	0.1	11.0	1.1	0.8	66	39	0.4	5	239	580	0.07	0.07	1.1	43
Scallion	89.4	36	1.5	0.2	8.2	(1.2)	0.7	51	39	1.0	5	231	[2,000]	0.05	0.05	0.4	32
Spinach	90.7	26	3.2	0.3	4.3	0.6	1.5	93	51	3.1	71	470	8,100	0.10	0.20	0.6	51
Squash:																	
Acorn	86.3	44	1.5	0.1	11.2	1.4	0.9	31	23	0.9	1	384	1,200	0.05	0.11	0.6	14
Butternut	83.7	54	1.4	0.1	14.0	1.4	0.8	32	58	0.8	1	487	5,700	0.05	0.11	0.6	9
Hubbard	88.1	39	1.4	0.3	9.4	1.4	0.8	19	31	0.6	1	217	4,300	0.05	0.11	0.6	11
Summer	94.0	19	1.1	0.1	4.2	0.6	0.6	28	29	0.4	1	202	410	0.05	0.09	1.0	22
Winter (all types)	85.1	50	1.4	0.3	12.4	1.4	0.8	22	38	0.6	1	369	3,700	0.05	0.11	0.6	13
Swiss Chard	91.1	25	2.4	0.3	4.6	0.8	1.6	88	39	3.2	147	550	6,500	0.06	0.17	0.5	32
Tomato	93.5	22	1.1	0.2	4.7	0.5	0.5	13	27	0.5	3	244	900	0.06	0.04	0.7	23
Turnips	91.5	30	1.0	0.2	6.6	0.9	0.7	39	30	0.5	49	268	Trace	0.04	0.07	0.6	36
Turnip Greens	90.3	28	3.0	0.3	5.0	0.8	1.4	246	58	1.8	—	—	7,600	0.21	0.39	0.8	189
Watercress	93.3	19	2.2	0.3	3.0	0.7	1.2	151	54	1.7	52	282	4,900	0.08	0.16	0.9	79
Yellow or Wax Beans	91.4	27	1.7	0.2	6.0	1.0	0.7	56	43	0.8	7	243	250	0.08	0.11	0.5	20
Zucchini	94.6	17	1.2	0.1	3.6	0.6	0.5	28	29	0.4	1	202	320	0.05	0.09	1.0	19

Food and Description	Water	Food energy	Protein	Fat	Carbohydrates Total	Carbohydrates Fiber	Ash	Calcium	Phosphorous	Iron	Sodium	Potassium	Vit. A	Vit. B_1 (Thiamin)	Vit. B_2 (Riboflavin)	Niacin (Nicotinic Acid)	Vit. C (Ascorbic Acid)
	%	*Cal.*	*Grams*	*Grams*	*Grams*	*Grams*	*Grams*	*Mg.*	*Mg.*	*Mg.*	*Mg.*	*Mg.*	*I.U.*	*Mg.*	*Mg.*	*Mg.*	*Mg.*
11. FRUITS and JUICES																	
Apples	84.4	58	0.2	0.6	14.5	1.0	0.3	7	10	0.3	1	110	90	0.03	0.02	0.1	4
Apple juice	87.8	47	0.1	Trace	11.9	0.1	0.2	6	9	0.6	1	101	—	0.01	0.02	0.1	1
Apricot	85.3	51	1.0	0.2	12.8	0.6	0.7	17	23	0.5	1	281	2,700	0.03	0.04	0.6	10
Avocado	74.0	167	2.1	16.4	6.3	1.6	1.2	10	42	0.6	4	604	290	0.11	0.20	1.6	14
Banana	75.7	85	1.1	0.2	22.2	0.5	0.8	8	26	0.7	1	370	190	0.05	0.06	0.7	10
Blackberries	84.5	58	1.2	0.9	12.9	4.1	0.5	32	19	0.9	1	170	200	0.03	0.04	0.4	21
Blueberries	83.2	62	0.7	0.5	15.3	1.5	0.3	15	13	1.0	1	81	100	0.03	0.06	0.5	14
Cherries	80.4	70	1.3	0.3	17.4	0.4	0.6	22	19	0.4	2	191	110	0.05	0.06	0.4	10
Cranberries	87.9	46	0.4	0.7	10.8	1.4	0.2	14	10	0.5	2	82	40	0.03	0.02	0.1	11
Currants	84.2	54	1.7	0.1	13.1	2.4	0.9	60	40	1.1	3	372	230	0.05	0.05	0.3	200
Dates	22.5	274	2.2	0.5	72.9	2.3	1.9	59	63	3.0	1	648	50	0.09	0.10	2.2	0
Figs	77.5	80	1.2	0.3	20.3	1.2	0.7	35	22	0.6	2	194	80	0.06	0.05	0.4	2
Grapefruit	88.4	41	0.5	0.1	10.6	0.2	0.4	16	16	0.4	1	135	80	0.04	0.02	0.2	38
Grapes	81.6	69	1.3	1.0	15.7	0.6	0.4	16	12	0.4	3	158	100	(0.05)	(0.03)	(0.3)	4
Kumquat	81.3	65	0.9	0.1	17.1	3.7	0.6	63	23	0.4	7	236	600	0.08	0.10	—	36
Lemon	87.4	20	1.2	0.3	10.7	—	0.4	61	15	0.7	3	145	30	0.05	0.04	0.2	77
Nectarine	81.8	64	0.6	Trace	17.1	0.4	0.5	4	24	0.5	6	294	1,650	—	—	—	13
Olives:																	
Green	78.2	116	1.4	12.7	1.3	1.3	6.4	61	17	1.6	2,400	55	300	—	—	—	—
Ripe	80.0	129	1.1	13.8	2.6	1.4	2.5	84	16	1.6	813	34	60	Trace	Trace	—	—
Orange	86.0	49	1.0	0.2	12.2	0.5	0.6	41	20	0.4	1	200	200	0.10	0.04	0.4	(50)
Orange Juice	88.3	45	0.7	0.2	10.4	0.1	0.4	11	17	0.2	1	200	200	0.09	0.03	0.4	50
Papaya	88.7	39	0.6	0.1	10.0	0.9	0.6	20	16	0.3	3	234	1,750	0.04	0.04	0.3	56
Peaches	89.1	38	0.6	0.1	9.7	0.6	0.5	9	19	0.5	1	202	1,330	0.02	0.05	1.0	7
Pears	83.2	61	0.7	0.4	15.3	1.4	0.4	8	11	0.3	2	130	20	0.02	0.04	0.1	4
Persimmon	64.4	127	0.8	0.4	33.5	1.5	0.9	27	26	2.5	1	310	—	—	—	—	66
Pineapple	85.3	52	0.4	0.2	13.7	0.4	0.4	17	8	0.5	1	146	70	0.09	0.03	0.2	17
Plum	81.1	66	0.5	Trace	17.8	0.4	0.6	18	17	0.5	2	299	[300]	0.08	0.03	0.5	—
Quince	83.1	68	0.4	0.5	15.5	—	—	10	21	0.6	2	201	0	—	—	—	13
Raisins	18.0	289	2.5	0.2	77.4	0.9	1.9	62	101	3.5	27	763	20	0.11	0.08	0.5	1

Rhubarb	94.8	16	0.6	0.1	3.7	0.7	0.8	96	18	0.8	2	251	100	0.03	0.07	0.3	9
Strawberries	89.9	37	0.7	0.5	8.4	1.3	0.5	21	21	1.0	1	164	60	0.03	0.07	0.6	59
Tangerines	87	46	0.8	0.2	11.6	0.5	0.4	40	18	0.4	2	126	420	0.06	0.02	0.1	31
Watermelon	92.6	26	0.5	0.2	6.4	0.3	0.3	7	10	0.5	1	100	590	0.03	0.03	0.2	7
12. SEA VEGETABLES																	
Agar-agar (*Kanten*)	20.1	—	2.3	0.1	74.6	0	2.9	400	8	5	—	*	0	0	0	0	0
Arame	19.3	—	7.5	0.1	60.6	9.8	12.5	1,170	150	12	—	3,900	50	0.02	0.20	2.6	0
Dulse	16.6	—	—	3.0	—	0.7	3.7	567	22	6.3	—	—	—	—	—	—	—
Hijiki	16.8	—	5.6	0.8	42.8	13.0	34.0	1,400	56	29	—	14,700	150	0.01	0.20	4.0	0
Irish Moss	18.8	—	9.4	—	57.6	2.2	14.2	—	—	—	—	—	—	—	—	—	—
Kelp	21.7	—	—	1.1	—	6.8	22.8	1,093	240	—	3,007	5,273	—	—	—	—	—
Kombu	14.7	—	7.3	1.1	54.9	3.0	22.0	800	150	—	2,500	5,800	430	0.08	0.32	1.8	11
Nori	11.4	—	35.6	0.7	44.3	4.7	8.0	260	510	12	600	*	11,000	0.25	1.24	10.0	20
Wakame	16.0	—	12.7	1.5	51.4	3.6	18.4	1,300	260	13	2,500	6,800	140	0.11	0.14	10.0	15
13. BEVERAGES																	
Amazake	—	50	1.1	0.25	10.4	0.27	0.42	6.1	93	1.1	1.9	76.8	0	0.13	0.03	1.9	0
Beer	92.1	42	0.3	0	3.8	—	0.2	5	30	Trace	7	25	—	Trace	0.03	0.6	—
Coffee	98.1	1	Trace	Trace	Trace	Trace	0.1	2	4	0.1	1	36	0	0	Trace	0.3	0
Gin, rum, vodka, whiskey:																	
80-proof	66.6	231	—	—	Trace	—	—	—	—	—	1	2	—	—	—	—	—
100-proof	57.5	295	—	—	Trace	—	—	—	—	—	1	2	—	—	—	—	—
Sake (Rice wine)	—	110	0.5	0	5.0	0	0	5	6	0.1	—	*	0	0	0	0	0
Tea (Brewed)																	
Bancha (Twig Tea)	7.0	—	20.3	4.3	61.0	19.0	5.4	720	200	37.0	60	*	9,000	0.08	0.89	9.0	130
Bancha (Leaf)	—	*	0	0	0	0	*	3.0	1.0	0.1	1.0	21.0	0	0	0.2	0.1	2
Black Tea	9.0	—	22.6	2.4	58.2	10.7	5.1	460	310	17.0	50	*	1,300	0.09	0.56	10.0	0
Green Tea	6.0	—	31.6	4.6	49.6	10.6	5.4	440	280	20.0	60	*	9,000	0.35	1.40	4.0	280
Wine:																	
Dessert (Alcohol 18.8% by volume)	76.7	137	0.1	0	7.7	—	0.2	8	—	—	4	75	—	0.01	0.02	0.2	—
Table (Alcohol 12.2% by volume)	85.6	85	0.1	0	4.2	—	0.2	9	10	0.4	5	92	—	Trace	0.01	0.1	—

Food and Description	Water	Food energy	Protein	Fat	Carbohydrates Total	Carbohydrates Fiber	Ash	Cal-cium	Phos-phor-ous	Iron	Sodi-um	Potas-sium	Vit. A	Vit. B_1 (Thia-min)	Vit. B_2 (Ribo-flavin)	Niacin (Nicotin-ic Acid)	Vit. C (Ascor-bic Acid)
	%	*Cal.*	*Grams*	*Grams*	*Grams*	*Grams*	*Grams*	*Mg.*	*Mg.*	*Mg.*	*Mg.*	*Mg.*	*I.U.*	*Mg.*	*Mg.*	*Mg.*	*Mg.*
14. SEASONING																	
Horseradish, prepared	87.1	38	1.3	0.2	9.6	0.9	1.8	61	32	0.9	96	290	—	—	—	—	—
Mayonnaise	15.1	718	1.1	79.9	2.2	Trace	1.7	18	28	0.5	597	34	280	0.02	0.04	Trace	—
Pepper	10.6	—	8.7	5.5	58.8	2.6	16.4	—	—	—	—	*	0	0	0	0	0
Tamari Soy Sauce	62.8	68	5.6	1.3	9.5	0	20.8	82	104	4.8	7,325	366	0	0.02	0.25	0.4	0
Tomato Catsup	68.6	106	2.0	0.4	25.4	0.5	3.6	22	50	0.8	1,042	363	1,400	0.09	0.07	1.6	15
Umeboshi	69.8	17	0.3	0.8	3.4	0.3	25.7	6.1	26	2.0	9,400	*	0	0.06	0.09	0.6	0
Vinegar	93.8	14	Trace	(0)	5.9	—	0.3	(6)	(9)	(0.6)	1	100	—	—	—	—	—
Tekka	40.0	249	9.0	5.2	42.8	2.0	3.0	150	250	60	*	*	0	0.10	0.15	1.5	0

An East West Reading List

There are numerous works—Eastern and Western, poetry and prose, old and new—that embody the way of health, happiness, and peace. The ones that follow are just a few of the many works that convey a spirit of adventure and self-discovery and are recommended for further study and enjoyment.

Books

- Aihara, Herman, *Learning from Salmon and Other Essays*, Oroville, Calif.: George Ohsawa Macrobiotic Foundation, 1980. Reflections on natural order by a perceptive and wise teacher of life.
- Akizuki, Tatsuichiro, M.D., *Nagasaki 1945*, London and New York: Quartet Books, 1981. Moving account of atomic bomb survivors in Nagasaki and how a Japanese medical doctor saved his patients from radiation sickness with a strict diet of brown rice, miso soup, and sea vegetables.
- Basho, Matsuo, *The Narrow Road to the Deep North*. A haiku master journeys through 17th Century Japan. Fine translations include those by Nobuyuki Yusa (Penguin, 1966) and Cid Corman and Kamaike Susumu (*Back Roads to Far Towns*, Grossman, 1968).
- *Bhagavad Gita*. The "Celestial Song" sung by Lord Krishna to Prince Arjuna, explaining the nature of ultimate reality and the supreme importance of food. There is no outstanding English translation, but those by Franklin Edgerton (Harvard University Press, 1944), Swami Prabhavananda and Christopher Isherwood (Vedanta Press, 1944), Juan Mascaro (Viking, 1962) and P. Lal (Writer's Workshop, 1965) are admirable. The Gita is part of the *Mahabharata*, the great Sanskrit epic about ancient India. J.A.B. Van Buitenan's translation (University of Chicago Press, 3 volumes, 1973–78) conveys the sweep of the original.
- *Bible*. Supreme judgment stands behind the Bible, from Genesis to the Book of Daniel, from the Gospels to Revelation, though it is not

always so easy to discern because of transcribing errors, editing, and interpolations. No English translation conveys the spirit of the original Hebrew and Greek. However, the King James Version is the most poetic. Luther's German translation is awesome.

• Black Elk, *Black Elk Speaks.* Powerful story of the Oglala Sioux holy man who as a young boy foresaw in a vision the destruction of the American Indian way of life. Edited by John Neihardt in 1932 (University of Nebraska Press, 1979). *The Sacred Pipe*, a sequel, edited by Joseph Epes Brown (Viking, 1953), delves more deeply into Native American spiritual practices.

• *The Book of Songs.* Chinese anthology of verse dealing with courtship, marriage, war, agriculture, dynasties, and friendship, dating to 600 B.C. and earlier. One of the five Confucian classics. Arthur Waley's translation (Grove Press, 1960) preserves the spirit of wonder and immediacy of the original.

• Buddha, Sakyamuni, *Hrdaya Sutra.* The simplest, clearest expression of the Buddha's teaching. Often referred to as the *Heart Sutra*, though no adequate English translation exists from the original Sanskrit. In Michio Kushi Spiritual Training Seminars, a translation is provided of the essence of this sutra based on the Japanese text *Hannya Shin Gyo.* In China and Japan, probably the most widely read Buddhist scripture is *The Sutra of the Lotus Flower of the Wonderous Law* (Lotus Sutra). It describes the ultimate nature of reality and how to practice and spread the teachings throughout the infinite universe. Translated by Bunnō Kato, W. E. Soothill, and Wilhelm Schiffer, Tokyo, Kosei Publishing Co., 1971. Nikkyo Niwano's *Buddhism for Today: A Modern Interpretation of the Threefold Lotus Sutra* (Tokyo: Kosei Publishing Co., 1976) provides an insightful commentary and introduction to Buddhism. Other basic Buddhist texts include the *Dhammapada*, dealing with ethics, and the *Jataka Tales*, stories of the Buddha's past lives.

• Butler, Samuel, *Erewhon*, New York: New American Library, 1960. Utopian fantasy by a 19th Century English novelist of a land where the sick are jailed, the criminals are hospitalized, and machines are kept in the museum. The inspiration for Erewhon Trading Company.

• Bunyan, John, *Pilgrim's Progress.* Allegorical journey from the City of Desolation to the Celestial City, from dualism to unity. Second only to the Bible for understanding the Puritan spirit that built America (Penguin Books, 1965).

• Carpenter, Edward, *Civilization: Its Cause and Cure.* Health and illness as the root of culture and its discontents by a 19th Century English artisan. Available from Greenleaf Books, San Diego, 1971.

• Carrel, Alexis, *Man the Unknown.* Reflections on the human condition by an early 20th Century French scientist. English translation published by Harper and Brothers, New York and London, 1935. Translated into Japanese by George Ohsawa in 1937.

• Carroll, Lewis, *Alice's Adventures in Wonderland* and *Through the Looking Glass.* Beloved children's classics and satirical portrait of the White Rabbit, the Mad Hatter, Tweedle Dee and Tweedle Dum, the Jabberwock, the Bandersnatch, the Red Queen, and many other inhabitants of modern society.

• Cervantes, Miguel, *Don Quixote.* The dream quest of the man from la Mancha. Samuel Putnam's version preserves the colloquial earthiness of the Spanish original (Viking, 1957).

• Confucius, *The Analects.* Reflections on life and the Order of the Universe by a man of righteousness. Worthy translations by Arthur Waley (Random House, 1966) and Ezra Pound (New Directions, 1969).

• Dante Alighieri, *The Divine Comedy.* Journey of a 13th Century Florentine poet through the Inferno, Purgatory, and Paradise. The first volume's description of the torments of the outer regions of the *Yū-Kai* cause many readers to give up, but the second and third volume follow the journey of the soul through the *Rei-Kai* and *Shin-Kai* where Dante's guide, Beatrice, explains the spiral nature of reality and "the love that moves the stars" and are sublime. If you can't read Italian, translations by Lawrence Binyun (Viking, 1947) and John Ciardi (Norton, 1977) convey a feeling of the majesty of the original. Dante's poignant childhood and youthful meetings with Beatrice are recounted in *La Vita Nuova* (The New Life), which is also available in several translations.

• Davis, Garry, *My Country Is the World,* Sorrento, Maine: Juniper Ledge Publishing Co., latest edition, 1985. Challenging story of an ex-American bomber pilot who gave up his nationality after World War II to become a world citizen. Davis's adventures appeared in Ohsawa's World Government newspaper in Tokyo and inspired the Kushis. Davis' more recent writings have been collected together in *World Government—Ready or Not* (Juniper Ledge, 1985).

• De Santillana, Giorgio, and Hertha von Dechend, *Hamlet's Mill,* Boston: David R. Godine, 1977. Absorbing study of early myths from around the world showing that they convey complex astronomical principles, especially the precession of the equinoxes and the Vega Cycle.

• Dufty, William, *Sugar Blues,* New York: Warner Books, 1975. The story of sugar and its effects on mind and body by a seasoned journalist, film writer, and macrobiotic author.

• Eckhart, Meister, *Sermons*. A 14th Century German mystic views life from the realm of infinity. Translated by Raymond Blakney (Harper and Row, 1941).

• Eliot, George, *The Mill on the Floss*. Mary Ann Evans's novels (written under her pen name) portray traditional Western society on the eve of the industrial revolution and display a deep understanding of natural order and the human heart. This novel is about a family which owns a grain mill and the river that divides and unites them. *Romola*, *Middlemarch*, and *Daniel Deronda* are also outstanding.

• Emerson, Ralph Waldo, *Essays*. The best presentation of the unifying principle by an American author, especially "The American Scholar," "Man the Reformer," "History," and "Nature."

• Epictetus, *The Golden Sayings*. Uncompromising courage and an absolute sense of justice in a first century Greek. Available in translation (Loeb Classical Library, 1965).

• Eschenbach, Wolfram von, *Parzival*. The romance of King Arthur's court and the quest for the Holy Grail by a 13th Century poet. Notable for its teachings of peace and harmony among Christians, Jews, and Moslems at the height of the Crusades. Translated from the German by A. T. Hatto, New York: Penguin Books, 1980.

• Esko, Wendy, *Introducing Macrobiotic Cooking*, Tokyo and New York: Japan Publications, 1978. A popular beginning cookbook. Its companion, *Macrobiotic Cooking for Everyone*, (Tokyo and New York: Japan Publications, 1980), includes a wider variety of recipes and an introductory section by Edward Esko on how to apply macrobiotic principles to daily life.

• Franklin, Benjamin, *Autobiography*. Commonsense reminiscences of the author's early days, including his decision to give up meat and eat primarily grains and vegetables. Available in many editions. Ohsawa published a life of Franklin for Japanese schoolchildren in 1952 based on material in this book.

• Fukuoka, Masanobu, *The One-Straw Revolution*, Emmaus, Pa.: Rodale Press, 1978. A Japanese farmer introduces the theory of no-till natural agriculture. *The Natural Way of Farming*, a sequel, offers gardeners and farmers practical advice on getting started (Japan Publications, 1985).

• Gandhi, Mohandas, *Autobiography: The Story of My Experiments with Truth*. Truthfulness and fearlessness in the early life of the father of modern India (Dover, 1983). *The Gandhi Reader*, edited by Homer A. Jack (Indiana University Press, 1956), an anthology of writings by and about the Mahatma, covers the second half of his life.

• Harding, Vincent, *There Is a River*, New York: Harcourt Brace Jovanovich, 1981. Powerful and moving account of how Black people in America kept alive their dream for freedom by a former director of the Martin Luther King Jr. Memorial Center and member of the Kushi Foundation advisory board.

• Hearn, Lafcadio, *The Romance of the Milky Way and Other Studies and Stories*. Pithy essays, ghost stories, and tales on traditional Japanese culture by a Western author who settled in Japan in the late 19th Century. This is representative of Hearn's works published by Tuttle Books (Rutland, Vt.), including *Glimpses of Unfamiliar Japan*, *Kwaidan: Stories and Studies of Strange Things*, and *Gleanings in Buddha-Fields*.

• Hippocrates, *Hippocratic Writings*, edited by G. E. R. Lloyd, translated by J. Chadwick and W. N. Mann, New York, Penguin Books, 1978. Selected essays by the Father of Western medicine.

• Homer, *The Iliad* and *The Odyssey*. Immortal Greek epics of war and peace and of a family's long separation and their enduring love. Odysseus's journey begins and ends in a field of grain, and an understanding of physical and spiritual nourishment is central to both epics. Superbly translated by Robert Fitzgerald (New York: Doubleday, 1974 and 1961). Michio Kushi and Alex Jack's *One Peaceful World* (St. Martin's, 1987) gives a brief macrobiotic interpretation of these works.

• Hufeland, Christoph W., M. D., *Macrobiotics or the Art of Prolonging Life*, Berlin, 1797. A classic on diet and health that is as inspiring now as when it was written almost two centuries ago. Available in the original German (*Makrobiotik, Die Kunst das Menschliche Leben zu Verlangern*, Munich: Matthes und Seitz Verlag, 1978) and in several 19th Century English translations in the library.

• *I Ching* or *Book of Changes*. The basic Far Eastern text on the philosophy of yin and yang and an inexhaustible source of insight and wisdom. Richard Wilhelm's German translation rendered into English by Cary F. Baynes is outstanding (Princeton: Bollingen Foundation, 1950) and includes Confucius's traditional commentary and a foreword by Carl Jung. However, for study purposes, it is enhanced by comparison with one or two others.

• Ineson, Rev. John, *The Way of Life: Macrobiotics and the Spirit of Christianity*, Tokyo and New York: Japan Publications, 1986. Reflections by an Episcopal priest, songwriter, and director of the Way of Life Center in Waldoboro, Maine. A book on macrobiotics and the spirit of Judaism by Sherman Goldman, senior macrobiotic teacher in Israel, will appear in 1987, with other world religions to follow in the future.

• Kabir, *Poems*. Penetrating verse by a 15th Century weaver from Benares who is acclaimed by both Hindus and Sufis. *The Kabir Book*, translated by Robert Bly, Boston, Beacon Press, 1977.

• Kervran, Louis, *Biological Transmutations*, Brooklyn: Swan House, 1972. The macrobiotic answer to the energy crisis. Exciting, dynamic theories and experiments by a French scientist.

• Kohler, Jean and Mary Alice Kohler, *Healing Miracles from Macrobiotics*, West Nyack, N.Y.: Parker, 1979. A warm-hearted account of how a professor of music healed himself of terminal pancreatic cancer with the love and support of his wife. Other books on the macrobiotic approach to cancer include: Virginia Brown, with Susan Stayman, *Macrobiotic Miracle: How a Vermont Family Overcame Cancer*, Tokyo and New York: Japan Publications, 1984. Inspiring story of how a nurse, with the support of her family, healed herself of fourth stage malignant melanoma. Elaine Nussbaum, *Recovery: From Cancer to Health through Macrobiotics*, Tokyo and New York: Japan Publications, 1986. Poignant story of a young woman's recovery from inoperable uterine cancer. Neil Scott, with Jean Farmer, *Eating with Angels*, Tokyo and New York: Japan Publications, 1986. A Texas bank robber sentenced to life imprisonment and suffering from untreatable colon cancer recovers his health and freedom.

• Kotzsch, Ronald E., Ph. D., *Macrobiotics: Yesterday and Today*, Tokyo and New York: Japan Publications, 1985. Engaging and lighthearted history of macrobiotics, especially the life and thought of George Ohsawa ("The World Journey of the Penniless Samurai").

• *Kojiki*. "Records of Ancient Matters" was presented to the Japanese emperor in A.D. 712, but its description of creation is timeless. Though these tales of Shinto deities are even difficult to follow in the original, English translations by Donald L. Philippi (Tokyo: University of Tokyo Press, 1968) and Basil Hall Chamberlain (Rutland, Vr.: Tuttle, 1981) are laudable attempts.

• Kushi, Aveline, *Lessons of Day and Night*, Wayne, N. J.: Avery Publishing Group, 1985. A child's garden of verses introducing yin and yang, with color illustrations by the author.

• Kushi, Aveline, *How to Cook with Miso*, Tokyo and New York: Japan Publications, 1978. Miso lore, recipes, and nutrient information, as well as how to make miso at home.

• Kushi, Aveline, with Wendy Esko, *The Changing Seasons Macrobiotic Cookbook*, Wayne, N. J.: Avery Publishing Group, 1984. Large-format cookbook with delicious, attractive, seasonal recipes and menus.

• Kushi, Aveline, with Alex Jack, *Aveline Kushi's Complete Guide to Macrobiotic Cooking for Health, Harmony, and Peace*, New York: Warners Books, 1985. Aveline's basic cookbook, distilling a lifetime of experience, teaching, and gathering macrobiotic recipes from around the world. Includes delightful stories about growing up in Japan, coming to America, and traveling with Michio, as well as haiku poems and illustrations by the author.

• Kushi, Michio, *The Book of Dō-In*, Tokyo and New York: Japan Publications, 1979. Introduction to the art of self-massage including breathing techniques, meridians and acupressure points, and exercises for physical and spiritual development.

• Kushi, Michio, *How to See Your Health: The Book of Oriental Diagnosis*, Tokyo and New York: Japan Publications, 1980. Introduction to diagnosis of facial features, lines of the face and hands, posture, and walking. *Oriental Diagnosis* (Red Moon, London, 1976) and *Your Face Never Lies* (Avery, 1983) cover the same subject in a more general way.

• Kushi, Michio, *Macrobiotic Home Remedies*, edited by Marc Van Cauwenberghe, M.D., Tokyo and New York: Japan Publications, 1985. Authoritative guide to making a ginger compress and other home cares, as well as the medicinal use of food. Includes a comprehensive discussion of ki.

• Kushi, Michio, *Natural Healing Through Macrobiotics*, Tokyo and New York: Japan Publications, 1978. General overview of the macrobiotic approach to disorders of the digestive, circulatory, nervous, endocrine, and reproductive systems. In 1985, the Kushis started a Health Education series of small books devoted to specific illnesses starting with *Diabetes and Hypoglycemia* and *Allergies* to be followed by two more every year. Companion volumes in the Food and Cooking Series provide recipes and menus for each condition. Published by Japan Publications.

• Kushi, Michio, *On the Greater View*, edited by Sherman Goldman, Wayne, N. J.: Avery Publishing Group, 1985. (Reprint of *Visions of a New Era.*) Essays on UFOs, the ancient world, and other social topics that appeared in *East West Journal* during the 1970s. *The Macrobiotic Way*, edited by Steve Blauer (Avery, 1985), offers a concise introduction to macrobiotic theory and practice.

• Kushi, Michio, with Alex Jack, *The Cancer-Prevention Diet*, New York: St. Martin's Press, 1983. The macrobiotic approach to preventing and relieving cancer, including the theory of its origin and development, a guide to twenty different types of cancer, current nutritional research, case histories of several dozen people who have successfully tried a macrobiotic approach, and 100 recipes and menus to get started.

• Kushi, Michio, with Alex Jack, *Diet for a Strong Heart*, New York: St. Martin's Press, 1985. The macrobiotic approach to preventing and relieving heart attacks, stroke, high blood pressure, congenital heart disease, and other cardiovascular conditions. Includes foreword by a cardiologist, the story of the macrobiotic experiments at Harvard Medical School, case histories, and recipes and menus.

• Kushi, Michio, with Alex Jack, *One Peaceful World*, New York: St. Martin's Press, 1987. The macrobiotic approach to creating a peaceful mind, home, and world community. Includes a biographical sketch of Michio's growing up in Japan, experiences during World War II and arrival in America, a comprehensive account of the spiral of history, case histories of macrobiotic projects in Latin America, the Middle East, the United Nations, and elsewhere, and songs of peace and harmony.

• Kushi, Michio, and Aveline Kushi, *Macrobiotic Pregnancy and Care of the Newborn*, edited by Edward and Wendy Esko, Tokyo and New York: Japan Publications, 1984. How to prepare for and take care of a new baby. *Macrobiotic Child Care and Family Health*, a sequel, continues through the childhood years (1986).

• Kushi, Michio, and Aveline Kushi, *Macrobiotic Diet*, edited by Alex Jack, Tokyo and New York: Japan Publications, 1985. Overview of the basic principles of the macrobiotic way of eating and their relation to personal health, social health, world peace, and spiritual development. Includes an in-depth look at the foods in the Standard Macrobiotic Diet, including their history, cultivation and harvest, processing, use, and nutritional value.

• Lao Tzu, *Tao Te Ching*. The way of heaven and earth in 81 transparent stanzas. The best Western version is by Richard Wilhelm, who also translated the *I Ching*. His original German translation and commentary was published in 1910 and only recently translated into English by H. G. Ostwald, (*Tao Te Ching: The Book of Meaning and Life*, London and Boston: Arkana, 1985). For study purposes, however, two or three other translations should be consulted for comparison, such as D. T. Suzuki and Paul Carus's *The Canon of Reason and Virtue* (Open Court, 1913), Witter Bynner's *The Way of Life According to Lao Tzu* (Putnam, 1944; Perigree, 1980), or R. B. Blakney's *Way of Life—Tao Te Ching* (New American Library, 1955).

• Mann, Thomas, *Joseph and His Brothers*. A modern retelling of the Biblical novelette. Translated from the German by H. T. Lowe-Porter (Knopf, 1934).

• Mao Tse-Tung, *On Practice* and *On Contradiction*. Two philosophical essays by the leader of the Chinese communist revolution describing the universal process of change based on an understanding of the complementary nature of opposites and their transformation into one another. Unfortunately, Mao's keen grasp of yin and yang did not extend to the biological dimension. Over the years his own health and judgment declined, and the People's Republic of China embarked on disastrous policies including the introduction of chemical fertilizers and pesticides, the abuse of human rights, the occupation of Tibet, and the Cultural Revolution. Translations of these early essays are included in *Selected Works, Volume 1* (Peking, 1965) and in many anthologies.

• Mencius, *Mencius*. One of the pillars of Far Eastern philosophy by a man of peace who lived in the 4th Century B.C. Translated by D. C. Lau, New York: Penguin Books, 1970.

• Mendelsohn, Robert S., M.D., *Confessions of a Medical Heretic*, Chicago: Contemporary Books, 1979. Impassioned critique of modern medicine.

• Milarepa, *The One Hundred Thousand Songs of Milarepa*. Poems and tales by an 11th Century poet and saint whose writings form a canon of Tibetan Buddhism. Translated in two volumes by Garma C. Chang, Boulder: Shambhala, 1977. Edwin Bernbaum's *The Way to Shambhala* (Doubleday, 1980) is a marvelous introduction to the wisdom of Tibet and Nepal and the mystical kingdom that is believed to be hidden in the snow-capped Himalayas. John Avedon's *In Exile from the Land of Snows* (Vintage, 1986) is a moving account of Tibet since the Chinese invasion. The Dalai Lama's autobiography, *My Land and My People* (New York: Potola, 1977), is very inspiring as are his essays and talks.

• Muhammad, *Qur'an* (Koran). The Qur'an is the sacred scripture of Islam, which means "submission" to God or the Order of the Universe. Translations by Mohammed Marmaduke Pickthall (*The Meaning of the Glorious Koran*, New American Library, 1970), Abdullah Yusuf Ali (*The Holy Qur'an*, International Book Center, Troy, Mich., 1983), Muhammad Asad (*The Message of the Qur'an*, New Era Publications, Ann Arbor, Mich., 1980), and Arthur J. Arberry (*The Koran Interpreted*, MacMillan, 1964) point to the majesty of the original Arabic. Mohammed's role as peacemaker and the Islamic view of a universal state are the subject of Afzal Iqbal's enlightening essay, *The Prophet's Diplomacy*, Cape Cod, Mass.: Claude Stark, 1975.

• Murasaki, Lady, *The Tale of Genji*. Novel dealing with Prince Genji and the Japanese court of the 10th Century. Translated by Edward Seidensticker, New York: Random House, 1976.

• Musashi, Miyamoto, *A Book of Five Rings*. A samurai of the 16th Century describes the way of the sword. Translated by Victor Harris, Overlook Press, New York, 1974.

• Needham, Joseph, *Science and Civilization in China*, 5 volumes, Cambridge: Cambridge University Press, 1959. Monumental study of Far Eastern thought, including philosophy and medicine, and its transmission to the West.

• Northrup, F. S. C., *The Meeting of East and West*, New York: Collier, 1966. A synthesis of Oriental and Occidental thought written in the 1940s by an educator at Yale. Translated into Japanese by George Ohsawa.

• Nostradamus, Michel de, *The Centuries*. Prophecies composed in the mid-16th Century by a French medical doctor, astrologer, and deeply religious thinker of Jewish and Catholic heritage. The enigmatic stanzas of rhymed verse have proved astonishingly accurate and perplexed each generation. Many predictions appear to refer to the end of the 20th Century. However, it is important not to rely on any one translation or commentary but use at least three different ones to see how widely interpretations can differ and then use your own intuition.

• Nguyen Du, *Kim van Kieu*. The national epic of Vietnam recounts the sorrows of a divided family. The heart and soul of Southeast Asia, true today as when it was composed by a Buddhist poet in 1802. *The Tale of Kieu*, translated by Huynh Sanh Thong, New York: Random House, 1973.

• Ohsawa, George, *Selected Works*. Ohsawa, the founder of modern macrobiotics, wrote over 300 books. Most of them are in Japanese and have not been translated. About a dozen have been rendered into French and/or English by the author or one of his associates. Those in English are available from the George Ohsawa Macrobiotic Foundation (G.O. M.F.) in Oroville, California. Ohsawa's mature writings have an irrepressible spirit of adventure and marvelously explain the principles of macrobiotics. However, some of his earlier work reflects the prejudices and misconceptions of his times. *You Are All Sanpaku*, edited by Bill Dufty (University Books, 1965), is perhaps the most accessible of Ohsawa's works in English. *Macrobiotics—The Way of Healing*, formerly published as *Cançer and the Philosophy of the Far East*, (French original, 1964; English translation, G.O.M.F., 1985) tells of George and Lima's adventures in Africa and visit to Dr. Schweitzer. *The Atomic Age and the Philosophy of the Far East* (French original, 1962; English translation, G.O.M.F., 1977), is a provocative critique of modern science and presents a new model of the atom. *The Unique Principle*, first published in 1929 in Paris (G.O.M.F., 1973), introduces the philosophy of yin and yang and shows Ohsawa's youthful attempt to bridge East and West. Three slender volumes, *The Book of Judgment* (1960; G.O.M.F., 1980), *Macrobiotic Guidebook for Living* (Japanese original, 1947; revised English translation, G.O.M.F., 1985), *Zen Macrobiotics* (Ohsawa Foundation, 1965), were very popular in the 1960s and early 1970s. However, Ohsawa's specific dietary guidelines, especially the emphasis on an all brown rice diet, are not suitable for Westerners who have a very different climate, environment, and background than Japanese. A more widely balanced diet is now observed by most macrobiotic people, and styles of cooking, use of salt and oil, and the application of other principles of food selection and preparation continue to evolve. Ken Burns' translation of *Jack and Mitie in the West* (French original, 1956; G.O. M.F., 1981) and *Gandhi—The Eternal Child* (1954; G.O.M.F., 1986) are dynamic and inspiring. Those who read French will enjoy *Le Livre des Fleurs* ("The Book of Flowers," 1931; 1972) and *Le Livre du Judo* ("The Book of Judo," 1952).

• Ohsawa, Lima, *Macrobiotic Cuisine*, Tokyo and New York: Japan Publications, 1985. A graceful collection of Japanese-style dishes and insights into the supreme art of cooking. Completely revised edition of *The Art of Just Cooking* (Autumn Press, 1974)

• Plato, *The Symposium.* The toughness and infinite appetite of Socrates are depicted in this dialogue. *The Republic*, Plato's vision of an ideal society guided by philosopher-kings, and *The Timaeus*, a discussion of cosmology and human origins, are also stimulating. Available in many translations.

• Rifkin, Jeremy, *Algeny*, New York: Penguin, 1984. Perceptive critique of modern science, biotechnology, genetic engineering, and the computer revolution.

• Russell, Walter, *The Universal One*, Waynesboro, Va: University of Science and Philosophy, 1974. Brilliant study of matter, energy, and consciousness based on the spirallic laws of the universe, originally written in 1927 after a visionary experience by a noted sculptor and architect. The author's shorter volume, *Atomic Suicide?* (1957), applies principles of dynamic change to contemporary political and environmental problems.

• St. Francis, *The Little Flowers of St. Francis.* Traditional biography of the 12th Century saint from Assisi who talked with the animals. Translated by Raphael Brown (Doubleday, 1958).

• Sattilaro, Anthony, M.D., with Tom Monte, *Recalled by Life: The Story of My Recovery from Cancer*, Boston: Houghton-Mifflin, 1982.

Dramatic account of how the president of the Methodist Hospital in Philadelphia healed his own terminal cancer with the help of macrobiotics and a renewed religious faith.

• Scott, Sir Walter, *Ivanhoe*. Best of the Waverly novels, all of which show a profound understanding of nature and human destiny. First published in 1820 and available in many editions.

• Shakespeare, William, *Collected Works*. The poet laureate of the human heart. For a macrobiotic introduction to Shakespeare and a dynamic understanding of traditional Western medicine and philosophy as reflected in the plays, including the doctrine of four elements and humors, see Michio Kushi and Alex Jack, "The Tragical Case History of Hamlet," in *Diet for a Strong Heart*, New York: St. Martin's Press, 1985.

• Shurtleff, William, and Akiko Aoyagi, *The Book of Miso* (Berkeley: Tenspeed Press, revised edition, 1983). History of miso and miso-making, along with recipes, and resource information, including a concise account of macrobiotics in North America. The authors' *Book of Tofu* (Ballantine, 1983), *Book of Tempeh* (Harper & Row, 1985), and *Book of Kudzu* (Avery, 1985) tell the story of other traditional foods popularized by macrobiotics.

• Sitchin, Zecharia, *The Twelfth Planet*, New York: Avon, 1976. Exciting, controversial story of contact between ancient Sumeria and an advanced civilization on a distant planet that is said to come into our part of the solar system once every 3,600 years. Robert K. G. Temple's *The Sirius Mystery* (London, Futura, 1976) looks at the Dogon of Mali, West Africa, whose traditions preserve knowledge from visitors from the Dog Star that has only recently been corroborated by modern astronomers. Charles Hapgood's *Maps of the Ancient Sea Kings* (Chilton, 1964) examines ancient and medieval maps showing the coastline and features of Antarctica before the last Ice Age. These are just a few of many books suggesting a unified world in ancient times and possible extraterrestrial contact.

• Spinoza, Baruch, *Ethics*. An all-encompassing view of reality by a 17th Century Dutch Jew. Translated by James Gutmann (Hafner, 1949).

• Sugimoto, Etsu Inagaki, *A Daughter of the Samurai*. Autobiography of a Japanese woman who observed the impact of Western culture, including modern food, on the Far East. The 1926 original was reprinted by Tuttle Books in 1966.

• Swedenborg, Emanuel. Visionary Swedish philosopher and prophet who lived in the late-17th to mid-18th Century and perceived the world of vibration and spirit. The Swedenborg Society publishes many of his works including *Spiritual Life—The Word of God*, *Heaven and Hell*, and *Universal Human and Soul Body Interaction.*

• Tagore, Rabindranath, *Gitanjali.* Verses of absolute commitment to the way of God by an early 20th Century Indian poet. An English translation by the author from Bengali is available from Macmillan, 1971.

• Tara, William, *Macrobiotics and Human Behavior*, Tokyo and New York: Japan Publications, 1985. The macrobiotic approach to mental health and psychological well-being by the former director of the Kushi Institute.

• Teilhard de Chardin, Pierre, *The Phenomenon of Man* (New York: Harper & Row, 1955). Stimulating reflections on evolution, cosmology, and spiritual development by a Jesuit priest from France who lived for many years in China and whose life and thought has helped to unify modern science and religion.

• Thomas, *The Gospel According to Thomas.* This newly discovered gospel shows Jesus teaching the Spiral of Life using the principles of movement and rest similar to yang and yin. Available in translation from the original Coptic by A. Guillaumont et al., New York: Harper & Row, 1959, and also in *The Nag Hammadi Library*, edited by James M. Robinson, New York: Harper & Row, 1977, an anthology of related writings, including *The Gospel According to Philip.*

• Thoreau, Henry David, *Walden.* Classic on self-reliance and being one with nature.

• Tolkien, J. R. R., *Lord of the Rings*, New York: Random House, 1965. The mythology of Middle Earth conveys endurance, faith, and other traditional virtues in terms that appeal to the modern imagination.

• Tolstoy, Leo, *War and Peace.* Monumental novel of Russian family life during the time of the Napoleonic wars. Prince Andrei's musings on the absolute, Pierre's discovery of the simple life and way of eating, and the old Russian general's strategy of nonaction imbue this epic with the spirit of infinity. The quality of translations varies greatly. Rosemary Edmonds's is enthralling (Penguin Books, 1978).

• *Upanishads.* The quintessence of Indian metaphysics, dating from the end of the Vedic Age. They present the unified relationship between the knower and the known, the individual soul and the world spirit, life and death. Fine translations exist by Swami Prabhavananda and Frederick Manchester (Vedanta Press, 1947), S. Radhakrishnan (Allen & Unwin, 1953), and Swami Nikhilananda (Harper & Row, 1963).

• Woolman, John, *Journals.* Diaries of an 18th Century American Quaker and man of peace. In addition to his gentle philosophy of life, the entries are notable for his decision to avoid sugar because of its manufacture by slave labor.

• Wu Chen-En, *The Journey to the West.* The rollicking saga of the Monkey King, Tripitika, Pigsy, and Sandy, written by a 16th Century Chinese poet, based on Chinese folk traditions and the real pilgrimage of a Buddhist monk to India in quest of scriptures. Arthur Waley's *Monkey* (Grove Press, 1958) condenses the essence of the tale in one paperback, while Anthony C. Yu's translation (University of Chicago Press, 1975–1983) covers the whole marvelous terrain in four volumes.

• Yamamoto, Shizuko, *Barefoot Shiatsu,* Tokyo and New York: Japan Publications, 1979. Introduction to acupressure massage by a student of George Ohsawa and the leading shiatsu practitioner in the West.

• *The Yellow Emperor's Classic of Internal Medicine.* Ancient Chinese medical text describing treatment by yin and yang and the five transformations. Unfortunately, the existing text is incomplete and often incomprehensible. Ilza Veith's condensation (Berkeley: University of California Press, 1949) gives a flavor of the original. Dr. Henry Lu's *A Complete Translation of Nei Ching and Nan Ching* in two volumes provides a complete English translation side by side with the Chinese (Vancouver: Academy of Oriental Heritage, 1978).

Periodicals

For further study, the following periodicals with original articles by George Ohsawa, Michio Kushi, and other macrobiotic teachers and students are recommended. Though many are out of print, some individual back issues are available at the Kushi Institute Library in Becket, Massachusetts.

• *East West Journal* (1971–), Brookline, Massachusetts

• *The Order of the Universe* (1967–1982), Boston and Brookline, Massachusetts

• *Michio Kushi Seminar Reports* (1973–1977), Boston, Massachusetts

• *Kushi Institute Study Guides* (1980–1982), Brookline, Massachusetts

• *Macrobiotic Archives* (1983–), Brookline, Massachusetts

• *The Macrobiotic* (1966–1983), Oroville, California

• *Macrobiotics Today* (1984–), Oroville, California

• *MacroMuse* (1982–), Rockville, Maryland

• *Le Compass* (1977–), Paris, France

Macrobiotic Educational and Social Activities

Educational Centers

Macrobiotics International, a network of educational centers in the United States, Canada, and around the world affiliated with the Kushi Foundation and East West Foundation in Boston, offers ongoing classes for the general public in macrobiotic cooking, traditional food preparation and natural processing, and One World studies. Instruction is also offered in Oriental and traditional Western medicine, shiatsu massage, pregnancy and natural childcare, yoga, meditation, science, culture and the arts. Macrobiotic educational centers also provide dietary and way of life counseling services with trained and certified consultants, referrals to professional health care associates, and cooperate in research and food service programs in hospitals, medical schools, prisons, drug rehabilitation clinics, nursing homes, and other institutions. In scores of other cities and communities, there are smaller macrobiotic learning centers, residential centers, and information centers offering some classes and services.

• Please contact Macrobiotics International in Boston for information on regional and local activities, as well as health referrals, whole foods outlets, and mail order sources. An annual directory available from the Kushi Foundation in Boston updates all national and international listings.

Macrobiotics International/Kushi Foundation
Box 850
Brookline Village, Mass. 02147
617–738–0045

Kushi Institute

For those who wish to study further, the Kushi Institute, an educational institution founded in Boston in 1979 with affiliates in London, Amsterdam, Antwerp, Florence, Lisbon, Barcelona, and Tokyo offers full- and part-time instruction for individuals who wish to become trained and certified macrobiotic cooking instructors, teachers, and counselors. Training is divided into four levels: 1) personal development (3 months); 2) community development (3 months); 3) planetary development (3 months); and 4) graduate training (1–2 years).

At the K.I.'s new campus in the Berkshire Mountains, a series of Spiritual Training Seminars has started under Michio Kushi's personal guidance. Ten to twelve levels (lasting about five days each) will be offered in the structure and nature of the spiritual world, prayer and meditation, and spiritual growth and development. Aveline Kushi has developed a short residential program, Aveline Kushi Cooking Intensives dealing with cooking, art, culture, and family relations.

Kushi Institute
Box 7
Becket, Mass. 01223
413–623–5742

One Peaceful World

In 1986 Michio and Aveline Kushi and their associates initiated a society to commemorate the beginning of One Peaceful World. The society's premise is that peace starts with each individual, family, and community through harmonizing with the environment, proper diet, and a more natural way of life and does not depend on governments, international treaties, societal reforms, or other institutional measures. Members receive an annual membership card, newsletter, discount on major macrobiotic seminars and events, and invitations to participate in peace education, quality food production and distribution, and other activities.

One Peaceful World
c/o The Kushi Foundation
17 Station Street
Brookline, Mass. 02146
617–738–0045

East West Journal

Ongoing developments are reported in the Kushi Foundation's publications, including the *East West Journal*, a monthly magazine begun in 1971 and now with an international readership of 200,000. The *EWJ* features regular articles on a more natural approach to health and nutrition, as well as ecology, science, psychology, the arts, and world peace. In each issue there is a natural foods cooking column and articles on traditional food cultivation and natural foods processing.

East West Journal
17 Station St.
Brookline, Mass. 02146
617–232–1000

North American Macrobiotic Congress

Since 1979, the North American Macrobiotic Congress has convened annually to discuss continental and global issues, including world peace. It has published guidelines in case of a nuclear emergency and other materials for distribution through East West centers and to the general public.

North American Macrobiotic Congress
c/o Kushi Foundation
Box 7
Becket, Mass. 01223
413–623–5742

U.N. Macrobiotic Society

At United Nations headquarters in New York, Katsuhide Kitatani, a senior development director, started a macrobiotic association after relieving his own case of terminal stomach cancer with the help of a more balanced diet. The group now includes several hundred members and chapters at U.N. agencies in Geneva. In addition to regular luncheon meetings and speakers, the group is lobbying to introduce whole natural foods in the U.N. cafeteria and U.N. development and relief programs.

United Nations Macrobiotics Society
Mr. Barish and Mr. Kawamura
1 United Nations Plaza
New York, N.Y. 10017
212–754–7969

Kushi Foundation Prison Project

The Kushi Foundation Prison Project has established a correspondence network with about 2,000 prisoners in 47 states. It also provides education and training to inmates for holistic self-development; food service support; study groups; and scholarships to the Kushi Institute. Information on the macrobiotic food service at Shattuck Hospital in Boston, and institutional whole foods cooking in general, is also available through this office. Meanwhile, in Virginia, Frank Kern has instituted macrobiotic food programs in the Tidewater Detention Center and Powhatan State Penitentiary.

Kushi Foundation Prison Project
Box 850
Brookline Village, Mass. 02147
617–566–0080

Frank Kern
Program Director
Tidewater Detention Center
420 Albemarie Drive
Chesapeake, Va. 23320
804–623–8949

Citizens for Dietary Responsibility

Citizens for Dietary Responsibility is an association of individuals and families, including many macrobiotic people, dedicated to preserving fundamental dietary and nutritional freedoms. Activities include public education and political organizing around issues such as freedom of choice in health care and dietary counseling, and the irradiation of foods.

Citizens for Dietary Responsibility
Box 494
Jamaica Plain, Mass. 02130
617–738–6557

AIDS Project

In New York City, a macrobiotic program to prevent and relieve AIDS started in the early 1980s. Activities include regular meetings of people with AIDS, along with family, friends, and supporters; meals and cooking classes; medical monitoring and research; and public outreach.

Wipe Out AIDS
Box 60
New York, N.Y. 10014
212–691–8309

Medical Health Care Network

The Medical Health Care Network is an association of medical doctors, nurses, nutritionists, and other health care professionals who are practicing or supportive of macrobiotics. Activities include seminars in Oriental medicine and philosophy with Michio Kushi, seminars in relating to the medical profession for macrobiotic counselors, and development and coordination of medical research.

Medical Health Care Network
c/o 62 Buckminster Road
Brookline, Mass. 02146
617–232–6869

One Peaceful World
c/o The Kushi Foundation
17 Station Street
Brookline, Mass. 02146
(617) 738–0045

Index